Conflict and Enlightenment

New approaches to the history of print have allowed historians of early modern Europe to re-evaluate major shifts in religious, intellectual, cultural and political life across the region. Drawing on precise and detailed study of the contexts of different types of print, including books, pamphlets, newspapers and flysheets, combined with quantitative analysis and a study of texts as material objects, Thomas Munck offers a transformed picture of early modern political culture, and through analysis of new styles and genres of writing he offers a fresh perspective on the intended readership. *Conflict and Enlightenment* uses a resolutely comparative approach to re-examine what was being disseminated in print, and how. By mapping the transmission of texts across cultural and linguistic divides, Munck reveals how far new forms of political discourse varied depending on the particular perspectives of authors, readers and regulatory authorities, as well as on the cultural adaptability of translators and sponsors.

Thomas Munck is Professor of Early Modern European History at the University of Glasgow where his research focuses on comparative European social, cultural and political history. A current member of a research group on cultural translation based in Germany, he is the recipient of research grants from the Carnegie Trust and the British Academy, and the author of *Seventeenth-Century Europe: State, Conflict and the Social Order in Europe, 1598–1700* (2005).

T0349745

Conflict and Enlightenment

Print and Political Culture in Europe, 1635–1795

Thomas Munck

University of Glasgow

CAMBRIDGE
UNIVERSITY PRESS

CAMBRIDGE
UNIVERSITY PRESS

University Printing House, Cambridge CB2 8BS, United Kingdom

One Liberty Plaza, 20th Floor, New York, NY 10006, USA

477 Williamstown Road, Port Melbourne, VIC 3207, Australia

314–321, 3rd Floor, Plot 3, Splendor Forum, Jasola District Centre, New Delhi – 110025, India

79 Anson Road, #06–04/06, Singapore 079906

Cambridge University Press is part of the University of Cambridge.

It furthers the University's mission by disseminating knowledge in the pursuit of education, learning, and research at the highest international levels of excellence.

www.cambridge.org
Information on this title: www.cambridge.org/9780521878074
DOI: 10.1017/9781139021289

First published 2019

Printed in the United Kingdom by TJ International Ltd. Padstow Cornwall

A catalogue record for this publication is available from the British Library.

Library of Congress Cataloging-in-Publication Data
Names: Munck, Thomas, author.
Title: Conflict and enlightenment : print and political culture in Europe, 1635–1795 / Thomas Munck, University of Glasgow.
Description: Cambridge, United Kingdom ; New York : Cambridge University Press, 2019. | Includes bibliographical references and index.
Identifiers: LCCN 2019019463 | ISBN 9780521878074 (hbk.) | ISBN 9780521701808 (pbk.)
Subjects: LCSH: Book industries and trade – Political aspects – Europe – History – 17th century. | Book industries and trade – Political aspects – Europe – History – 18th century. | Printing – Influence. | Enlightenment – Europe. | Europe – Intellectual life – 17th century. | Europe – Intellectual life – 18th century.
Classification: LCC Z124 .M94 2019 | DDC 338.4/76862094–dc23
LC record available at https://lccn.loc.gov/2019019463

ISBN 978-0-521-87807-4 Hardback
ISBN 978-0-521-70180-8 Paperback

Contents

Figures

Acknowledgements

Printed texts are never merely what they appear to be. In the early modern period, the versatility of printing as a means of communication opened up new possibilities, but as with the internet and social media today, authorship, intended audience, implicit content and possibilities of dissemination all require careful analysis before we can be reasonably sure we understand what is being communicated and why. Movable-type printing, when it was first developed for commercial purposes in the fifteenth century, may have been regarded primarily as a means of making religious texts more widely accessible, but these texts (and their translation) soon generated religious disagreement and controversy, and, by extension, a more critical approach to textual transmission in other fields of knowledge and imagination. Questions of a political nature, including good governance and the purpose of civil society, were unavoidable in the Reformation debates themselves, but it is one of the core arguments of this book that political controversy in print became much more sustained and belligerent from the 1630s onwards, creating imaginative new formats and styles of writing intended to reach a wider readership.

Traditional research agendas in the history of ideas, and in intellectual history, have greatly enhanced our understanding of the early modern period. But intellectual attribution is rarely an exact science, least of all in politics and the study of civil society, where less readily definable influences, symbolism and even public opinion may be equally significant. Seventeenth- and eighteenth-century writers, at least when writing for a scholarly audience, liked to cite sources from antiquity, but they tended to be less specific when writing for a wider audience and more selective in citing or attacking their own contemporaries. We may end up speculating whether Hobbes influenced Rousseau's concept of the general will, or whether Lessing was in any real sense a Spinozist, but we are unlikely to find conclusive evidence if we restrict our study solely to a narrow selection of recognised major texts in the intellectual history of the seventeenth century and the Enlightenment.

Instead, this book seeks to explain how information, ideas and opinions were disseminated, adapted and transformed through print, and how the mechanisms of the print market changed the ways in which a wider reading public might seek to understand the extraordinary political challenges during a period of 160 years, spanning both the English civil wars and the French Revolution. We may often lack precise evidence on who could access which texts and we have only sporadic indications of how readers might interact with the texts they did access. But we do have scope for re-examining the material culture of print and the circumstances of production, and we can to some degree track the physical dissemination of books, pamphlets, newspapers and other printed media. We also have a vast range of contemporary translations, responses and refutations, which help us understand how important it was (and is) to read between the lines on the page, while remaining alert to any unstated cultural assumptions and intentions relevant to the context in which each text was produced and read. If we do all that for as wide a sample of printed material as possible – well beyond the 'great works' of recognised innovators – we may be in a better position to understand how a whole range of political notions, from the highly traditional to the dangerously subversive, were interpreted by a widening reading public, many of whom (especially from the 1640s onwards) had never had access to political texts before.

While the huge growth in the use of print for political purposes in this period can hardly be disputed, it was far from linear or predictable across Europe. This book adopts a resolutely comparative and thematic approach, focusing on print as both the richest, but also the most problematic, uncontrollable and irrepressible of any media available to those who might acquire an interest in current affairs and good governance. Given the specific focus on print and dissemination, some recent historiographical debates regarding this period will not figure prominently – notably disagreements concerning the 'radical' Enlightenment, or questions surrounding the influence of certain groups such as freemasons, whose discussions were not made public in print. The focus throughout this book is on what we might see in print, even (and not least) when it was censored, popularised, fictionalised or plagiarised.

It is a great pleasure to record the inspiration, help and assistance I have received during the many years it has taken to complete this book. The editorial and production teams at Cambridge University Press have been helpful from the start, and I am very grateful both for their seemingly inexhaustible patience during many delays and their efficiency when the book was finally ready. The University of

Glasgow, where I have worked for most of my academic career, has been generous in allowing periods of research-leave for detailed field work. I would like to thank the ever-helpful staff of the wonderful Special Collections of rare books in Glasgow University Library, giving me ready access to a wealth of pre-1800 print. Many other major libraries have also provided invaluable assistance, either directly in letting me examine original printed texts, or in providing evermore digitised texts allowing comparisons between variant editions beyond the holdings of any one library. In particular, I would like to thank the Herzog August Bibliothek in Wolfenbüttel for awarding me a senior fellowship and subsequently hosting hugely productive research workshops on Translating Cultures.

A great many friends, colleagues and researchers in early modern history have helped along the way. I would like to thank in particular Karin Bowie, Michelle Craig, Lionel Glassey, Rachel Hammersley, Henrik Horstbøll, Gaby Mahlberg, Mike Rapport, Steven Reid, Hamish Scott, Alex Shepard and Don Spaeth, not to mention many others cited in footnotes or in the Bibliography. I am also grateful to the graduate students and colleagues who have made the Early Modern Work in Progress seminar at Glasgow so enjoyable over the past decade. It goes almost without saying that none of these are responsible for any remaining errors or misinterpretations in this book, but they have contributed immeasurably by providing fresh insights, discussing key ideas and, in some cases, reading sections and putting me back on track when at times the project seemed overwhelming. I would also like to thank the many students who have taken up the challenge of undergraduate and graduate courses in which I tried out some of these ideas: they too have helped me understand the complexities of early modern political culture and the impossibility of summing up the intellectual life of the seventeenth century and the Enlightenment in simple terms.

This book is being completed as Britain struggles to understand its relationship with the rest of Europe. The Brexit crisis has convinced me, more than ever, that a thorough understanding of our shared European history and culture is essential for all of us, including everyone in Britain. As someone who grew up in Copenhagen and in Geneva and first came to Britain when commencing undergraduate studies at the University of St Andrews, I have had the privilege of a great many friendships where a mix of languages and cultures were continuously and unforgettably enriching. Above all I have had the companionship and support of Meg (a Scot) and our son and daughter, Neil and Rhona, who now live in different countries, but are always there when needed – as when I recently struggled to come to terms with having to reapply for 'settled status' in a country which has been my home for many decades. I hope this book may be at least a token of thanks to my family, friends and colleagues. Perhaps it may also add just a little to our understanding of the rich inheritance we all enjoy from our shared European background.

Introduction

In the early modern period, printing was the only means of disseminating a text or message reliably to a large number of people. Print could serve all kinds of purposes, ranging from religious education to scientific debate, from state propaganda to open political subversion, from proclamations and the reporting of news to the provision of entertaining fictional reading. But the printing industry was also one of the most complex, labour-intensive and investment-dependent sectors of the early modern economy, involving a huge range of very specialised and skilled manual labour as well as a range of associated trades (see Figure 1). It required considerable infrastructure, management and marketing skills, and was subject to severe market fluctuations with high risks. These conflicting pressures were not matched by any substantial technological change in the printing industry from the middle of the fifteenth century right through to the Napoleonic period. So despite gaining a solid footing in the economies of many large prosperous cities, the increase in the use of print for particular purposes was unsteady, and its geographic spread surprisingly uneven.

If we turn our attention from the production of print and its distribution, and focus more on physical presentation, content and intended readership, we encounter a number of different and additional variables. For example, in order to meet the expectations of readers with different levels of disposable income, a publisher could do little to change the unit costs, beyond making appropriate choices of page size and qualities of paper, and by experimenting with layout, font sizes and title pages. However, very short texts could be sold in a cheap paper cover – it was often the buyer who arranged for the actual binding of larger works – so authors and printers soon realised they could create and meet a different kind of demand by producing texts aimed specifically at readers with relatively modest resources and possibly different interests. Bearing in mind that a printed text was never really cheap, gaining a socially wider reader base was a matter of experimentation and innovation in format. To make the most of variable market demand, printers therefore rarely specialised in any one genre, and made sure they could easily switch between

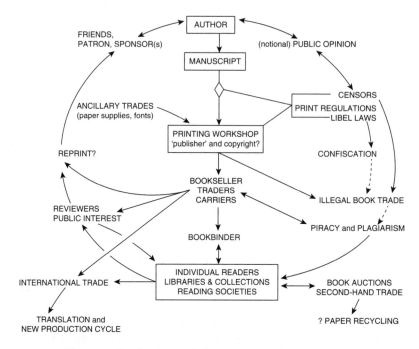

Figure 1: Production and dissemination of print

different types of work. In any case, books, newspapers, pamphlets, journals and printed flysheets were all produced in much the same way, and
looked very similar. Publishing opportunities depended very much on
cultural, political and social context; but the relationship between these
factors is so complex that a serious study of print history now requires
close scrutiny of the specific environment in which authors, printers and
distributors operated. Each book or pamphlet had a history of its own, and
each genre had distinct roles to play in political communication.

Since the publication in 1979 of Elizabeth Eisenstein's seminal work[1] on
the cultural impact of printing, historians have looked more closely at some
of the many questions that arise from its early history. There is no doubt
that Gutenberg's ingenious combination (around 1452) of a mechanical
wooden press with the use of movable type did mark a fundamental change
in the way texts could be duplicated mechanically and reliably in large
numbers. Yet this technological leap did not result in as sudden a change in

---

[1] E. Eisenstein, *The printing press as an agent of change: communications and cultural transformations in early-modern Europe* (Cambridge, 1979).

communication and dissemination as one might have expected. At first, printing was meant to produce pages that looked like quality manuscripts, primarily for large Bibles and other devotional texts aimed at a limited institutional market. The economic advantages either to the printer or the user were not immediately obvious – and indeed Gutenberg himself struggled financially. But over the next century others exploited the market more effectively. In the second quarter of the sixteenth century, Luther and other advocates of religious reform grasped the huge potential of printing as a way of transmitting their ideas to a much wider audience by means of short catechisms, collections of psalms, as well as polemical and belligerent tracts. Yet the scope for other kinds of reading material was not recognised as quickly, and some printers struggled with uneven demand and at best only modest growth. A small print run (perhaps less than 100 copies) was not cost-effective, so handwritten copying remained commonplace well into the eighteenth century – and indeed much later, in some smaller language communities. In any case printing technology initially remained confined to prosperous cities, notably those that were situated on the great trading axis of early modern Europe running from northern Italy, along the Rhine to the Netherlands, and in cultural centres such as Paris and subsequently London.[2] Even there, the output and content of print fluctuated considerably, boosted during the major religious conflicts of the second half of the sixteenth century, but still dependent on an unpredictable market. As we will argue in Chapters 1–2, it was only from the 1630s that a new wave of innovative printing came about, this time spectacularly fuelling, and fuelled by, the political upheavals which continued through the 1640s and 50s.

If the early history of the production and dissemination of print has proven less linear than it once seemed, its effective cultural impact has also been the subject of intensive research. Half a century ago, Robert Darnton questioned the traditional assumptions about the 'great' works of the Enlightenment. He focused on ways of determining what kinds of books were the real bestsellers of the later eighteenth century, and in particular noted the 'grub-street' polemics that most clearly met reader demand – more so than the 'canon' of famous texts which with hindsight have assumed the status of landmarks of the Enlightenment.[3] His work

---

[2] For the impressive but uneven growth of print before 1600, see notably A. Pettegree, 'Centre and periphery in the European book world', *Transactions of the Royal Historical Society*, 18 (2008), 101–28.

[3] This historiographical development was heralded by R. Darnton, 'The high Enlightenment and the low-life of literature in pre-revolutionary France', *Past & Present*, 51 (1971), 81–115. Further work will be cited in later chapters, but see also H. T. Mason, *The Darnton debate: books and revolution in the eighteenth century* (*SVEC* 359, Oxford, 1998).

has had enormous impact on how historians try to assess the real dissemination of different kinds of printed material, and on the kinds of evidence which may throw new light on the complex business practices of printing and bookselling.[4] In effect in recent years the intellectual and cultural history of the early modern period has shifted substantially, partly in recognition of the fact that many of the texts that were widely read at the time of publication (but have since fallen into obscurity) can now be recognised as important historical evidence. Research on this more diverse reading material has given us a much clearer understanding of the role of those texts which were profitable, sold well in particular contexts, generated public discussion, or possibly contributed to the growth of what we would now call 'public opinion'. As we will see here, some works still stand out as major landmark texts with both an immediate and a longer-term impact, but they did not achieve such impact in isolation. Research in intellectual history which focuses solely on 'great' writers and thinkers and how they influenced each other misses at least half the story. We now have to recognise the need for a much more comprehensive re-evaluation of the precise cultural and historical context and dissemination of all kinds of print, using detailed research into the bibliographical evidence, as well as assessments of the 'life' of each particular text, its physical appearance in extant copies, its immediate and/or enduring impact on readers, as well as the many factors that may have affected its dissemination, reprinting and physical survival.

This enormous research agenda is what makes the history of early modern print such a dynamic and increasingly interdisciplinary field. From the small handful of texts that have so far been studied in sufficient depth, we have gained insights into the processes of dissemination and communication that printing made possible and how it affected public discussion. We have also learnt a great deal about the increasing tangle of censorship and other restraints on freedom of expression which authors and publishers had to navigate. Printing did not displace the use of manuscript, but by the seventeenth century printing affected all aspects of cultural interaction and communication in urban communities, including controversies within and between religious groups, many aspects of central and local government, and the nature of power-relationships in civic society more generally. Not surprisingly, the incentives to learn to read were enhanced accordingly, affecting everyone who wanted to participate in urban life.

---

[4] See notably R. Darnton, *The business of the Enlightenment: a publishing history of the Enclyclopédie 1775–1800* (Cambridge, MA, 1979).

This book cannot explore the full range of cultural change attributable to the use of print, nor will it provide a survey of the origins and impact of intellectual change in general. Rather, it takes as its starting point a question which is central to our understanding of cultural, political and social communication in early modern Europe: what functions print could perform in engaging a widening circle of readers who had not previously had much opportunity to access texts of their own choice; and in particular, how communication in print might change some of the key parameters of political life broadly defined. Of course all participants in any form of social organisation invariably come into contact with some forms of power, and political awareness would no doubt have been enhanced by the very long European tradition of contestation through petitions, riots and demonstrations, as well as by simple refusal, disobedience or even legal challenge. But print provided a very powerful additional tool of communication and, when used skilfully, a means of fundamentally transforming public discussion. Historians of the late seventeenth and eighteenth centuries have been aware of these questions for some time, and as a result have substantially reshaped their definition of major cultural shifts such as the Enlightenment.[5] This book, however, encompasses a broader period going back to the 1630s, and focuses on ways in which print could provide crucial information and conflicting interpretations, in formats that could be accessed consistently by a much larger number of readers, and could be cited and challenged – thereby facilitating critical analysis of the use of power, the nature of legitimate authority, and the ordering of civic society itself. In a way, print became an essential component in the emergence of demands for political accountability, representation and ultimately some experimental forms of democracy in the 1790s.

Historians now recognise that in the early modern period what we call 'political culture' – awareness of the structures of power and authority in civic society – was much more widely diffused and more complex than the normative language of a hierarchical and deferential society might lead us to assume. Before 1789, the specific words 'politics' and 'political' were used in a mostly theoretical and narrow context derived directly from the writings of Aristotle and Plato, and referring to classical ideals such as the Greek 'polis' (city-state), the Latin 'politia' and its adjective 'politicus'. Derivative forms (and spellings) of the root word were absorbed into many European languages by the fourteenth century. Variants such as

---

[5] For an admirably concise survey, see J. Robertson, *The Enlightenment: a very short introduction* (Oxford, 2015). Wider dissemination and reader access is discussed in T. Munck, *The Enlightenment: a comparative social history 1721–1794* (London, 2000).

'polity', 'politie' or 'policie' were used to denote civil society in general, the processes of civil and ecclesiastical government, and ultimately the range of policies and public regulations creating the framework for social and economic relations ('good police' or public policy), most frequently in respect of early modern towns and markets. As a more abstract adjective or noun, 'politic[s]' could denote public affairs and the nature of government – the study of which was originally regarded as part of moral philosophy, but by the eighteenth century was often treated as a subject in its own right focusing on theories of government, state-craft (*Staatswissenschaft*) and administration. John Locke wrote in 1690 of 'Divinity, Ethicks, Law, and Politicks, and several other Sciences', while David Hume noted that 'Politics consider men as united in society, and dependent on each other'.[6]

As we explore other usages of this cluster of related words, we meet some surprises: the word 'politic', for example, could be used in the sense of 'judicious' and 'sensible', but also (already by the sixteenth century) in a more derogatory sense of 'expedient', 'crafty', 'scheming', or 'cunning', to describe someone lacking principles, even a hypocrite. In French, 'politique' might denote a pragmatic middle way, but also acquired strong undercurrents of cynicism when used in the contexts of court politics and civil war, so, by extension, was applied to men who were engaged in politics (politicians). Not surprisingly, the root word came to acquire further connotations, often in certain combinations – notably as 'body politic' in the sense of 'commonwealth' (a word which also had a very long history, widely used as a synonym for 'res publica' or the whole nation/ community gathered together). By extension, 'politic' came to be used for decision-making at lower levels, not just town councils (or even church meetings), but also, more rarely, in the household – as when Henry Fielding refers to the reading of 'a lecture on prudence, and matrimonial politics' to a young woman.[7] Clearly, concepts of private and public, 'natural' or normative authority, and the 'people' in relation to the community or the 'nation' – all components of what might nowadays be regarded as 'political culture' – meant different things in different

---

[6] J. Locke, *An essay concerning humane understanding* (London, 1690), book 2, ch. 22, p. 135; see also his use of terms such as 'community', 'commonwealth' and 'civitas' in his *Second treatise of government: an essay concerning the true original, extent, and end of civil government* (London, 1690), chs. 8, 10, 15 and *passim*; and [D. Hume], *A treatise of human nature* (London, 1739), Introduction, p. 5. For an overview of the history of political concepts, see M. Pappenheim, 'Politique', and R. Monnier, 'République, républicanisme, républicain', which constitute vol. 21 of R. Reichardt (ed.), *Handbuch politisch-sozialer Grundbegriffe in Frankreich 1680–1720* (Berlin, 2017).

[7] H. Fielding, *The history of Tom Jones* (London, 1749), vol. III, book 16, ch. 7, p. 214.

contexts. In this as in other respects, the 'linguistic turn' in early modern historical research has been hugely valuable and productive.[8]

Authority, power relationships and effective control in civil society could be expressed verbally in many different and sometimes oblique ways – notably so in past societies where there were immense and often implicit or hidden restraints on what could be openly said or written. Some forms of authority were obvious and unmistakeable, projected visually, spatially and culturally by rulers and state institutions. But real agency might well be delegated to others (local authorities, landowners) or exercised jointly with, for example, the church. The reality therefore rarely corresponded to the theoretical ideals and ideological constructs of a strictly hierarchical social order – a mismatch both in words and practical implementation which we will notice frequently in the course of this book. Out of practical necessity, some words such as 'culture' will be used here in the modern sense, since ambiguity is unlikely to arise. But more unstable terms such as 'public' or 'private', the meanings of which were themselves contested in the early modern period, will where appropriate be used with cautionary quotation marks to highlight alternative meanings. Other keywords, such as 'representation' and 'sovereign', became such central concepts during the seventeenth and eighteenth centuries that explanations will be provided as necessary. One of the central arguments of this book, however, is that many commonly used terms became so widely contested, and could be used to denote such different (and sometimes incompatible) ideals, that language itself became a key tool of authors and publishers who wanted to reach a new audience. Already from the time of Erasmus and Luther, print had helped to demonstrate the fundamental fluidity of many keywords. But during the seventeenth century, as Latin was gradually displaced by French as the common language of the educated elite, new possibilities opened up. Even more important, the translation into other vernacular languages enriched the vocabulary of everyone. Print could serve both to enhance and to standardise common usage of words and concepts in all linguistic communities. This textual legacy in turn allows historians to understand early modern political cultures in a much more precise context, and on a much

---

[8] Key work includes J. G. A. Pocock, *The Machiavellian moment: Florentine political thought and the Atlantic republican tradition* (Princeton, 1975); Q. Skinner, *The foundations of modern political thought*, 2 vols. (Cambridge, 1978); M. van Gelderen and Q. Skinner (eds.), *Republicanism: a shared European heritage*, 2 vols. (Cambridge, 2002); G. Mahlberg and D. Wiemann (eds.), *European contexts for English republicanism* (Farnham, 2013); A. Brett, 'Political thought', in H. Scott (ed.), *The Oxford handbook of early modern European History 1350–1750* (Oxford, 2015), vol. II, 29–55.

wider scale, than what is reflected in the formal rhetoric and projection of traditional authority.

In theory, at least, early modern political ideals were based on traditional Old Testament patriarchy, buttressed by notions of a severe and judgmental God. In practice, however, authority was exercised by a whole array of variable power relationships, visible at all levels of society and far more dependent on tacit agreement and apparent consensus than normative descriptions of the hierarchical social order might suggest. Yet direct physical expressions of power were also very obvious. Amongst the most extreme manifestations were the military and naval codes of conduct, using violence and displays of force to suppress internal disorder, to exploit overseas maritime commerce and to legitimise occupation of foreign territory. During the early modern period military manpower was acquired primarily by two means: the use of mercenary soldiers, and a more systematic implementation of coercive military impressment. Both required elaborate financial mechanisms to extract resources, and a clear projection of the non-negotiable power of the state. The forcible extortion of supplies and revenue from occupied territories (your own, or foreign, wherever your army was operating), the development of military entrepreneurial networks for equipment and organisation, and the difficult consolidation of more permanent fiscal and administrative mechanisms to sustain the inevitable increase in military demands were the most obvious indicators of what we now call the process of 'state formation' in this period. The impact on every member of society was inescapable, whether it came in the form of huge increases in the tax burden (leading to the 'fiscal state'), demands for personal military service from able-bodied males (conscription and other labour service), or unpredictable pillage by marauding troops (the booty of war). Armies and navies were themselves run on norms of ferocious internal discipline which replicated the hierarchy of civil society but added extreme levels of physical violence, well beyond what would have been acceptable in terms even of the harsh standards of early modern civil law. No state during this period secured anything like a monopoly of violence, but the projection of political power was an essential means towards that end.

Some of the other formal principles underpinning power in early modern society were equally explicit, not least in terms of institutions, deferential use of space and appropriate forms of speech, all of which could serve to mark out the many intricacies of status, rank and power. Important as these were, however, they should not blind us to the many more tacit assumptions and symbolic reinforcements of inequality that sometimes emerge from closer scrutiny of a wider range of source material. We need to be acutely aware of the connected but not identical

concepts of legitimate authority (including sovereignty), legitimate traditional power and coercive power – and the attendant (reinforcing but not
always explicit) political assumptions that held civil society together most
of the time. In trying to conceptualise early modern political culture,
therefore, we may want to keep in mind the many ways in which power
might be represented in different contexts: in the language of legal processes and arbitration, and the ceremony or spectacle of social discipline
(including criminal punishment); in the many ambiguities inherent in the
power relationships of landowners with their workforce (peasant tenants,
cottagers, labourers); in the very different civil relationships existing
within those urban societies that could preserve some degree of autonomy
and self-government; and (in so far as visions of civil society reached that
far) in the norms of (ostensibly pious) discipline which were supposed to
prevail within household and family structures. Much of the evidence
relating to these complex cultural systems never made it into print, and
for some of these areas of interaction body language and speech were at
least as important as handwritten texts.

If there are many forms of evidence reflecting the higher levels of power
and authority of rulers, church leaders, judges, landowners, town councils, guilds and corporations, it is sometimes more difficult to evaluate at
the lowest level of everyday experience, especially where patriarchy was
most firmly entrenched, within the individual household.[9] There, actual
relationships were not on continuous open display, and most of those on
the receiving end of regulatory discipline or even physical abuse never had
a chance to describe their side of the story, let alone challenge any
coercion. Normative sources, ranging from church and civil law to moralising advice manuals recommending appropriately decorous behaviour,
always assumed that authority belonged unequivocally to the head of
household (typically an older male), who was culturally and explicitly
the key link in a hierarchy of power reaching all the way down from the
head of state to the individual. Male household authority was not only
unquestioned, but also in practice nearly unrestrained even in law (except
in cases of extreme violence). Accordingly, within the family, there was
effectively no scope for legitimate contestation by other members of the
household – least of all by women, whose ability to engage in decision-
making either in the household or in the local community was habitually
regulated by senior males in the family. Such a hierarchy of power applied
in principle at all social levels, from the aristocracy down to the great

---

[9] See C. W. Brooks, *Law, politics and society in early modern England* (Cambridge, 2008),
352–84, regarding the law in relation to the household. For a wide-ranging discussion of
patriarchy in cultural context, see C. Cuttica and G. Mahlberg (eds.), *Patriarchal moments:
reading patriarchal texts* (London, 2016).

majority of households where occupational and economic constraints made women an essential (if often unacknowledged) part of the labour force, and where gender inequality was taken for granted.

In a formal sense, the household was not in the public eye, and its relationships were deemed private and unaccountable. By convention, the textual portrayals of household relationships fictionalised the domestic sphere: a profusion of satirical ballads circulating in oral culture and sometimes in print; privately published sermons and devotional literature amongst non-conformist groups; actual fiction (including by the eighteenth century the all-important category of novels); new types of family-oriented reading material such as the moral weeklies and *Spectator*-type journals; and not least (for those who could afford it) imaginary representation in opera and theatre. Much of this material tended to rely on stereotypes, or even caricatured aberrations – leaving many questions unanswered. Far more detail is found in the manuscript material and administrative archives of law courts, municipal government and parish churches, where we find ample evidence of quarrelsome partners, disputed property rights both within marriage and involving outsiders, unruly servants, rebellious children, tiresome or complaining elderly relatives, physical and verbal abuse which offended against moral and religious precepts and, not least, illicit sexual relationships with or without the consent of both participants.[10]

Some types of first-person account from this period survive. They range from simple annotations in printed almanacs, autobiographies, memoirs, family histories and diaries, to more elaborate travel accounts or fictionalised storytelling based on real-life experience – categories of writing which were only developing at the time, and not all stabilised into recognisable forms. First-person accounts are by definition always exceptional, their authors taking an extraordinary decision in writing anything at all.[11] Apart from letters, the relatively few personal writings that survive conventionally focus on devotional and spiritual life, or, amongst the aristocracy, typically about family and lineage. But during the eighteenth century, memoirs with political content became more

---

[10] A few legal records made it into print. The *Proceedings* of the Old Bailey in London, published from 1674 and almost serialised, were never detailed accounts, but rather summaries intended for those with an interest in the law, and for the general public. This venture was exceptional: in London and elsewhere, the publication of legal briefs became more common only in the later eighteenth century. In Paris such publications became fashionable in the 1780s, also serving as publicity for the lawyers themselves: S. Maza, *Private lives and public affairs: the causes célèbres of pre-revolutionary France* (Berkeley, 1993).

[11] An excellent analysis with particular focus on lower social levels is found in J. S. Amelang, *The flight of Icarus: artisan autobiography in early modern Europe* (Stanford, CA, 1998).

common amongst those of high social status and sufficient educational attainment, including a few accounts by women. By the time of the French Revolution, there is a substantial range to choose from, including such well-known examples as the fragmentary memoirs of Madame Roland (wife and personal assistant of a government minister). Many participants in the French Revolution left personal accounts, but often in the form of edited memoirs rather than actual diaries. A highly informative example is the account of Louis-Philippe, son of the Duc d'Orléans, edited at the end of his long and politically complicated life, acutely aware of his national political role as officer in the French revolutionary armies and as a member of a very elevated aristocratic family with a claim to the throne. Neither Madame Roland nor Louis-Philippe intended to do more than merely 'put the record straight', probably for their family and friends.[12] But writing (in any form) is inevitably a kind of engagement with more readers than one might know, even when there was no initial intention of going into print or addressing a wider unknown 'public'. How much we can read into such accounts has been debated extensively in recent years.[13] But we are left in no doubt how intricate and problematic family relationships often were: clearly the evidence is anything but straightforward.

Petitions stand out, in early modern Europe, as a very voluminous (and so far underused) type of source material which allows historians a more clearly placed insight into ongoing disputes and difficulties of all kinds. They were a normal form of communication between individuals at all levels of society, usually addressed to a superior (landowner, church authority, local government official, or territorial ruler). Unlike the records of the law, usually recorded by trained lawyers or court officers, petitions were typically written by the petitioner him- or herself, or from dictation or personal summary to a clerk paid by the petitioner. Petitioning had always been a normal process in most communities, and commonly served as a safety valve for social, economic and political grievances everywhere, recognised by petitioner and superior alike. In some parts of Europe, attempts were made by governments to restrict what sometimes seemed a flood of petitions, but such restrictions were always resented and deemed contrary to the relationship of trust that was

---

[12] English versions are found in E. Shuckburgh (transl. and ed.), *The memoirs of Madame Roland* (London, 1989); J. Hardman (transl. and ed.), *Louis Philippe Memoirs 1773–1793* (New York and London, 1977).

[13] Indicative examples include: S. C. Seelig, *Autobiography and gender in early modern literature: reading women's lives, 1600–1680* (Cambridge, 2006); A. Smyth, *Autobiography in early modern England* (Cambridge, 2010); O. Niethammer, *Autobiographien von Frauen im 18. Jahrhundert* (Tübingen, 2000).

supposed to exist between subject and ruler. Elsewhere, notably in Denmark and in the Habsburg lands, petitions to the crown became an important mechanism whereby the crown could check on its own local officials, and occasionally intervene in order to reinforce public perceptions of a fair and impartial ruler serving the interests of stability and security for all.[14] Significantly, however, it was very dangerous to print a petition, since that could well be interpreted as a breach of the trust that was at the centre of the petitioning process. A petition was meant to be a personal request for help, recognising the relative status and influence of each part, and reinforcing the mutual but personal interests of both parties. Once a petition went into print, however, you were by definition addressing a wider public, and not respecting the rules of an interdependent and deferential society: a printed petition might therefore appear either conspiratorial or even an incitement to sedition. As we shall see in Chapter 2, the printing of petitions in civil war England changed the political parameters in ways that had fundamental repercussions.

The early modern state became increasingly aware of the value of detailed records and administrative information, but very little of it was published. The uneven manuscript records of actual parliaments or other representative assemblies (where such still existed) can be frustratingly summary, and only in exceptional circumstances available to readers at the time. Extraordinary parliamentary events, however, might create major public interest, as happened in France in 1789, when the formal request by the crown in connection with the first meeting of the Estates General for nearly two centuries led to the compilation of detailed books of grievances (*cahiers de doléances*) from all over France. The French *cahiers* were in a way just another and more specific version of collective petitions. But the compilation process itself generated substantial discussion within the French nobility, the divided clergy and the better-off amongst the commoner Third Estate, and even led to some 'model cahiers' being published and circulated. Even if hardly any of the actual *cahiers* were printed at the time, they undoubtedly formed a substantial and formally recognised summary of public perceptions of problems in the political, social and economic structures of the kingdom.[15]

---

[14] D. Beales, 'Joseph II, petitions and the public sphere', in H. Scott and B. Simms (eds.), *Cultures of power in Europe during the long eighteenth century* (Cambridge, 2007), 249–68; T. Munck, 'Petitions and "legitimate" engagement with power in absolutist Denmark 1660-1800', in *Parliaments, Estates and Representation*, 38 (2018), 378–91, and other articles in that issue.

[15] The estimated 40,000 surviving *cahiers* have so far only been analysed on the basis of systematic samples, but nevertheless reveal levels of political engagement at all levels of society which readily dispel any assumptions that the majority of French commoners, hitherto devoid of any political role in government, were not capable of putting together

The use of print for isolated political texts had been initiated much earlier, often by individuals who were no longer in positions of authority. We need only think of the political upheaval in Florence leading to the trial and execution of Girolamo Savonarola in 1498, and the precarious republican government that followed. During this period, a senior official in the republic, Niccolò Machiavelli (1469–1527), was able to acquire a range of insights into the mechanics of high-level government. These are reflected in his best-known work, *The prince*, completed in 1513 shortly after he had been imprisoned and then exiled by the restored Medici ruling family. When the book was eventually published in 1532, after Machiavelli's death, it established itself (along with his *Discourses*) as one of the most influential political tracts of the Renaissance, widely disseminated and later translated,[16] with long-term impact not just on his immediate patrician readers but also on the writings of later political theorists.

The religious movements of the Reformation also brought political questions into much sharper focus. Since all the main variants of Protestantism, as well as groups of reformers within the Catholic church, were bound to challenge established religious authority in some way, it is hardly surprising that many key participants, including the leading reformers themselves, were ambivalent and at times alarmed at what they had unleashed. Luther reacted fiercely against the Peasants' Revolt of 1525, and Calvin's Geneva created a model theocracy where parishioners appeared to have little scope for independent judgment, let alone actual agency. 'Liberty', in short, was a dangerous concept, and free will in religious terms was in many eyes tantamount to heresy or libertinism, to be avoided at all costs, and if necessary forcibly suppressed.[17]

Almost everywhere we look in later sixteenth-century Europe, there were manifestations of the divisive politics of religion. In France and England in the later sixteenth century, Calvinist influences pushed some reformers even further, towards fully fledged religious resistance theories. The French wars of religion demonstrate the violence

---

some very ambitious political agendas. See notably J. Markoff, *The abolition of feudalism: peasants, lords and legislators in the French Revolution* (Philadelphia, 1996); G. A. Kelly, 'The machine of the Duc d'Orléans and the new politics', *Journal of Modern History*, 51 (1979), 667–84, notes that draft or model cahiers were circulated in print, providing cues for those compiling the actual documents.

[16] A French translation of *The prince* appeared in 1613, and an English one in 1640, each with further editions. For a recent analysis, see P. Stacey, 'Free and unfree states in Machiavelli's political philosophy', in Q. Skinner and M. van Gelderen (eds.), *Freedom and the construction of Europe* (Cambridge, 2013), vol. I, 176–94.

[17] See also Skinner and van Gelderen (eds.), *Freedom and the construction of Europe*.

inherent in such confrontations, and its worst events, such as the massacre of Huguenots on St Bartholomew's Day 1572, caused flurries of pamphlets and arguments on both sides,[18] demonstrating the scale of public anxiety. The deeper impact became apparent over the following years, with a cluster of texts analysing not only conflicting Catholic and Calvinist beliefs, but also the limitations of princely power. Some of these writings took political resistance to its ultimate extreme, advocating the right to kill a tyrant ruler: the monarchomachs (as these more radical writers were later called) thereby provided religious justification for direct actions that Luther or his followers would never have sanctioned. François Hotman (1524–90) had been a close associate of Calvin, but by the time he published his *Francogallia* in 1573 (translated into French and German soon afterwards) he was probably more influenced by Calvin's successor, Theodor Beza (de Bèze), who himself wrote a (less widely disseminated) tract on the power of magistrates (*Du droit des magistrats*, 1574). Even more blunt in circumscribing the rightful powers of rulers and magistrates was the anonymous tract *Vindiciae contra tyrannos* which appeared in 1579 (with numerous Latin editions over the following years, as well as a French version and sections in Dutch).[19] These works made clear the unconditional right of resistance against a ruler imposing decisions counter to the judgment of individual religious belief and biblical interpretation.

The repercussions on ideals of political authority were enormous. The distinctive and cautious arguments presented by Jean Bodin in *Les six livres de la république* (1576) carefully distinguished legitimate undivided royal power from tyranny, and recognised a right to resistance only within defined limits. Bodin first appeared in French, clearly aimed at Calvinist readers, but went through a large number of editions, and was rendered in Latin and German in the following decades, thereby reaching across the educated and more conservative elite of Europe. In Scotland, a striking variant of Calvinist resistance theory was published in Latin by George Buchanan, notably in his *De jure regni apud Scotos Dialogus* (1579), and to a lesser extent his *Rerum Scoticarum Historia* (1582). *De jure regni* acquired so much notoriety in Scotland that it was banned, and had to be printed on the continent, sustaining numerous editions in the Netherlands and Frankfurt, but no English translation

---

[18] R. M. Kingdon, *Myths about the St. Bartholomew's Day massacres 1572–76* (Cambridge, MA, 1988).

[19] 'Stephanus Brutus' [Anon], *Vindiciae contra tyrannos* ('Edinburgh' [Basel], 1579). The authorship of this tract remains uncertain, but could have been Philippe Duplessis de Mornay or Hubert Languet.

until 1680 (significantly, reprinted in 1689).[20] By contrast, the less original compilation by Justus Lipsius (1547–1606), his *Politicorum sive civilis doctrinae* of 1589, followed a much more cautious line of argument, using quotes from Cicero, Tacitus and the earlier Christian writers to shore up traditional authority. Probably more important was the Calvinist political theorist Johannes Althusius (1563–1638), whose *Politica methodice digesta* of 1603 provided important arguments for devolved government, but even so it was not widely translated and appears to have had little impact outside scholarly circles. As we will see in Chapter 3, Latin remained the habitual language for major work well into the seventeenth century: the use of French by Beza and Bodin already in the 1570s may therefore signal a desire to reach a different readership.

The division of power between civic government and the church was key to the great political crisis that struck the determinedly independent Venetian republic, when in 1606 the Pope excommunicated the Doge and the Senate of Venice because of a long-running conflict regarding jurisdictional rights and the power of civic government in ecclesiastical affairs. Amongst the most effective theorists and advisers to the patrician Venetian government was Paolo Sarpi (1562–1623), a prelate and canon lawyer with extensive experience of ecclesiastical politics all over northern Italy and Rome, whose understanding of politics turned him into an exceptionally well-informed and outspoken advocate of authoritarian civic governance and the subordination of the church to Venetian law. He gave edge and sophistication to a lively public discussion, playing a major role in weakening the impact and credibility of the papal interdict, challenging papal prerogative powers and ultimately ensuring that the Venetian clergy largely stayed loyal to the government. Such a fundamental confrontation necessarily entailed an extensive use of propaganda on both sides (including print), in what became a very public dispute. The botched attempt by the Papacy to have Sarpi assassinated (1607) merely demonstrated how vicious the power struggle had become. Sarpi remained an influential adviser to the Venetian government, a prolific writer and a patron of a number of scientists including Galileo. His outstanding and critical *History of the Council of Trent*, published in London under a pseudonym in 1619, was translated into English in 1620 and into French the following year, whilst his no less controversial study of the Inquisition, written around 1613 just for the Venetian government, was published in 1638, translated into English

---

[20] C. Erskine and R. A. Mason (eds.), *George Buchanan: political thought in early modern Britain and Europe* (Farnham, 2012).

the next year and into Latin in 1651.[21] He can readily be credited as one of the most effective intellectual publicists for republican government, his ability to see church and state politics in starkly realistic terms winning him many readers across Europe.

Religion and politics remained an explosive mix right through the seventeenth century and beyond. It substantially changed the way governments operated everywhere, sometimes fundamentally so, as in Elizabethan England in the 1580s[22] and in the Netherlands in 1618. Calvinist communities particularly had great difficulty drawing a line between liberty and the right of resistance on the one hand, and the risks of 'libertine' deviance and political disloyalty on the other.[23] In religious terms, liberty and free will, even for those not wholly committed to the doctrine of the elect, was no more than the freedom to do what God intended (guided by anything ranging from free will to an assumed or explicit covenant with God). In political terms, liberty might involve freedom from slavery or imprisonment, freedom to do something, being given (or taking) liberty in a specific context, or (as in Locke's *Two Treatises*) a more generic right to live under a government instituted by the common consent of those who were part of the political nation. That in turn explains why 'liberties' was a word often used to mean privileges to which (some) individuals were entitled – for example the established citizens of an urban area – whilst to more radical thinkers 'liberty' acquired connotations of rights to which everyone was entitled, on the basis of ancient precedent or even a notional (mythical) 'constitution' of a free people, and ultimately on broader natural rights arguments.

With all these qualifications in mind, we may now recognise that the modern term 'political culture' is indeed widely applicable to the period before 1789, despite the fact that the early modern period was an age of ostensibly restricted and undemocratic politics. In 1987 Keith Baker, in the Introduction to a four-volume compilation on the French Revolution, suggested that:

Political culture comprises the definitions of the relative positions from which individuals and groups may (or may not) legitimately make claims one upon another, and therefore of the identity and boundaries of the community to which they belong (or from which they are excluded). It constitutes the meanings

---

[21] Sarpi's writings need further research, but see J. Kainulainen, *Paolo Sarpi: a servant of God and state* (Leiden, 2014), and D. Wootton, *Paolo Sarpi: between Renaissance and Enlightenment* (Cambridge, 1983).

[22] See notably A. Walsham, *Catholic reformation in Protestant Britain* (Farnham, 2014).

[23] J. Coffey, 'The language of liberty in Calvinist political thought', in Skinner and van Gelderen (eds.), *Freedom and the construction of Europe*, vol. I, 296–316.

of the terms in which these claims are framed, the nature of the contexts to which they pertain, and the authority of the principles according to which they are made binding. It defines the institutional (and extra-institutional) processes by means of which these claims are formulated, the strategies by which they are pressed, and the contestations to which they give rise. It shapes the constitutions and powers of the agencies and procedures by which contestations are resolved, competing claims authoritatively adjudicated, and binding decisions enforced.[24]

Historians analysing the power structures of early modern Europe may therefore legitimately start by defining 'political culture' to include all accepted ideas, institutions, systems of shared assumptions, commonly accepted negotiating practices and legal structures underpinning the exercise of civil authority and legitimate power at all levels of society. With such a broad definition, we have no difficulty in recognising many forms of political consciousness across the whole social spectrum, from central government down to parish officeholders, from royal advisers down to craft guild members, in an age where 'politics' was rarely defined but power was universally recognisable. Elaborate cultural constructs were used to express and project social and political hierarchies – in words, buildings, the use of space, in the ubiquitous observance of deference and rank, styles of dress and forms of address, as well as in the complex webs of patronage and personal connection, some of them implied rather than stated. Social assumptions and religious conventions certainly reinforced ubiquitous and inescapable inequality, but could also serve as a guarantee against abuse. Powers that were exercised in ways that manifestly exceeded what was accepted as legitimate and 'fair' (by the standards of the community) might be openly challenged, whether by unruly apprentices, revellers, rioters or hard-pressed peasants, or even by members of the political elite itself. Power was constantly renegotiated, often through elaborate rituals. If accepted norms appeared to be flouted beyond acceptable bounds, collective action might emerge, justified in terms of commonwealth, consensus or even collective responsibility, and underpinned by hypothetical ancient rights of a 'free' people, an imagined 'constitution', or perhaps by local custom or long-established tradition.

It will be clear from this overview of early modern political culture, that print was a particular form of communication and dissemination, but by no means the only one. However, since print had already earlier changed the whole nature of religious controversy and religious belief across Europe, it is worth asking whether it had an equally dramatic

---

[24] K. M. Baker (ed.), *The French Revolution and the creation of modern political culture*, vol. 1 (Oxford, 1987), xii.

impact also on political culture, power relationships and concepts of a stable civic society. We have noted some of the authors who by 1620 had tackled fundamental issues of good governance, so print was already recognised as a powerful tool in political confrontations. What makes the period covered in this book different is the scale, diversity, deliberate social outreach and extraordinary inventiveness of political print gaining momentum from the 1630s, and leading to near-anarchy in political culture in some parts of Europe in the 1640s. In some of the conflicts of the mid-seventeenth century the parameters of public controversy changed irreversibly, and quite suddenly. The scale of political upheaval in England, in particular, not only attracted a socially much broader range of urban readers, but also catapulted authors into writing texts that would have been inconceivable earlier. This book seeks to demonstrate that controversy in print now became a regular feature of major political crises – a process that was not at all continuous, but helped to create a shared cross-cultural awareness of how civic society and good governance might work. Print also fostered a truly international and many-sided exploration of what kinds of authority were creditable and legitimate, and how political power might serve to moderate and balance the conflicting interests of both the individual and society as a whole.

First of all, Chapter 1 outlines ways in which we may attempt to quantify changes in printed outputs across the more important European markets, measuring both the quantity and the content of different types of publication, and how changes in style and content could be accommodated within the print industry. As we will see, we still lack systematic overview of total print output for many parts of Europe, so alternative methods of assessment may be needed. But where we do have reliable bibliographical data (Short-Title Catalogues or other forms of comprehensive listings) a range of useful research techniques can be applied. Access to the actual content is much more cumbersome, except for the very small proportion of all early modern printed texts that have so far been fully digitised. Those that have can be subjected to additional systematic analysis of vocabulary and style of argumentation.

This lays the foundations for the rest of the book. Chapter 2 examines the political crises across much of Europe between 1635 and 1660 in terms of the publication of new kinds of texts, and their wider dissemination. In England during the 1640s, print played an unprecedented and unique role in raising a host of political and religious questions for a wider public. Print became the most powerful tool available to polemicists, political activists and loyalists alike, and no-one with an interest in re-stabilising civic society could ignore what was being published.

During the 1640s and beyond, an impressive range of questions were raised regarding scriptural authority, royal power, parliamentary and representative authority, the politics of military force (discussed in extraordinary army council meetings), individual rights, and those natural rights that might be inherent in all civilised communities and therefore guaranteed against political manipulation. Much of the controversy dissipated after 1660, as the various political crises in England and other parts of Europe subsided. But English exiles in the Netherlands helped to keep key ideas alive, and they became relevant once more when religious and political instability resurfaced in the Netherlands, France and England in the 1670s and 1680s, in particular when Louis XIV in 1685 revoked the Edict of Nantes and so wrecked any hope of religious compromise. It is difficult to overstate the impact of the resulting flight of probably several hundred thousand Huguenots to neighbouring Protestant countries, aggravated by a series of territorial wars. A huge amount of print was generated by those who set up whole communities of highly skilled and well-educated French-speaking exiles in the Netherlands and elsewhere. Chapter 3 therefore includes quite detailed discussion of both the religious and the broader civil implications of these challenges, and how long it took before arguments for toleration could gain even limited traction in the eighteenth century.

The international upheavals from 1685 to 1721 had major repercussions not just in terms of political exiles, but also on the transmission of news, discussion of civil society, and above all a broadening of political discussion beyond the bounds of particular crises. The works of Locke, Fénelon, Montesquieu and others acquired a transnational significance, and since Latin was only accessible to a learned minority, translation became increasingly common. Chapter 4 examines both the tools available to translators (including dictionaries and reference works) and the way contemporaries became more explicitly conscious of the importance of language and mutual understanding in order to reach beyond the traditional republic of letters. We can identify a more open international community of readers who relied primarily on their own native language. Again, printing was a crucial component in 'democratising' the dissemination of information and understanding, but translation also unavoidably required transcultural understanding and sometimes a significant degree of adaptation to suit the needs of its new readers. Some years ago, Peter Burke alerted us to the historical significance of cultural translation.[25] Current research

---

[25] P. Burke, 'Cultures of translation in early modern Europe', in P. Burke and R. Po-Chia Hsia (eds.), *Cultural translation in early modern Europe* (Cambridge, 2007), 7–38; and P. Burke, *Languages and communities in early modern Europe* (Cambridge, 2004).

suggests not only that a whole new market for translated books developed from the 1690s onwards, but also that political languages across Europe became more standardised and more mutually intelligible thanks to this transnational dissemination of texts. Patterns of transmission through translation created new (if uneven) context-sensitive networks of dissemination. But translation also provides the historian of print with major new and precise evidence: a book translated into Danish, for example, can be located much more accurately in time and place than a frequently reprinted French original read all over Europe by the small francophile elite.[26]

Rapidly changing political circumstances after 1748 created the framework for the last two chapters. Chapter 5 focuses on the enormous changes in political thinking, governmental practice and public discussion which developed during the mid-century wars and after the peace settlement of 1763. A few years later, the American wars of independence led to a sensational experiment in constructing a new republic according to the political ideals of the late Enlightenment. News reports and commentaries were read with growing interest across the old world. The wars had already alerted all governments to the urgent need for rational reform, but some were better than others at recognising the value of active engagement with public opinion. The impact of the American revolt was naturally felt most strongly in Britain, where soul-searching was accompanied by an increasingly dynamic recognition amongst a wider public of the need for domestic social and economic improvement, as well as electoral reform. In Britain and in France there was also widespread interest in the potential for better fiscal management, and awareness of the damaging effects of factional politics and court patronage. In response, the British and the French governments tried very hard (by different means) to stifle domestic political controversy by controlling what could be said in newspapers and other publications, but neither had more than partial success. In France the censorship system became so intricate and self-contradictory that, as we will see, it virtually collapsed under its own weight. Censorship could in any case easily become counterproductive, merely by attracting attention to contentious publications.

Both before 1789 and in the early 1790s, the British and French reading public demonstrated some interest in political developments on the other side of the Channel. Chapter 6 uses the example of radical political activism in Paris to illustrate how far the new politics originated

---

[26] For practical purposes, nearly all quotations included here have been translated into English (by the author, except where otherwise stated). The irony of comparing translations – by retranslating texts into English – will not be lost on readers of this book, but wherever possible the footnotes will help locate the original version for further study.

in ideas from earlier printed texts, brought back into consideration by urgent political quandaries. Across much of Europe, despite reinforced censorship, Parisian political free-thinking was reported extensively, and led to renewed discussion of good governance and social inequality. Significantly, however, the disintegration of civil government in France into wartime Terror not only fundamentally changed the nature of the domestic newspaper industry and what it could print, but also appears to have damaged commercial printing in France very severely, to the extent that the publication of substantive independent texts was less likely to be profitable or even viable. Perhaps the premature deaths in 1794 of two of the greatest figures of the late French Enlightenment, Condorcet and Lavoisier, were symbolic of more than just a huge personal loss. But in any case the very severe repressive measures taken against writers in Britain, France and across much of the rest of Europe between 1792 and 1795 undoubtedly mark the end of reasonably open political discussion, both in print and in public.

It goes without saying that a single volume cannot encompass political discussion in print across all of Europe during these distinct periods of political change and turbulence. Such a discussion would, for a start, require thorough bibliographical research (encompassing all reprints and translations before 1800) for a much larger sample of texts. Instead, the aim is to discuss representative or extreme examples with a view to documenting broader patterns of change. The sample of texts used here has grown throughout the years it took to write this book, but remains largely confined to those parts of Europe where the market for political texts (including translations) was strongest. As will be clear, politics often shaded into religious beliefs as well as other cultural norms, and print was not the sole vehicle for wider dissemination of political awareness – not even the most important one for some types of personal communication. Public opinion was also directly affected by prevailing attitudes to social hierarchy, norms of decorum and deference. But a rapidly growing legacy of controversial texts increasingly scrutinised all kinds of characteristics and problems in civil society. By the eighteenth century, scientific research and interest in the social sciences ('the science of man') created even more reading material.

All this makes for a complex canvas, where different types of printed material can be read as evidence both of changing political perceptions and of the changing priorities of political reformers, political scientists, visionaries and polemicists, or merely the curious voracious reader. The texts, studied in their specific context, of course throw light both on authors and on the expectations of readers. But all kinds of printed material also form a hugely important resource in assessing changes in linguistic usage and the adoption of more diverse conceptual vocabularies. Since no language can ever be static until it is dead, we can use keyword searches on printed material to map out some of these changes and usages more systematically, and to help us understand how textual communication might actually have worked. In what follows, comparative analysis is invariably the preferred approach: what may be lost in terms of specific detail may, perhaps, be compensated for in terms of insights gained through a transnational perspective. Even if we cannot always compare like with like, differences can be just as helpful in revealing significant shifts in political culture.

Indicative Note on the Value of Money in Britain and France

Printed material was never cheap, but a case for a widening readership would in part rest on relative costs. The following approximate reference points regarding wages and prices may help place the price of printed material in some kind of context.

The English pound sterling was divided into 20 shillings (20s.) and each shilling into 12 pence (12d.). The French livre was valued at just short of one-tenth of the pound sterling, but was also divided into 20 sous, each of 12 deniers.

Wages

Basic wage rates amongst ordinary craftsmen and workers varied significantly by season (daylight hours and availability of work), size of the market (rural or urban) and the overall state of the economy. Any general summary, as well as particular examples, must be treated as very approximate representations of a much wider range of actual earnings.

In late seventeenth-century England, a male labourer's wage might be in the range of £10 to £20 per annum. Gregory King set the poverty line (for a family of two adults and two children) at around £20 per annum (based on calculations from the 1680s), but actual poor relief payments under the poor law in 1748 were typically around £14 per annum. By the 1760s, Adam Smith estimated that skilled workers might earn up to £37 per annum (but less in the provinces and in lower-skill trades).

In France in the 1690s, a period of severe economic instability, the well-informed marquis de Vauban estimated rural labourers and weavers might earn 90–120 livres per annum. By 1790, the government's Comité de Mendicité estimated an annual subsistence wage (again for a family) at 435 livres (with inflationary erosion accounting for a significant part of the apparent increase since Vauban). We may also note that during the eighteenth century a compositor in a printing workshop could earn 650 livres per annum if he was working full time. Diderot, as editor of the *Encyclopédie*, earned 2600 livres per annum.

Cost of Books

The format of books varied to suit the market. Substantial works were often first published in quarto or larger formats to meet the expectations of wealthier readers. Reprints and more popular texts typically economised on paper and were printed in smaller formats (octavo or less), often with correspondingly smaller fonts, and sometimes issued in paper covers to ensure lower prices and wider accessibility.

In the seventeenth century, the plays of Corneille might sell at just over 2 livres (but only a quarter of that, 10 sous, in pirated versions). Hobbes's *Leviathan* cost 8s. on publication in 1651, but the price rose dramatically after the book was banned. By contrast, shorter pamphlets (8–24 pages) and chapbooks (blue books, *livres bleues*) were typically priced between 2d. and 4d. in England, or around 2 sous in France.

In the early eighteenth century, novels were often 1s. in England. In France some novels might be slightly more expensive, depending whether they were authorised or not: by the 1780s prices were often in the range 1–2 livres. Rousseau's lengthy *Nouvelle Heloïse* at first cost 8 livres wholesale.

By the later eighteenth century non-fictional books tended to be in the range 3s.–£1 in London. A duodecimo volume of Hume's *Philosophical essays* initially sold at 3s. in 1748, but his very successful *History of England* sold in 1762 at 30s. for the two-volume set in quarto. William Robertson's *History of the reign of the emperor Charles V* was published in three quarto volumes in 1769 at a cost of £2.12s. unbound, and over £3 bound. The two volumes of Adam Smith's lengthy *Wealth of nations* (1776) sold at £2, again in quarto. Paine's *Rights of man*, part 1 (1791), sold at 2s. 6d. in a relatively upmarket octavo version, but was soon reprinted at a much lower price (or given away for free) – invariably cheaper than the text it attacked, Burke's *Reflections on the Revolution in France*, typically selling at 5s. In 1792, Mary Wollstonecraft's *Vindications of the rights of woman* sold for 7s., but the following year William Godwin's upmarket (quarto) and slightly longer *An enquiry concerning political justice* sold at twice that price.

A seat in the upper gallery of a theatre might cost 1s. in London, or 1 livre in Paris.

In England, a single engraved print typically sold at 6d. or 1s., but could be as much as 4s. depending on size (and possibly hand-colouring). By 1789 a single issue of a newspaper might cost 3d., or slightly higher in London.

1 Print, Production, Authors and Readers

By the early seventeenth century, the printing industry had become a well-established, complex and investment-intensive part of the urban economy in the more prosperous parts of Europe, particularly in the Rhineland area, the Netherlands and in major capital cities. Yet it is worth noting that, following Gutenberg's creation of a fully working movable-type printing workshop by 1452, production methods and the core technology of printing did not change substantially for centuries, until experiments with cast-iron presses gained momentum around 1800. At most, during the seventeenth and eighteenth centuries, there were incremental refinements in the practical design of printing presses, improvements in the design and clarity of typefaces, marginal reduction in costs to meet an expanding market, as well as some stabilisation of the all-important ancillary trades such as paper manufacturing, distribution, bookselling and bookbinding (see Figure 1). The only significant reduction in actual unit costs arose from improvements in paper production (including the growing use of mechanical water-powered mills to treat the rags constituting the core raw material in the manufacture of paper). Since paper remained the most expensive component of the printing industry, publishers were often cautious when printing a new work: significantly, it remained more cost effective to reset and reprint repeatedly if demand was high, rather than run off a larger number of copies first time. This gives historians a vital clue to market demand, but of course did not make texts which were in great demand any cheaper.

The quite dramatic but uneven increases in the quantity and types of printed material in many parts of Europe during the seventeenth and eighteenth centuries cannot therefore be explained primarily in technological terms: such increases, as we will see in this chapter, had far more to do with diversification in the kinds of texts that were printed, and rising demand from a socially more diverse range of readers. Authors and publishers recognised the potential for development beyond the traditional modes of communication, and successfully experimented with particularly adaptable forms of output such as pamphlets and shorter books, newspapers and fiction. In order to understand changes in the role of print as a vehicle for political awareness, we need to be more aware of the types of printed material that used to be considered 'ephemeral' or marginal, including short polemical works published in very specific contexts and therefore quickly losing their apparent relevance. Understanding actual dissemination processes requires more complex research techniques. This chapter will use the comprehensive databases of printed material currently becoming available online, notably the so-called short-title catalogues (STCs) designed to give full bibliographical data for all extant printed items from before 1800.[1] In such searches, clues arising from the physical (material) aspects of print become very important: the smaller formats used to save on paper costs, the different layouts intended for different types of readers and of course the language and content of the texts themselves.

The many interests that characterise the complicated relationships between authors, printers, booksellers, readers, censors and church or state authorities, in different cultural environments across Europe, pose major challenges in terms both of evidence and historical interpretation. Restraints (and self-restraints) on freedom of expression are evident everywhere, but were erratic and very context-sensitive. Despite recent progress, the process of gathering reliable data on actual print output and distribution is very time-consuming, and we still lack comprehensive and reliable national bibliographical information for many parts of Europe. Incunabula (movable-type books printed before 1500) have been examined more systematically than the much larger quantity and diversity of print produced during the turbulent sixteenth and early seventeenth centuries. The trade networks that connected printers and readers are difficult to document in any detail: even though printed material remained a relatively expensive and context-sensitive commodity to produce and sell, reliable trade records from before 1760 (if they ever existed) rarely survive, and even those from the later eighteenth century may be atypical.[2]

---

[1] STCs are more reliable (for the purposes of this chapter) than the many digitised collections of historical texts now being developed for many European languages. Although such collections have the advantage of rendering texts in full, they are invariably very selective: that selection process is not normally based on systematic sampling techniques, so the resulting collections of digitised texts do not represent overall print output as accurately as comprehensive STCs.

[2] See the current debate (which may be called 'the Darnton debate') surrounding the records of the later eighteenth-century STN (Société Typographique de Neuchâtel), as discussed by R. Darnton, 'The forbidden books of pre-revolutionary France', in C. Lucas (ed.), *Rewriting the French Revolution* (Oxford, 1991), 1–32; S. Burrows, 'French banned books in international perspective 1770–1789' (SVEC 2013: 15, Oxford, 2013), 19–45; M. Curran, 'Beyond the forbidden best-sellers of pre-revolutionary France', *Historical*

On the consumer side, the questions are no less formidable: historians have debated the evidence from many parts of Europe regarding rates of literacy, and have faced comparable methodological challenges when drawing tentative conclusions from inventories, sales of second-hand books, the catalogues compiled for the big book fairs and (by the later eighteenth century) the records of lending libraries. Before the arrival of review journals in the eighteenth century, evidence of the actual response of readers (and indications of *how* they read) is almost impossible to discern except in a few rare cases, such as where individuals commented on their reading to others, or were hauled before law courts to account for their illegal reading. Accordingly, we have to accept that considerable uncertainty persists when we try to map changing demands and the patterns of dissemination of different types of politically oriented printed material in the seventeenth and eighteenth centuries, within and across different language communities.

Formal regulation of the printing industry varied substantially across Europe. The importance of printing as a means of disseminating new ideas, and its ability to respond rapidly to changing demand, led to a universally perceived need for censorship and regulation. Various methods were in concurrent use. The most common was direct pre-publication censorship, which required authors to submit their manuscript to an authorised censor for review and possible correction before it could be published legally. This process was workable as long as there were only a few printers in operation, and the censors knew what they were doing, but it was time-consuming, unpredictable and liable to become highly subjective. In some parts of Europe a more indirect approach developed, where the authorities relied more on denunciation and post-publication prosecution, using church consistories, law courts, magistrates, or other agents. This was essentially a reactive process, and as such was almost bound to be uneven, relying largely on a deterrent effect to intimidate authors and publishers. Some governments and church authorities went to great lengths drawing up lists of prohibited texts as a guide to the clergy, local authorities and booksellers, but this was again reactive. Lists of prohibited books could also, in the wrong hands, serve as an advertisement for texts that were deemed unacceptable. Indeed all censoring and regulative processes risked simply drawing attention to books that the authorities wanted to ban.

Journal, 56 (2013), 89–112; L. Seaward, 'The Société Typographique de Neuchâtel (STN) and the politics of the book trade in late eighteenth-century Europe, 1769–1789', *European History Quarterly*, 44 (2014), 439–57; M. Curran, *The French book trade in Enlightenment Europe, I: Selling Enlightenment* (London, 2018); S. Burrows, *The French book trade in Enlightenment Europe, II: Enlightenment bestsellers* (London, 2018).

Southern and Catholic Europe probably had the most organised and most effective systems of censorship, based on one of several versions of the Index of prohibited books formally authorised by the Papacy in 1557–9, revised by the Council of Trent and regularly reviewed thereafter by church authorities in the Italian and Spanish territories. Practical enforcement tended to be directed by officials of the Inquisition (Holy Office), widely feared because of their reputation for systematic use of investigative powers including torture. Even the Venetian Inquisition, while intermittently claiming some degree of operational independence from Rome, was for most practical purposes closely aligned to standard inquisition policies. France, however, had no Inquisition and was not subject to the Papal Index of prohibited books (though some might see the Index as advisory). Instead from 1563 a separate censorship system was introduced, managed on royal authority by the theologians of the Sorbonne, and strengthened from 1618 through direct guild regulation of printers and booksellers. The primary aim was to prevent the dissemination of unacceptable religious ideas, but criticism of the state, or of powerful individuals, soon also became a focus of attention.

England acquired restrictive policies even earlier, when Henry VIII in 1529 reacted to perceived threats by establishing a formal list of prohibited books. The work of London printers was made increasingly delicate and complicated by the major lurches in religious policy during the later years of Henry's reign and again on the successions of each of his three children. His daughter Mary chartered the Stationers Company in 1557, instituting an ostensibly indirect system of control where the Company did the censoring on behalf of the crown, in return for an exclusive privilege to control the entire printing trade and its profits. This ensured a form of routine pre-publication censorship, since a member of the Company was meant to check each manuscript before it was registered. By the early seventeenth century, monarchs began to interfere more: James VI/I was unpredictable and subjective in his response to print, sometimes acting on personal whims, sometimes failing to notice a problem. Delegation to the Stationers Company was no guarantee of clarity or firmness of purpose.[3] As elsewhere in Europe, control of print relied more on brutal example than on consistent policy. Even so, the Court of Star Chamber confirmed and extended the powers and monopoly of the Stationers Company in 1637. During the civil wars and interregnum, when the abolition of the Star Chamber left the Stationers Company in limbo, there was formally no regulative relaxation: on the contrary, repeated attempts to extend controls and spell out punishments

---

[3] C. S. Clegg, *Press censorship in Jacobean England* (Cambridge, 2001).

for infringement were made in successive new printing acts, notably those of 1643 and 1649. But enforcement became very difficult.

In the Netherlands and the Holy Roman Empire, where central authority was relatively weak and religious policy had effectively been devolved to the many component jurisdictions, pre-publication censorship could work only sporadically. In the southern (Spanish) provinces of the Netherlands, the Catholic church continued to operate inquisitorial controls in line with those of the Papacy. But once the northern provinces gained independence (*de facto* in the 1580s and in 1609, formally in 1648) the growth in prosperity in the autonomous great cities of the Netherlands created a decentralised environment ideal for a relatively free printing industry. In the Holy Roman Empire, the extraordinarily complicated mosaic of jurisdictions also ensured huge variations in policies and enforcement: even before the outbreak of war in 1618, it had become feasible to escape censorship and prosecution simply by moving to a more congenial neighbouring jurisdiction.

Although enforcement and consistency varied hugely across Europe, there were no general demands before 1640 either for freedom of expression or for the deregulation of the printing industry: the need for doctrinal unity and political conformity was deemed absolutely essential to any stable state. Printed texts could disrupt the monopoly on information, disseminate ideas that might be at odds with official beliefs and, worst of all, reach ordinary readers who were not meant to have independent views of their own. Later chapters will examine more closely the different kinds of censorship and self-regulation experienced in the growing markets for print in the seventeenth and eighteenth centuries. However, in those areas where the printing industry did not develop so quickly or in such innovative directions (notably parts of eastern Europe, Spain and especially the Ottoman Empire), there are still large gaps in the research, making comparisons more difficult.

This chapter will examine both the quantitative evidence of how the printing industry worked round these restraints, on what scale they did so and what types of text were involved. Equally important, but far more difficult to answer, is the question of demand: what kind of people may have had – or acquired – the taste and time for independent reading. Historians have argued at length about the problematic evidence on literacy, but most now agree that commonly cited signature evidence (the ability to sign marriage contracts or other official documents) is totally misleading: reading and writing were taught as separate skills, and writing was taught only to those intended for careers requiring clerical skills (thus invariably leaving out women). It is easy to understand why some historians have assumed low levels of reading skills: primary education in the countryside was often extremely basic or non-existent, focusing on religious rote-learning rather than on transferable skills. Equally, while most types of evidence suggest that reading skills were significantly more common in towns than in remote rural or economically static areas, we rarely get a clear indication of how contemporaries themselves understood the sliding scale of practical reading – from laborious and hesitant access to already familiar or simple texts, through gradual familiarisation (perhaps listening to others reading unseen texts), to fluent, habitual or even voracious personal reading of more substantial and unfamiliar texts. Both the scale of reading fluency and the probable shift from intensive reading (of a few texts) to extensive reading across a wider range are particularly important in considering adult learning, but are never adequately represented in the historical evidence. We know that the urban environment provided far more incentives for adults to learn, but only rarely do we get a glimpse of what and how much they may have read – a particularly acute problem with respect to women readers, but to some extent also for men of lower social standing. This is not the place to revisit the contested ways in which we might get round some of the problems in the evidence.[4] But even if actual reading skills before 1750 cannot be measured accurately, it is worth noting that the growing quantity and range of printed material throughout this period was itself a major incentive to adult learners, especially in towns where daily contact with print became almost unavoidable.

Quantifying Print Output from the Reformation to 1800

During the first 150 years of printing, most production was concentrated in urban markets connected by trade routes from northern Italy, the Rhine valley and major centres in the German lands, to the Netherlands and Paris. By 1600 the most important printing firms were still located there: the output of printers from France, the Netherlands, the German lands and northern Italy account for nearly nine-tenths of all known printed works by that date, with England and Spain accounting for most of the rest. As we would expect, there were fluctuations – in the case of French printers notably during the civil wars of the later sixteenth century and for the Netherlands a slowing down in printing during the wars against Spain – but most production remained concentrated in the big cities and along the main commercial arteries.

---

[4] A good range of the older research is noted in R. A. Houston, *Literacy in early modern Europe: culture and education 1500–1800* (London, 1988; rev. edn 2002); see also T. Munck, *The enlightenment: a comparative social history 1721–1794* (London, 2000), 46–59.

In spite of the uneven geographic spread, total print output grew impressively in the sixteenth century, both in the total number of editions and (especially in the German-and French-language communities) in the degree of experimentation with new genres such as newsbooks, pamphlets on current affairs and other examples of news-related printing. The virulence of religious controversy during the Reformation was a major factor in this growth: Lutheranism made striking use of print in the German lands from the 1520s, as did Calvinism notably in the 1560s in France and Netherlands. This in turn had a big impact on the use of print for political purposes, both in polemical tracts and more academic studies. Despite market disruptions, such publications proliferated in periods of political instability – very clearly so in France in the 1570s and 1580s, when some of the greatest works on political thought, legitimate authority and the right of rebellion (both in French and in Latin) were produced in the aftermath of the St Bartholomew Massacre (1572), as part of the controversies around Calvinist resistance theory.[5]

We are still some way short of a complete STC for French-language publications in the seventeenth century, and the main catalogue of the Bibliothèque Nationale de France (BNF) is not an adequate substitute. In practice, the increasingly complicated regulatory system of pre-publication censorship forced many authors to rely on illegal printing or on printers outside the borders of France, notably in the Netherlands and along the Rhine frontier, making the print industry exceptionally decentralised and opaque. With as yet very uneven data, overall quantitative summaries for the seventeenth century must be regarded as very approximate – no doubt under-representing ephemeral output that might have been lost, but also marred by problems of duplicate or secret editions whose imprint is misleading. For the later eighteenth century, we have a wider range of source material and a firmer research base. With French the recognised international language, disparate data on French-language material produced outside the kingdom is being collated from library holdings across Europe, as well as information from sales catalogues and journals, which will give us more reliable quantitative estimates.

All that taken into account, if we agree that the BNF catalogue, while far from comprehensive, may give some indication of the overall broad trend, the annual average number of printed titles (mostly books, not yet including short pamphlets or flysheets) seems to have risen fairly gradually from minimum estimates of just under 100 to around 200 titles per

---

[5] A. Pettegree, *The French book and the European book world* (Leiden, 2007) and his *The book in the Renaissance* (New Haven and London, 2010) provide a new understanding of European data up to 1600. See also the Universal Short Title Catalogue, project directed by Pettegree at the University of St Andrews.

annum during the early seventeenth century, with sudden temporary surges to over 250 in the early 1640s and again in the 1660s. There were surges during years of political uncertainty, notably 1649–52, and further instability in the book market during the consecutive economic and military crises towards the end of the reign of Louis XIV from the 1690s onwards. During the eighteenth century – again judging from the BNF but this time including a greater share of smaller works – overall output may have increased fivefold between 1710 and 1789, reaching a cautiously estimated 2000 new titles per annum just before the Revolution, probably more. Of these, it is interesting to note that less than half were produced legally, whilst the rest consist of *permission tacites*, totally illegal underground publications, or French-language works published abroad.[6] We can currently only guess at the changes in printed output during the Revolution itself (see Chapter 6).

The huge diversity of political, cultural and economic structures in the Holy Roman Empire means that, as for France, accurate quantification of German-language texts is difficult. The new STC of seventeenth-century German-language material, currently under development, promises to combine aggregate bibliographical information from the holdings of most major German research libraries. Yet even as it stands at present, we can draw some significant conclusions. Thus, in terms of geography, it is clear that cities such as Frankfurt and Leipzig supported very dynamic publishing industries after 1600, and although suffering visible setbacks during the Thirty Years War, recovered quite quickly after 1650. In Frankfurt, the average annual output of titles (new and reprints) dropped from over 250 items at the start of the seventeenth century to less than 100 in the 1640s, gradually recovering to its pre-war total by the 1680s. Leipzig, being within electoral Saxony, suffered slightly less during the war: like Frankfurt, it had an average annual output of around 250 titles in the decade before 1618, which fell to half during the 1640s, but then recovered more quickly, reaching pre-war totals already in the 1650s and growing to an average of over 400 titles per annum in the 1690s. By comparison, other cities such as Strasbourg, Augsburg and Hamburg had a much smaller average output, with cities such as Erfurt, Mainz and Cologne trailing even further behind. As we would expect, profiles

---

[6] H.-J. Martin, *Livre, pouvoirs et société à Paris au xviie siècle* (Geneva, 1969), 1062; H.-J. Martin and R. Chartier (eds.), *Histoire de l'édition française*, vol. II (Paris, 1984), 95–103. The totals from the seventeenth and eighteenth centuries are not based on fully comparable data. As is clear from the Darnton debate, all estimates almost certainly significantly underestimate a growing proportion of illegal printing in the eighteenth century, making numerical estimates of short-term fluctuations very problematic. See also Chapter 5 below.

within the printing industry varied significantly across the German-speaking lands, dependent on the prevailing religious orientation and on political and economic restrictions. In terms of language distribution, it is no surprise to note that Latin (including reprints of imported works) remained easily the dominant language for theology throughout the century, whilst in fields such as politics and history German was relatively stronger, with substantial increases in output after 1650.[7] French did not become a major component of the publishing industry in the German lands until the eighteenth century.

Mapping the output of German publishers during the eighteenth century to a high level of detail is not yet possible, but general trends are clear. In terms of subject matter, for example, there are some significant overall shifts. Theology, which may have constituted around 40% of all titles in the second half of the seventeenth century, dwindled to 31% in 1745, 20% in 1775 and a mere 6% by 1800; whilst philosophy, the sciences and education followed a nearly mirror image increase, reaching 40% of the total by 1800, with comparable increases in travel literature and history. Fiction, by contrast, constituted an insignificant part of total production even at the start of the eighteenth century, but may have exceeded one quarter by the 1790s.[8] But we need to remember that these proportional changes occurred within what was a substantial increase in overall output in German. For example, the total number of titles classified as theological did not decline in absolute terms, merely as a proportion of the whole. The lists from publishers and bookshops, and catalogues from the big book fairs, also suggest that there were substantial differences between north and south. When Schirach's *Politisches Journal* in 1786 reported on trends in published writings in Germany, the total number of new titles in all languages available at the Leipzig Easter book fair came to 2423, including a large range of journals, 326 new works in theology, 294 fictional works and poems (of which 125 were novels), 176 titles in medicine, 175 in education, 134 in history, with politics and statistics accounting for 124 titles, jurisprudence also 124 and political economy and commerce 95. The journal noted that over the two annual book fairs at Leipzig around 5000 new books were available, but noted with relief that Germans were not as interested as the French in 'bad books', thus keeping the totals down.[9] Going by such data, the big German book fairs were offering ten times as many titles in 1786 as they had a century earlier.

---

[7] These figures are from the online *Verzeichnis der im deutschen Sprachraum erschienenen Drucke des 17. Jahrhundert* (VD17), last accessed in October 2018.

[8] R. Wittman, *Geschichte des deutschen Buchhandels* (Munich, 1991), 83–5.

[9] *Politisches Journal*, Jahrgang 1786, issue 6 (June), 555–62. This conservative monthly journal, published in Hamburg, is discussed further in Chapter 5 below. The journal estimated that

Even allowing for fuzzy data, the overall shifting trends are clear, and the growing market both for practical informative books and for literature designed to be accessible to a wider readership is particularly noticeable.

In the Netherlands, although the output of print had fluctuated significantly in the later sixteenth century because of the war against Spain, the combination of a highly volatile political environment with an exceptional degree of urbanisation and economic development soon created ideal conditions for the growth in print. The absence of central institutions of control again makes it difficult to link this growth directly to censorship regulations and changes in the response of local authorities.[10] However, the Dutch Short Title Catalogue is now sufficiently developed to allow us to draw conclusions regarding patterns of publication prior to, and during, the major upheavals of the seventeenth century. The total number of titles printed during the 1560s and 1570s averaged a fairly modest 48 items per annum (three-quarters of them in Dutch), rising in the following decades to an annual average of 115 in the 1580s and early 1590s, then increasing rapidly around 1600 (a rise accounted for both in Dutch-language and Latin publications) and staying in the range 350–410 during the early years of the truce with Spain from 1609.

A surge in publications accompanied the political crisis of 1618–19, which culminated in a showdown between the military-political ambitions of the *stadtholder* (Stadhouder, an office of military leadership, held by Maurice of Orange-Nassau) and the mercantile interests of the major cities including Amsterdam. Altogether 557 titles are listed for 1617, 676 for 1618 and 552 for 1619, still with a very high proportion in Dutch. The extraordinary arrest (August 1618), political trial and public execution (May 1619) of the 71-year-old leader of the province of Holland, Oldenbarnevelt, was undoubtedly one of the focal points for the growth in political texts. But as we shall see in the next chapter, both religion and foreign policy remained focal points of contestation. The total printed output (number of titles) averaged around 425–500 during most of the 1620s and 30s, but rose again during the 1640s to a peak of 996 in 1650 and another peak of 1237 titles in 1672, both neatly coinciding with the biggest political crises of those years. For most of this period, at least two-thirds of these titles were in Dutch, and that continued during the

the total number of books available annually in Paris was around 10,000, which (even if including unspecified 'bad books') must be regarded as a very unreliable estimate.

10 For an overall view, see J. Kloek and W. Mijnhardt, 'The printed word', in E.F. Shevlin (ed.), *The history of the book in the west 1700–1800*, vol. III (Farnham, 2010), 431–52; and for the later eighteenth century, J. D. Popkin, 'Print culture in the Netherlands on the eve of the Revolution', in M. Jacob and W. Mijnhardt (eds.) *The Dutch Republic in the eighteenth century: decline, Enlightenment and revolution* (Ithaca, NY, 1992), 273–91.

following decades, despite the significance of Latin and French for some kinds of publications. The total output levelled after 1672, usually in the range of 800–1050 titles per annum (all languages) right through to the 1760s, and with less dramatic fluctuations than during the seventeenth century. The number of titles increased slowly from 985 in 1763, to an average of 1640 titles per annum in the 1780s, then falling slightly in the 1790s (except for the peak year in 1795). Throughout this period Dutch remained the dominant language (often three-quarters of the total output or more), but French only outnumbered Latin texts in a few years, no doubt because of the continuing use of Latin for academic theses and commemorative orations.[11]

By comparison, estimates based on the Dutch-language holdings of major collections such as Amsterdam University Library may provide approximate indications of general trends. Even if these undoubtedly under-represent ephemeral or small publications, such estimates may serve to illustrate broad shifts in subject area in the more upmarket kinds of print. On that basis, we note that the output of major religious texts was steady but unremarkable into the early decades of the seventeenth century, followed by a rather higher output in the period 1640–70, and again during the 1680s at the time of the expulsion of the Huguenots from France. During the eighteenth century religious titles seem to have remained fairly steady, except for a temporary increase during the middle years of the century. As we would expect, major history titles were more volatile: less than 10 per decade at the start of the seventeenth century, rising to around 30 at mid-century, and continuing to increase after 1720 to reach around 50 titles per decade in the 1740s and 1750s, then doubling to nearly 100 (that is, averaging 10 history titles per annum) during the volatile final two decades of the eighteenth century. Given inconsistencies in subject classifications in all library catalogues, estimates for what we might now call the social sciences are not feasible. In any case we need to be cautious about drawing conclusions from Dutch-language publications alone, since part of the printing in the Netherlands was in French, serving the illegal French market as well as bilingual Dutch readers.[12] Provisionally, however, we might conclude that the overall upward trend is clear enough, whilst context-specific fluctuations in output seem less pronounced than one might expect from for example the English experience.

---

[11] Figures drawn from the Short Title Catalogue Netherlands (STCN), last accessed in October 2018, but also using language filters from earlier versions of this database. Again no allowance is made for either duplicates or lost titles.

[12] Data in this paragraph is based primarily on the online catalogue of the University of Amsterdam, using modern subject classifications.

The most detailed and comprehensive aggregate bibliographical database so far completed for any language is the English-language Short Title Catalogue (ESTC). Compiled over many years on the basis of major library holdings on both sides of the Atlantic, this database can now be regarded as a near-comprehensive catalogue of virtually all surviving printed material in the English language before 1800, and of texts in other languages that purport to have been printed in the English-speaking world (even where the imprint is likely to be false). The ESTC unavoidably includes a significant number of duplicate entries (printed items located in different libraries which appear to be the same edition, but cannot be proven to be so until thorough physical examination and comparisons have been made). In any case the way books were printed in the early modern period, with sections sometimes shared between different workshops and corrections made in mid-production, make it more difficult to define what constitutes a single edition or printing of a work. The overestimates resulting from counting duplicates may, however, be compensated by the items that are known to have existed but for which no copies appear to have survived. So, even if complete accuracy is unattainable, the ESTC provides comprehensive and detailed bibliographical data which allows historians to measure the scale and dynamics of English-language printing as accurately as early modern production and distribution methods allow.

As in most other European countries, printing in England had initially concentrated on religious texts (including Bibles, collections of psalms and devotional literature), almanacs, formal government proclamations, poetry, ephemera (such as funeral orations, celebratory publications, or sensational accounts notably of executions), and any other texts for which there was a predictable and steady demand. All of these types of publication continued to sell well throughout the seventeenth and eighteenth centuries, but do not account for the sudden change in the role of print which can be observed notably in England from the late 1630s onwards, when the collapse of royal power was mirrored in the weakening of the hitherto tight controls over printing. This growth is much more dramatic than in most other parts of Europe, and has been explained primarily in terms of the major upheavals of the English civil wars. Raw data clearly indicates that the total number of publications issued in London rose slowly and quite steadily through the sixteenth century until around 1640, rising from an annual average of 250 titles in the 1590s to around 500 titles in the 1630s.

From 1640, however, the patterns changed dramatically, with 742 titles in 1640, 2334 in 1641 and a staggering 3902 in 1642. The civil war years resulted in some decline, but never to pre-1640 levels – with predictably high output again in 1647–9, levelling at around 1150 new titles on average during most of the 1650s and another peak at 2816 titles in 1660. As we would expect, the Restoration in 1660 calmed the print market somewhat – or brought it under more effective control – with London totals declining even before the Great Fire, averaging 625 for each of the years 1666–9 and just over 1100 for most of the 1670s. The pattern during the civil war period, therefore, was exceptional.[13] Joad Raymond observes that the extraordinary surges of print in the 1640s and 50s 'reflect the fierce and contestatory book culture of the civil wars in Britain, and the use of books by parties involved in those wars in order to recruit public opinion'. He also emphasises that a significant part of the increase consisted of pamphlets, cheap tracts, news-sheets and printed petitions, rather than more substantial works.[14] At the same time, civil war conditions militated against actual preservation of printed material as such, even more than in peacetime, so the numbers are if anything likely to be underestimates. And even if we adopt a conservative estimate of the average number of copies made in each print run, London alone in the early 1640s will have had a total printed output probably exceeding two million copies every year.

A fairly clear correlation between political instability and the quantity of new titles becomes apparent again during the early 1680s, as public opinion focused on a number of major issues and concerns. As we would expect, particularly high annual output in London was reached during the years 1688–90 (with 2475 titles recorded in 1689), before stabilising in most of the 1690s around an average of 1580 titles per annum (but rising to 2040 in 1695). In Scotland, in the 1640s and 50s the increase in print was much less pronounced than in England,[15] but by the 1680s there was a sharp increase, with Scottish printers evidently responding to public interest in ways similar to those south of the border. Neither Scottish printers, nor those working in Dublin, were subject to English regulation,

[13] The quantitative data given here and in the following paragraphs (except where otherwise stated) has been compiled directly from the ESTC: it takes account neither of any duplicate titles (multiple printings of a given title in the same year, which may be distinguishable on closer scrutiny), nor of those more ephemeral outputs that are now lost or have not yet been identified. London totals are used, since English-language printing in Scotland, the Americas and elsewhere varied for different reasons. Even during the 1640s and 1650s, London accounted for the vast majority of printed outputs in England.

[14] J. Raymond, 'The development of the book trade in Britain', in J. Raymond (ed.), *The Oxford history of popular print culture: cheap print in Britain and Ireland to 1660* (Oxford, 2011), 59–61.

[15] See also J. Raymond, *Pamphlets and pamphleteering in early modern Britain* (Cambridge, 2003), especially ch. 5.

and their total output increased substantially from the later seventeenth century onwards, in part to undercut the London market with cheaper reprints.

The precise role of print in the English-speaking world during and after the political upheavals of 1688–9 have not yet been analysed as thoroughly. The definitive lapse of the Licensing Act in 1695 meant that subsequent estimates produced from within the London printing trade itself are not comprehensive: estimates by the printers themselves of a fairly steady and modest output of about 500–600 titles per annum in London until around 1760 is clearly too low, probably because small and supposedly ephemeral items were not counted.[16] The raw ESTC totals again indicate an output of 1500–2000 separate titles per annum (with some adjustment for duplicates) in London in the early half of the eighteenth century. There was a slight drop in the 1740s and 1750s, and only a modest growth in the first few years after the conclusion of peace in 1763. Partly because of the revolt of the American colonies, the 1770s brought an increase in new titles (averaging 2190 in London over the decade), sustained in the 1780s. Including the output from provincial presses and English-language printing in the Americas, the total output from all English-language printers probably surpassed 5000 in the later 1780s and exceeded 9800 in 1795. London alone averaged 2600 titles per annum in the 1780s and 3800 in the 1790s, with significant increases in output also in Edinburgh, Dublin, Philadelphia, Boston and elsewhere. Even for a long-standing centre of printing such as London, the 1790s total amounted to at least a sevenfold increase compared with the early 1630s.[17]

An equally striking impression may be gained from the ESTC if we look at cities other than London itself: there, duplicates are much less common, so total output is much easier to measure accurately, and tells an equally important story. The number of provincial centres with their own printing presses increased significantly during the eighteenth century, including in the Atlantic colonies – a process which may have somewhat reduced the total amount of print sent out from the older main printing centres. The overall trend is very clear. In cities such as Edinburgh, already producing over 30 new titles every year in the 1660s and 70s, there was a very marked growth from the later 1690s up to and including the time of the Union of 1707 (reaching 230–300 titles annually in the last stages of the union debate). Output settled at around 160 titles per annum in the early eighteenth century (with a peak in 1745), rose to over 400

---

[16] W. St Clair, *The reading nation in the Romantic period* (Cambridge, 2004), 455.

[17] Print numbers are again based on the ESTC database. For comparable estimates, see also J. Raven, *Judging new wealth: popular publishing and responses to commerce in England 1750–1800* (Oxford, 1992), 31–41.

briefly in the 1760s but then dropped again. The years 1789–94 brought a new increase, peaking at over 400 titles per annum, confirming the pattern of fairly close correlation with major political and social confrontations in a city which, although now only a regional capital, continued to serve as a centre for all kinds of printing including legal and scientific work. In Glasgow, although printing only began in the late 1630s and was subsequently boosted disproportionately by the rapid growth in size and wealth of the city, there were equally significant shifts both in terms of the quantity of print and the kind of work that was printed: again, from just over 50 new titles in the middle of the eighteenth century, the output doubled in the 1790s. Dublin closely rivalled Edinburgh in terms of total output, but its output grew even faster in the last decades of the eighteenth century, with a steep rise in the 1790s predictably reaching a peak somewhat later, in the years 1798–9 in connection with the Irish revolt. So as far as English-language publishing is concerned, there is no doubt that significant political developments are reflected directly in the quantity of pieces appearing in print: in each of the upheavals, from the early 1640s through to the impact of French and Irish upheavals of the 1790s, the correlation seems clear.

As we would expect, smaller language communities could at best sustain print markets commensurate with their economic prosperity, levels of urbanisation and levels of political and cultural openness. In Denmark, printing was heavily concentrated in Copenhagen and (as one would expect from a composite state) included texts in Danish, Latin, German, Icelandic and, by the eighteenth century, also in French. Given the relatively small total output, and without a fully researched short-title catalogue, it is possible to use existing library catalogues for the Royal Library in Copenhagen to indicate change over time, though as always some flysheets and other smaller outputs will have been lost. It would appear that the average annual total number of titles produced in Denmark increased eightfold, from roughly 75 in the 1620s to around 550 in the 1790s, with a marked acceleration in the second half of the eighteenth century. Consistently throughout the period, roughly one-sixth of these were in German, but the proportion in Latin fell from over one-third in the seventeenth century to one-tenth or less in the late eighteenth.[18] It is likely that, in the process, the average size of books also diminished to meet the demands of a broader and cheaper market, but this cannot currently be confirmed from the available bibliographical

---

[18] Estimates based on manually checked retrievals from the online catalogue of the Royal Library in Copenhagen, using the filter of the older Bibliotheca Danica catalogue. The language counts are manual, since the online language filter is not reliable.

data. What is clear, however, is that works of a religious and devotional type were to some extent displaced by a growing interest in fiction, history and politics.

For Sweden we can use relatively detailed bibliographies of early printed material available online at the Royal Library in Stockholm. These suggest a pattern quite similar to Denmark, as we would expect from the similar total populations and reading cultures in these two solidly Lutheran states. The annual average number of titles rose from around 55 in the 1630s to 65 during the more turbulent 1640s, dipping during the wars of mid-century, but climbing again from the 1670s to an average of around 75 titles per annum in the early eighteenth century. From then on it becomes possible to do more detailed quantitative summaries, suggesting a fivefold increase in total annual output between 1710 and the 1770s, with noticeably high points during the years when the Swedish parliament was in session. We note a particularly impressive outpouring of pamphlets and socio-political analysis during the 1760s – clearly the high point of public discussion in Enlightenment Sweden. The political coup by Gustavus III in 1772 brought a very visible slump in total print output, falling from a peak of 944 titles in 1770 alone, to below 300 for most of the ensuing years up to the revolutionary upheavals in France. Equally interesting is the large proportion published in Latin in the first half of the seventeenth century, sometimes exceeding the number of Swedish titles, whilst by the eighteenth century four-fifths were in Swedish, alongside a modest number of reprints in French or German.[19]

Basic groundwork needs to be done on the Italian and Spanish print markets, and on areas of east-central Europe after the Thirty Years War, before we can draw any wider sustainable quantitative conclusion. As Gary Marker noted some years ago, printing in Russia was very closely state-regulated, remaining so under changing intellectual conditions during the reign of Peter I (the Great) and his successors. Catherine II was willing to allow some measure of commercial printing, and in 1783 formally allowed private printers to operate in Moscow and St Petersburg. As a result, the total number of titles rose to nearly 500 in 1788. This relative freedom did not last, however, as Catherine reacted against the fear of French revolutionary upheaval. The great printing entrepreneur Nikolai Novikov published much less after 1789, and was arrested in 1792. Although the total number of Russian publications did

---

[19] National Library of Sweden, Databases: Swedish bibliography for the seventeenth century (Collijn) and the Swedish bibliography (*Svensk Bibliografi* SB17) 1700–1829, used alongside the detailed online catalogue. See also A. Jarrick, 'Borgare, småfolk och böcker i 1700-talets Stockholm', [Swedish] *Historisk Tidskrift* (1990), 191–227.

not drop off immediately, conditions for printers were so hostile that independent printing with political relevance became almost impossible.[20]

Reliable comparisons between the major national print cultures, and across the whole early modern period, will not become possible until we have more consistent short-title catalogues for all the major printing centres. But it is clear that printing was very *unevenly* spread across Europe – with very high levels in the most literate and economically buoyant (often urbanised) parts of north-western Europe, much lower levels in parts of southern France, southern Italy and south-eastern Europe, and probably no independent commercial printing at all in the Ottoman Empire. In other words, the estimates noted here for different language communities in the more literate parts of Europe probably represent the strongest parts of the market. If so, some conclusions do appear inescapable: there was a remarkable increase in the total number and diversity of printed items from the early seventeenth century to the period of the French Revolution, which may amount to as much as a tenfold increase in titles overall, and which in some languages shows dramatic fluctuations during periods of change or political instability. These increases were far greater than the relative increases in population for the areas concerned: in other words, there were significantly more titles, per head of population, at the end of our period than at the start. We can observe a consistent relative shift away from Latin towards the local vernacular languages, which, when combined with evidence of the development of many new types and genres of publication, including shorter and cheaper popular ones, indicates an unmistakeable (if not yet quantifiable) broadening of the readership beyond the educated elite. More detailed investigation of the available data suggests an equally striking spread of printing to smaller cities and towns – a trend which would almost certainly be replicated in the proliferation of bookshops, if reliable data were available.

Printed Newsletters and Visual Imagery

Any attempt to define precisely what sorts of reading material might have most impact on contemporary political awareness is probably doomed to failure. Seeing political implications in a text depended very much on the eye of the beholder – and might be found as much in religious works, travel, history and scholarly reference works, as in fiction and poetry – so

[20] G. Marker, *Publishing, printing and the origins of intellectual life in Russia 1700–1800* (Princeton, 1985), 103–9 and 184–211.

we need to discard any pre-ordained categorisations or assumptions that might exclude some genres of printed material. That said, some widely sold popular texts might not seem likely to figure prominently in a study of the dissemination of political ideas: almanacs for example (a mainstay of many printers, using recycled material based mostly on stereotypes, folklore and the partisan marking of historical anniversaries), devotional literature of the more traditional kind (conventional pious house reading, rather than sectarian or polemical religious writings with obvious political implications), or accounts of the crimes and punishments of ordinary criminals (even though the spectacle of punishment itself was intended as moral and political propaganda).

The early advertisers and corantos ('currents') might not at first glance look very political either, being essentially periodical or serial publications intended to provide commercial information relating to markets, shipping and the promotion of new products. During the early seventeenth century, however, this kind of serial developed significantly, introducing new forms of content clearly relevant in any attempt to map the dissemination of political ideas in print: the conveying of news about war and its resulting economic disruption, lists of fluctuations in exchange rates and indications of instability as well as topical information about foreign states and overseas markets more generally. Throughout the early modern period, publication of any information relating to domestic events was regarded as highly sensitive, and rapidly subjected to very strict political control, but the authorities were usually more relaxed about news of events in foreign countries provided these had little domestic political relevance. It is not difficult to see why news-sheets of any kind – first as manuscript letters circulated within personal networks, but soon developing into printed serialised newsletters containing a range of current news and information and sold to the general public – would meet an obvious demand for commercially valuable information in the bigger urban markets of Europe.

Historians have traced prototype newspapers right back to the earlier sixteenth century, notably in reports and broadsheets relating to the Protestant reforms, or one-off pamphlets addressing specific events. These in turn triggered a series of responses, resulting in more systematic reporting of major incidents such as the confrontation with the Ottoman Empire at the Battle of Lepanto in 1571, or the St Bartholomew's Massacre in France the following year. Such news, even if reported in purely narrative form, was politically sensational and liable to generate wider discussion. Explicitly regular (that is, serialised or periodical) printed news media came into their own a little later, in the early decades of the seventeenth century, boosted especially by the demand for information regarding the Thirty Years War from 1618 and the closely related second phase of the Dutch Wars of Independence from Spain from 1621. The Dutch, as the most powerful commercial agents of the time, had an obvious interest in compiling European-wide information, and their corantos were reused in translation in neighbouring countries, notably in London and other markets with a lively demand.[21] The development of public mail services with regular routes across many parts of continental Europe also made both the collection and dissemination of news easier and more dependable. However, it may not be entirely helpful to describe the growing postal services as a 'communication revolution': although transmission networks were certainly consolidated along the main trading routes, improvements took a long time, varied enormously across Europe according to local and private initiatives and were very vulnerable to disruption in war zones.[22] It is worth noting that news-sheets were nearly always published in the local language (not Latin), and were intended not just for the social elite, but for a wider readership of people whose actual practical influence on politics would be minimal, but whose interests were becoming more wide-ranging and more insatiable.

Apart from the Netherlands, those parts of the German lands that escaped the worst wartime destruction also had a good provision of newspapers. Several major German cities had by 1618 acquired serial newsletters, typically taking the form of short narrative accounts of important events, and sometimes incorporating official news (peace treaties, court events). The emphasis was very much on summary information: value judgments and analysis (if included at all) would conform to the expectations of the intended readers, no doubt more self-censored and subdued than in, say, private correspondence. Because of the need for subscriptions, serial publications were naturally much more vulnerable to reprisals from the authorities than single news-sheets, so their survival depended on strict observance of politically acceptable self-restraint and conformity with prevailing opinion. It is reasonable to assume that readers would have used serial news-sheets and short pamphlets both for information and as entertainment. The interests of the publisher, if commercial, would no doubt have centred on making a profit, securing a reputation and trying to win more readers by

---

[21] A. der Weduwen, *Dutch and Flemish newspapers of the seventeenth century*, 2 vols. (Leiden, 2017); see also B. Dooley and S. Baron (eds.), *The politics of information in early modern Europe* (London, 2001); and B. Dooley (ed.), *The dissemination of news and the emergence of contemporaneity in early modern Europe* (Farnham, 2010), for a range of papers on the emergence of news reporting across Europe.

[22] W. Behringer, *Im Zeichen des Merkur: Reichspost und Kommunikationsrevolution in der frühen Neuzeit* (Göttingen, 2003); J. Caplan, *Postal culture in Europe 1500–1800* (SVEC 2016: 04, Oxford, 2016).

projecting a gratifying impression of the importance of their collective identity. Civic governments also soon realised the potential of such media: in the German lands and the Dutch Republic semi-official publications exploited such demand, for obvious political purposes.[23]

Monarchical or major princely states, being intrinsically more secretive, had greater difficulty managing the news media to their satisfaction, and also had difficulty retaining some degree of control. In England, the government of James VI/I had to strengthen the Stationers Company in 1621 in order to regulate those printers who saw no benefit in registering experimental newsletters. Paris acquired its first weekly newspaper in 1631 on the initiative of the philanthropist Théophraste Renaudot (1586–1653), but the government provided sponsorship in order to maintain control. Such developments would suggest that news media were soon perceived as a potential threat in terms of influencing public opinion. However, actual assessment of the reality of that threat, or the impact of news media, is problematic: reactions and comment were muted, the evidence scattered and necessarily weak, except when governments reacted openly.

The potential for using visual imagery, if necessary combined with textual explanation, was also clearly recognised in the search for wider communication across social barriers. Any image was bound to attract attention simply because there was so little of it (except in churches and as shopfront signs). Images had the great advantage that interpretation was in the mind of the beholder, and thus not only capable of escaping legal prosecution but also inherently liable to foster discussion. Woodblock printing (designs cut into the end-grain of wooden blocks) could be combined with movable-type text and printed together on the one press; the much finer detail and shading that could be obtained in copperplate engravings, however, could not be printed together with movable-type texts, requiring instead a roller press with much higher pressure. As a result, newspapers and other texts were not normally endowed with images other than the simple woodcuts that could be recycled from one text to another. Detailed engraved images required a different production process, and accompanying texts had to be engraved by hand in reverse mirror-image, making such images much more costly.

This explains the sharp differentiation between the simpler woodcut images typically used for ballads and flysheets from the sixteenth century onwards, and the quite remarkable number of high-quality copper-plate

---

[23] T. Schröder, 'The origins of the German press', in Dooley and Baron, *The politics of information*, 123–50, and *passim* in that volume; V. Bauer and H. Böning (eds.), *Die Entstehung des Zeitungswesens im 17. Jahrhundert* (Bremen, 2011); J. E. E. Boys, *London's news press and the Thirty Years War* (Woodbridge, 2011).

engraved images distributed during the Thirty Years War as part of well-co-ordinated (and expensive) propaganda campaigns financed by some of the more powerful belligerents. As we will see in Chapter 2, these routinely combined vivid images with varying levels of textual commentary (either engraved, or printed in movable type by means of a second impression), and their ability to combine news with heavy political propaganda was unprecedented and extravagant. They threw light on current issues and exploited highly provocative symbolic representations of power and conflict, using striking imagery of contrasting religious beliefs, alongside allegorical representations of good and evil, strong government and anarchy, virtue and sin.

Such material was clearly intended to foster awareness amongst those who had a chance to view them, whether literate or not. Once the war spread, the prints acquired a surprising level of graphic detail. The Swedes in particular, when they became major belligerents from 1630 onwards, appear to have employed the best Dutch engraving techniques to produce propaganda prints of outstanding detail and sophistication. Events such as the siege and destruction of Magdeburg in 1631 generated a range of representations, including both visual images of the atrocities and more symbolic representation of the abuses of power and trust that made this event so controversial. Whilst it is interesting to speculate just how widely distributed such costly prints would have been, and precisely who commissioned them, there is no doubt that those who sympathised with the core message may well have been tempted to display the larger prints in public places (for example in churches or town halls), and they may even have been kept as collector's items. In most cases, we can only guess what kind of impact these sheets would have had, but judging from frequent reuse of certain images (sometimes reprinting from the same plates), it is clear that those who commissioned and designed this kind of propaganda regarded it as important and effective. Both the range of motifs and the quite staggering development in thematic content of the imagery during the period of the war itself suggest that such visual material may have contributed more than newspapers to a growing awareness of demonstrably conflicting views on the legitimate or good use of power, on the need for religious and social stability, and even on the false promises of princes and soldiers struggling for control in this increasingly complicated and irreconcilable conflict.[24]

---

[24] J. R. Paas, *The German political broadsheet 1600–1700*, vols. I-XIII (Wiesbaden, 1985–2016); S. S. Tschopp, 'Rhetorik des Bildes: die kommunikative Funktion sprachlicher und graphischer Visualisierung in der Publizistik zur Zerstörung Magdeburgs im Jahre 1631', in J. Burkhardt and C. Werkstetter (eds.), *Kommunikation und Medien in der Frühen Neuzeit*, in *Historische Zeitschrift*, Beiheft 41 (Munich, 2005), 79–103.

Such sophisticated and divisive political commentary was possible in Germany only because there were a number of opposing governments in continuous conflict, each with substantial resources and with a need to try to win loyalty, secure fiscal support, or at least dampen open resistance. In most other parts of Europe, even if such strong pressures to engage in political propaganda did not materialise until later, changes in demand were nonetheless visible. The London printers who created the first weekly newspapers from 1621 exploited a demand for news regarding the wars on the continent, and in particular the public interest in the fate of Elizabeth, daughter of James VI/I and wife of the deposed Elector Palatine and King of Bohemia, Frederick. By 1632 the crown was sufficiently concerned about the increase in domestic English information that it used the Court of Star Chamber to impose bans. It is worth noting that Charles I generally failed to grasp the opportunities he had in the 1630s for influencing public opinion through the media – often reacting negatively, or too late, hesitating to overcome his natural reluctance to allow any kind of independent discussion in matters of foreign policy and ultimately domestic affairs.[25]

During the English civil wars visual print was at first not as prominent as we might have expected, given the levels of activity noted during the Thirty Years War, yet the demand for news was predictably high. As noted above, London publishers quickly seized the exceptional opportunities for development that arose with the collapse of royal government in 1641. It is of course impossible to assess the relative impact of news reports compared with other kinds of printed communication (such as printed petitions or the growing output of printed images).[26] But major disagreements concerning the legitimate role of the king, parliament and other participants certainly created ample material to feed regular serial publication, not least as those in positions of power deliberately flouted older restraints by appealing to a broader public opinion. All forms of news media flourished in such a climate: pamphlets and newsbooks, broadsheets, journals of various kinds and newspapers with distinctive identities and political leanings on both sides of the conflict. As Raymond has argued, newspapers such as the *London Gazette* or the *Mercurius Politicus* sold as well as some of the great individual political pieces of

[25] Boys, *London's news press*, 210–76; N. Brownlees, 'Narrating contemporaneity: text and structure in English news', in Dooley (ed.), *The dissemination of news*, 225–50.

[26] M. Mendle, 'News and the pamphlet culture of mid-seventeenth-century England', in Dooley and Baron (eds.), *The politics of information*, 57–79; C.J . Sommerville, *The news revolution in England* (Oxford and New York, 1996); D. Zaret, *Origins of democratic culture: printing, petitions and the public sphere in early modern England* (Princeton, 2000), 184–97.

the age, such as *Eikon Basilike* (the best-known royalist apologia, issued just after the execution of Charles I).[27] The distinctions between different types and formats of publication remained blurred and the instability of the market meant that many serial titles had only a brief life, but for those who had the right instincts for journalism, the scope for inventiveness and profit in news was unprecedented.

Understandably, the London market slackened a little in the subdued political climate of the early 1650s, as self-censorship once more became necessary. But the appointment of John Milton as licenser for newsbooks (in effect a poacher turned game-keeper) surely signalled a degree of flexibility which increased when the political uncertainty from 1657 gave news publishing greater urgency once more. Those aiming at personal power, and who knew how to exploit the new media, could make the most of it, as did General Monck in the run-up to the Restoration. Consequently the restored monarchy of 1660 brought fresh calls for more systematic government control of print, and measures such as the 1662 Printing Act were used to curtail both religious and political dissent. Yet the Pandora's box of news media could never be completely shut: recurrent political difficulties ensured a lively public interest, amply demonstrated in the turmoil from 1679–82 and 1685–9.[28] In any case, the legal framework for prosecutions changed definitively after the fortuitous lapse of the Licensing Act (1679–85 and definitively after 1695), as a result of which the authorities increasingly relied on libel prosecutions rather than pre-publication control. By then, the government had also followed French precedent by attempting to secure reliable dissemination of its own version of news through a government-sponsored newspaper, the *London Gazette*, from 1665.

Newspapers and Periodicals as Political Texts in the Century after 1660

Given the dramatic events all over Europe between 1618 and 1660, it is hardly surprising that serialised news-sheets (newspapers) continued to develop a market of their own. After the return of stable government in France in the 1650s, the official *Gazette* exercised a monopoly of domestic news, but was challenged in the 1680s with the appearance of several French-language gazettes published outside French jurisdiction by Huguenot exiles in the Netherlands and elsewhere. However, since

[27] J. Raymond, 'The development of the book trade in Britain', in *The Oxford history of popular print culture*, vol. I, 63; see also J. Raymond, *The invention of the newspaper: English newsbooks 1641–49* (Oxford, 1996),127–83 and *passim*.

[28] J. Sutherland, *The restoration newspaper and its development* (Cambridge, 1986).

these were necessarily expensive to buy within France, they did not represent a major threat to royal control. Other periodicals, such as the scholarly *Journal des Sçavants* (from 1665), had little political significance. Manuscript news-sheets also diminished in importance because of their very limited circulation and high costs. Elsewhere in Europe, except in the Netherlands and parts of northern Germany, the scope for publication of politically sensitive domestic news was subject to similar strict controls.[29] Nevertheless, given the interest in foreign news, the serialised publishing of news-sheets became a more durable component of the print industry from the late seventeenth century onwards, gradually becoming a normal part of urban life and coffee-house sociability in the more prosperous parts of Europe.

In Britain, the records arising from the Stamp Act of 1712 (requiring a tax to be paid on all newspapers) name twelve London newspapers for that year, with a total weekly output of around 50,000 copies; by 1776 the number of titles had substantially increased, and the total output was nearly a quarter of a million – a figure which of course does not include the unmeasurable but significant output of papers that evaded the tax altogether. Northern Germany also sustained a huge growth from the early eighteenth century, ranging across many different types of dailies, weeklies and periodicals. The high-quality *Hamburg Correspondent* increased its circulation from 1600 copies in 1730 to 30,000 by 1800, and journals specifically intended to provide political overviews became commonplace in the last quarter of the eighteenth century, including titles such as Schirach's *Politisches Journal* or Schlözer's prestigious *Staats-Anzeigen*. In France, demand was dampened by heavier censorship, leading to the appearance of a number of openly critical papers in French, such as the *Gazette de Leyde*, published within easy reach just across its northern and eastern borders, or Linguet's widely influential journal *Annales politiques, civiles et littéraires* published mostly from London and Brussels. But there was also a significant growth within France: the official *Gazette de France* had acquired a circulation of around 12,000 copies before the Revolution, and around 80 other titles had become reasonably well established by 1785. Again, the political instability of the Maupeou Crisis (1771–4) clearly guaranteed a growing demand for printed news

[29] See for example P. Arblaster, 'Policy and publishing in the Habsburg Netherlands 1585–1690', in Dooley and Baron (eds.), *The politics of information*, 179–98, and other papers in that volume, and in Dooley (ed.), *The dissemination of news*; systematic studies of newspaper publishing in Spain and Italy are sparse, but see A. C. Gomez, ' "There are lots of papers going around and it'd be better if there weren't": broadsides and public opinion in the Spanish monarchy in the seventeenth century', in M. Rospocher (ed.), *Beyond the public sphere: opinions, publics and spaces in early modern Europe* (Bologna and Berlin, 2012), 227–48.

in France, a trend that continued until 1789 and soon became an explosive factor in the Revolution itself. These and many more examples will be examined more closely in changing political contexts in later chapters.

With the trend towards comprehensive and organised news networks increasingly firmly established during the eighteenth century, newspapers and other seemingly ephemeral forms of print came to play a significant role in public discussion. However, newspaper and periodical journalism remained a highly experimental and often risky process: the large number of failures (titles that lasted only a short while) demonstrate how difficult it was to secure a sustained demand whilst at the same time avoiding reprisals from local authorities or central government. The need to retain a large audience ensured that most actual newspapers in the later seventeenth century and into the early eighteenth concentrated on basic summary narratives of events, often copied from other newspapers, added to as much official news as they could muster, while avoiding editorial positions that might be construed as openly critical or even analytical. Advertisements, commercial news and sensational stories kept many papers going, even if they offered little or no political commentary. In other words, the survival of a newspaper required a great deal of pragmatism and adaptability. Those that focused on political material were particularly vulnerable to variations both in political climate and public demand. In recognition of all these factors, historians have tended to disregard estimates of total circulation (often based on questionable contemporary claims), or counts of new titles, as insufficient on their own. More useful as a guide to public significance, perhaps, is a detailed exploration of the innovative presentational techniques and the range of new types of journal created to engage a wider public.

One striking development was the emergence of periodicals which, on the surface, did not carry political news as such, but which nevertheless created scope for some kinds of indirect political commentary. We will encounter many such ventures later, but for now it is worth noting just one outstanding example, the *Tatler*. Appearing anonymously from April 1709, it adopted a number of brilliant literary devices, not least its fictional character, Mr Isaac Bickerstaff. He could ostensibly report what he had heard in various London coffee houses – in effect giving free rein to commentaries on a number of subjects including international affairs, domestic news, moral issues and humorous misunderstandings. The *Tatler* also used real or fabricated letters to the editor as pegs from which to hang discussions of general interest. Significantly, the periodical was addressed to women as well as to men, its moderate tone designed to entertain rather than provoke. The venture came to an end with the last issue of 1710, when Richard Steele finally owned up to being its editor.

But shortly afterwards, he and Joseph Addison launched an equally successful (but slightly less overtly political) daily journal, the *Spectator*, each issue of which often revolved around a thematic essay rather than a range of different stories. This, too, had a short lifespan, lasting only until December 1712. By then, however, the two successive ventures had set a new standard for imaginative and accessible journalism, widely imitated in various 'moral' journals, not only in Britain but also in France, the Netherlands and Germany. Fashionable and lighthearted, rather than intellectual or confrontational, these ventures were a really popular component in the emergent public sphere of coffee houses, inns, theatres and other venues of sociability. Although total circulation figures were rarely large (often in the range 600–1500, short of the *Spectator*'s peak at 3000), the proliferation of new titles and the trouble most governments took to keep an eye on them attest to their perceived significance and impact.

The abandonment of formal pre-publication licensing in Britain after 1695, and the resulting greater reliance on direct legal prosecution of printers and authors under various kinds of charges including libel – combined with the gradual acceptance of political disagreement as part of normal parliamentary and local politics – go some way towards explaining why English newspapers continued to have more innovative scope and seemingly more vitality than in most other parts of Europe. After the Hanoverian succession, with foreign news usually not attracting government sanction (as long as national interests were not affected too obviously), publishers naturally explored how far they could go in reporting of domestic politics. It became apparent that although for example the Walpole administration used a number of repressive tactics (as well as buying favourable press coverage), it was increasingly difficult to secure successful prosecutions in law against critical newspapers (especially in jury trials). The 1731 guilty verdict against Richard Francklin, regarding his paper the *Craftsman*, for example, generated so much public criticism that it was counterproductive: admittedly the *Craftsman* ended publication in 1736, but as with other prosecutions of critical authors, there was a very substantial measure of public support for political freedom of expression. Similarly, in 1738, when *The Gentleman's Magazine* (founded in London in 1731) ostensibly bowed to pressure to stop its featured short narrative summary of parliamentary proceedings, it merely substituted reports of the debates in the Parliament of Lilliput – a transparent ruse which not only relied on the universal familiarity with Swift's *Gulliver's Travels* (first published in 1726, and a text with obvious political symbolism to which we shall return), but also proved financially shrewd since the profits from sales far outweighed the potential repercussions of the penalties imposed through the invoking of increasingly despised legal restraints. Although we should not underestimate the severity of the threats used by the British government against newspaper publishers, and the degree of defensive self-censorship which resulted, nevertheless well-connected editors were increasingly able to make a show of their defiance, and by mid-century even exploited slogans proclaiming liberty of the press as a political right.[30]

As we shall see in later chapters of this book, the struggle to control and influence public opinion remained unresolved through the eighteenth century. Newspapers, as serial publications, had to avoid being so controversial that they would incur prosecution or suppression, but a reputation for accuracy also mattered. The reliance on strategically located 'correspondents', and unashamed reuse of material published in other papers, lent a certain structure to politically oriented newspapers and allowed editors to use headings and develop multi-column printing to attract the reader. Even though many newspapers continued to resemble pamphlets in actual appearance, some distinct characteristics of serial newspapers were now well established: normally an aim to be comprehensive (meeting the needs of different readers by covering all kinds of current affairs), extreme caution in respect of particular issues (to avoid alienating readers and censorship) and of course open commercialisation (including more extensive use of advertisements). By the early eighteenth century, newspapers were becoming firmly established with a seemingly insatiable urban demand. But they remained less flexible, and less independent, than the well-established vehicle for controversial political print, the pamphlet.

Pamphlets

Cheap print came in many forms and, while serialised newsletters were an innovation of the early seventeenth century, one-off polemics and pamphlets had long since become an established part of the print market. Inexpensive short texts had the obvious potential to create a socially wider market and may even have provided a direct incentive to learn to read. Nevertheless we need to resist the temptation of assuming that cheap print was within reach of everyone: as Joad Raymond has reminded us, printing (and paper itself) remained relatively costly and even the cheapest items were not really 'popular' in the strict sense of being readily

---

[30] *The Gentleman's Magazine*, July 1738, p. 331ff; but attempts to prevent the publication of accounts of the proceedings of the House of Commons continued at least until 1771. See also B. Harris, *Politics and the rise of the press: Britain and France, 1620–1800* (London, 1996) and H. Barker, *Newspapers, politics and English society 1695–1855* (London, 2000).

accessible to everyone.[31] The formats and presentational styles of printed material owed much to equivalent handwritten forms of communication, but printers and publishers who wanted to make the most of market opportunities were not slow to experiment. Already by the late sixteenth century, there were many forms of text with political potential: 'libels', petitions, broadsheets (single-sheet texts) and the slightly longer chapbooks, 'booklets' or 'blue books' (from the cheap paper used as covers), almanacs, letters, 'pasquils', tracts, and other texts that were not serialised and therefore easy to produce and sell on the unregulated market.[32] The simplest texts were printed on just one sheet (each sheet making 8 pages in quarto, or 16 pages in octavo format), but pamphlets typically have several sheets folded and stitched together to make booklets, and so ranging from 16 to 48 pages, or by the eighteenth century even longer. Pamphlets as a genre were not at all clearly distinct from other forms of cheap print, and could be either serious or scurrilous, a tall story or a supernatural account. But pamphlets were also ideal for a context-sensitive confrontation – typically around just one key issue or story, produced very quickly to ensure topical relevance and intended for a broad readership. Unlike newspapers, pamphlets were not serial, which meant that both printers and authors could if necessary conceal their identity.

Pamphlets were both more flexible and much more difficult to control or suppress than, say, newspapers, and were therefore ideally suited to stir discussion and controversy about any contentious issue. From the time of Luther, and in France and Britain from the 1570s onwards, pamphlets had been used extensively (and increasingly systematically) by those seeking religious reforms, challenging established authority, wanting to stir dissent and unrest, or reinforcing a particular political solution. As a result, such texts were soon recognised as a weapon to focus the attention of the reading public – and hence as a challenge which called for a response (if necessary, from other pamphleteers hired by those who felt challenged). Printing simply extended the range and impact of such polemics, particularly in urban environments where more purchasers could be found, but potentially also further afield, distributed by hawkers and itinerant pedlars. We can never know the actual print run (number of

---

[31] J. Raymond, 'Introduction: the origins of popular print culture', in *The Oxford history of popular print culture*, 4–7. By mid-seventeenth century, in London, it was common for a cheap booklet of 24 pages to sell for one penny, or around one-twelfth of a typical day's wages in the urban labour market. See also the overview of prices and wages above, p. 22f.

[32] D. Bellingradt, *Flugpublizistik und Öffentlichkeit um 1700: Dynamiken, Akteure und Strukturen im urbanen Raum des Alten Reiches* (Stuttgart, 2011), 11–19 and *passim*, has called for a clearer historical definition of these overlapping types of popular print. More consistent cataloguing in library collections is also needed.

copies) of any individual text, but if you could sell even a few hundred copies printing was financially viable.

If printed pamphlets were hardly a new invention, historians agree that they turned into a deluge in certain parts of Europe at critical junctures in the early seventeenth century, notably in the cities of the Netherlands, England and France, when religious and political issues were particularly pressing. There, as we will see in the next chapter, cheap print came to be regarded by some observers in the 1640s and 50s as a menacing torrent threatening to destabilise society, or conversely a tool of empowerment for those whose voices had not previously been audible. In the Netherlands, for example, the total output of distinct pamphlets (as measured from surviving collections) ranged from a few dozen in relatively calm years, to more than a thousand in the crisis year 1672, when Johan de Witt resigned as Grand Pensionary and, with his brother, was lynched by a mob whipped into a frenzy by the threat of French military invasion. Well over half of these pamphlets were printed in Amsterdam, but significantly there were publishers in every Dutch city and town of any significance, some of whom plagiarised newly issued polemics from elsewhere, whilst others commissioned local writers to give the argument a particular slant. Many pamphlets were anonymous, but amongst those that were not it is interesting to observe how many different individuals became authors, and how adversarial the arguments often were. The Dutch invasion of England in 1688 also resulted in a lively range of polemics, but this time included much stronger arguments put out by the government itself, at the behest of the *stadtholder* William of Orange, to generate support for his ambitious foreign policy. In the next chapters, we will look more closely at the links between political crises and print, but the general trend is clear enough. The Dutch market for polemics was volatile and buoyant, displaying all the characteristics of a wide-reaching and controversial medium. Whilst we cannot identify the actual readers with any degree of certainty, we may at least suggest that they are likely to have been no less diverse than the authors themselves.[33]

The most dramatic example of how instability could generate major change in the market for print is that of England in the 1640s and 50s. As we noted earlier on the basis of the ESTC, the total quantity of separate titles increased almost tenfold from the late 1630s to 1642, and although numbers fluctuated through the 1640s and 50s (with predictable peaks

[33] G. de Bruin, 'Political pamphleteering and public opinion in the age of de Witt', in F. Deen, D. Onnekink and M. Reinders (eds.), *Pamphlets and politics in the Dutch Republic* (Leiden, 2011), 3–30; D. Onnekink, 'The revolution in Dutch foreign policy (1688)', ibid., 143–71; M. Reinders, *Gedrukte chaos: populisme en moord in het rampjaar 1672* (Amsterdam, 2010).

again in 1648 and 1660), the role of print had clearly acquired unprecedented importance. Much of this growth was made up of a distinct shift from relatively long texts to shorter publications, notably newspapers and pamphlets.[34] Producing this kind of print became a mainstay of the printing trade, especially for those workshops that tried to evade the continuing but inconsistently enforced censorship and regulatory systems. It is important to note that some readers clearly regarded newsbooks and pamphlets not as disposable material but as items to be collected and kept for future rereading. The London publisher George Thomason carefully collected 22,000 items during the twenty years from 1640 to the Restoration, and there were many others who found the new reading irresistible – including (as we will see in Chapter 2) some women active as authors, sellers and even printers, as well as self-confessed 'addicts' of pamphlet-reading such as the woodturner Nehemiah Wallington and the ironmonger Henry Walker.[35]

We can also see the emergence of pressure groups capable of sustaining religious or political campaigns in print over a period of time, from the early Scottish Covenanters in 1638 to the radical religious groups of the 1650s such as the Ranters and Quakers, or from the Levellers and republican polemicists to the royalists before and after the execution of Charles I. As Jason Peacey has noted, discussions that had previously been 'closed', in oral conversation, were now documented and disseminated through pamphlets, providing specific detailed political or religious information to anyone who was interested.[36] Not surprisingly, such information was far too controversial and 'dangerous' to leave uncontested, and the only possible response (when regulation failed) was to commission more authors to write responses. Significantly, protestations of loyalty or dissent could be reinforced by an innovative adaption of a long-established form of communication, the petition: after 1640, political activists developed the tactic of mass printed petitions to generate (and demonstrate) wide public support for particular causes, particularly amongst the lower orders in the bigger cities.[37] Further analysis below, in Chapter 2, will attempt to explain these changes more fully, for France

---

[34] J. Raymond, 'The development of the book trade in Britain', in *The Oxford history of popular print culture*, 59–75; and his *Pamphlets and pamphleteering in early modern Britain* (Cambridge, 2003).

[35] Raymond, *Pamphlets and pamphleteering*, 192–6; J. Peacey, *Print and public politics in the English Revolution* (Cambridge, 2013), 75–6; on the role of women up to the mid-seventeenth century, see H. Smith, *'Grossly material things': women and book production in early modern England* (Oxford, 2012).

[36] J. Peacey, 'Pamphlets', in *The Oxford history of popular print culture*, 453–70; Peacey, *Print and public politics*, 29–91.

[37] Zaret, *Origins of democratic culture*, 216–65.

and the Netherlands as well as England. But it would appear that the age of public dialogue and disputation of power in print had truly arrived.

The Printing Workshop: Production, Costs, Sales and Workflow

Important though it is, core quantitative data regarding the growing market for newspapers, pamphlets and other forms of print is not the only way of evaluating the processes whereby print changed contemporary strategies of communication. Important evidence can also be found in the physical object itself, the printed text. The material culture of printing, and the 'life story' of a single book or pamphlet, allows us to approach questions of origin, marketing and dissemination (or provenance and reception) from the object itself. The print industry was one of the most complicated, high-skill and labour-intensive sectors of the early modern European economy. It relied on a number of inter-linked specialist trades and suppliers, including paper manufacturing and long-distance trade (see Figure 1). Large capital investment was needed just to get started: in later eighteenth-century France a new printing press could be obtained for 400 livres (the subsistence wage for a manual labourer for a year), but the cases of fonts (in several sizes and styles) were expensive. The entire cost of the equipment needed to produce one newspaper in Paris in the 1790s was typically reckoned at 2000 livres. Book production required a bigger range of fonts, and usually several presses, but that could also lead to some economies of scale and efficiency in production.[38] Bookbinding was a separate process controlled by different guilds, usually negotiating independently with the buyer. Shipment and sale of texts (bound or not) carried further costs, but books normally also retained a significant resale value (as evidenced in auction and sales catalogues).

Every stage in the printing of a book is liable to have left some physical marks, some of them the direct result of technical restraints in the production process itself. Most books were printed in modest print runs on initial publication, typically ranging from a few hundred copies to upwards of one thousand, and if that sold well, reprints might in large markets be even larger. The cost of paper, and its vulnerability if kept for any length of time, meant that it was normal business practice to meet higher market demand by resetting a text soon after first publication, rather than by printing more stock copies and storing for months in anticipation of future sales. The size of a print run could not easily be increased once production had started, except by resetting and reprinting

[38] H. Gough, *The newspaper press in the French Revolution* (London, 1988), 183–7.

those sheets that had already been completed. However, resetting a text meant repeating nearly all the production costs, from typesetting and actual printing, to breaking up the type from completed pages and resorting all the units. Accurate typesetting was itself a highly skilled and labour-intensive job requiring decent light and good eyesight.

An efficient team of two men could print up to 200 sheets per hour (sustained over a 10-hour working day), but each sheet of paper had to be turned over and printed again for the other side, and hung up to dry before it could be folded. Because of the quantity of font required, only a limited number of pages could be typeset at any one time, before the movable type was sorted and reused for subsequents sections. To keep one press going fairly continuously, therefore, would normally require at least four people: two taking turns to work the press and feed the paper, one compositor setting the type and one or more assistants cleaning the printing frames, breaking up and resorting the type back into the right cases when the print run had been completed, and sorting the printed sheets carefully. Significant efficiency savings could be made if more presses were operated in parallel, with a number of compositors, pressmen, apprentices and assistants working where most needed, but that required careful organisation. For best results, a workshop had to be laid out with sufficient space and enough light for everyone, but also with paper supplies and storage space readily to hand.

Closer examination of printed texts often yields additional evidence. Very short texts, such as newspapers, might require only half a sheet of paper, such that two copies could be produced in parallel in one pressing. By contrast, because of the vast number of separate letters needed for a text of any length, substantial books were usually produced one or two gatherings at a time, sequentially. Each sheet of paper had to be run through the press twice, once for each side (twice for each side if it included coloured letters). And since each sheet was large enough to take several pages of finished text (when folded), the layout of each page within a single frame had to be correct so that the sheet would make a sequential set of pages the right way up when folded (or would make appropriate sequences, if folded with one or more additional sheets within a single gathering). A folio volume required each sheet to be folded just once (making 4 pages), quarto twice (8 pages, each page a quarter of the size of the original sheet), octavo three times (16 pages), and so on down to various small-format texts. At some stage, sample sheets would also need to be proofread, either by the author or by some other careful reader, and mistakes in the typesetting corrected before the print run was continued.

The production of blank paper was a separate and complex industry, involving the milling and bleaching of rags and the preparation of size, culminating in the delicate operation of turning the pulp into uniform sheets of paper by means of a wire screen mounted in a frame (a fine-meshed sieve on which the pulp is drained), followed by pressing and drying of each sheet. The manufacture of movable type was also done by specialists, requiring skilled design of the steel dies used to make the matrix and moulds for every letter, in every size, upper and lower case, for casting in a softer metal alloy. Both paper and fonts can sometimes help identify where a text was produced, and (especially for illegal publications) may help us identify the printing workshop itself.[39] But for the workshop manager, dealing with movable deadlines and sometimes problematic supply lines, production of any sizeable text required careful co-ordination of a number of essentially different and technically demanding processes. Glitches could easily occur anywhere, even in the proofreading stage, potentially stalling production.

The standard methods of production provide historians of print with important additional evidence. Because print runs were usually small, but the actual number of copies hardly ever recorded, the rate and frequency of reprinting is the most reliable way of measuring market demand. Since a text that was reset in movable type would never turn out exactly the same (minor differences in alignment and minor spelling errors being unavoidable), careful comparison of printings even from the same publisher within the same stipulated year can readily confirm how many reprints there were. Physical comparison of individual copies may also reveal other historically significant evidence, such as changes made in the course of one print run (mid-printing), or inconsistencies of layout indicating parallel printing of different parts of the same text across several printing houses (for speed). Occasionally there is crucial evidence of secret printing of an unauthorised text, or illegal reprinting of a book which had been banned – and could therefore only be sold if disguised with a false title page or as a remnant copy of the original printing. There are even instances of illegal works started in one city, with printing shifted to another location altogether to avoid confiscation by the authorities. To check, ideally we need a census of all surviving copies of a particular text

---

[39] The manufacture of paper, the design and large-scale production of font, and other links in the production cycle are described for example in A. Johns, *The nature of the Book* (Chicago, 1998), 74–136. Detailed material on early modern printers is rare, but see the entry 'Imprimerie' in vol. VIII of Diderot (ed.), *Encyclopédie* (1765). See also R. Darnton, *The great cat massacre and other episodes in French cultural history* (New York and London, 1984), which includes discussion of Nicolas Contat's 1762 manuscript *Anecdotes typographiques*.

(including reprints, pirated versions, translations and adaptations) and their provenance – a huge task for modern researchers. Old marginal annotations and other indications of use may also become significant. Ultimately all this evidence allows a fresh evaluation of which books were most successful in market terms, where, and when. That in turn allows historians of print to move away from making assumptions about a 'canon' of texts now deemed important (most often in terms of content) merely on the basis of historical hindsight.

Printers and publishers did not specialise in any one particular sector of the market, and would regard newspapers, pamphlets and books as work to be done interchangeably, to make the most of variable demand and available opportunities. In terms of layout, paper supply, production and distribution, there was little need for specialisation. Although serialisation made more forward planning necessary, newspapers, pamphlets and books otherwise shared common physical characteristics (including page size and fonts), and were produced in the same way. In times of political disturbance, individual one-off productions such as pamphlets could have as much market potential as newspapers. What distinguished different kinds of text was primarily a matter of content and intended readership: flysheets, ballads and newspapers were meant to attract all buyers, and often had direct connection to a specific controversy or incident. Newspapers had to be sold fairly quickly, before they lost value, but most other genres had an unpredictable shelf life. By contrast, substantial tracts, books or even reference works intended to appeal to wealthier readers might be produced at a more leisurely pace, complete with decorative title page, perhaps an inserted engraving rather than a woodcut image, and more spacious printing on better-quality paper. In assessing the transmission of political culture, therefore, we need to remember that production was highly flexible, with printers changing priorities to suit changing demand.

Really successful printers could operate on large budgets with complex credits and loans. But few could rival the state-funded Imprimerie Royale in Paris, which in the eighteenth century occupied a large building and outhouses, with up to fifty presses and a workforce of well over 100. With little change in the basic technology, however, it was possible to operate at any level: small print shops had to be agile and efficient to survive, while large ones required substantial management as well as good social and political connections. Since printing was the only medium of mass communication, it comes as no surprise that the industry quickly became the target of increasingly complex government regulation everywhere. The agility (almost portability) of small printing presses made them ideal for use in times of political crisis or instability. Printing also created new legal problems and the scope for endless litigation regarding privileges and copyright, often requiring compromise settlements between major entrepreneurs, family printing dynasties, publishers and governments. Such issues, alongside the increasingly elaborate censorship systems operating with questionable efficiency across Europe, provide significant additional information regarding the impact and dissemination of particular texts.

Copyright, Intellectual Property and Dissemination

State or local regulatory mechanisms clearly did intrude into the working practices of printing workshops, but the evidence of how and where is uneven. Formal permissions to print, usually confirmed by some kind of privilege granting exclusive copyright, were unlikely ever to benefit the author, even if they could be enforced. The normal practice was for a printer or publisher to buy a manuscript, thereby also acquiring the full intellectual property rights in a work (unless agreed otherwise in the sales contract with the author). These rights came to be defined in law in various ways across Europe, with variable degrees of enforcement. In France the author or printer might apply for a royal privilege through the Chancery, a process that also involved approval by a royal censor. In England print jobs were meant to be registered through the Stationers Company, a corporation of printers and publishers sanctioned until 1695 by means of successive Licensing Acts, whereby the Stationers Company itself acted as a proxy censorship system. After 1695, the status of intellectual rights was uncertain, but a new copyright law in 1709–10 attempted to give perpetual copyright legal basis. This was challenged and overturned by 1774, after a great many legal disputes. But in any case English copyright law did not apply to Scotland or Ireland, so neither authors nor publishers had effective protection against piracy there.

The many different legal and political systems operating across Europe inevitably fostered different legal frameworks for the control and regulation of print. Legislation was needed to secure property rights, intellectual rights and financial interests, as well as to regulate what could be printed in the first place, and determine libel and liability where necessary. In practice, the stakes were often far too high, the scope for evasion or piracy too great and the financial interests too enticing to secure any real stability in the major centres of printing. There were so many inherently conflicting vested interests in the whole publishing sector: authors no doubt wanted to be heard, and gain a reputation, but could rarely make a living as writers; printers and publishers, having bought the manuscript, wanted to make money and get predictable returns on their investments in equipment and skilled workmen; local, church and state authorities wanted to ensure that print would not disturb the established order, and would only reach 'responsible' readers; book traders and their shipping agents would aim to circumvent local regulations and evade customs checks; readers, on the other hand, once they started looking, might want to search out new texts with interesting content, even if that meant buying on the black market or relying on friends with underground networks. Print was truly a great medium for any of these purposes.

Clearly printing and its auxiliary trades, together with marketing and bookselling, created a valuable economic sector of growing importance. But there is a second dimension to printing which also deserves closer investigation: the reception of a text, its reviewers, those who wrote in response and the resulting but elusive reputations of all the participants in any resulting arguments. Once again, as in the commercial aspect of publishing, the author was often in a vulnerable position, having to defend both the substantive content and his public reputation. As we shall see, the author was an obvious target for censors, but might also find that if the book had a significant impact, critics might publish full-scale responses or engage in critical polemics. Sometimes these were published anonymously, whether supportive or critical, but as ever might involve unintended misunderstandings or deliberate manipulation of the arguments. Bitter disputes had already become frequent in matters of religion, but from the 1640s were fought out in other fields as well. Every individual case has a story of its own, but print evidently created much scope for corrosive confrontations.

In those parts of Europe where comprehensive short-title catalogues and other digital resources have become available, we now have the potential to collate evidence of impact. For example, we may identify reprints of individual texts that had had some initial impact when first published, but had since fallen into obscurity, outside the canon of 'great' texts. Digital technology may also facilitate searches for turns of phrase and distinctive forms of political expression. As we will see in the next chapter, such search techniques are invaluable for the 1640s and 1650s, when the collapse of regulatory mechanisms in many parts of Europe, and the surge in the number of shorter printed texts, created opportunities for new forms of political thinking and writing. It has become apparent that some of these texts were read by, even occasionally written by, the 'middling sorts' who had hitherto rarely engaged visibly with political texts. Such broader political engagement may have been partly reversed after the re-establishment of order in many parts of Europe in the 1660s, but if so only temporarily. In the 1680s, and definitely from the early eighteenth century onwards, we have additional evidence from book-trade catalogues, journal reviews, commercial and public library holdings, and other data, allowing us to construct a more complex picture of the processes of dissemination.

Translation into other languages is evidence of a different kind of dissemination, just as important as reprinting, but for different reasons. Translation took on much greater practical significance when political discussion increasingly moved from Latin (as a lingua franca) to native vernacular languages accessible to all readers. The abandonment of Latin for political polemics began in the great controversies over Calvinist resistance theory[40] arising after the Massacre of St Bartholomew in France in 1572, but only became the norm after 1640 during the political confrontations in England and upheavals in other parts of Europe. For a while, French served as a new international language, but only for the educated elite. Given that many authors wanted to address a wider domestic readership, the use of native languages became an important strategic choice available to authors, typically accompanied by a more accessible style of writing. In other words, use of the vernacular for first-time publication, and translation of texts into other vernaculars, not only served the needs of a wider readership, but changed the intended purpose of print.

As we will see in Chapter 4, translations are of enormous importance in the history of print, for two reasons: first, they provide tangible geographic evidence of how a book spread (Latin editions could be traded anywere); and secondly, with careful analysis of the actual translation, we are able to understand how contemporaries would have read a particular text and explained its meaning in terms intelligible to a different cultural community. Furthermore, since there is no such thing as an 'accurate' translation that stays completely faithful to the original, any translation might well to some extent be adjusted or substantially modified to suit its new readers. Translations may even have helped to create a new political vocabulary in the host language. The interpretative aspect of early modern translation can be very informative in itself, providing the historian with a mirror (of variable quality) showing how contemporaries might have understood (or misunderstood) a new text. Some further degrees of garbling would have been almost unavoidable if French was used as a bridging language – for example when the translator was unable to read the original, and instead relied on a French translation as intermediary. Although decisions whether to publish a translation may have as much to do with accident and the business interests of printers, by the eighteenth century

[40] Amongst the major contributors, for example Bodin published his *Six livres de la république* (Paris, 1576) in French, while George Buchanan preferred Latin for his *De iure regni apud Scotos* (Edinburgh, 1579).

increasingly rapid translation between the major European languages became the norm, and this process of translation and adaptation itself became the object of detailed and fruitful discussion amongst contemporaries.

Authors and Intended Readers: Milton, Hobbes and Spinoza

The many issues discussed so far affected all kinds of texts, including some of the most impressive or detailed works of analysis. Amongst the many authors who wanted to contribute to the political arguments in England during the 1640s and 50s, two stand out in terms not just of their impact but also their careful choice of language and publication strategy: Thomas Hobbes and John Milton. Of the two, Milton (1608–74) was much more polemical in style, becoming in effect a very confrontational critic of the established clergy, a spokesman for resistance to the king and a key intellectual speaking for Commonwealth government. Apart from tracts on clerical abuses (1641) and education, divorce and censorship (1644), he published *The tenure of kings and magistrates* (1649) and *Eikonoklastes* (1649): all texts which, while essentially maintaining the tone of intellectual analysis expected by its English readers, were written in a muscular prose, provocatively outspoken in their support of republican government, the trial and regicide. To this he added the more substantial *Pro populo Anglicano Defensio* (1651) – published in Latin because it was intended for the European market, but later translated into English as *A defence of the people of England*, and he added a second *Defensio* in 1654. Both of these tracts were part of a major international polemic, and constitute the most significant rebuttal of royalist arguments of their time.

In later life Milton became best known across Europe for his *Paradise lost* (1667) and his *Paradise regained* (1671) – the former of which, in particular, enjoyed very frequent reprinting as well as regular translation into French (with at least 14 editions during the eighteenth century), German (8 editions), Dutch (5), Danish and Italian. Although also about power, these canonic texts are perhaps less important in the present context than his earlier overtly political writings. His 40-page polemic on censorship (*Areopagitica, a speech of Mr John Milton for the liberty of unlicensed printing*, 1644) was reprinted in 1698 as part of a complete edition of Milton's writings, and again in 1738, 1772, 1791 and 1792. It was also adapted for a French version by Mirabeau in 1788, reprinted in 1792 because of its relevance to the French political controversies of the time. Milton's first *Defence* of the English republic (1651), possibly reprinted seven times within the year, had two further reprints in the 1650s and, although accessible to continental readers because it was in Latin, also had a Dutch translation in 1655. Its significance for a wider readership is demonstrated by the English translation of 1692, in turn reprinted in 1695 and in the complete edition of 1698, no doubt because of its continuing political relevance. More striking, perhaps, is the fact that although there were no translations of this work in most parts of eighteenth-century Europe, the French rediscovered it in a translation in 1789 and were keen enough to support reprints in 1791 and again in 1792. Milton's *Defence* was thus a book which after 150 years had suddenly found a receptive foreign readership.[41]

Milton's slightly older contemporary, Hobbes (1588–1679) gained notoriety for a rather different kind of writing. His first major published work directly focused on politics and government, *De cive* (1642), was written in Latin when Hobbes had escaped to Paris from civil-war England. It was published anonymously in a restricted edition, but was later reprinted a number of times in Amsterdam (1647, 1657, 1669) and had at least a further three eighteenth-century editions. An English translation was published in 1651 (as *Philosophical rudiments concerning government and society*) but was not authorised by Hobbes and was of such poor quality that it was never reprinted. More important was the French translation prepared and published by Hobbes's friend Samuel Sorbière (1649), which was reprinted at least twice before Hobbes died, followed by another translation in 1660 and other versions in the following years. It was the French version that was most widely read on the continent and which, alongside the Latin original, made Hobbes known amongst political theorists. There was also a Dutch version published in 1675, used by some German readers.

For the English reading public, however, Hobbes's most forceful and contentious work was his *Leviathan* (1651). Regarded by scholars as the greatest work on politics in early modern Europe, this was also the book that caused Hobbes real personal difficulties. Written in very forceful and clear English, and headed by one of the most memorable frontispiece plates in book history, it was clearly intended to be read by the political establishment in England, and as such its impact was deliberate and dramatic. We will consider some of the radical implications of Hobbes's landmark arguments more fully in subsequent chapters, but for now we should note that *Leviathan* not only made the overwhelmingly pessimistic case for the need for authoritarian government, for which it is primarily

---

[41] The data on the reprinting and translation of Milton's work is based on the ESTC and on the respective catalogues of the main European research libraries.

known today, but also provided the most sophisticated argument to date for the absolute necessity of separating church and state. It combined this with a detailed and systematic analysis of the Bible itself, as a historical text, intending thereby to explain why belief in any divine sanction for government was unnecessary and irrational. That *Leviathan* remained an extremely controversial work, both before and after the Restoration of 1660, is therefore unsurprising. Understandably, it was the religious challenges that seemed initially to exercise his contemporary critics most,[42] even though the political implications also caused difficulties for Hobbes as he tried to make peace first with the Commonwealth government, then after 1660 with the monarchy.

The writing, publication and diffusion of *Leviathan* have justifiably been the focus of much recent research. Hobbes was already 60 when the book appeared, and although it might originally have been intended as a revision for English readers of his *De cive*, it clearly turned into something much bigger, intended for a different purpose. It was clearly meant as a direct warning against the dangers of weak and changeable government, but its message was far too complex and analytical for the book to loose its relevance quickly. Recent scholarship indicates that Hobbes may have started thinking about *Leviathan* in 1646, but did most of the work during the climactic years 1649–50. He probably did not write in a linear way: he had an overall framework in mind, but (as his friend John Aubrey noted) would work out the detail in his head while going for long walks and write it out in a sequence which was neither particularly systematic nor necessarily very logical. The result is what one scholar has called a 'layered text', where new parts were added that do not always match corresponding sections elsewhere in the book: *Leviathan* needs to be read as if it were an archaeological site.[43] To traditional historians of ideas, this may seem an obstacle, in that we do not have a single definitive statement of some of the main arguments. But for those historians who recognise the urgency and power of Hobbes's response to the problems he saw around him, and the understandably hostile criticisms he knew would come from churchmen, republicans and monarchists alike, such textual archaeology becomes an essential means of understanding what he was trying to do. For that reason, we need to thoroughly understand the history of the book, including reprints and translations.

---

[42] S. Mintz, *The hunting of Leviathan: seventeenth-century reactions to the materialism and moral philosophy of Thomas Hobbes* (Cambridge, 1962); J. Parkin, *Taming the Leviathan: the reception of the political and religious ideas of Thomas Hobbes in England 1640–1700* (Cambridge, 2007).

[43] D. Baumgold, 'The difficulties of Hobbes interpretation', *Political Theory*, 36 (2008), 827–55.

There are several slightly different but significant original versions of *Leviathan*. We have one authentic manuscript copy (the Egerton manuscript in the British Library). This was a professionally made presentation copy done by a scribe in Paris from Hobbes's own working text, complete with a hand-drawn version of the frontispiece, and it was given to the exiled prince Charles (whom Hobbes had been tutoring in mathematics). Hobbes's original working text has not survived, nor has the copy sent to the printer in London (likely to have differed slightly in matters of detail from the presentation copy, since it was not prepared at the same time). We also have two, and possibly three, superficially identical but totally distinct printed editions from within the author's own lifetime, all of which have potentially significant textual variations. These are known by the different emblems they display on the title page: the original 'Head' edition of 1651, the so-called 'Bear' edition, which must have been printed before 1678, and the 'Ornaments' edition, which is much more difficult to date with any degree of accuracy. The precise differences between these versions, and an exhaustive account of the likely history of each, are provided by Noel Malcolm in his definitive edition of the text.[44] However, as Malcolm has now made clear, it is not enough to look at these three variant English printings alone: Hobbes almost certainly also wrote the Latin version which appeared in Amsterdam in 1668 as part of a complete edition of Hobbes's work. During these difficult years after the Restoration, Hobbes was in real danger of being brought to trial for blasphemy. His book was explicitly named by the special House of Commons committee of 1666 set up to review 'the former Laws against Atheism, Profaneness, Debauchery and Swearing; and to examine whether ... there be any Neglect in putting the Laws into Execution...' Hobbes was acutely aware of the very serious charges against himself, on account of *Leviathan*, and would have chosen his precise wording for the Latin version with care. Some important sections diverge substantially from the English original, or are summarised, perhaps because Hobbes thought foreign readers would not want so much material of primarily English significance. In key respects, however, the Latin version was no less combative and certainly no less likely to stir up religious controversy. The print run and dissemination of the Latin version has not been fully documented, but even if it was in less demand than the English original, it did help give the international scholarly community access to most of his argument at a time when few readers on the continent read English.

[44] Thomas Hobbes, *Leviathan*, edited by Noel Malcolm (3 vols., Oxford, 2012), the first volume of which provides full editorial comment, with the remaining two volumes providing an English text with all significant variants (including the Egerton manuscript) as well as a parallel text of the Latin version of 1668.

A Dutch translation was published in 1667, reprinted in 1672, and banned two years later by the otherwise relatively lax Dutch authorities.[45]

As far as English readers are concerned, we know that the original 1651 edition, although probably issued in quite a large print run,[46] had by the 1660s become expensive and difficult to find. Originally sold at 8 shillings and 6 pence, a copy was acquired by the diarist Samuel Pepys on 3 September 1668 for three times that price, 'it being a book the Bishops will not let be printed again'.[47] Given efforts formally to proscribe the book and even bring the author to trial, reprinting would be very dangerous, but also potentially lucrative. The 'Bear' edition was undoubtedly an attempt to exploit this demand: it had to be printed in secret, but the production was interrupted and aborted in London in 1670, then transferred to Amsterdam for completion. It has been suggested that the 'Ornaments' edition may also have been planned during Hobbes's last years, but is now regarded as being later – most likely an attempt to meet continuing demand arising from the political disruptions of the 1680s, or perhaps exploiting the gap left by the final lapse of the Licensing Act in 1695.[48] What matters most in the present context is the fact that an English version of the book remained in demand for half a century or more, so much so that reprintings were organised despite conditions liable to make careful proofreading very difficult and open sale dangerous. That the Latin version seems to have had only a modest diffusion may be because the French version of *De cive* had a firmer hold, or because German readers used the Dutch translation. Equally, many continental publishers (even in the Netherlands) would have had good reason to regard reprinting as dangerous and demand unpredictable.

The detailed publication history of Hobbes's great work illustrates how complicated both the compilation and dissemination of such major works could be, especially when the text was highly critical of contemporary cultural, religious and political norms. His decision to make the text available in a fully revised version in Latin, for an international audience, not only reflects his awareness that some essential aspects of commonwealth government were liable to be forgotten after 1660, but also his bravery in sticking to his political principles (especially the necessity of separating church and state) when they had become not only

---

[45] N. Malcolm, 'Hobbes and the European republic of letters', in his *Aspects of Hobbes* (Oxford, 2002), 457–545.

[46] Estimated by Malcolm at 1200–1500 copies, judging from the number that still survive: Malcolm, (ed.), *Leviathan*, vol. I, 225.

[47] R. Latham and W. Matthews (eds.), *The diary of Samuel Pepys* (London, 1970–83), vol. IX, 298.

[48] G. A. J. Rogers and K. Schuhmann (eds.), *Thomas Hobbes Leviathan* (London 2003), vol. I, 155–81; Malcolm (ed.), *Leviathan*, vol. I, 258–71.

unfashionable but also downright dangerously subversive. Both Hobbes and Milton were masters of forms of expression designed for a wider (if still intellectual) readership, but their role as public intellectuals also required a finely tuned strategy: Milton was boldly provocative but quite impulsive in much of his work from the 1650s, whilst Hobbes calculated his language to perfection to give it lasting relevance and a general applicability that made him dangerous to all governments without leaving him vulnerable to charges of rabble-rousing.

We have much less detailed information about the ways in which other seventeenth-century writers constructed their published work. However, it is difficult to avoid making direct comparisons with the most dangerous of all texts published during this period, Spinoza's *Tractatus Theologico-Politicus* of 1670. Spinoza was in recurrent and at times very lengthy correspondence with Henry Oldenburg, secretary of the Royal Society in London, from the early 1660s to 1676, and was also a member of the circle of radicals who organised both the Dutch and Latin versions of *Leviathan,* so he cannot have avoided contact with the ideas in that book; but whether Hobbes knew of Spinoza is more difficult to establish. It is worth noting, however, that Spinoza was more cautious than either Hobbes or Milton. As we will see in Chapter 2, he had good reason to beg his friends *not* to go ahead with a Dutch translation of his treatise, for fear of a public outcry. His worries were amply confirmed when even the Latin *Tractatus* was suppressed in 1674 (alongside the Dutch version of Hobbes). The necessary secrecy also means that the edition of Spinoza's complete works, published by his friends after his early death in 1677, has not yet been mapped successfully. There are several versions purporting to be printed in Hamburg in 1677 (actually underground, in Amsterdam), but we do not know when they were really published, and what the print run may have been. Nor can we be sure about the diffusion of the various translations: the French versions of the *Tractatus Theologico-Politicus* (seemingly printed in Amsterdam in 1678, probably in several print runs, some copies with a deliberately misleading innocuous title), the English one of 1689 (reprinted in 1737), or the belated Dutch version of 1693. The Latin version, like the French translation, appears to have gone through several editions, but these cannot yet be accurately enumerated.[49]

These three exceptionally powerful writers demonstrate why we need to know how each author worked and how he gauged his language to avoid the worst reactions from their contemporaries. However, we clearly

---

[49] Malcolm, *Aspects of Hobbes*, 40–52 and 480–6; see also J. Israel, *Radical Enlightenment; philosophy and the making of modernity* (Oxford, 2001).

also need to look beyond the circumstances of each single work and the process of dissemination in order to fully understand their significance. All three writers discussed here triggered strongly worded attacks from contemporaries, often going into such detail that one may wonder whether the effect on readers was the opposite of what was intended. By trying to demonstrate the errors in a given text, after all, the critic had to discuss (and even cite) it in some detail. Some authors acquired reputations that went well beyond what they actually wrote. For example, after his death Spinoza became a shorthand label for so many forms of subversion, including anarchy, heresy and atheism, that one suspects some of those who referred to him may never have read his books. In other words, authors and their books became symbols even when not read, and (as always happens) their ideas were often taken out of context, misinterpreted and at times selectively adapted by others for many different purposes.

Hobbes and Spinoza created such extreme political, religious and social agendas that few Enlightenment writers dared follow them openly. But from now on it was manifestly clear to all that the use of print, and the style and form in which arguments were presented, were indispensable means of gaining influence. John Locke, Samuel Pufendorf, Pierre Bayle and several other major writers struggled to provide durable answers to some of the many questions thrown up by the profound political challenges of the mid-seventeenth century – their work in turn providing the springboard for much of the lively political discussions pursued in enlightened circles throughout the eighteenth century. As we shall see, Locke's work also had a durable impact on political thought, not just immediately from 1689, but also through recurrent reprints and translations, some of which became foundation texts for those with an interest in how mankind could and should live in a stable and civilised society.

The Changing Dynamics of Print and Dissemination

This chapter has raised more questions – qualitative as well as quantitative – than it has provided answers. Only a small proportion of the core bibliographical data that we need on first editions, reprints, dissemination and translations has so far been collated. More uncertainty arises when we attempt to classify this uneven data by types of publication (books, pamphlets, flysheets, serials, newspapers – let alone woodcuts and engravings), and it is clear that such categorisation can never be rigid or clear-cut. Classifying print by subject matter (religious/devotional reading, philosophy, history, current affairs and news, politics, science, travel, fiction) is equally problematic, not least since we risk imposing definitions and distinctions that would not have been obvious to contemporary readers. And finally, trying to understand the communication process – how (and how far) authors were responding to the context in which they found themselves, who financed their work, who bought it and how readers might have understood and interpreted what they read – compels us to tackle questions about the specific location of each publication in its historical and social context with as much precision as possible. We can never be certain who might have read a particular text, and we can only guess at its overall impact from the incidental evidence we have from citations, explicit reference in correspondence and other personal testimony, or the records of censors and the law courts. We can draw more robust conclusions about the longer-term success of a publication on the basis of reprints (or in the case of periodical publications, survival) – and in the case of translations, we have a much clearer indication of cross-cultural dissemination and interpretation. In short, the history of print presents us with a monumental range of methodological and technical problems.

The following chapters will tackle these challenges from a number of different thematic perspectives, and for distinct chronological periods and cultural/linguistic areas. As we noted in the Introduction, discussion of early modern politics and the use of power took a variety of forms, oral as well as written, and print did not displace manuscript. That said, print was indisputably becoming recognised as the most effective way of collectively reinforcing, confronting, debating and analysing power. The mechanics of the print industry, its growing versatility and its growing impact in terms of employment and profits created very strong undercurrents of vested interests below the surface of cultural and political change. But, as the work of Milton, Hobbes and Spinoza show, the political stakes were also very high. In Chapter 2 we will see how a number of restraints on the discussion of politics in print were broken down during the unstable 1640s and 1650s, with lasting repercussions over the following decades. Central governments, local and church authorities increasingly struggled against authors and printers finding new and imaginative ways round various regulatory obstacles – also making the historian's task considerably more challenging.

The surviving evidence does not readily tell us who the readers were. As we noted at the start of this chapter, reading skills cannot be measured reliably in this period: signature evidence is demonstrably misleading, particularly for women, and while we have important alternative indications in the shape of church inspection and visitation records, early public library lending records and a range of incidental evidence, they tend to tell us more about overall trends than precise readership. It is clear that much of what follows relates primarily to urban populations in those parts of Europe that were affluent enough to support some kind of print culture. We know that most schools and higher educational establishments worked within very conservative and cautious agendas, but we should not on those grounds alone underestimate the growing proportion of urban middling sorts who became modestly habitual readers, incentivised to do so when political crises created obvious questions and inescapable uncertainties of immediate relevance. This, coupled with the evidence of a proliferation of cheap print (shorter pamphlets, newspapers, broadsheets, abridged and popularised texts), is perhaps sufficient explanation for why we need to look more closely both at the role of print in feeding contemporary curiosity and inquisitiveness and also at the emergence of a recognisable public opinion, despite the misgivings and warnings of contemporaries against both these trends.

2 Instability and Politicisation (1630–77)

The Thirty Years War (1618–48) has long been recognised as a period of acute (if uneven) social, economic and political destabilisation in many parts of Europe, brought about in part by the damaging direct impact of prolonged warfare and ill-disciplined armies, inefficient and abusive fiscal regimes, severe disruption of trade particularly in northern Italy and parts of central Europe, outbreaks of epidemic disease, religious disputes and persecution, and the disarray or even collapse of stable government – compounded in the 1640s and 50s by a deterioration in climate which resulted in the most prolonged and far-reaching harvest failures of the century. The repercussions on almost every aspect of European society were enormous: permanent changes in the power structures of Europe as experienced both at international and regional or local levels, institutional disruption or change, substantial movements of population in some parts of Europe, a further entrenchment of religious and ideological divisions, and a long-term shift of economic power from the Mediterranean to north-western Europe (with concomitant changes in sea power, overseas colonial expansion and financial power). In such an unstable environment, it is hardly surprising that print was used as a major means of questioning and of attempted reinterpretation. In Chapter 1 we noted the quantitative and material evidence pointing towards substantial, and sometimes quite sudden, changes in the overall output of printed material, notably in the 1630s and 40s. This chapter will explore the extent to which print became more diversified both in style and content, potentially appealing to a wider range of readers keen to understand the power structures which they experienced.

The manifest social and political instability witnessed by contemporaries may be sufficient explanation of the growth of certain kinds of print during this period, but we might also look for other possible factors to help explain specific changes in relation to precise context. Historians have to strike a difficult balance between looking for changes in political awareness, where that may genuinely have occurred, whilst at the same time recognising the risks of reading too much into the (often veiled) language of discontent, or even over-emphasising texts which at the time were merely marginal. Each generation and each political culture had its distinctive and very strong normative expectations in public speech and writing, matching the finer gradients of authority, legitimacy and social status, but these changed over time. For example, the continuing interest in formal rhetoric during the later sixteenth and early seventeenth centuries imposed certain expectations, as represented notably in great set speeches by monarchs and other prominent individuals, other 'speech acts',[1] or actual writings of similar intent. Even so, innovation and imagination were crucial components in the kind of dialectic presentation which was meant to lead listeners inevitably to a balanced but conclusive point of view. It is interesting to observe how rhetorical skill was cultivated and valued in all formal settings, from sermons in Protestant churches to speeches in law courts, assemblies and parliaments, all composed in language and sentence structures designed to conform to specific ideals, yet capable of both originality and creativity.

Normative language continued to be enhanced in the formal speeches and announcements of monarchs such as James VI/I or Gustavus Adolphus, as well as by other figures asserting religious/political authority, and these forms of expression lent themselves equally well to dissemination in print. The finer nuances of conventional language were all the more important because some of the key concepts no longer went uncontested. Alternative political visions were readily available, notably in the potentially oppositional implications of Calvinism dating back to the big controversies on the right of resistance in the 1570s,[2] or in the wonderfully rich and constantly renegotiated language of individual or collective petitions – an almost routine form of communication across all of Europe, where expressions of overt deference sometimes veered towards veiled threats if the assumed mutual obligations of petitioner and recipient were not respected. Naturally, where traditional authority seemed weak or more vulnerable to challenge, there was bound to be more experimentation and innovation in language and symbolism: power was subject to constant renegotiation – but not necessarily in terms that we can take at face value.

---

[1] A. Hunt, 'Recovering speech acts', in A. Hadfield, M. Dimmock and A. Shinn (eds.), *The Ashgate research companion to popular culture in early modern England* (Farnham, 2014), 13–29.
[2] See above [Introduction], p. 14.

Power and Propaganda Visualised in the Thirty Years War

Although the multi-layered religious grievances, territorial disputes and political uncertainties that triggered the outbreak of war in the German lands from 1618 were mostly long-standing, there were significant developments in the ways in which some of the key issues were represented to a wider audience. Visualising power was not itself new: paintings, statues, heraldic ornaments and formal processions had been used for this purpose for generations, but these could never reach beyond a limited audience. For those who were not physically present, printed textual descriptions might make a vicarious impression – in this case limited by reading skills and access. By contrast, the distribution of multiple copies of printed images opened up new possibilities for propaganda: images were so rare in early modern Europe that they were bound to attract everyone's attention, and an image could be designed (with just minimal textual explanation or a title) to convey ideas in ways accessible even to those who could not read.

The power of printed images was already well established: traditional woodblock prints, cheap and versatile, had been used for illustrative and decorative purposes from the earliest days of printing. Woodblock images and decorations were cut as positive relief, so required relatively little pressure to transfer the ink to the paper: they might even be made to fit alongside movable type within the standard printer's frame for a single page. Skilled craftsmen working on the end grain of suitable wooden blocks acquired the ability to reproduce extraordinarily fine detail, as demonstrated notably in the work of great artists such as Albrecht Dürer (1471–1528). But images carved in wood could not easily be altered, so tended to be recycled with scant relevance to the text they accompanied. It was also difficult to make large images, since the wooden blocks themselves were liable to warp or split over wider areas of end grain. By contrast, engraving was a fundamentally different process: indentations were made in a hard surface (usually a sheet of polished copper) by means of a burin or other steel tool, the plate was inked and then wiped, so that only the residual ink in the indentations was left to mark the paper when plate and paper were passed through a roller press. Engraving was more suitable for larger images, limited only by the capacity of the press and the availability of sheets of copper. The manual skills were very different from those of woodblock carving: if the artist learnt these skills himself, he could work directly with his image rather than relying on a wood-carving craftsman. As the techniques of copper-plate engraving developed from the later fifteenth century, the reproduction of very fine detail and nuances of shading became possible.

It is interesting to observe how some of the great printmakers of the early Reformation period, including Albrecht Dürer himself, experimented with both woodblock printing and engraving (as well as variants such as etching and drypoint) to produce images of great emotional power and individuality – images which, though reproduced in large numbers, were in effect all original (and identical) works of art. However, unlike woodblock images, printing from an engraved copper plate required far great pressure (to make sure the paper made contact with the ink in the indents), so the use of a totally different roller press was essential. That meant that engraved images could not be used alongside movable-type text on the same page, except by means of two separate printing operations (and a careful alignment of the paper): to achieve a combination of image and text in one printing, the text itself would need to be engraved by hand (and of course in mirror image). Despite these limitations, there were great advantages in copper-plate engraving: fluency of line, extremely fine detail, actual editing and correction of the image or engraved text (by smoothing out the copper plate itself), easy storage of the plate for later reprinting and much more scope for large formats. These characteristics mean that copper-plate engraving lent itself well to complex images and single-sided broadsheets designed for posting on doors and public places where they could be seen by a large number of people. The fact that copper-plate images wore down noticeably when approaching one thousand impressions was not a problem, since larger print runs were rarely required for propaganda images and broadsheets with one-off distribution and topical relevance. Really successful prints were in any case vulnerable to piracy, so reprinting was rarely commercially viable.

Broadsheets, 'pasquils', libels and flysheets (some of the interchangeable terms used to denote single-sided prints made using either movable type, woodblock images or copper-plate engraving)[3] seem to have flooded the market during periods of instability. They played a major role in the Lutheran Reformation and later in the French civil wars and, because they could be printed and distributed quickly, were difficult to censor or control. Contemporaries complained about the flood of scurrilous unauthorised material, but whether they had any real grounds for concern is difficult to tell. Since most sheets were inherently ephemeral, and highly vulnerable to damage, we have even less reliable quantitative data than we do for pamphlets and books. There is no way of knowing how many distinct prints ('titles') were available in any one year or place, let alone

---

[3] D. Bellingradt, *Flugpublizistik und Öffentlichkeit um 1700: Dynamiken, Akteure und Strukturen im urbanen Raum des Alten Reiches* (Stuttgart, 2011), provides clearer definitions of these overlapping categories of print.

the print run of any one item, so any analysis of change over time must necessarily be based on samples of uncertain reliability. Only when a particular image was reprinted, retouched or pirated can we be reasonably sure that demand was high enough to indicate a really successful sheet.

Allowing for this uncertainty, it would nevertheless appear that printed visual imagery became more politically innovatory from around 1618 onwards. Previously, the core message had often been delivered in fairly conventional ways, typically underlining a commonplace religious (devotional, moral) or secular (often scurrilous) theme, to form a narrative as if from a neutral observer. The Reformation had quickly led to strikingly sectarian imagery including personal attacks on prominent figures such as the Pope or Luther, or moral messages complete with monsters and devils, but the broader political propaganda was perhaps less explicit. Sensational stories relating to major international events, such as the battle of Lepanto in 1571, or the assassination of Henry IV in 1610, were embellished to serve as descriptive propaganda, rather than to initiate fresh political controversy. This changed from the start of the Thirty Years War: topical but divisive political themes became significantly more common in periods of uncertainty, notably in connection with the political crisis in the Netherlands in 1618, the Bohemian War 1619–22 and above all the spectacular military intervention of Gustavus Adolphus 1630–3.[4] Descriptive broadsheets continued to appear, such as those giving accounts of major battles, often requiring detailed textual explanations alongside images. Other sheets, however, began to use more striking visual imagery to dispense with all but the most basic textual labels. In 1620, Frederick of the Palatinate became the focus for polemics on both sides, some questioning his basic motivations, others lampooning the Calvinist 'Palatine catechism' as contrary to the interests of stability and security. Outright criticism of all the participants as power-hungry opportunists came to the fore in broadsheets from 1621. One idea could be recycled in many versions (suggesting unusually high demand), as in depictions of the battle over Bohemia as a fight between a number of different participants, each represented as a different animal with distinct symbolic attributes, against a backdrop which showed not only the

---

[4] A recently completed compilation of political sheets has as many images from the years 1620–1 as for the whole period 1600–19: J. R. Paas, *The German political broadsheet 1600–1700*, vols. I–XIII (Wiesbaden, 1985–2016), where vol. III covers the Winter War, vols. V–VII the Swedish phase. See also W. A. Coupe, *The German illustrated broadsheet of the seventeenth century* (Baden-Baden, 1961), 65–91; and M. Schilling, *Bildpublizistik der frühen Neuzeit: Aufgaben und Leistungen des illustrierten Flugblatts in Deutschland bis um 1700* (Tübingen, 1990).

vulnerable cities of the Holy Roman Empire but also a Dutch lion eagerly picking rich spoils from a huge spider's web in which major assets had been trapped.[5] With very little explanatory text, these images would clearly attract attention, highlighting the breakdown of moral stability and legality in politics, whilst leaving substantive issues of interpretation to the mind of the observer.

The most impressive shift in the deployment of propaganda broadsheets came with the entry of the Swedes into the German war in 1630. Coming after a disastrously unsuccessful intervention by Christian IV of Denmark (who, as Duke of Schleswig-Holstein, was at least a legitimate participant in the affairs of the Holy Roman Empire), the Swedish landing was greeted with some hostility even amongst those north-German princes who shared the strict Lutheran faith of Gustavus Adolphus. The resulting extension of the war may help to explain a quite remarkable propaganda campaign orchestrated by Sweden and its allies, and directed at both German and international audiences (with German and Latin captions). It began in 1630 by exploiting the centenary of the Augsburg Confession to celebrate the core religious values of the Lutheran faith, using traditional forms of elaborate imagery incorporating the Bible as a textual foundation, a tree of the true faith based in Christ and sustained by the visible hand of God, sometimes with a lion repelling the forces of evil. The lion was of course a common political symbol (then as now), but was used extensively by the Swedish monarchy, and figured in an array of subsequent broadsheets which sought to justify the Swedish mission to rescue the true Christian church by slaying the dragons of Counter-Reformation encroachment.[6] The Catholic capture and destruction of the city of Magdeburg in 1631 provided the material not only for atrocity stories, but also for allegorical depictions of the 'maiden' of Magdeburg surrounded by an array of 'suitors'.[7]

At the same time, Gustavus Adolphus himself appeared in broadsheets, clearly recognisable from his moustache and pointed beard, often dominating the scene as Hercules, as a morally upright military commander fighting a just war, or even as a mediator and ally amongst the quarrelling princes of the Empire – invariably guided by the hand of God.[8] The symbolic and thematic imagery is varied and unprecedented in its sophistication, symbolic content and careful presentation. The prints themselves testify to a high-quality propaganda machinery that may have

---

[5] Paas, *The German political broadsheet*, vol. III, prints 784–90, and additional print PA 171.
[6] See for example Paas, *The German political broadsheet*, vol. V, prints 1263, 1269–71, 1294–5 and 1370–73.
[7] Paas, vol. V, prints 1335–69.
[8] Paas, vol. V, prints 1426–7, 1430–6, 1541–8, 1565–72; vol. VI, prints 1657–63.

combined Swedish finance with skilled Dutch and German engravers, relying on the consolidation of a north-German network of allies who were gradually (if sometimes reluctantly) persuaded to see Swedish military strength as the only effective way of restoring Protestant interests in the war. At the same time, anti-Catholic prints portrayed both Wallenstein and Tilly as flawed and failed military commanders: for this purpose, more explanatory text might be needed, as in a broadsheet comparing Tilly with the mythical Icarus, defying his father's orders and flying too high, losing his wings (as the adhesive wax melted in the sun) and falling to his death.[9] Such allegories would no doubt have been intended for a predominantly literate audience, in contrast to the simpler self-sufficient images of Gustavus Adolphus. It is interesting to observe that after the death of Gustavus Adolphus in battle in 1632, the resulting stream of laments drew on an impressive array of hagiographic images, but also reverted to more substantial texts, some of them printed in striking symbolic shapes (for example a dense text elegantly aligned to take on the graphic outline of an hourglass) which might attract the attention even of those who were not habitual readers.[10]

We can speculate on the circumstances that led to this extraordinarily voluminous and innovative pro-Swedish propaganda campaign – and why there was very little effective Catholic response. As the war dragged on, high-quality imagery continued to be used in connection with major events, notably around the abortive Treaty of Prague and the protracted peace negotiations from 1644 to 1648, but the basic message tended to revert to a more politically neutral, narrative or traditionally moral mode seeking an end to the war. Individual leaders might still be praised or targeted, but a full-scale politicised propaganda campaign such as that deployed on behalf of the Swedish intervention was not repeated by anyone else (not even by the Swedish regency government itself after 1632). We can only conclude that Gustavus Adolphus or his closest advisers recognised the value of this kind of broadsheet propaganda[11] – uniquely so by comparison with his contemporaries and would-be allies Christian IV or James VI/I, let alone the Bourbon and Habsburg dynasties. But there may also have been important contingent factors: one

---

[9] Paas, vol. IV, print 1463–4; for Wallenstein, see also print 1958.

[10] Paas, vol. VI, prints 1875–8; vol. VII, prints 1898–1912, and additional prints PA 304–5; J. R. Paas, 'The changing images of Gustavus Adolphus on German broadsheets, 1630-33', *Journal of the Warburg and Courtauld Institutes*, 59 (1996), 205–44.

[11] Comparisons can be made with his major set speeches to his own subjects, such as the one he delivered on 19 May 1630 to the Swedish Riksdag, before leaving for the German war – translated in M. Roberts, *Sweden as a great power 1611–1697* (London, 1968), 13–16, from the Swedish transcript in C. G. Styffe, *Konung Gustaf II Adolfs skrifter* (Stockholm, 1861), 628–33.

might speculate about the role of Dutch expertise not only in exploiting sophisticated engraving skills already available in the major German print centres, but also in helping to finance what must have been an expensive large-scale printing and distribution network. At a more practical level, the large-scale use of engraved broadsheet propaganda relied on a supply of rolled copper sheets: the Dutch were certainly instrumental in developing the Swedish copper-mining and smelting industry, turning Sweden into the dominant European exporter of copper from 1613 onwards.[12] Despite the fact that copper was the third most precious metal available in this period, there would clearly have been no difficulty for Sweden or its allies in obtaining both the copper and the skilled craftsmen who could produce this kind of a work.

That said, there are still a number of uncertainties surrounding the large-scale use of political broadsheets during the war years. Many of the allegorical themes were not intrinsically new or unfamiliar, but the way they were exploited would have seemed surprising to contemporary observers. Just as with texts, we have very little evidence – except in the prints themselves – regarding the intended audience, the actual reception and impact of the prints, the social position of the most likely readers/observers, or their levels of functional literacy. It is not yet clear how these broadsheets were financed, and whether they were genuinely independent commentaries on current events or (more likely) government-sponsored efforts to project certain key messages. It would appear from the scarcity of effective Catholic response that northern German (predominantly Protestant) centres of print were more active, but an explanation based on the main religious divisions does not at first sight account for the aggressively negative campaign against Frederick of the Palatinate whilst he was still a valuable Calvinist asset for his Dutch supporters. However, we would reach a different conclusion if we take into account the fact that many of the Lutheran princes in the Empire were profoundly hostile to Calvinism and anxious to restore the earlier confessional balance. Such an ambivalent position was certainly characteristic of Johann Georg, Elector of Saxony, who tried to position his staunchly Lutheran territories alongside the Catholic Habsburg Emperor in defence of the now outdated principles of the Peace of Augsburg of 1555, in which Calvinism had no place. In this interpretational framework, the surge of pro-Swedish propaganda may acquire primary tactical significance, necessary to win over the foot-dragging

---

[12] Significant copper mining and milling continued in northern Germany and Flanders, but not on a scale comparable to that of Sweden and its Dutch investors and trading partners. The other big producer of copper was Japan, but its output reached Europe only in very limited quantities. See J. Israel, *Dutch primacy in world trade 1585–1740* (Oxford, 1989).

north-German princes themselves. Many of these princes, whether Calvinist or fellow-Lutheran, feared being outflanked by Swedish military successes, and the Lutheran ones were so anxious to avoid a fundamental destabilisation of the traditional imperial constitutional complexities that they needed to be pushed quite hard. If we pursue such an explanation a little further, both the 1620 and the 1630–2 surges in political propaganda may ultimately have been the result of the divisions and deep-rooted political conservatism within the Empire itself. That, in turn, would explain why those behind each of these propaganda campaigns found it convenient not to claim explicit ownership, since doing so would merely have emphasised the deep tactical and personal divisions amongst the different Protestant interest groups. If so, we might conclude that the printed visual propaganda deployed on behalf of Gustavus Adolphus was not merely another indication of his exceptional skills of political self-projection and leadership, but probably a decisive strategic breakthrough in the divided German lands comparable to his innovations in military organisation.

Pamphlets and Politics in England in the 1640s

The contested outcome of the war in the Palatinate and the loss of the Bohemian crown by Frederick and Elizabeth (Stuart) was a major unresolved international issue which troubled both Elizabeth's father James VI/I, and her brother Charles I, and could readily be perceived as damaging the interests of the English monarchy. Taken in conjunction with the major impact of the Thirty Years War as a whole on English commercial and religious interests, it is hardly surprising that there was a growing market in the 1620s and 30s for continental news, conveyed by broadsheets and other printed material imported via the Netherlands or produced in London.[13] While domestic political reporting was of course rigorously censored, information from abroad could be reprinted more freely, and might serve (for those trying to understand high politics) as some kind of proxy for domestic news. Visible difficulties arose in the later 1630s over a whole range of religious and administrative matters, culminating in the prayer-book riots in Scotland in July 1637 and the formation of a revived covenanting movement around a revised confession of faith (later known as the National Covenant) which was circulated from 1638 for public subscription.

[13] J. E. E. Boys, *London's news press and the Thirty Years War* (Woodbridge, 2011); M. Mendle, 'News and the pamphlet culture of mid-seventeenth-century England', in B. Dooley and S. A. Baron (eds.), *The politics of information in early modern Europe* (London 2001), 57–79.

It is hardly surprising that the demand for information and analysis increased, especially in London itself. When the Court of Star Chamber was abolished in 1641, the validity of regulations regarding the control of print and the registration of all master printers became legally questionable, and pre-publication censorship (through licensing) became impossible to enforce. Even though a new licensing law was implemented in 1643, there appears to have been confusion over powers, jurisdictions and implementation. In any case the open split between king and parliament created even more questions around the location of sovereign authority itself, and the outbreak of actual civil war in 1642, making the political stakes much higher, also generated by far the biggest increase in new print.

This is not the place to review the very protracted debate amongst historians over longer- and shorter-term factors in the complex and unprecedented sequence of political crises in England in the 1640s. But we might remind ourselves that there was a pre-existing and exceptionally long thread of disagreement (verbal and in writing) over the nature of civil government and stability, which had first come into the open in the confessional divides of the English Reformation, and was subsequently aggravated by extreme and traumatic policy changes under successive monarchs. Despite the grand declarations and claims of James VI/I,[14] these questions did not go away under Stuart rule, but resurfaced with even greater urgency as soon as Charles I appeared to be challenging the traditional balance of power and consensus in the late 1630s: in other words, there was a well-established precedent for substantive if cautious political discussion, and a vocabulary to suit.

Intransigence ensured that some of the practical problems experienced during these years became more contentious. The range of potential points of dispute was impressive:[15] a sovereign who did not accept that anyone had the right to challenge his authority and royal prerogatives, and who had already demonstrated a willingness to disregard agreements that he himself had signed; members of the political nation who had not

---

[14] James left no-one in doubt as to his claims to be God's representative on earth, as in his writings and speeches to Parliament, such as that of 21 March 1610, reproduced in J. P. Kenyon, *The Stuart constitution* (Cambridge, 1966), 12–14. James was clearly also aware of the power of print, formally sanctioning the 'catechism' compiled by R. Mocket, *God and the King: or a dialogue shewing that our Soveraigne Lord King James being immediate under God doth rightfully claime whatsoever is required by the oath of allegiance* (London, 1616), the subtitle of which indicated its divine-right royalist claims. This 90-page booklet was made compulsory reading, with booksellers forced to hold stock at a fixed price, to their cost. See A. Mann, *The Scottish book trade 1500–1720* (East Linton, 2000), 21.

[15] For a recent overview, see M. J. Braddick (ed.), *The Oxford handbook of the English Revolution* (Oxford, 2015).

forgotten the way parliament had been misled in 1628 over the Petition of Right, but who were at the same time anxious to preserve the existing political order; immediate and practical issues of revenue and taxation, which rapidly became acute once the Scots army occupied northern England in 1640 and required a military response; a dramatically curtailed Short Parliament in 1640, followed by an even more recalcitrant Long Parliament which increasingly felt compelled to publish its responses to royal demands and justify extensions of parliamentary authority which appeared increasingly autocratic and unaccountable; severe religious polarisation, with Charles seen as a threat both by many Scots and by a varied array of English religious factions, who could nevertheless rarely agree amongst themselves; a near-universal lack of willingness to consider any kind of religious compromise or tolerance as anything other than 'ungodly', colouring almost all political discussion with undercurrents of mutual hostility between high-church royalists, presbyterians and an ever-widening array of religious radicals and independents. Tensions in Ireland were equally complicated and, since the strong Catholic interest there had to rely on Charles for any hope of protection, the outbreak of open rebellion in Ireland in 1641 had military repercussions across the British Isles and protracted contingent costs. To this explosive mix should be added the external aggravating factors of recurrent economic crises (including repercussions from the continental wars) culminating in the terrible years of hardship of 1647–50. None of these problems were susceptible to easy resolution, and each was liable to generate significant discussion by word of mouth, in handwritten letters and of course in all kinds of print both in London and elsewhere, including a profusion of newspapers.

We have already noted (Chapter 1) how the number of new separate items (all kinds of text) going into print increased dramatically from 1640 onwards, reaching a peak of around 4000 in 1642 – or more than seven times the average annual output in the period 1632–9. The pattern over the following years was uneven, but never fell back to earlier levels, and predictably had renewed peaks in 1648 and 1659–60.[16] Such extraordinary fluctuations in print output obviously call for closer scrutiny. The highly skilled printing workforce

[16] R. Raymond, *Pamphlets and pamphleteering in early modern Britain* (Cambridge, 2003), 161–8. These figures can be compared with ESTC totals for London: although the ESTC totals include some titles that may well be duplicates rather than actual reprints, these are probably more than offset by items where no copies survive (and therefore not in the ESTC). Attrition is likely to be greater amongst the shorter polemics of the 1640s. London is taken as indicative of the overall pattern of print in England, since the output of presses in Oxford and Cambridge (and York from 1642) is extremely small by comparison. Dublin printing was even smaller in scale at this time, so the Irish dimension is not

in London could not have increased total output on such a scale, and paper supplies would have run out, if a large proportion of the new print had not on average been denser and much shorter in length (and often more hurriedly and inaccurately printed) than had been the norm earlier. In other words, the rapid increase in the number of titles is at least partly accounted for by pamphlets often taking up just a few printer's sheets, in quarto or smaller format, often stitched to make booklets typically of 24 or 48 pages, but without a cover, and sold at prices that started around a penny or two.[17] At that price, a pamphlet would be within comfortable reach of a skilled artisan, and occasionally even of a labourer on a builder's wage (typically just over one shilling a day). Parliamentarians and royalists were deeply concerned about the rabble-rousing, divisive and subversive potential of such cheap unregulated print, whether visual or textual, and repeatedly (if hardly successfully) attempted to dampen demand and regulate content. The Stationers Company itself, nominally responsible for the registration of all printed material, was legally in limbo from 1641. Regulation of the many short and anonymous new publications proved particularly difficult, as they often lacked indication of printer or precise location – but these were the texts intended for a wider range of readers.[18]

Initially, the Scots may have given impetus to some London radicals. The Scottish Covenanting movement had coalesced in 1637–8 in openly belligerent opposition to the imposition by Charles I of what were deemed Arminian or papist reforms of, and threats to, Scottish presbyterianism. The Covenanters relied heavily on manuscript texts read out loud at local meetings, followed by collective oaths of adherence or personal subscription. The Covenant was also printed, but this seems not to have been the primary form of dissemination and relatively few printed versions

represented adequately in print, being skewed heavily (in London) towards atrocity stories and scaremongering around alleged Catholic plots. See also D. F. McKenzie, 'Printing and publishing 1557–1700: constraints on the London book trades', in J. Barnard and D. F. McKenzie (eds.), *The Cambridge history of the book*, vol. IV: 1557–1695 (Cambridge, 2002), 553–67.

[17] J. Peacey, 'Pamphlets', in J. Raymond (ed.), *The Oxford history of popular print culture, vol. 1: cheap print in Britain and Ireland to 1660* (Oxford, 2011), 453–70, provides a succinct overview of the genre in Britain.

[18] J. McElligott, *Royalism, print and censorship in revolutionary England* (Woodbridge, 2007), 183–224, has called for a new understanding of the nature and impact of censorship during the 1640s and 50s, noting that its effectiveness varied greatly with the specific political context, and in any case should be judged not by the number of actual suppressions or prosecutions, but by the exemplary deterrent effect that a single severe punishment of author or printer could have. We cannot assume that contemporaries were no longer frightened into silence, even during periods of apparently lively radical controversy.

survive.[19] However, significant amounts of Scottish religious propaganda came to England from 1638 (much of it printed in London or in the Netherlands) and this distribution greatly increased with the Scottish military invasion and occupation of northern England in 1640. Some Scottish presbyterians argued that the covenant with God was strictly separate from their contract with the king, and long-established Calvinist resistance theories from the 1570s could now be revived to substantiate that case (including a new English edition in 1648 of the famous Huguenot tract *Vindiciae contra tyrannos* of 1579). Some of the Scottish texts attracted sufficient interest and support in London to merit reprinting in large quantities – noted, with great alarm, by the king's advisers, including archbishop Laud (before he himself was imprisoned in 1640 and brought to trial). But there were important differences of viewpoint in England which called for direct responses to, or development of, the Scottish arguments. Some groups in London pursued distinct lines of argument which diverged from Scottish-presbyterian reasoning towards a notably more radical decentralised form of church governance or 'Independency' (in its specific religious sense, but with wider political potential, designed to ensure more self-government within individual congregations and hence better protection of individual consciences). The scope for vigorous discussion, verbally, in writing and in print, was expanding, and although real freedom of expression could never prevail, regulation was very uneven in the rapidly moving political context from 1640.

One of the illegal presses producing new texts, the so-called 'Cloppenburg press', was once assumed to have been Dutch, but recent research suggests that it was actually operating secretly in London in the period 1640–1 (until it was located and raided by the authorities). It produced both Scottish-based presbyterian propaganda and some distinctively English commentaries. Although printed anonymously (and sometimes identifiable solely on the basis of distinctive features of presentation and typeface), some of these texts have now been attributed to a range of authors from the relatively conservative William Prynne to the future Leveller John Lilburne. There were occasional glances back to the notorious Marprelate tracts of 1589, but more often distinctly new arguments for extreme Independency (now insisting on the separation of individual congregations or groups from the established church and from any presbyterian attempts to secure negotiated compromises with

---

[19] L. Stewart, *Rethinking the Scottish revolution: covenanted Scotland 1637–51* (Oxford, 2016) argues that there was a substantial widening of the politicised public in Scotland as a result of the Covenanting movement, despite its lack of coherence or durability and its limited outreach in print.

the establishment). But arguments of this kind could go well beyond matters of just church organisation: thus the pamphlet *Englands complaint to Jesus Christ against the bishops canons* (in circulation by November 1640) not only detailed the threats to the true church, but also put forward arguments based on an 'ancient constitution' guaranteeing the 'traditional rights' of Englishmen, noting how the king himself had broken the contract with his subjects by imposing 'absolute Monarchie' and turning them into slaves. As David Como has argued, this pamphlet created clear foundations for arguments based around universal political rights and the importance of challenging tyranny. As he notes, it also raises questions for those revisionist historians who have argued that the English civil wars were provoked primarily by short-term concerns rather than by longer-running issues of principle and legality. A case can now once more be made for the emergence already in the early 1640s of fundamental political arguments that may in part have been initiated in response to the Scottish Covenanting movement, but quickly developed further. Here we might also note an intriguing link, in that one of the key people in the short visible life of the 'Cloppenburg press' was probably the future Leveller writer Richard Overton.[20]

Given the surge of printed polemics (let alone unquantifiable handwritten sheets and scribal copies), it is almost impossible to map out who influenced whom, what texts were most widely read and what impact they may have had. Yet individual case studies may still throw light on the resulting 'virtual community' of readers and polemicists: on the public discussion conducted amongst readers and listeners who did not know each other, would probably never have met, but could relate to certain ideas which they shared in print. One notorious book which acquired a large readership, the tract *Gangraena*, has been examined in wonderful detail by Ann Hughes. Written by the self-proclaimed presbyterian preacher Thomas Edwards, and appearing in three parts in 1646, its full title gave a clear indication of its purpose: *Gangraena: or A Catalogue and Discovery of many of the Errours, Heresies, Blasphemies and pernicious Practices of the Sectaries of this time.* It was essentially a catalogue trying to define the many beliefs that Edwards thought deviated from the narrow presbyterianism he wanted to impose on all. Part 1 claimed to define altogether 176 such heresies and errors; parts 2–3 followed in quick

---

[20] D. R. Como, *Radical parliamentarians and the English civil war* (Oxford, 2018); D. R. Como, 'Secret printing, the crisis of 1640, and the origins of civil war radicalism', *Past & Present*, 196 (2007), 37–82. Como also notes evidence of dissemination of these texts, which for example reached the insatiable (but by no means radical) London woodturner Nehemiah Wallington. The significance of the Scottish impact on the printing of polemics in London is also discussed by Raymond, *Pamphlets*, 161–201.

succession, adding more errors and more alleged evidence, in what could have become a never-ending cumulative diatribe had Edwards' health not failed shortly afterwards. His rambling discussion was based on sermons he had heard, tracts he had read, discussions pursued, reports received – some of them clearly misunderstood or wilfully misrepresented. Enough detail was provided to create an impression of scholarly reliability, but the key purpose was to dramatise all kinds of perceived deviance or dissent and at the same time oppose any arguments for toleration of any kind of dissent, particularly amongst fellow puritans who might lean towards Independency. He often named his opponents and sources, quoted selectively and had no qualms in suggesting full use of blasphemy legislation, book-burning and even capital punishment for 'offenders', so it is hardly surprising that his deliberately provocative stance stirred up both enthusiastic support and vitriolic counter-attacks.[21]

Amongst the many contemporaries he cited were equally vitriolic and intolerant preachers such as John Goodwin, members of other religious groups such as the Baptist Thomas Collier, the poet and pamphleteer John Milton and two future Levellers, John Lilburne and William Walwyn. Some responded only briefly, or passed Edwards over in silence, but others responded in kind. Goodwin said Edwards 'hath spread a table for Satan with the shame and sorrowes of the Saints . . . yea he hath made Belzebub himself drunk with the bloud of the Saints', while another respondent noted that 'his Gangrenous Epistle testifyes, by his Going, Writing, Eavesdropping, his Sending his Spyes, Emissaries, Agents, and factors abroad, to pry into the haltings, failings, infirmityes, and naked-ness of his Brethren . . . exposing them to a publique sale, to the view of all men, even to his own shame'.[22] Although much of the argument was about religious beliefs, the political implications were inescapable not just in terms of church governance and the role of the magistrate in regulating beliefs, but also in the wider legitimate use of power by the state and by local authorities. Clearly, *Gangraena* made a big impact – but, typically in this profusion, not a lasting one. Parts 1 and 2 were each printed twice and again as a single volume, but part 3 had only one printing, suggesting that the book had already lost momentum as an 'ephemeral best-seller'.[23]

Books such as this not only give us ready access to those individuals who were named as participants in the controversies, but also show us

---

[21] A. Hughes, *Gangraena and the struggle for the English Revolution* (Oxford, 2006). For an overview, see also A. Hughes, 'Religious diversity in revolutionary London', in N. Tyacke (ed.), *The English Revolution c.1590–1720* (Manchester, 2007), 111–28.

[22] Hughes, *Gangraena*, 256.

[23] For a thorough discussion of the controversy in print arising from this book, see Hughes, ibid., 222–317.

something of the language used to discuss these matters and to draw in new participants. Edwards always insisted he was writing to consolidate the true faith, but like so many of his kind was visibly vulnerable to accusations that he was simply promoting himself by courting interminable controversy. That his writings were soon forgotten reminds us again that evaluating the overall importance and impact of any one writer or text is almost impossible to do objectively: the quantifiable evidence (for example number of copies sold or read, or the number of citations by others) is very incomplete, and research on longer-term reception (use by later readers) is still fragmentary. For the moment we may rely primarily on content analysis, combined with circumstantial evidence, to draw conclusions about authorial intentions, likely readers and overall reception. In the case of well-known prolific disputants such as John Milton we can trace how a single writer adapted to the unsettled environment. We have already noted Milton's substantial contributions to the polemics of the 1640s, but in the present context it is worth emphasising that this marked a complete departure from his earlier writings, consisting of poetry and celebratory writings. Milton continued to publish poetry (with a collection appearing in 1645), but his close contacts with the world of printers and publishers meant that he was now able to engage emphatically with current political and religious disputes, notably in his repeated attacks on the established church from 1641 and his formidable criticism of pre-publication censorship in his *Areopagitica* of 1644 – a tract which appears to have had only a modest impact amongst readers when published, but became a standard point of reference for later exponents of freedom to print right up to the French Revolution.[24] In short, he turned himself quickly into an effective and radical campaigner across a wide range of contentious issues in the 1640s, writing in his most accessible English style in the 1640s, before turning to a more exclusive (and Latin) readership in the 1650s which gained him a European-wide reputation.[25]

The language used during the 1640s gives some indication of the main ideological battlefronts. Since regulation became intermittent, sometimes almost non-existent, authors could risk expressing themselves

[24] Milton's *Areopagitica* (London, 1644) was cited by reformers in the 1770s, and adapted in a French version by Mirabeau in 1788, in turn reprinted in Paris in 1792. For its significance in the 1640s, see R. Robertson, *Censorship and conflict in seventeenth-century England* (Philadelphia, 2009), 100–29; and H. Gatti, *Ideas of liberty in early modern Europe from Machiavelli to Milton* (Princeton, 2015), 140–57.

[25] J. Raymond, 'Milton', in Barnard and McKenzie (eds.), *The Cambridge history of the book*, 376–87, explains how Milton adapted to the changing market for print, but also served as Licenser of books in the Commonwealth government. See also S. B. Dobranski, 'Principle and politics in Milton's *Areopagitica*', in L. L. Knoppers (ed.), *The Oxford handbook of literature and the English Revolution* (Oxford, 2012), 190–205.

more openly. Consequently we have a unique opportunity of getting closer to the real intentions and conceptual mindset of those who went into print than arguably at any other time or place in early modern Europe (except perhaps the Netherlands). Even a cursory glance at the range of keywords used in the titles of publications suggests distinct shifts in emphasis from the 1630s to the 1640s. Adjusting for the fact that there are on average four times as many separate printed items published yearly in the period 1642–6 than in the period 1632–6, we notice that the word 'England' comes up noticeably more often, 'authority' twice as often and variants of 'power', 'tyrant' or 'tyranny' nearly three times as often. Interestingly, references to 'monarch' or 'king' do not increase (if anything fall slightly, proportionally), while 'nation' and 'civil-' are also fairly static, and occurrences of 'god' or variants of 'divine' are less frequent. Some of the words that now appear much more frequently in the titles of publications are perhaps even more revealing: thus the word 'petition' comes up nearly fifteen times more frequently, variants of 'oppress' and 'just' are each five times more common, while (not surprisingly) terms such as 'covenant' and variants of 'remonstrance' (which had been almost invisible in the mid-1630s) are now used very frequently. Variants of 'violence' are hardly ever found in titles in the 1630s, but become relatively common in the 1640s, and 'assemble' or 'assembly', which hardly ever appear in titles in the 1630s, are in hundreds of titles every year in the 1640s. Naturally, titles containing derivatives from 'vote' and 'voting' are extremely rare in the 1630s, but occur in abundance in the 1640s because of obvious public interest in the votes held in parliament and other assemblies. Such quantification is of course only a crude measure of intended focus and does not place these keywords in context, but it can provide a means of searching through less well-known material, and gives us a clearer impression of what a contemporary reader might have noticed if he was looking through the stock of a London bookseller. If such a reader paid attention to the full (often lengthy) text of the titles, he would also readily observe that an emotive word such as 'tyranny' – which in the 1630s was often used either in connection with popery or in historical contexts from the classics to Richard III – had acquired much wider and more precise applications in the 1640s. It was now used against bishops, presbyterian government, Independents, cavaliers, factions of all kinds, and of course the king himself, but was also deployed to denounce high-handed parliamentarian decisions, rebellion of any kind and alleged abuses of power by individuals within local communities. 'Tyranny' was also deployed as a catch-word to expound the rights of individuals against unfair prosecution and imprisonment, and as justification for a call for the restoration of 'common liberties'. In short, the word 'tyranny' had become an emotive term applied directly to current affairs: as befits polemical writings, it was defined in wildly different ways right across the political spectrum.[26]

An innovative use of such a word appeared on the title page of a tract published in 1649 (ostensibly in Rotterdam): *Tyranipocrit, discovered with his wiles, wherewith he vanquisheth. Written and printed, to animate better Artists to pursue that Monster*. It described the 'marriage' of tyranny and hypocrisy 'amongst such false Christians as inhabit Europia' and emphasised the exploitation of the poor by the rich – even though the 'Magistrates duty is, equally to divide and share such goods, as God hath given them a power to dispose of, and when they have done that, they have done their duty'. This densely printed 42-page pamphlet had no author's name and made few precise references to contemporary events or places. Yet it noted that 'It is not enough, that some Tyrants bee removed, but all tyranny must freely bee forsaken...' and suggested that in England a key problem was the judicial system:

They call them Courts of Iustice; but God knoweth if there bee one just court in all the land, for till that just foundation bee laid, all rules and ordinance whatsoever they bee, are nothing else but tyrannical injunctions ... yes, those impious theeves which doe robbe the poor, doe make lawes, as they call them, to hang the poore people, when they themselves doe deserve double hanging.[27]

Such a text could have been written by someone associated with the Levellers, presumably just after the execution of the king. As Rachel Foxley has recently affirmed,[28] the Levellers were at best a 'movement' rather than a 'party', with only a minimal organisation and no clearly defined membership. They were driven by 'agitators' within the lower ranks of the New Model Army and by London radicals of artisan or the middling sort, but were led by individuals who never held significant power except through what they wrote and said. Those who took the lead in producing the key texts that kept the Leveller movement together from 1646/47 to 1649 had all been active publicists for some time. John Lilburne first appeared in print in 1638, and petitioned against imprisonment as early as 1639, but he attracted much more attention from 1645 partly by his huge output of publications, partly by getting into

---

[26] The quantification in this paragraph is based on ESTC, accessed recurrently up to December 2018.

[27] Anon, *Tyranipocrit, discovered with his wiles, wherewith he vanquisheth* (Rotterdam [?], 1649), 33–9.

[28] R. Foxley, *The Levellers: radical political thought in the English Revolution* (Manchester, 2013).

recurrent (and often well-publicised) confrontations with the authorities, mostly over issues of free speech and arrest. He was sufficiently well versed in law, and so skilled in winning popular support, that on two occasions, when imprisoned and formally charged with politically subversive activities, he secured his own acquittal (1649 and 1653). Richard Overton and William Walwyn appear to have been less prolific (though they, too, were imprisoned in 1649): Overton had a very unusual style of polemic which made him nearly as distinctive as Lilburne, but it seems Walwyn preferred to publish anonymously and keep a low profile, whilst maintaining contact with the MP Henry Marten and colonel Thomas Rainsborough. Upwards of 250 publications and reprints in the period 1645–9 may be attributable to Lilburne, Overton and Walwyn alone,[29] amongst them some of the most subversive and famous texts of the 1640s.

The Leveller leaders drafted a number of landmark collective petitions to the House of Commons (notably March 1647 and September 1648), and were involved in at least the later redraftings of three versions of the constitutional blueprint known as *An Agreement of the People* (October 1647 to May 1649), a rudimentary constitutional contract which was to have been the formal basis for a new system of governance and was meant for formal signature by all adherents. The first Agreement was discussed in Putney (28 October to 1 November 1647) in closed debates organised by the General Council of the Army.[30] The transcripts of these extraordinary Putney Debates, constituting the sole surviving evidence of what was actually said there, were made by the Council secretary William Clarke in 1662, from shorthand notes taken at Putney, but they were not published at the time, nor were summaries printed in the newspapers. Already on 3 November, however, and before the resulting negotiations had been completed, the Agreement appeared in print, leading to an armed stand-off outside London between different parts of the army, defused by the army grandees led by Fairfax. More political agitation resulted from the second Agreement a year later, whilst the third Agreement of 1 May 1649 (with 20,000 copies distributed free, despite the fact that the Leveller leaders who had drafted it were already in prison) was in effect the final call for popular revolt against the army leadership

---

[29] Raymond, *Pamphlets and pamphleteering*, 226–34.

[30] E. Vernon and P. Baker, 'What was the first Agreement of the People?', *The Historical Journal*, 53 (2010), 39–59, have argued that this first version was more closely associated with Henry Marten, John Wildman and Maximilian Petty (the last two civilian London representatives at Putney), than with Lilburne or Overton – in other words, the first Agreement may have been primarily an internal army document rather than an essentially Leveller text. Wildman later became an associate and friend of Lilburne, but may not have had much contact with the Leveller leaders before Putney.

coupled with an array of fundamental constitutional demands.[31] No wonder that the Levellers came to be regarded as a dangerous threat to stability and the social order: they clearly knew how to combine fundamental political principles with a mass appeal which clearly threatened army discipline, the social order and existing if rapidly shifting power structures. It is not surprising, either, that the Leveller leaders openly attacked Cromwell and Ireton explicitly, in print, when the army leadership severely restricted petitioning within the army and punished soldiers who contravened these restrictions (6 March 1649) – a step which the Levellers saw as betrayal.[32]

The published Leveller output (both anonymous collective texts and those from named individuals) has been analysed so extensively by historians as to require no further overview here.[33] It is nonetheless important to observe that although they are by no means easy texts to read, either in terms of concepts or language, they were written in a compact and clear style evidently intended for maximum outreach, and structured in such a way as to lend themselves readily to extracted quotation and further discussion, whilst at the same time setting an aggressively innovative agenda. But if the substance of the Leveller socio-political reform programme was radical even for these unpredictable times, their communication strategies and use of print really just followed existing patterns. The printing of government decrees had been commonplace for years, but already in 1640 there were indications that key political leaders, royalist as well as parliamentarian, might now also be committed to use print as propaganda, in order to attract public support. The bluntly titled *A large declaration concerning the late tumults in Scotland, from their first originalls: together with a particular deduction of the seditious practices of the prime leaders of the Covenanters collected out of their owne foule acts and writing, by which it doth plainly appeare, that religion was onely pretended by those leaders,* published in 1639, was compiled by Walter Balcanquhall, but according to its own title page also authored 'By the king', and amounted to a 430-page diatribe whereby Charles tried to justify his forthcoming war against the rebellious Scots.[34] On the parliamentarian

---

[31] I. Gentles, 'The *Agreements of the people* and their political contexts, 1647-1649', in M. Mendle (ed.), *The Putney debates of 1647: the army, the Levellers and the English state* (Cambridge, 2001), 148–74.

[32] [Attrib to J. Lilburne], *The Hunting of the foxes from New-Market . . . to White-Hall, by five small beagles (late of the Armie)* (London, March 1649; Thomason Tracts, E.548/7).

[33] See notably G. E. Aylmer (ed.), *The Levellers in the English Revolution* (Ithaca/NY, 1975); and Foxley, *The Levellers.*

[34] ESTC; see also M. Kishlansky, 'A lesson in loyalty: Charles I and the Short Parliament', in J. McElligott and D. L. Smith (eds.), *Royalists and royalism during the English civil war* (Cambridge, 2007), 16–42.

side, the Grand Remonstrance of 1641 similarly called for a public answer, in effect launching an argument in print. There were many other instances, ranging from *The Humble Petition and Advice of both Houses of Parliament of 1642*, to the *Answer* formulated by the king's advisers and the Solemn League and Covenant of 1643 itself. Details of the controversial negotiations between king and parliament from 1646 were also published, including those leading up to the highly problematic Treaty of Newport in October 1648. In January 1649 the king was called to defend himself before the High Court of Justice, acting explicitly on the authority of the (purged) House of Commons.

The extraordinary exchanges between the king and the prosecuting Solicitor General were of course recorded. But the decision also to publish the 'official account' was recognised by everyone as a necessary public justification for what was a totally unprecedented formal trial of a reigning monarch. What appears to be a verbatim transcript of the trial was not only serialised in print (distributed two days after the events described in each section), but also reissued as a continuous narrative immediately after the end of the trial. The reading public would have learnt that Charles was brought before the High Court at three successive hearings, in each of which he was asked formally to answer to the charge of high treason, the details of which had already been read out to him in full. It was made clear to him that, if he refused to answer 'either by way of Confession or Negation', the charge would be deemed to stand, by tacit admission. Charles, on the other hand, asserted that 'a King cannot be tryed by any Superiour Jurisdiction on Earth'. When, on 23 January, the Lord President warned him of the authority of the Court, 'which Authority requires you in the name of the People of England, of which you are Elected King, to answer them', Charles immediately responded by asserting that 'England was never an elective Kingdom, but an Hereditary Kingdom for neer these thousand years'. He persisted in his refusal to plead, even when the Lord President rebuked him with the words 'Sir, this is the third time that you have publikely disown'd this Court, and put an affront upon it'. The terrifying inevitability of confrontation between two fundamentally incompatible political ideologies is palpable even in the printed text and must have had an extraordinary impact not just on all those present, but also on those reading the text as the trial unfolded.[35]

---

[35] *The charge of the Commons of England, against Charles Stuart, king of England* (London, 1648 [=1649 new style]); *A perfect narrative of the whole proceedings of the High Court of Iustice in the tryal of the King in Westminster Hall, begun on Saturday January 20. and ended on Saturday Jan. 27. 1648* (originally published in three instalments, dated 20 Jan, 25 Jan

The transcript of the trial was of course published in order to pre-empt any royalist counterclaims. Raymond has noted how such sequential patterns of 'official' comment and response between crown and parliament not only acquired techniques and vocabularies of their own, but also in effect changed the very framework for discussion: in addressing the public directly, both sides made it legitimate for outsiders to enter into the 'discussion' and escalation was almost inevitable. The fact that so many participants lamented their opponents' strategies of appealing to a wider reading public merely confirms that we are dealing with processes of politicisation which many regarded as unwarranted and dangerous.[36] There was even a cartoon in 1642 entitled *The world is ruled & governed by opinion*, showing a tree hung with tracts, with a scribbler underneath watering it.[37] Once started, the process of commitment to print was difficult to control. Consequently, when the king fled from London in 1642, he quickly had to establish a printer at his new headquarters in York (with significant results identifiable in the ESTC). Equally, the New Model Army itself acquired a printer in 1647 specifically to facilitate full political engagement.[38] Even documents intended as the basis for secret negotiations were published by the opposition as a deliberate tactical disclosure, or to put the record straight, inevitably creating a war of words. The printing and dissemination of supposedly personal letters was used by both sides.[39]

Political legitimacy now had to be argued in print – either directly, or by commissioning a willing author to assist. In the periods when the formal control of printing appeared ineffectual, authors might merely temper their words to reduce the risk of prosecution. With hindsight, a large proportion of publications in the 1640s appears ephemeral or even imprecise, and very few of them have been studied in any depth in terms of their success in the print market, but we would be wrong to underestimate the impact these tracts had on their readers right across the political spectrum. Some of the oppositional texts seem to have stood out – the most famous example being the royally sanctioned *Eikon Basilike* published right after the king's execution in January 1649, in response to which the

---

and 29 Jan, after each stage of the trial, and reprinted as a single text of 48pp, London, 1648 [1649]). There were several printings (varying only in details of spelling and layout), recording what was said at each of the king's appearances before the court, emphasising the king's refusal to recognise the court itself and hence his refusal to answer the charges brought against him.

[36] Raymond, *Pamphlets and pamphleteering*, 206–24.

[37] British Museum/Research/Collection online/museum number 1850,0223.244.

[38] D. Zaret, *Origins of democratic culture: printing, petitions and the public sphere in early-modern England* (Princeton, NJ, 2000), 199–216.

[39] D.G. Barnes, *Epistolary community in print, 1580–1664* (Farnham, 2013), 103–35.

Council of State commissioned John Milton to write *Eikonoklastes, in Answer to a Book Intitl'd Eikon Basilike.*[40] But we need far more studies of individual texts before we will be in a position to evaluate whether such well-known publications acquired their iconic status at the time, or merely with hindsight and retrospective 'canonisation'.

It is now clear that any view of the conflict as essentially two-sided – parliament against the crown – must be a serious oversimplification of what was really a many-sided and fluid search for order, legitimacy and authority. Especially in the uncharted political territory of the questionable negotiations with the king from 1646 onwards, allegiances and arguments on all sides (high and low) were bound to be susceptible to change. As several historians have recently demonstrated, some royalist supporters adopted points of view that, in context, were not entirely at odds with those of the radical critics of parliament. This made good political sense: an increasingly authoritarian parliamentary government and a politically assertive but divided military were by the later 1640s no longer the obvious 'middle ground' between royal claims and populist demands. As so often in early modern Europe, the crown could (in traditional mythical garb) be presented as the true guarantor of the common welfare (commonwealth) against the narrow interests of the parliamentarian and military-political elites, or the pretensions of 'aristocratic' faction. In other words, we need to be careful not to use terms such as 'royalist' or 'democrat' in ways that obscure the more complex political ideas and alignments of the 1640s, especially when the tactical or secretive manoeuvres of key participants were liable to alienate their own supporters, and when the nature of the 'commonwealth' (common weal) itself was still very open to questioning.

The royalist camp was particularly vulnerable to divisions, not least when Charles himself appeared to be giving away key powers in the Treaty of Newport, negotiated belatedly in October 1648.[41] But royalist sympathisers could also (and not without reason) claim that parliament had usurped powers that it was not entitled to and was rapidly becoming

---

[40] The *Eikon Basilike* (London, 1649) appears to have gone through thirty-five editions in England in the first year, and was translated into Latin, French, Dutch, German and Danish, according to F. Madan, *A new bibliography of the Eikon Basilike* (London, 1950). Milton's response, published late in September or early October 1649, was by then less topical and was reprinted only once, a year later, with planned Latin and French translations probably never completed: see N. H. Keeble and N. McDowell (eds.), *The complete works of John Milton*, vol. VI (Oxford, 2013), 253–77.

[41] See notably M. Mendle, 'The royalist origins of the separation of powers', and S. Kelsey, '"A no-king, or a new": royalists and the succession, 1648–1649', both in J. McElligott and Smith (eds.), *Royalists and royalism during the English civil war*, 175–91 and 192–213 respectively.

more narrow and factional than either religious and political tradition warranted. Such views evidently gained resonance even amongst some members of the House of Commons itself. As Peacey has argued, moderate royalist writers could at the very least publish details of parliamentary debates and committee decisions that revealed how self-serving and exclusive parliamentary government had become. One royalist, Roger Twysden, even expressed open sympathy for Leveller demands for annual parliaments, stronger grass-root accountability of all MPs to their constituents (as in the Netherlands) and proper transparent processing of petitions. Such arguments were not just a tactical manoeuvre: rather they demonstrate that the discussion of power, accountability and stability in the 1640s really did explore core issues along pathways that do not conform to a simple binary view of the conflict between crown and parliament. In short, a highly complex 'public opinion' was developing, with many variant points of view represented in texts serving a great many causes and interests, at a time when there were no obvious solutions and few effective means of restricting what was offered to readers.[42]

Once more, as in Germany and the Netherlands, visual prints acquired new importance for the dissemination of both propaganda and subversion or dissent, in that images could convey both more powerful and more ambiguous messages than text. Compared with the relatively conventional use of engravings in the 1620s to describe and provide hagiographic reinforcement of existing values,[43] visual imagery during the English civil wars acquired a wider and more ambivalent role. Most of the methods of propaganda offered by traditional royal ceremony and processions became unworkable, as did the allegorical masques so vigorously promoted at court by Charles I to reinforce royalist values. Visual propaganda, however, was developed in new directions by all the participants in the civil wars, both to sanctify monarchy in its terminal phase and, in a less ornate fashion, in support of parliament and key military commanders.[44] In contrast to what we observed in the major crises in Germany earlier,

---

[42] J. Peacey, 'Pamphlets relocated: royalist politics and pamphleteering of the late 1640s', in A. Hessayon and D. Finnegan (eds.), *Varieties of seventeenth- and early eighteenth-century English radicalism in context* (Farnham, 2011), 51–68; and other papers in that volume; J. Peacey, *Politicians and pamphleteers: propaganda during the English civil wars and interregnum* (Aldershot, 2005); J. Peacey, *Print and public politics in the English Revolution* (Cambridge, 2013).

[43] See for example M. Jones, 'The common weales of canker worms, or the locusts both of church, and states: Emblematic identities in a late Jacobean print'; and A. Bellamy, 'Buckingham engraved: politics, print images and the royal favourite in the 1620s', both in M. Hunter (ed.), *Printed images in early modern Britain: essays in interpretation* (Farnham, 2010), 193–213 and 215–35 respectively.

[44] K. Sharpe, *Image wars: promoting kings and commonwealths in England 1603–1660* (New Haven, CT, 2010), 285–537.

English prints in the 1640s covered a wider thematic range, using more colourful imagery than we might have expected if they had been sponsored solely by the major power brokers. It is also worth noting that both cheap woodblock printing and more expensive engraved images were common, no doubt in part to supply different parts of the market and secure wider impact. Critical and subversive broadsheet printing became even more sophisticated than what could be seen in the Netherlands – and as we would expect, the Commonwealth government was unable to develop effective controls over this elusive medium of communication. Demand for such prints became a fairly permanent feature of the London market: even after the Restoration, scurrilous and seditious cartoons and broadsheets often re-appeared during successive political crises, a trend which continued into the 1680s and the early years of the eighteenth century.

Decoding the precise meaning of visual political satires, however, can be difficult. Sponsorship by diverse political factions and patrons played an important role in the production and dissemination of all kinds of political sheets, so we certainly cannot take these at face value, nor can we assume they are straight representations of a 'public opinion'. Actual impact is also difficult to evaluate, compared with texts: possible quotation or plagiarism is much more difficult to follow, and we hardly ever have reliable indications of print runs or even the number of surviving copies. For the moment, conclusions drawn with regard to the impact of such visual material in the mid-seventeenth century may have to remain tentative – and given the costs of production, it seems likely that the deployment of high-quality visual material could never be an option for individuals with modest resources.[45]

Print during the Commonwealth and Protectorate

Once the new republican Commonwealth was in place in England, the Council of State tried to reinstitute effective control of print by means of the detailed and more restrictive Printing Act of 20 September 1649. With a single government now uncontested, this legislation may actually have been more effective than its predecessors. The forcible suppression of the Leveller movement and imprisonment of its leaders, combined with the overbearing military power of the new regime, made discussion of alternative political proposals both pointless and dangerous and may well have induced some writers to silence. The raw ESTC annual totals

---

[45] For recent work on this, see H. Pierce, 'Images, representation and counter-representation', in Raymond (ed.), *Cheap print in Britain and Ireland to 1660*, 262–79.

of items printed in London show a sharp decline during the period 1649–51, from over 2300 titles in 1648 to just over 1000 in 1651. Print output then stayed quite level (averaging 1160 pa) through most of the 1650s, but by 1658 renewed political uncertainty once again brought a spike in printing, with nearly 2000 items in 1659 and 2800 in 1660. Soon, however, the Restoration (and a new Printing Act in 1662) dampened output, settling to a broad trend in annual outputs comparable to what we would expect by projecting forward the figures from the 1630s (above, p. 36).

If the quantity and types of printed material produced during the 1640s and 1650s indicate a period of exceptional volatility, where printers responded rapidly to changing political, religious and social circumstances, there may also be significant overall differences between the two decades. The confrontational public use of print by the army, parliament and the crown in the 1640s inevitably became much more subdued once the Commonwealth government was perceived to be firmly in control: certainly the prominent role of the armed forces in subduing both Ireland and Scotland (and crushing active supporters of the Stuart claimant, prince Charles) left no-one in doubt about the military capabilities of the new state. That said, royalist sympathies of various kinds did not dwindle as much as one might have expected, and the recurrent difficulties of Cromwell in securing negotiated settlements with powerful groups, including the Long Parliament and its leaders on the Council of State, indicate that major differences across the political spectrum persisted. These were represented somewhat differently in print compared with the rich harvest of the 1640s, but were clearly visible. While we need to be cautious not to overstate the impact of print, or indeed the effectiveness of its dissemination, there are clear indications that the political establishment itself continued to regard print as a challenge. The underlying and no doubt much richer layers of oral communication – ranging from gossip to radical preaching and seditious demonstrations – no doubt had comparable subversive potential, and the authorities certainly remained acutely vigilant in this area, too.[46]

The style and substance of polemical writings during the 1650s have not been analysed as thoroughly as for the previous decade. Judging from the extraordinary collection of an enthusiastic reader such as the London bookseller George Thomason, the diversity of polemical reading material would appear to have declined somewhat during the Commonwealth, but his collection, though very extensive, is not necessarily representative of

---

[46] See notably D. Cressy, *Dangerous talk: scandalous, seditious and treasonable speech in pre-modern England* (Oxford, 2010), 132–202.

all the new trends in print culture.[47] We know that some writers demonstrated great skill in adapting to changing circumstances, to the point where (as with Marchamont Nedham) they seemed blatantly opportunistic and mercenary. It is also clear that relatively few were prosecuted just for what they wrote: John Lilburne was again one of them, in 1653, but was acquitted in what his supporters could regard as a great victory for the public interest. The fact that many of the polemicists of the 1640s did not give up, at this point, is a useful reminder that the creation of the new Commonwealth government (and the military machine that kept it in place) left many outsiders frustrated and angry, keenly aware either of those ideals of participatory or devolved politics that seemed increasingly out of reach, or of the continuing lack of stability in the new order. Not surprisingly, this led to a number of distinctive developments: a significant follow-up of royalist writings and counterarguments after the success of the *Eikon Basilike*; state-sponsored efforts to explain and strengthen the new order, notably in the writings of Milton, Nedham and others; major new works of independent and original political analysis, of which Hobbes's *Leviathan* was undoubtedly the most powerful but not the only voice; and more radically, a search for a simpler and purer form of community existence based on religious beliefs – as practised in ever more varied ways ranging from the Diggers and Ranters to the irrepressible Quakers.

The *Leviathan* (1651) is beyond doubt the most powerful political book of the early modern period. It was not a polemical tract directly favouring either monarchy or republican government – or indeed offering any kind of specific suggestions on the practical operation of government in England – but instead amounted to a pessimistic analysis of human nature and the failings of civil society, arguing that a strong sovereign authority was an indispensable means to the preservation of limited peace and security. As we noted earlier (Ch. 2 above, pp. 63–7), the book quickly established itself as a pivotal text which all other substantive political thinkers had to confront, not just in Commonwealth and Restoration England, but also subsequently in the Netherlands and (through Hobbes's own Latin translation) across Europe. In the present context, however, we need to consider how accessible it was to a broader readership in England in the 1650s, whatever their political horizon may have been. Hobbes clearly envisaged the book as a detailed theoretical analysis of civil government, intended for those in power or for those entering

---

[47] Raymond, *Pamphlets and pamphleteering*, 192–6; see also the *Catalogue of the pamphlets, books, newspapers and manuscripts collected by George Thomason* (2 vols., British Museum, 1908).

a career in law or government, presenting his arguments in a clearly structured sequence of succinctly titled chapters with informative marginal notes, as in a conventional textbook. The book was printed in quite generous format and, at an original price of 8 shillings for 400 pages of text, could never be mistaken for a typical polemical tract of the 1650s. A casual reader, however, would have been struck not only by its extraordinary frontispiece, portraying the sovereign body in superhuman form looming over both civil and ecclesiastical government. Even more surprising was the fact that the work was written in forceful and plain English – a remarkable choice for Hobbes, given that Latin remained the academic language of choice and that most of his own works to date had been in Latin.[48]

Thus encouraged, a reader would have had no difficulty locating some extraordinarily powerful and concise statements leading to closer engagement with the whole work. For example, at the start of chapter 12, on religion, the reader was confronted by the blunt statement that 'Seeing there are no signes, nor fruit of *Religion*, but in Man onely; there is no cause to doubt, but that the seed of *Religion*, is also onely in Man...' Chapter 13 starts with an equally bold statement that:

Nature hath made men so equall, in the faculties of body, and mind; as that though there bee found one man sometimes manifestly stronger in body, or of quicker mind then another; yet when all is reckoned together, the difference between man, and man, is not so considerable, as that one man can thereupon claim to himselfe any benefit, to which another may not pretend, as well as he.

Part 2 of the work, 'Of Commonwealth', explains the purpose of the restraints of civil society in terms of enlightened self-interest, and although the fundamental social contract handing power to the sovereign is irreversible, chapter 19 contains a sophisticated analysis of how that power can operate, and chapter 21 a detailed discussion of the liberty of subjects. Part 3, 'Of a Christian Commonwealth', again opens uncompromisingly, stating that 'I have derived the Rights of Soveraigne Power, and the duty of Subjects hitherto, from the Principles of Nature onely...', adding at the end of chapter 32 that 'Seeing therefore Miracles now cease, we have no sign left, whereby to acknowledge the pretended Revelations, or Inspirations of any private man...' A detailed analysis of the Bible follows, and the work is rounded off with Part 4, 'Of the Kingdome of Darknesse', which immediately (chapter 44) confronts 'Of Spirituall

---

[48] Hobbes had also hoped for a full French translation, to suit his large circle of contacts in France during his years of exile there, thereby underlining its topical relevance in both countries – but no French translation was completed, and his French readers would have had to rely on Samuel Sorbière's 1649 translation of his *De cive* instead.

Darknesse from Misinterpretation of Scripture'. No wonder that neither royalists nor republicans could be sure of Hobbes's support for their cause, and that adherents to established religious beliefs were terrified by the prospect of ordinary laymen reading this text: it bristles with statements that would seem extraordinarily controversial and thought-provoking to contemporary readers. Such a work could only have been published in the uncertain times of 1651 (it was proscribed in England in 1666 and the Dutch translation was banned in the Netherlands in 1674). Hobbes clearly took great risks by publishing such a fundamental and broad-ranging agenda in English.

John Milton was as adamant in his own beliefs as Hobbes, but once he had become an employee of the Commonwealth government in March 1649 he was more cautious in terms of language and context than he had been in the 1640s.[49] Unlike Hobbes, who used both English and Latin for his other publications in the 1650s, Milton's major work in the 1650s was in Latin – notably his *Pro populo Anglicana Defensio* of 1651, explaining why the king had been executed and a republic established, and the *Defensio secunda* of 1654. Latin was a natural choice, since Milton was now Secretary for Foreign Tongues, and his text was intended for an international readership rather than for Londoners. His official duties would no doubt also have prevented him from engaging extensively with the polemics of the 1650s, so his English publications amount essentially to just two short pieces from 1659 and, belatedly, *The readie and easie way to establish a free Commonwealth; and the excellence therof compar'd with the inconveniencies and dangers of readmitting Kingship in this Nation* of 1660, which needs no further explanation (but suffered from bad timing and heavy style). After the Restoration, Milton, like many others, was in considerable danger of reprisals, having to resort to subterfuge, protective friends and innate persuasive skills first to survive, then to resume tentative writing (albeit within much stricter limits and avoiding politics). Such retrenchment was no doubt a potentially creative limitation: Milton's *Paradise Lost* of 1667 is of course the best example of him making the most of difficult circumstances. Hobbes, too, was forced to change tack: he wisely chose to publish his reworked Latin

---

[49] K. Sharpe, '"Something of monarchy": Milton and Cromwell, republicanism and regality', in his *Reading authority and representing rule in early modern England* (London, 2013), 173–91. Milton's *The tenure of kings and magistrates*, written during the king's trial and published around the time of his execution, was a short polemic (42 pages in its first printing, slightly revised for a second edition within a year); his *Eikonoklastes* (London, 1649, 242 pages in its first edition, with one immediate reprint, and a French translation) was much more elaborate, but as a detailed critique of another text and scornful rejection of royalist 'idolatry' it was part of a polemic and not a text intended to be read on its own.

version of *Leviathan* in the Netherlands and left his *Behemoth* unpublished until the very end of his life (1679). James Harrington, author of a major work on pure republicanism, *The Common-Wealth of Oceana* (1656), was permanently silenced.

Other writers had a far less predictable career, famously so in the case of Marchamont Nedham (1628–78). Sometimes regarded as an opportunist, Nedham started his journalism with the parliamentarian newsbook *Mercurius Britanicus*, was imprisoned for seditious libel, became royalist in 1647 publishing his *Mercurius Pragmaticus* and, after a short spell in prison in 1649, came round to supporting Cromwell through his weekly *Mercurius Politicus*. In this newsbook, and in a number of pamphlets, Nedham managed to adapt his language to that of a populist spokesman for the government, gaining the support of Cromwell's powerful intelligence officer John Thurloe. His newspaper was strong on international and commercial news, but also gained a reputation as a commercially viable advertiser. Not surprisingly, he had to go into hiding after the Restoration, but appears to have negotiated a pardon. Historians have debated precisely what made him such a political survivor, but any explanation must give due credit to his powerful journalism (making him valuable to each successive regime) and his own pragmatic judgment in searching above all for a stable government, limited religious toleration and the marginalisation of false godliness amongst his contemporaries. His admission of a change of mind, in his republican tract *The Case of the Common-Wealth of England Stated* (1650), is frank and clear: with his pragmatic and utilitarian approach to politics and common sense, he was no doubt at least as influential in shaping political opinion in the 1650s as his more austere contemporaries Hobbes and Milton. His colourful life as a journalist and pamphleteer certainly demonstrates how difficult it is to demonstrate clear connections in the rapidly moving political disputes of the 1650s, or indeed to impose twenty-first-century ideals of consistency on thinkers working within such a complex environment.[50]

Nedham's political pragmatism is perhaps as remote as can be from the austere other-worldly writings of the religious visionaries

---

[50] R. Foxley, 'Marchamont Nedham and mystery of state', in G. Mahlberg and D. Wiemann (eds.), *European contexts for English republicanism* (Farnham, 2013), 49–62; J. Raymond, 'Marchamont Nedham', in Knoppers (ed.), *The Oxford handbook of literature and the English Revolution*, 375–93; S. Kelsey, *Inventing a republic: the political culture of the English Commonwealth 1649–1653* (Manchester, 1997); for the longer-term impact of republican writings, see R. Hammersley, *The English republican tradition and eighteenth-century France* (Manchester, 2010).

of the 1650s. Amongst these, Gerrard Winstanley positioned himself as a direct heir to the Leveller cause, his Digger community becoming a symbol of an alternative lifestyle which abandoned individual property rights (but, somewhat inconsistently, maintained patriarchal authority in the family without even a hint of equality for women).[51] An effective writer and publicist himself,[52] Winstanley naturally also attracted a great deal of adverse comment amongst other writers. So did the Ranters, a fleeting group of anarchists whose real identity and existence was partly obscured by the flood of hostile and hysterical (mostly fabricated) print coverage they attracted. They became ready targets under the new Blasphemy Act of 1650, both for the incoherently mystical writings of one of their spokesmen, Abiezer Coppe, and for their alleged indulgence in uninhibited sex in connection with meetings for worship.

If some of these colourful and eccentric sects had a sensational but fleeting impact on contemporary opinion, the same cannot be said for the Quakers. They had also absorbed a number of Leveller ideas, but by 1652 engaged more effectively in print to help provide a focus for what was otherwise a barely coherent ideological movement committed to the 'inner light' and strongly individualist religious-philosophical beliefs. Since they required no church for meetings of worship, and openly despised all forms of hierarchy or external authority, outsiders regarded them as heretical anarchists. This reputation was reinforced by their willingness to regard men and women as real equals: a few Quaker women gained a unique role as preachers and community leaders, and many more spoke regularly in meetings for worship (as men might do) or in public gatherings. Quaker women also constituted a disproportionately large share of women authors overall, from the 1650s onwards.[53] The early Quakers displayed a kind of 'enthusiasm' and visionary otherworldly plainness which made them highly controversial, and exposed them to reprisals from more traditional believers. Accordingly, although early Quaker leaders such as George Fox, James Nayler, Sarah Blackborow and Esther Biddle had strong personal followings, their impact through print may at first have been largely negative, at least amongst those readers who were not already sympathetic to the Quaker

---

[51] A. Hughes, '"Gender trouble": women's agency and gender relations in the English Revolution', in M. J. Braddick (ed.), *The Oxford handbook of the English Revolution* (Oxford, 2015), 347–62.

[52] A. Hessayon, 'Gerrard Winstanley, radical reformer', in Hessayon and Finnegan (eds.), *Varieties of seventeenth- and early eighteenth-century English radicalism*, 87–112.

[53] P. Crawford, 'Women's published writings 1600–1700', in M. Prior (ed.), *Women in English society 1500–1800* (London, 1985), 211–82; Raymond, *Pamphlets and pamphleteering*, 276–322.

ideals.[54] Even more unacceptable to most readers, no doubt, were the visions of the Fifth Monarchist mystic Anna Trapnel, some of which were printed in the 1650s.

Women were generally not frequent contributors in the outpouring of political print in the 1640s and 1650s. Except for a few aristocratic women who held titles or voting rights as widows or heiresses, women were traditionally excluded from almost all forms of active political life. Female authors were by custom supposed to restrict themselves to the traditional female sphere of interest, going into print mostly in their devotional writings, and otherwise relying on manuscript communication, diaries and private letters. Accordingly, it is difficult to determine what their role may have been, informally, in the print culture of this period. We know that several Leveller wives acted for their husbands when in trouble, notably Elizabeth Lilburne and Mary Overton (who was herself imprisoned in Bridewell).[55] Equally, we have evidence of wives being actively involved in their husbands' printing activities, as happened most notably in the case of Samuel and Katherine Chidley, but such roles were traditionally acceptable as part of the normal functions of a household. Conventional social norms, however, did allow women to engage in political life as petitioners.

A remarkable development in the use of print for political purposes was the emergence of collective printed petitions. Personal handwritten petitions had been a mainstay of political communication as far back as we can see, a crucial way of implicitly or explicitly negotiating power relations between people of widely different social standing: between subject and lord or subject and king, between congregations and ecclesiastical authorities, and even between individuals who felt that the appropriate intervention of authority could restore traditional social relationships and fair treatment. Petitions could serve as declarations of support for specific groups, or even statements of loyalty to a ruler or local authority – though often couched in normative language that might well to modern eyes appear almost a caricature, or at least ambiguous. We cannot, of course, assume that the wordings of petitions represent political 'reality', but they do give us insights into contemporary perceptions of what was right and wrong, and what the boundaries of grievance and political agitation

---

[54] On the continuing influence of the Quakers in the late 1650s, see for example K. Peters, 'The Quakers and the politics of the army in the crisis of 1659', *Past & Present*, 231 (2016), 97–128.

[55] A. Hughes, 'Gender politics in Leveller literature', in S. D. Amussen and M. A. Kishlansky (eds.), *Political culture and cultural politics in early modern England* (Manchester, 1995), 162–88.

were perceived to be.[56] Handwritten petitions were essentially private supplications for help, according to standard formulae: in effect a form of personal negotiation. Collective petitions were bound to have a more 'public' character and would inevitably turn the request into an open and potentially more threatening demand. This may explain why petitions hardly ever made it into print before the 1620s: the kind of 'public opinion' implied in printed petitions could easily be seen as untrustworthy and manipulative, no longer part of the normal privileged and reasoned negotiation of power.

It is striking how few petitions went into print in London even in the 1630s: the actual word 'petition' appears in the titles of at most four items in any one year, and there were even fewer with words such as 'grievance', 'remonstrance' or 'complaint' in the title. In 1641 'petition' appeared in the title of 265 items recorded in the ESTC (including pamphlets that responded to others using the word), climbing to 678 in the year 1642 alone, then fluctuating widely during the following years, before settling around an average of 40 per annum in the 1650s. Since title words are not in themselves sufficient to locate texts that in effect amounted to a petition, we need to be cautious in regarding such figures as anything more than just one indicator of a trend. Nevertheless, the rapid adoption of print for what had originally been a 'private' form of communication is astonishing. Activists soon realised that print created new opportunities for reaching a wider audience. By 1643 there were printed broadsheets informing the public where they would find a petition to be able to sign it personally,[57] clearly a cost-effective way of getting as many signatures as possible. For some petitioners, the number of signatures was intended to add weight to the demand, or create safety in numbers: although we cannot take claims of thousands of personal signatures entirely seriously, one petition to the House of Commons as early as 1641 was said to have 20,000 subscribers.[58] Printed petitions for peace, common from the autumn of 1642, often aimed to maximise support by including an invitation for more subscribers. Not surprisingly, therefore, we also find printed declarations denouncing a particular petition as false or illegal, presumably when the petitioning momentum appeared to have got out of

---

[56] Again petitions in the 1640s and 50s have not been studied as exhaustively as they deserve, but a very influential discussion is found in Zaret, *Origins of democratic culture*, 217–65; and for the Restoration period, M. Knights, *Representation and misrepresentation in later Stuart Britain: partisanship and political culture* (Oxford, 2005), 114–6 and 127–35.

[57] An early example has a self-explanatory title: *All sorts of well-affected persons, who desire a speedy end to this destructive warre* were invited in to appear at a designated place on 19 July 1643 to sign up.

[58] *The petition of the citizens of London to both Houses of Parliament*, single sheet (London, 1640).

hand, or critics of collective petitioning wanted to vent their disapproval of the manipulative nature of collective petitioning.[59] It clearly mattered who signed, and the names of prominent subscribers were often included in the printed titles to add credibility and weight. Equally, the political purpose might be underlined, as when *A remonstrance or declaration of the Army presented to the House of Commons on Munday Novemb. 20. 1648* publicised 'an agreement for all the kingdome to signe, which shall be above law', and would form a constitutional contract which would be used to exclude non-signatories from citizenship.

Already in 1641 we get an early impression of how such petitioning might develop. In *The petition of the weamen* [sic] *of Middlesex ... to the High Court of parliament,* the organisers decided to withhold (but nevertheless print) their text 'untill it should please God to endue them with more wit, and lesse non-sense'[60] – even though they claimed they already had 12,000 signatories. Clearly, petitions were becoming part of a complex process of open negotiation, explicitly designed to influence public opinion, in which women could take part within certain norms. Overt acceptance of traditional gender roles continued in the 1650s, but there is no doubt that women exploited what opportunities they had. The women's petitions in April–May 1649 in support of the imprisoned Leveller leaders, that of October 1651 regarding the treatment of debtors and that for John Lilburne in June 1653, all broke new ground in terms of politicised language, and all were circulated in print to gain as large a number of signatories as possible.[61] Although not ostensibly structured as a petition, a tract calling for a parliament of women (1656) is an even more striking indication of how far radical thinking might develop.[62]

Is there a risk of exaggerating the impact of print on political awareness and opinion in England during the 1640s and 50s? We still cannot be sure how big the print runs were, or who read these texts in London, let alone the provinces. But we now have a clearer idea of who the authors, writers, polemicists and orators were, and on that basis at least we can dispel some older assumptions. Historians have long since given up any clear

---

[59] As in *A new found stratagem framed in the old forge of Machivilisme* [sic], [London?], April 1647. On ambivalent contemporary attitudes to 'public' collective petitioning, see also Chapter 1 above.

[60] *The petition of the weamen of Middlesex* (London, December 1641).

[61] P. Crawford, '"The poorest she": women and citizenship in early modern England', in M. Mendle (ed.), *The Putney debates of 1647: the army, the Levellers and the English state* (Cambridge, 2001), 197–218, especially p. 216; see also M. Bell, 'Women writing and women written', in Barnard and McKenzie (eds.), *The Cambridge history of the book,* vol. IV, 431–51.

[62] *Now or never: or, a new Parliament of women ... with their declaration, articles, rules, laws, orders and proposals,* 8 pages, Thomason collection (London, August 1656).

separation of elite from popular culture in this period, recognising instead that, in spite of strong notions of social status and rank in early modern society, there was a fluid range of writing styles, language and content which linked the interests of readers across a wide spectrum. The Diggers may have been one of the groups trying to cross social barriers by seeking support from the poorer sorts, but the Quakers were notorious for their complete disregard of social conventions and their deliberate assumption (as voiced by George Fox and many others) that everyone, man or woman, with or without formal education, could and should interpret what they read using their innate intelligence. All the Leveller leaders deployed substantial erudition in their polemics, whilst explicitly denying that formal education on its own provided any guarantee of good sense or independent reasoning. Although it may be the case that visionary religious enthusiasm had greater appeal to people of humble background, the Quaker movement amply demonstrates both how subversive such ideas could be and how effectively they reached across all social barriers. Equally, although only one prominent Quaker writer, Samuel Fisher, is known to have had a university education, some other radical polemicists had, including the Ranter leader Abiezer Coppe and the Leveller Overton.[63]

So, although printing technology had been available for two centuries and was not an intrinsically new medium of communication, the use to which it was put in the 1640s and 50s genuinely could (and did) help reach out across social barriers. It is difficult to resist the conclusion that print became an innovatory and indispensable tool in the unprecedented power confrontations and political culture of civil war and Commonwealth England – not just responding to the demand for more information, but also enhancing political awareness and hence providing incentives to active political participation. Equally clear is the extraordinary shift from traditional kinds of texts to far more short items, authored by people who would never have gone into print in normal years, and dealing with issues of immediate religious, political and social significance.

Revisionist historians of the English civil wars and Commonwealth period tended to marginalise the impact of radical writers, regarding them as serving a fairly small minority of like-minded readers. Recent work on the history of print, however, has located this colourful array of noisy, disruptive, argumentative polemicists, and their often unprecedented demands for political participation, as direct participants in political life. In particular,

---

[63] For a full discussion of this crucial social contextualisation, see notably N. McDowell, *The English radical imagination: culture, religion, and revolution, 1630–1660* (Oxford, 2003).

Jason Peacey has noted how evidence of private purchase and extensive market distribution confirms that polemical texts did reach a broad readership even outside London, enhanced by borrowing, manuscript copying, as well as by sponsored or free distribution. He also notes highly significant indications that readers were becoming sufficiently familiar with a wide range of opinions that they no longer took what they read as simple truth, and were capable of critically evaluating the origins and purpose of polemics and at times incorporating them into communal discussion. Peacey has also investigated precisely how such popular reading material changed the nature of parliamentary politics itself – with readers evaluating factions, key demands, actual parliamentary speeches and overall political processes. We even find complaints by the political elite itself that members of parliament might risk being held to account by their constituents. As a result, lobbying and petitions acquired a clearer purpose, pressing popular demands in search of a true commonwealth. That search encompassed all kinds of causes, traditional and conservative as well as radical and populist, and print became an indispensable and versatile tool serving them all. But printing did not merely help disseminate, it also changed fundamental political practice: for example petitions, letters, protestations and proclamations became something quite different when they were taken out of the private and formal arena into something much more public and inclusive.

The many strands of thought that came into the open during these years defy simple categorisation. Some polemicists called for a return to the past, some saw scope for a religious-inspired society, while others dreamt up new idealised forms of civil society based on divergent views that reached right across (and sometimes beyond) the existing political spectrum. Kingship and absolute rule was analysed, negotiated and ultimately (if reluctantly) discarded by some as unreliable; different versions of the separation and balance of powers in government were explored systematically, in ways anticipating the more formal principles of the Enlightenment a century later. In England, principles of parliamentary representation and accountability were put to the test as never before; local authority was open to challenge; the dangers of military dictatorship became all too visible at times; but in the process (and for a limited time) an extraordinary experiment in army organisation and 'democratisation' was also allowed to take place, whilst claims were made for universal male suffrage and for some fundamental human rights deemed to be constant and beyond the reach of parliamentary legislation. Rights of property were questioned by a small radical fringe of visionaries; many more explored a bewildering array of religious and sectarian options, some of which had the effect of deepening and entrenching the already significant religious divides which England had experienced for a century. And last but not least, unprecedented steps towards equality became possible for the strong women of the early Quaker movement, even if they had a long struggle ahead of them. As we shall see, such ideas, once in print, could not entirely be suppressed even after the Restoration of 1660.

Print in France during the Fronde

A study of political print in France during the 1640s and 50s, on as systematic and comprehensive a level as for England, is not possible. We do not yet have a French equivalent of the English Short Title Catalogue, and the catalogues of the Bibliothèque Nationale substantially under-represent total French-language output. Quantitative estimates of changing overall output therefore remain impressionistic, and it is difficult to identify representative samples of print. Only one specific period has been studied in any depth: the troubles which confronted the regency from 1648, five years after the death of Louis XIII in 1643 and that of his first minister Richelieu a few months earlier. Significant grievances had been building up for some time, notably regarding the unbearable fiscal burden of protracted warfare (causing huge peasant revolts in the 1620s and 30s), harvest failures, economic disruption and the seemingly overbearing policies of cardinal Richelieu. France experienced the full brunt of the climate disruption and catastrophic agricultural crises of 1647–9 which caused unrest all over Europe. Continuing war with Spain (until 1659) ensured there was no relief, so the regency (headed by Anne of Austria and cardinal Mazarin) soon became the target of political intrigue from ambitious factions contesting who could speak for the king. By the time these challenges erupted into the Fronde (1648–53) there was no single authority that could enforce print regulations effectively.

The numerous *libelles* and pamphlets published during these unstable years, the so-called Mazarinades (a collective name given to some 5500 political tracts from the period 1648–53), have been studied by a number of historians as a distinct set of texts which reflect political controversy during the Fronde.[64] Attacks against the regency and its political mastermind cardinal Mazarin came from both the law courts and the aristocracy, so the top levels of the political nation are strongly represented. France had already had a recurrent history of challenges from princes of the blood, who (as in other European

---

[64] H. Carrier, *La presse de la Fronde (1648–1653): les Mazarinades:* vol. I: *La conquête de l'opinion* (Geneva, 1989); and vol. II, *Les hommes du livre* (Geneva, 1991); M. Bannister, 'Mazarinades, manifestos and mavericks: political and ideological *engagement* during the Fronde', *French History*, 30 (2016), 165–80.

monarchies) could claim a right to be consulted whenever the crown was under regency or appeared insecure. Any regency, however, also had major implications for constitutional law and the rightful exercise of sovereign power.

There were two separate constitutional bodies of potential overall political significance in France: the Estates General (which had served as a kind of national assembly until 1614 and was nearly recalled in 1648 to provide a central focus for the disparate provincial Estates) and the Parlement de Paris (the leading legal institution amongst nine provincial *parlements* and some other special 'sovereign courts'). The French *parlements* originated as one of a number of variant forms of assembly (royal councils, law courts and representative Estates) which were becoming institutionalised in many parts of Europe in the thirteenth century. Although not essentially a representative body, the Parlement of Paris self-consciously claimed a more overt political role as a final court of appeal across all the distinct jurisdictions which made up the kingdom of France and as a council formalising royal legislation (including taxation), either approving it or occasionally challenging it by means of remonstrances. The Parlement of Paris even aired abstract ideas of 'representing' the kingdom in all matters of law, especially when the Estates General was not in session and only some of the provincial Estates continued to operate. However, these representative claims were tenuous, partly because the *parlementaires* were not elected (being lawyers appointed for life), partly because constitutional principles were rarely argued with anything resembling the political creativity of the English parliament. But the Parlement of Paris did claim the right to print and distribute its memoranda and decisions independently of the crown and without prior censorship. In some situations this could create the potential to undermine the exclusive control which the crown exercised over 'privy' (private and privileged) information.

In contrast to England at this time, however, the institutions of the French monarchy itself were rarely explicitly questioned – not even by the most radical of the late Frondeurs, the group known as the Ormée in Bordeaux 1651–2. Rather, the Mazarinades tended to focus on factional power struggles, challenging the legitimacy of those claiming in various ways to act on behalf of the young king. Historians have noted the importance of the wealthy and aristocratic patrons who sponsored many of the publications, but have found few indications of any broad-based engagement with the fundamental questions of the time – established religious beliefs and the power of the church, the hierarchical order of society, or notions of a political contract comparable with what we saw in the case of England.[65] Accordingly, the Fronde has been regarded as essentially a sequence of power struggles caused by the uncertainties of a regency, rather than a fundamental turning point in public political discussion. That, however, may be an oversimplification: when, in September 1651, Louis XIV became old enough (after his thirteenth birthday) to be declared of age, the regency nominally ended, and many could now openly exhort the young king to assert his personal authority in accordance with traditional concepts of kingship. But both the fighting and the polemics in print continued for at least another year, until it became clear to the leaders of the main factions that nothing further could be gained. By early 1653, the flood of polemical prints disappeared, leaving just the bitter memories of violence and disorder which the king could use later as justification for a further consolidation of royal absolutism.

Hindsight is easy, however, and we should not dismiss the Mazarinades (or other political texts of this period) as insignificant because they were part of what has sometimes been called a 'failed revolution'.[66] It would be equally unsatisfactory, having selected them precisely because they are polemical pamphlets, to dismiss them as insufficiently innovative or analytical. Understanding what the texts were trying to do, whose views they may reflect and what impact they may have had can still provide insights into contemporary political opinion, conceptual frameworks, grievances and expectations in the main centres of unrest. Many pamphleteers complained bitterly about the 'manipulation' of information, the spread of rumours and the deliberate use of misinformation to distort political judgment. Clearly one of the keys to Mazarin's own success at holding on to power (even when he temporarily left the court in what was a tactical manoeuvre) was his information network – including not just agents with an ear to the ground, but also good diplomatic contacts providing him with updates on the English situation. Direct intervention in England (as demanded by the wife of Charles I, Henrietta Maria, now sheltering in France) was quite beyond the reach of a weakened French state and not in Mazarin's political interests; influencing the flow of information in Paris itself, on the other hand, was crucially important.

Until 1648, French news-sheets reported events in civil-war England without much analysis. However, the trial and execution of Charles, occurring as it did at the height of the Fronde *parlementaire*, led to more

[65] C. Jouhaud, *Mazarinades: la Fronde des mots* (Paris, 1985); for a comparison of English and French visions of kingship, see R. Asch, *Sacral kingship between disenchantment and re-enchantment: the French and English monarchies 1587–1688* (New York, 2014).

[66] H. Carrier, *Le labyrinthe de l'état: essai sur le débat politique au temps de la Fronde* (Paris, 2004), 376–8 and *passim*.

substantial coverage in the official *Gazette de France* (the monopoly news-paper which Théophraste Renaudot had launched in 1631). A number of significant separate publications also appeared, organised by Henrietta Maria and other members of the high aristocracy anxious to try to shape public perceptions of royalty. Some English texts were even translated into French, amongst them the *Eikon Basilike,* whilst works in Latin, including Milton's, were available to more learned French readers. Hobbes was amongst those who had strong personal connections in Paris, from his years of exile, but we should remind ourselves that a French version of the *Leviathan* did not materialise at this stage (even though an attempt was made to produce one). We should not assume that knowledge of English developments would have a direct relevance for, or impact on, French thinking. France did not face anything like the reli-gious disunity of England (and significantly, the Huguenot communities understandably kept a low profile in public controversies); the structures of local authority worked very differently in France from those in England; the French political elite did not have to contend with the fundamentally difficult issue of negotiating or controlling the authority of an adult ruling monarch; and the *parlementaires* themselves, as lawyers rather than national representatives, were often at pains to distance themselves from the radical policies of the English parliamentarians.[67]

The mechanics of pamphlet production and distribution are quite difficult to track. Around four-fifths of the texts were anonymous, many probably compiled by hacks sponsored by leaders of the political factions. Details of printer and place of publication occur slightly more often, and the year of publication, if not explicitly stated, may sometimes be guessed from references in the text. The first and largest outpouring of polemics (some 2000 texts in 1649 alone) mostly concentrated on the arguments raised by the *parlementaires,* even questioning the legitimacy of the regency itself.[68] The market seems then to have been less buoyant for a while, as total output dropped to around 600 per annum during the years 1650–1, but it surged to 1500 in 1652, when Mazarin's political survival was again at stake and aristocratic factions were particularly active.[69] Authors lingered on the evils of factional self-interest, lamented the violence and social breakdown, and occasionally had recourse to

---

[67] P. A. Knachel, *England and the Fronde: the impact of the English civil war and revolution on France* (Ithaca, NY, 1967) provides a narrative overview of the diplomatic and high-level contacts between the two countries, but does not explore the outreach of print in any detail.

[68] Notably the 8-page satirical *Catéchisme des courtisans de la cour de Mazarin* ([no place], 1649). Interestingly, it was recycled in 1668.

[69] For example, the 22-page *Les cauteles de la paix* ([no place], 1652), directed primarily at Mazarin himself.

broader political thought in proclaiming the need to preserve liberty against the threats of tyranny.[70] Some looked to traditional authority to regain stability, often in the name of the young king. No obvious summing-up occurred when polemic output rapidly dropped towards the end of 1652 and into 1653. Over these five years, the length (number of pages and layout) varied from single sheets to book-length quartos intended for more learned readers, with some 8-page pamphlets sold for as little as one sou (one-twentieth of the livre). The occasional inclusion of cheap woodcut illustrations points towards the popular market, and some Mazarinades were presented in the form of sheets printed on just one side – in other words placards that could be posted outside on walls or doors. The repetition of common themes – embroidered narratives indicating intrigue, or accusations of misrepresentation, deception and violence – suggest that the market had built up a populist momentum of its own, no doubt fuelled by uncertainty. But does this amount to a broadly based participatory political culture?

Questions of style, language and narrative confirm that authors no doubt had specific kinds of readers in mind. In order to appeal to a wider audience, some texts raised obvious popular grievances, not unlike the fiscal burdens and accusations of economic exploitation that had been a common thread in the petitions and manifestos of popular revolt since the 1620s. By contrast, according to Christian Jouhaud, French translations of contemporary Leveller texts imported from England had virtually no identifiable impact – not even amongst the most famous group of revolutionaries in the Fronde, the Bordeaux radicals of the Ormée in 1652.[71] A relatively rare text, *Le manifeste des bourdelois* (1652) describes how a decree issued on the authority of the Parlement of Bordeaux was challenged by an ordinance issued in the name of the Ormée assembly, carrying a wax seal embellished with the phrase 'vox populi, vox dei'. *Le manifeste* is sprinkled with references to Greek and Roman precedents, and argues that in France the princes and magistrates are accomplices of tyranny. Since legitimate authority has to come from the people, the Ormée has set up a new 'democratic government' with appointed office-holders and commanders of the armed forces, as well as instituting a simple machinery of justice that

---

[70] For example, the 24-page pamphlet *Le caractère de la royauté et de la tyrannie* (Paris, 1652). Although keyword counts on titles of texts published in France cannot be very reliable, it is interesting to observe that the occurrences of 'roy' (king) in titles increase two to five times during the years 1649–52, by comparison with the average frequency for the rest of the 1640s and 50s; it occurs most frequently in the titles of works published in 1649.

[71] C. Jouhaud, *Mazarinades: la Fronde des mots* (Paris, 1985), 162 and 185–208.

does not rely on advocates and procurators. This, the text optimistically concludes, will become the model for the government of all of France.[72]

There were plenty of pamphlets explicitly blaming key figures ranging from Anne of Austria and Mazarin, to Cardinal de Retz, the Prince de Condé and Gaston d'Orléans, not to mention the pretensions of the Paris and provincial robe (*parlementaire*) leaders themselves. All factions had their share of criticism, legitimate or otherwise, and all woke up (sooner or later) to the potential for engineering support by means of the war of words. An imaginative example is the 58-page pamphlet entitled *L'esprit du feu Roy Louys XIII, à son fils Louys XIV*, dated 1652 but written as if the deceased king was addressing his son from beyond the grave. It blamed the queen mother, Anne of Austria, for falling under the spell of Mazarin, putting her love of the cardinal above the interests of the kingdom and of her son. Predictably, it advised the young king to seize back the decision-making powers that he was traditionally entitled to hold. Another tract from this late stage of the Fronde, *Les cauteles de la paix* (1652), distinguished Mazarin himself from what it called 'mazarinisme' and elaborated on the dangers of a secret deal between the regent and the princes. At the same time, in more populist mode, it attacked the burdens of continuing civil war, insisting that all contributions from the people are by nature and origin a voluntary concession which could therefore be withdrawn when those in power were not promoting the true interests of the kingdom. The pamphlet also noted how the fall of the monarchy in England had produced two different reactions: for some, it was proof that sovereigns needed to treat their subjects with more consideration, but for others, it demonstrated that the best way of safeguarding the crown was to rule with more force and 'to weaken subjects to such an extent that they cannot lift their arms to overthrow that force'.[73]

A number of texts explored distinctions between legitimate monarchy and the usurpations of tyranny, without going into much detail.[74] A few, however, provided more substantive analysis of the consequences of different kinds of abuse of power. *Le dereglement de l'Estat* (1651) set out, already on its title page, a composite framework of explanation for the current disorders in France:

(1) Contempt for religion apparent in the disagreements between its teachers, in the politics espoused by preachers, and the bad example set by the magnates; (2)

---

[72] Anon, *Le manifeste des bourdelois* (Paris, 1652: Bordeaux City Library), 8 pages.

[73] Anon, *Lex cauteles de la paix* (Lyon City Library, no place or year of publication, but probably 1652), 8–9 and 16.

[74] Anon, *La mercuriale* (Paris, 1652), which also argues that Mazarin and the princes are all condoning the usurpation of power from a legitimate ruler, leading to tyranny or despotism.

The disorder of the three Estates, the uncontrolled ambition of the clergy, the abuse of nobility, and the self-indulgence of the people; (3) The criminal impunity of public office-holders; (4) The excessive abundance of riches amongst church-men; (5) The bad habit in politics of following Italian maxims contrary to the simplicity of the French.

The text itself noted how easy it was to assume that popular politics and factional recriminations were all to blame. Each of the themes listed on the title page were then discussed in sequence, including the underlying problems created by amoral self-interest, disputes exacerbated by variant beliefs (including Jansenist and Molinist disagreements) and the need for a better understanding of the natural hierarchy and functional differentia-tions within society in order to restore harmony between the three estates. In language reminiscent of the proclamations of the popular protest movements of the 1630s, the pamphlet pointed to the irresponsibility and impunity of ministers and office-holders (including Mazarin), and in its final section focused on a broad range of political malpractices and abuses of power.[75]

A more outspoken critique is found in a pamphlet from 1649, *Catechisme des partisans*. In a short preface, the reader is reminded how, if answers to core questions had been given a generation earlier, some of the current problems could have been avoided. The argument then takes the form of a 'catechism', with questions and answers evolving along a very pointed line of enquiry. The very first question asks 'what is the king', to which the answer immediately sets the tone:

You would have pleased me more, if you had asked what is God, for, following the example of an ancient scholar, and after taking time to formulate an answer, I would give up by admitting my ignorance. For nowadays flattery places royalty on such a pinnacle, while self-interest, ambition and avarice form such a strange idea of it, that if God came down to earth ... he would scarcely find a place amongst the lackeys of a royal favourite, let alone in the house of the king himself.

A clear distinction is made in response to a question whether the king is master of the life of his subjects: 'yes, but not in the manner understood in the politics of Machiavelli, but rather as taught in the Bible, that is, ... in accordance with the laws of God, and not otherwise'. Maxims that allow the king to go further than that are 'impious, damnable and abominable, and would be neither approved nor authorised amongst the most barbar-ous or unnatural of peoples'. In similar outspoken language, the pamphlet proceeds to explore power-broking, office-holding, those who profiteer from state finances, and other partisan interests. It suggests that it is not

---

[75] Anon, *Le dereglement de l'Estat* ([no place], 1651), 39 pages, reprinted in H. Carrier (ed.), *La Fronde: contestation démocratique et misère paysanne* (Paris, 1982), 2 vols.

enough for them to compensate the state: corruption needs to be tackled properly, not merely at the top but right down through the hierarchy and machinery of power.[76]

Have historians, in concentrating on the Mazarinades as a predefined corpus of texts, risked missing the full range of political controversy in print? And, given that most of the detailed work on this group of texts was done some time ago, have key groups of contributors (such as women) been overlooked? We might remind ourselves that the Mazarinades were defined retrospectively (in the nineteenth century) as a genre of polemical texts intended to argue specific factional and political points of view. They inevitably shared common turns of phrase and plagiarised or recycled existing stories, but may have been less concerned with more fundamental analysis of political thought and structures. Elite readers at the time recognised openly that polemics of this kind had the potential to destabilise, at critical moments, but were unlikely to have a lasting impact. Recurrent efforts to repress unauthorised texts suggest that the subversive potential of print was feared, without anyone actually analysing how it might work.

To get a more balanced view of French political culture at mid-century, therefore, we may want to consider a wider range of printed material (whilst remembering that petitions and manuscript material may have had significant impact too). What other texts may have helped readers make overall sense of the Fronde? As noted above, even Parisians appear to have taken little interest in English developments. More surprising is the diminishing interest in Bodin's great classic from the 1570s, *Les six livres de la république* of 1576: it had been reprinted in French at least eighteen times by 1600 (not counting seven editions of Bodin's own Latin translation, a Spanish translation and an English version in 1606) and had had three new editions in the early years of the seventeenth century (1608, 1610 and 1629), but it was not reprinted at all during the 1640s and 50s, perhaps because real politics had moved on under Richelieu.[77] Similarly, we might expect the *Essays* of Michel de Montaigne (1533–92), regularly reprinted in the half-century before the Fronde, to have acquired further readers, but demand did not go beyond one reprint in 1649 and possibly two in 1652. We should of course not rely solely on reprinting data as

---

[76] Anon, *Catechisme des partisans, ou resolutions theologiques, touchant l'imposition, levées & employ des finances* (Paris, 1649, avec permission, 32 pp.), 3–6, reprinted in Carrier (ed.), *La Fronde: contestation démocratique*.

[77] W. F. Church, *Richelieu and reason of state* (Princeton, NJ, 1972), 268–76, notes how Cardin le Bret, in his *De la souveraineté du Roy* (Paris, 1632), provided the most convincing re-interpretation of political power as exercised on behalf of the crown by an ever-more unchallengeable Richelieu. (I am grateful to Professor Hamish Scott for alerting me to this point).

evidence of the continued relevance of ideas – reformulation in new publications may have been just as important – but it is nevertheless surprising that such major older works did not catch the eyes of more readers in these troubled times.

In contemporary theatre, Pierre Corneille avoided core political questions, but one might plausibly argue that political themes gave an edge to the successful plays of Cyrano de Bergerac, notably in *Le ministre de l'état* (1649) and perhaps especially *La mort d'Agrippine* (written 1647, published 1653). By contrast, the philosopher Blaise Pascal, whose life also straddles this period (1623–62), did not finish or publish his great *Pensées* in his own lifetime, and we struggle to identify political connections in his fragmentary manuscript notes. It does seem as if the Fronde, whilst creating countless opportunities for pamphleteers, did not leave as deep a mark on the political culture of France as one might have expected, except as a warning of what might happen if central authority was undermined.

Access to Politics: the Netherlands

The Dutch market for political print was stronger and more sustained than in France, having developed already from the 1570s to underpin the long struggle for independence from Spain. The 12-year truce (1609–21) created scope for widening public discussion of foreign policy, trade and religious freedom, much of it represented in print. Fundamental disagreements over political direction and leadership came to a head in the politically determined trial and public execution of the long-serving and elderly *Landsadvocaat* Jan Oldenbarnevelt in 1619. The power struggle had a core religious component which focused on the dispute between Remonstrants and Counter-Remonstrants in the Calvinist church, on predestination theology and Arminian willingness to allow marginal doctrinal dissent. The Synod of Dordrecht (1618–19) had addressed this issue, but its hardline orthodox Calvinist decisions did not bring any durable resolution – there were too many dissenting religious interest groups to make a single answer widely acceptable. Besides, in the many prosperous urban communities of the coastal provinces, civic pride and participation in local self-government tended to produce highly variable levels of compliance. So, if the political crisis of 1618–19 created an opportunity for the *stadtholder* (*stadhouder*) Maurice of Orange-Nassau to assert his military control over the Dutch Republic, a bewildering array of devolved government structures ensured that political disunity would erupt again as soon as there were new stress points. The Dutch continued to enjoy a degree of political involvement which seemed incomprehensible to most visitors. Government at all levels was hugely complex, republican yet conservative in practice – effectively a loose confederation of prosperous towns keen to preserve their traditional autonomy and privileges, less hierarchical than any other strong state, economically dynamic, yet more prone to political instability and institutional upheaval than any other part of Europe, and riddled with ideological and local fracture lines which became all too apparent in further crises in 1650 and in 1672. It is hardly surprising that in such a volatile environment, thriving urban communities could sustain quality news networks and pamphleteers working with enterprising publishers and booksellers, and that no consistent control mechanisms could be enforced for any length of time. High levels of functional literacy, as well as ready access to north-German and French markets, made Amsterdam and other large cities ideal markets for print of all kinds.

One of the striking aspects of Dutch printing was its geographic decentralisation. With no particular need for subterfuge, most of the time, the majority of Dutch publications carried details of printer and location. As early as 1608, out of a total of 210 Dutch-language publications identified in the Short Title Catalogue Netherlands (STCN), two-thirds specify a place of publication, and these are spread over twenty-three different towns. A predictably large number of items came from Amsterdam, The Hague, Leiden, Middelburgh, Rotterdam and Antwerp, but even relatively small towns such as Arnhem and Zwolle had a printer. Of these, the Dutch component fluctuated more noticeably, sometimes dropping to just half the total output (1597–9), but more typically constituting at least two-thirds of the total, not least during the periods of acute political crisis around 1618 and 1672. Smaller printing centres such as Leiden naturally show patterns that are more erratic (both in absolute numbers and in terms of language distribution), but certainly confirm that the market for print was both very robust and significantly decentralised. The total number of Dutch-language publications (from all cities) had doubled between 1595 and 1608, doubled again from 1608 to 1644 and doubled once more by the peak year 1672. Whilst such crude numbers can only be regarded as approximations, and do not tell us what kind of printed material gained popularity or large print runs, they confirm that the Dutch Republic had by far the most buoyant and decentralised print market anywhere in Europe (as well as being one of the main European suppliers of print in Latin and French). This success was reflected in a reputation for quality, speed of delivery, improvements in lay out and fonts, and overall quality.

Recent research has provided hints of the kind of effect these many polemics might have had. As in the case of France, we should be cautious about the term 'pamphlet' itself: contemporaries did not see broadsheets, newsbooks, *libelles*, ballads, ambiguously worded stories, poems with implied topical relevance and other such context-specific publications as belonging to stable categories or clearly distinguishable genres. Roeland Harms has argued that, during the political crisis of 1650, Dutch polemics changed significantly, in step with the political crisis. When *stadtholder* William II tried to manipulate public opinion in Amsterdam by means of printed propaganda (the true purpose of which was uncovered by the city government), other writers responded by publishing the details of this deception, whilst claiming to regret that they had been forced by William's actions to resort to such tactics. In other words, demonstrably false printed stories were met with direct polemical responses that ensured the deception became public knowledge. The political consequences would have been more serious had William not suddenly died from smallpox.

Equally, poems (probably also meant for singing, as ballads) and images were used as a way of questioning the motives of political actors: poems could not so easily be proven to be libellous and by definition they required the reader to engage more directly with the process of understanding multiple layers of meaning. Such elusive writing had been used by broadsheet- and ballad-writers for generations and was a key component of polemical tactics. In the Dutch context, there is no doubt that the polemics caused anger on both sides – clearly contributing directly to the conflicts themselves, rather than merely reporting them. In the run-up to the yet more violent crisis of 1672, frighteningly aggressive polemics were deployed against the de Witt brothers, and – after they were murdered by a lynch mob – against their allies. Evidence of reprinting, plagiarism and explicit rebuttals show that such texts played a significant role in mobilising political awareness, often in an inflammatory way; but we cannot assume that printed polemics actually caused, rather than merely aggravated, the violence already stirred by preaching, rumour and verbal communication.[78]

If we broaden our search beyond pamphlets, we would expect the successive political crises and instability in the Dutch Republic to have fostered more substantive writings, too. The lawyer Hugo Grotius (Hugo

---

[78] R. Harms, 'Thievery of literature: consequences of the interaction between politics and commerce for the form and content of pamphlets'; and G. de Bruin, 'Political pamphleteering and public opinion in the age of de Witt (1653–1672)', both in F. Deen, D. Onnekink and M. Reinders (eds.), *Pamphlets and politics in the Dutch Republic* (Leiden, 2011), 37–57 and 63–95; for the broader background to the 1672 upheaval, including the role both of print and of oral discussion in exacerbating political division, see M. Reinders, *Gedrucktes chaos: populisme en moord in het rampjaar 1672* (Amsterdam, 2010) and his *Printed pandemonium: popular print and politics in the Netherlands, 1650–72* (Leiden, 2013).

de Groot, 1583–1645) had been an assistant and supporter of Oldenbarnevelt until their arrest in 1618, but he escaped the death penalty by giving evidence against his patron, was imprisoned and later fled to France. His best-known work, *De jure belli ac pacis*, published in exile in France in 1625, argued for a system of universal international law based on natural ethical principles (natural law) rather than explicit divine sanction. Yet, although the book became a landmark text to legal scholars, no Dutch or French translation became available soon enough for it to have secured a wider readership beyond its 1631 and 1651 Amsterdam Latin reprints.[79] In 1635 the English scholar John Selden (1584–1654) had drafted a response to Grotius, also in Latin, but it was not available at all in print until it was translated into English by Marchamont Nedham in 1652, shortly before Selden's death, and published under the title *Of the dominion or ownership of the sea*. Scholarly reputation was of course no guarantee of popular appreciation: in reality, during his lifetime Grotius may have been more widely read for his contributions to the Arminian controversy within the Calvinist church and Selden for his historical and archaeological works. In any case neither was accessible to a general audience, and the reputation of Grotius in international law and government was only secured through Pufendorf's work (see below, Chapter 3).

We evidently need to look elsewhere for major texts with a long-term impact on Dutch political awareness. The wealthy merchant Pieter de la Court (1618–85) published a number of very successful pamphlets after 1660, including *Consideratien van staat, ofte politike weeg-schaal* (1660, with five editions by 1662), *Interest van Holland* (1662, with a German translation 1665), other political essays (some possibly by his younger brother Johan, who had died in 1660) and works of history. As a committed supporter of the government led by Johan de Witt, and writing in an accessible vernacular style, de la Court became a household name in the 1660s, as an effective exponent in print of a republican government based on a decentralised federation of semi-autonomous towns preserving their traditional commercial interests. We should remember that city magistracies and the councils of individual provinces used print extensively, releasing *Deductie* (Deductions), *Declaratie* (Declarations) and *Bedenkingen* (Memoranda) regularly for public information and generating responses published either anonymously or by named authors. De Witt himself was involved in these

---

[79] Amongst contemporaries, Grotius was read (and translated) more for his religious works than for his writings on law. *De jure belli ac pacis* was available mainly in Latin editions: the first English translation appeared in 1654 (*Of the law of warre and peace*, translated by Clement Barksdale), but it was not rendered in French until 1687, and there was not even a Dutch translation in his lifetime.

sometimes lengthy policy explanations (as in his *Deductie* of 1654). Newspapers naturally culled much of their material from these publications, incorporating details into their domestic reports. It is difficult to see this as anything other than a remarkable public discussion of domestic politics. The evidence suggesting that the decentralised censorship mechanisms available to the authorities had only limited effect may suggest either that authors were aware of the need for self-censorship, or simply that the extent of illegal books in the Netherlands still needs further research. But it seems incontestable that print had now become one of the normal means of channelling and negotiating power relationships and policies. Much of what appeared in print was of a kind which in most other states would have been regarded as scurrilous, scandalous or manipulative. But in the Netherlands it was a fact of life at least until 1672, when the young *stadtholder* William III started imposing tighter restrictions on at least some sensitive areas of discussion such as foreign policy.

Scholars have disagreed over the extent to which English and Dutch political writers and polemicists may have influenced each other. On the face of it, there should have been plenty of scope during the 1650s, when both were resisting the claims of Stuart-Orange hereditary rights and princely power. But the great majority in the Netherlands were appalled by regicide and had no sympathy for the radical political solutions discussed in England before and after 1649. In any case the commercial rivalries between the Dutch and the English, which flared into naval confrontation over the Navigation Acts and the colonial ambitions of both sides, directly affected the Dutch patrician families who controlled both the Estates General and individual provincial and municipal governments. This could help to explain why Hobbes was of greater interest to the Dutch than Milton and why Harrington in his own works did not discuss Dutch republican government in any depth. Many English and Scottish radical pamphlets of the 1640s were translated and disseminated in Dutch, but significantly the initiative for such transmission appears to have come mostly from the English side, and some texts appear to have had little impact amongst Dutch readers. Surprisingly few of the major English political writings seem to have been translated into Dutch: Hobbes's *Leviathan* was the outstanding exception, alongside a few of Algernon Sidney's writings and a Dutch translation of the *Eikon Basilike* itself. And while the Latin writings of Milton were of course intended for a European readership (his *Defensio secunda* was reprinted in The Hague) they appear to have had a less enthusiastic readership in the Netherlands than the conservative reply penned by the Huguenot polemicist Claudius Salmasius in his *Defensio Regia* (1649, translated into Dutch in 1650 following a government ban). Few in the Netherlands could read English, so the vast output of polemics produced in London in the 1640s and 50s would have had no direct impact on the Dutch. In any case, English royalism and republicanism, alike, were deemed highly dangerous in the very unstable political environment of the Dutch Republic itself in 1650.[80]

Recently, however, Hans Blom and others have reminded us that an author does not have to be translated and reprinted in order for some of his ideas to have an impact. There was ample opportunity for informal contacts between Dutch and English writers and thinkers throughout these troubled years, not least after 1660 when many radicals (including some regicides and a significant number of Quakers) fled from England and settled in the Netherlands, integrating well with some of the radical religious groups there.[81] Here we have an important example of influences crossing linguistic barriers in ways that cannot easily be documented directly in print, but are nonetheless visible enough in the creative adaptations seen in the writings of many of the leading polemicists on both sides. These influences, of course, need not have been in actual sympathy with any of the strands of the English radicals: it is important to note that many Dutch writers were very critical of the insubordination of the London activists, both in religious and political terms, and might see them as something to be avoided rather than embraced. Such negative influences are nonetheless important.

This was the context and intellectual climate in which Spinoza worked. As one of the most original thinkers of his age, but also one of the most controversial and elusive, his actual influence on contemporary discussion is very difficult to define with any degree of precision. He was evicted from his own Portuguese-Jewish community in Amsterdam in 1656 for what appears to have been ill-defined heresies: we may assume the Jewish community leaders feared his dangerous ideas might cause disturbances of a kind that could jeopardise their hard-earned tolerated status in the United Provinces. Amongst the strict Dutch Calvinist clergy, Spinoza also soon came to be regarded as dangerously subversive. Yet he shared friendships and intellectual companionship amongst the more liberal

---

[80] H. J. Helmers, *The royalist republic: literature, politics and religion in the Anglo-Dutch public sphere, 1639–1660* (Cambridge, 2015).

[81] H. W. Blom, 'Popularizing government: democratic tendencies in Anglo-Dutch republicanism', in G. Mahlberg and D. Wiemann (eds.), *European contexts for English republicanism* (Farnham, 2013), 121–35, and other chapters in that volume; W. R. E. Velema, '"That a republic is better than a monarchy": anti-monarchism in early modern Dutch political thought', in M. van Gelderen and Q. Skinner (eds.), *Republicanism, a shared European heritage* (Cambridge, 2002), vol. I, 9–25.

dissenting circles of Collegiants, Mennonites and other radical groups, in a network which after 1660 also included Quaker refugees from England. Spinoza was not socially well connected: although his family had run a successful business in Amsterdam, his expulsion from the Jewish community there damaged his economic position and he ended up making a living as a lens-grinder and freelance writer. In the early 1660s he worked mostly on a critique of the Cartesian philosophy, but it was his *Tractatus Theologico-Politicus* (published anonymously in 1670) which earned him public notoriety. This work was written in defence of traditional Dutch republican-democratic government, if not explicitly in support of de Witt. Although the argument is presented in generic and theoretical terms, the reader could scarcely have missed the strong case made against the proto-monarchical authoritarianism of the office of *stadtholder* (an office which was almost hereditary in the Orange family, but unfilled since 1650). In order to avoid popular controversy, Spinoza wrote in Latin and chose to lay out his text in the form of a complex reasoned argument, gradually drawing the reader to specific conclusions by means of carefully guarded steps rather than by provocative assertions. If the *Tractatus* was meant to be a technical philosophical text, the reaction was nevertheless so fierce that Spinoza deferred publication of his other contentious work – his *Ethica* (which he had started drafting earlier) and his more concise and accessible *Tractatus Politicus*. Both of these were published in Latin after his death in 1677, as part of the complete edition of his works (under a false Hamburg imprint) secretly compiled by his friends and rushed into print to ensure the authorities could not impound and suppress his legacy.

It is clear Spinoza's writings were not meant for a broad readership: his style was much less accessible than that of Hobbes or Milton, the argument a deductive philosophical process comprehensible only to the educated elite. Once he saw the hostile reaction to the Latin text, he reputedly discouraged his friends from publishing a translation. After the murder of the de Witt brothers, he naturally had to be even more cautious in avoiding public controversy. That said, he was in contact with many leading thinkers of his day (including Henry Oldenburg of the London Royal Society, Christian Huygens and Leibniz) and was even offered the chair of philosophy at the University of Heidelberg, which he refused. His *Tractatus Theologico-Politicus* of 1670, although issued with false printer's details, appears to have had at least six and possibly eight reprints in Latin by 1678, a French version under several misleading titles, followed by English and Dutch versions in 1689 and 1693 respectively – all in spite of the fact that the Latin version of the book had been officially prohibited in the United Provinces in 1674 alongside the work of Hobbes and had met vehement disapproval elsewhere.[82] Since these texts were all prepared surreptitiously, their diffusion is sufficiently obscure that historians, while recognising Spinoza's enormous importance as a philosopher and scientist, have disagreed not just on the extent of his influence on contemporary political confrontations in the 1670s, but also on the real importance of his work for the longer-term development of radical democratic republicanism and the rights of individuals within civil society.

Some of Spinoza's ideas originated in his detailed analysis of Cartesian thinking, but the challenging questions raised by the English civil wars and by the powerful arguments of Hobbes[83] – combined with observation of the difficult political balancing act of the Dutch Republic through repeated political crises to 1672 – enabled Spinoza to construct an entirely different vision of a democratic, consensus-based and rational civil society. This visionary society was free and egalitarian, requiring active participation by an educated citizenship, eliminating the need for any authoritarian religious establishment or state church and discarding most religious dogmas in favour of a few universal ethical principles. Following Hobbes, Spinoza did not build God into his political system as a guarantor or even final judge, but rather preferred to think of human society as part of a vast natural universe. We cannot see precisely how this might work: the level of argument remains highly abstract, and in any case Spinoza's premature death in 1677 prevented him from finishing his most concise book, the *Tractatus Politicus*. Tantalisingly, it stops precisely in the middle of a crucial discussion of democratic government and the role of ordinary men and women in civil society.

---

[82] Israel, *Radical Enlightenment*, 275–94.

[83] Spinoza published a study of Descartes in 1663. Although rarely citing other authors who influenced him, Spinoza was clearly also responding directly to Hobbes: he had a copy of Hobbes's *Elements* in his own library and was a close friend of Abraham van Berckel, who translated the *Leviathan* into Dutch in 1667. The following year Spinoza would also have had ready access to Hobbes's own Latin translation of the *Leviathan*, printed (as were other texts by Hobbes) in Amsterdam. On the close links between the arguments of Hobbes and those of Spinoza, see also T. Verbeek, *Spinoza's theological political treatise* (Farnham, 2003), 9f; N. Malcolm, 'Hobbes and Spinoza', in J. H. Burns (ed.), *The Cambridge history of political thought 1450–1700* (Cambridge, 1991), 547–55; and S. Nadler, *A book forged in hell: Spinoza's scandalous treatise and the birth of the secular age* (Princeton, 2011), 27–30, 119 and *passim*. On the printer who acted as publisher and literary executor for Spinoza, see C. G. Manusov-Verhage, 'Jan Rieuwertsz, marchand libraire et éditeur de Spinoza', in F. Akkerman and P. Steenbakkers (eds.), *Spinoza to the letter: studies in words, texts and books* (Leiden, 2005), 237–50.

Political Volatility and Print in the Mid-seventeenth Century

One of the factors limiting public political debate in the seventeenth century was the relative weakness of representative assemblies (parliaments) in many parts of Europe. It goes without saying that no assemblies were democratic in nature: it is more appropriate to see their role in terms of protecting aristocratic and elite rights to advise the ruler, protect 'liberties' (in effect privileges) and provide a framework for political consensus amongst the 'political nation'. Assembly participants had variable levels of access to inside information, but such information was always regarded as confidential, preventing non-participants from gaining any precise knowledge of detailed proceedings except by way of private contacts with members. Nearly all information of a political nature in early modern Europe was regarded as exclusive to the sovereign and covered by special privilege: printing or distribution of any detail was censored. As we have seen especially in the case of England in the 1640s and 50s, in times of political crisis, such secrecy could not be maintained effectively. But parliaments elsewhere never acquired such exceptional powers.[84]

In Sweden, with its exceptional broad parliamentary representation in four separate Estates, uncertainty remained over the precise powers of each. In particular, there were long-standing disagreements about whether deputies from the lower elected Estates could serve on key committees. It was also unclear whether the commons (third and fourth estate) should speak or vote in the collective national interest, as plenipotentiaries, or rather act merely as mandatories acting on behalf of their specific constituency. A subdued, but nonetheless significant, disagreement became visible in the run-up to the crucially important meetings of the Estates General in Sweden in 1649 and 1650. These meetings had to confront the issue of taxation and wartime expenditure, and in particular peasant fears of erosion of their status, highlighting deep social divisions aggravated by the burdens of the Thirty Years War. The formal records of the Estates of 1650 give some account of these differences, with the lower

---

[84] Comparative studies of parliaments in early modern Europe include G. Griffiths, *Representative government in western Europe in the sixteenth century* (Oxford, 1968); H. G. Koenigsberger, *Estates and revolutions: essays in early modern European history* (Ithaca, NY, 1971); M.A.R. Graves, *The parliaments of early modern Europe* (London, 2001). Recent analyses of individual assemblies include: J. R. Young, *The Scottish parliament: a political and constitutional analysis* (Edinburgh, 1996); K. Brown and A. J. Mann (eds.), *Parliament and politics in Scotland 1567–1707* (Edinburgh, 2005); K. M. Brown, 'Toward political participation and capacity: elections, voting and representation in early modern Scotland', *Journal of Modern History*, 88 (2016), 1–33.

Estates launching a vigorous demand for fiscal fairness and specifically for protection of freehold peasants alienated from the Crown as part of the pay-off to nobles and officers in the Swedish army during the Thirty Years War. We get a detailed impression from a sharply worded pamphlet which was circulated in manuscript form. This text was probably written in 1649, but was not published until more than a century later, in 1769, when it was (possibly wrongly) attributed to a commoner, Edward Philipsson Ehrensteen (in 1649 a tutor to a noble family, later an office-holder in the central administration). The text indicates how far political attitudes had changed even since 1630: it launches a strongly worded attack on behalf of the lower orders against the privileged nobility, who are accused of deliberately grinding their newly acquired freehold peasants into poverty by extracting as much revenue and labour from them as possible. The pamphlet noted that this process was against the law and the Swedish constitution, infringing not only the rights of the peasantry but also the crucial consultative role of the Estates.[85] We do not know what impact such a pamphlet may have had; but it clearly represented a division between privileged landowners on the one hand and lesser landowners, officeholders and the lower Estates on the other – a division which built up during further meetings of the Estates in 1652 and 1654 and led ultimately to the drastic initiative of 1680, where ownership rights of much alienated crown land was reviewed and a substantial part returned to the crown. But the Swedish Riksdag of 1680 also acknowledged the shift in the political balance of power by voluntarily surrendering authority to the king to act on exclusive information.[86]

In Sweden as elsewhere, surviving assembly records often merely outline received grievances and petitions, or other formal demands, and summarise the official decisions reached at the end.[87] We rarely have

---

[85] [Edvard Philipsson Ehrensteen, attrib.], *Oförgripeliga bewis emot adelens rättighet öfwer skatte-gods* (written in 1649, but published in Stockholm in 1769 – now once again relevant); 108 pages in print, this extract is translated in M. Roberts, *Sweden's age of greatness 1632–1718* (London, 1973), 98–100.

[86] The sessions of the Swedish parliament are well documented, by comparison with other parliaments in seventeenth-century Europe, but further study of the meetings of 1649–54 is needed. It is interesting to note that the three commoner Estates often seemed more united than the noble Estate and that the commoners were essentially royalist. In 1680 the aristocratic council was outmanoeuvred by the monarchy, but Charles XI himself seems to have been driven by duty more than by political ambition. See A. F. Upton, 'The Riksdag of 1680 and the establishment of royal absolutism in Sweden', *English Historical Review*, 103 (1987), 281–308; and his *Charles XI and Swedish absolutism* (Cambridge, 1998), especially 31–9.

[87] For a helpful comparative overview of parliamentary petitioning, see B. Kümin and A. Würgler, 'Petitions, *gravamina* and the early modern state: local influence on central legislation in England and Germany (Hesse)', *Parliaments, Estates and Representation*, 17 (1997), 39–60.

actual minutes of the discussions themselves, or any other detailed records summarising what was really said. Equally significantly, in many cases not even the actual participants would have had access to the kind of detailed information needed for informed political discussion. The strictly limited nature of 'public' information merely emphasised, even to contemporaries, the private and confidential nature of political life. Most assemblies were in any case dominated by the titular and propertied elite and so had no interest in disseminating any information that might publicise the social inequality on which the early modern state was built.

Given the material discussed in this chapter, it is nonetheless clear that the range, content and impact of public awareness in the 1640s and 1650s widened substantially in some communities, notably in England, and more slowly but still very significantly in the Netherlands and France. It is often difficult to trace the many paths by which new ideas and reinterpretations are disseminated, absorbed, modified, applied, or even discarded. This is even more the case in the middle years of the seventeenth century, when the absence of strong government made regulation inconsistent and often unenforceable. The first reactions to a particular text (at the time of publication) are often strikingly different from the significance attributed to it with hindsight, and as historians we ought to be at least as interested in the former as in the latter. So far, only a very small proportion of the huge quantity of contentious printed material from the mid-seventeenth century has been subjected to detailed historical scrutiny in terms of context and immediate reception.

That said, some broader observations are in order. It is clear that, during the years of political instability in the 1640s and 50s across many parts of Europe, an understandably strong demand for information ensured that existing means of communication (oral and written) were significantly enhanced by the imaginative strategies of printers and booksellers eager to exploit any opportunities of circumventing both state and church controls. The use of printed images with explanatory texts went through rapid development in the traumatised conditions of the Thirty Years War. Yet the decisive breakthrough in terms of critically analytic texts must be attributed to the extraordinary political developments in England in the 1640s and 50s and (briefly but less conclusively) to the disruptive years of the French Fronde. The prospering Dutch Republic added another dimension, partly because of its recurrent political crises, but also because its intrinsic political decentralisation made it a relatively safe long-term haven for the printing of more 'dangerous' texts – a well-placed but relatively unregulated information hub with links across much of Europe.

The role of print in all this can now be documented more clearly, using large-scale digital resources and the research techniques of the new history of print. We have a much better understanding of how authors, printers and booksellers responded to the challenges they faced and how rapidly the market developed and changed (most notably in England in the early 1640s) to meet demand – a demand which, at least in the more economically developed urban communities, seemed at times almost insatiable. Even though there were no fundamental changes in core printing technologies, paper manufacturing, or the cumbersome mechanisms of sale and distribution of printed material, there is no denying that print now provided a formidable and adaptable tool in the hands of government propagandists, religious dogmatists, philosophers, rabble-rousers and political subversives alike – all of them finding enthusiastic readers and even inspiring first-time authors to have a go themselves. Yet the processes of dissemination were not continuous, and it is remarkable how new styles of writing and presentation fluctuated rapidly with circumstances. This instability was hugely challenging for those willing to take on the heavy investment and overhead costs required in the printing industry, but clearly did not stop them.

Given that we are dealing with material compiled in an age of powerful conformism, extremely strict religious vigilance and a universal reluctance to allow freedom of speech, the content of printed texts evidently cannot be taken at face value. Knowing the context is essential to understanding what is being communicated. We need to locate a much wider sample of printed texts in their precise social and political context – including texts that appear with hindsight to have taken unconvincing turns or have fallen into oblivion. None of the political controversies discussed in this chapter had a clear outcome and many of the resulting ideas were dramatically suppressed in the more conservative climate of the decades after 1660. Both in England after 1660 and in the Dutch provinces after 1672 republican thinking became unfashionable, not least because decentralised government seemed irrelevant in an age of heavy militarisation and warfare. Groups who had temporarily gained a political voice – religious radicals and political visionaries in England, France and the Netherlands – had to moderate their tone, restrict or avoid going into print again, or hide.[88] The huge personal risks taken by many of the authors noted here, from Hobbes, Milton and Harrington, to Pascal, Pieter de la Court and Spinoza, would confirm that any progress towards freedom of expression might well have seemed illusory. Many activists found themselves outside the accepted bounds of political thinking, or at

---

[88] See notably Hammersley, *The English republican tradition and eighteenth-century France.*

best struggled to navigate either the troubled waters of Restoration England or the repressive authoritarianism of Louis XIV's France. Such confrontations, however, also contributed to wider dissemination of some ideas spread by refugees and exiled activists who, as we shall see, helped to ensure that the political culture across many parts of Europe became visibly more complex. The communicative potential of print was being put to good use.

3   Subversive Print in the Early Enlightenment

The major political upheavals in different parts of Europe in the middle years of the seventeenth century left many unresolved issues, not all of which could be brushed aside after the return to relative stability in the years from 1660. Examples could be cited from right across Europe, but a few obvious ones will suffice. The Peace of Westphalia of 1648 had rounded off a period which permanently decentralised the Holy Roman Empire, contributed directly to recurrent political crises in Sweden (1652–1721) and precipitated a complete regime change in Denmark (1660–5). Both France and England had come close to disintegration in the late 1640s and had to reconstruct from the 1660s onwards, but with very different outcomes for monarchy over the next half-century. In France, the huge fiscal burdens of Louis XIV's over-reaching foreign policy became a chronic liability, especially after 1683 when Colbert was no longer there to provide reliable information and financial restraint.[1] The disastrously misjudged revocation of the Edict of Nantes in 1685 had little of the propaganda effect Louis intended: rather, it caused significant economic loss for France and consternation all over Protestant Europe – fears that were reinforced by the many Huguenots who fled from France and settled in clusters in Protestant cities across northern Europe, from Amsterdam and London to Berlin, Copenhagen and Stockholm. In England, the revocation also directly aggravated anxieties surrounding the succession of James II in 1685: his open adherence to the Catholic faith confirmed the fears of Catholic resurgence which had already manifested themselves in the Popish plot, the Exclusion Crisis (1679–81) and some rebellions during the last years of Charles II. Public opinion in the Dutch Republic, already severely destabilised by the French invasion of 1672, was left in disarray by the resulting six-year war against France. When the *stadtholder* William III invaded England in

---

[1] For the availability to governments of reliable fiscal, economic and other information in France, see J. Soll, *The information master: Jean-Baptiste Colbert's secret state intelligence system* (Ann Arbor, 2011).

1688, and he and his wife Mary were given the English crown, domestic politics in both England and the Dutch Republic changed profoundly, as did the mutual relationship between these two major commercial powers.

In addition to these major changes in national and international affairs, there was also much in local and domestic politics to help generate public discussion. Severe economic dislocation, climate instability and resulting underemployment across much of Europe in the 1690s and early 1700s, reminiscent of the years around 1650, contributed substantially to a widespread mood of insecurity. All this was compounded by French aggression against the Holy Roman Empire which resulted in further turmoil from 1680: the War of the League of Augsburg (1688–97), the destructive Wars of the Spanish Succession (1701–14) and the Great Northern War (1700–21). Most of Europe was involved in these conflicts in one way or another, and the domestic costs were inescapable. Internal royal succession issues in several European monarchies added further complications: in Britain, the death of Queen Anne (1714) leading to the succession of a branch of the Stuarts through the Elector of Hanover (in accordance with the Act of Settlement of 1701); in France the death of Louis XIV (1715) and the succession of his five-year-old great grandson under a regency; in Sweden, a disputed succession when Charles XII was killed in a siege in 1718, leading to substantial constitutional change and real parliamentary sovereignty.

This chapter focuses on the profound repercussions these confrontations had on the substance, shape and processes of politics, as discussed in print, and on the factual news reporting which increasingly fuelled public interest. In England, some feared a return to the political instability of the 1640s and 50s, but elsewhere, too, commentators tried to make sense of the many difficulties of the years from 1685 to 1715. Significantly, religious disputes were greatly exacerbated not only by the French revocation of 1685, but also by persistent disunity within both the Catholic and several Protestant churches. As we will see, these religious disputes focused not just on church organisation and clerical powers, but also on the fundamental issues of belief which, as always, proved irreconcilable. Public disunity made it easier for governments and local authorities to claim that the maintenance of stability required stricter regulation of print. In effect, some controversies went underground (especially in England and the Netherlands), or shifted to less overtly political arenas. Yet heated argument continued around fundamental and fiercely contested visions of religious peace and a stable framework for civil society. At the same time, mass starvation and economic dislocation across much of Europe around 1696 and 1709 also focused attention on policies that might enhance prosperity and social utility.

Given how writers treated these strands in different but overlapping ways, it is difficult to categorise particular types of printed texts within distinct subject areas: fiction and non-fiction were often blurred, just as religion and philosophy overlapped with politics and the sciences. Yet changes in the overall annual number of printed items in Britain, France and the Netherlands show some distinctive patterns: as we noted in Chapter 1, the total number of new titles and reprints stabilised temporarily in the years after 1660 in those countries where we have the means to measure such trends with reasonable accuracy. In London, the annual average number of titles fell in the 1660s to around the 1640 level, picking up slightly in the 1670s. But during the 1680s annual output averaged twice that of the 1660s, reaching totals of over 2000 titles per annum, not unlike the levels of activity seen in the 1640s. The annual totals then dropped somewhat, with just a modest (and short-lived) increase in 1695 (the year the Licensing Act expired). Although we lack reliable figures for most of continental Europe, we know that in the Netherlands total output was fairly stable from the mid-1650s to 1671, but spiked in 1672, 1684 and 1688 (when the annual output increased temporarily by 50 per cent to over 1200 titles), then settling during the last decades of the century and the early 1700s. Provisional figures from the main German publishing centres confirm that the total production of printed items increased only very gradually in the 1670s and 1680s, before levelling off again. No doubt conflicting pressures would have affected most markets: a huge demand for news and information, set against the greater risks of publishing and distribution in a context of war.

Censorship and other mechanisms to restrict or suppress unacceptable printed material varied across Europe, depending in part on the state of civil and ecclesiastical power and their ability to collaborate. Measures of control were not particularly difficult to implement in cities where government was centralised, theological unanimity somehow maintained, economic growth modest and the market therefore relatively unadventurous – as for example in the two Scandinavian capitals, Copenhagen and Stockholm. By contrast, the relatively autonomous commercial cities in the Holy Roman Empire, such as Hamburg and Frankfurt, benefited from more commercially oriented local power structures where profit and free trade might be considered a higher priority than political subservience. However, it is worth noting that even in the most commercialised and independent towns of the Rhineland and the United Provinces, church and civil authorities continued to exercise substantial powers: in the Netherlands, for example, the ban on Hobbes and Spinoza in 1674 may have had only modest effect, but constant uncertainty undoubtedly forced radical authors, printers and booksellers to take elaborate protective measures to avoid the risk of imprisonment. The fate of the brothers Adriaen and Johannes Koerbagh reminds us that even the cosmopolitan Amsterdam authorities could be extraordinarily brutal: both brothers were imprisoned and interrogated by the city magistrates in 1668, accused of heresy and political subversion in print. Adriaen was given a huge fine with a ten-year prison sentence in the Rasphuis (workhouse), where he died shortly afterwards, in 1669, aged 37; his brother Johannes was eventually released, for want of clear evidence, but he never published anything again and died three years later.[2]

In practice, once stable governments were back after 1660, no place in Europe had anything approaching freedom of expression, and offenders, if caught, could expect harsh punishment intended as a deterrent to others. Nevertheless, cases continued to occur in those regions where subversive print and political dissent had already been in evidence in the middle decades of the seventeenth century. The newly assertive French monarchy of Louis XIV organised a police force from 1667, directed by La Reynie, whose ambitions can be gauged by the regulatory mechanisms he tried to impose on Paris and its printing industry. By the eighteenth century French authors faced a hugely complicated system, loosely (and not always effectively) organised by a Director of the Book Trade and operated by an army of unpaid volunteer censors – a system which we now know to have become almost unworkable and certainly extremely accident-prone, already by mid-century (below, Chapter 5). In practice, anywhere in Europe, censorship was bound to have more of a deterrent effect than any actual success in locating and repressing books: at best, the censorship system would make an example of a particular author or publisher who was caught, in the hope that the punishment (often very severe personal penalties and destruction of stock) would serve as a deterrent in general. But in France as elsewhere, the regulations were (probably deliberately) unclear and often inconsistent, and their implementation invariably haphazard and arbitrary, so fear of unpredictable punishment ensured that many authors had to exercise continuous and careful self-censorship.

In England after the Restoration, regular licensing through the Stationers Company was re-established by law (from 1662 onwards), but subject to renewal by parliament every two years. The legislation lapsed in 1679, was reinstated in 1685 and lapsed definitively in 1695.

[2] Israel, *Radical Enlightenment: philosophy and the making of modernity 1650–1750* (Oxford, 2001), 193–6; M. Wielema, 'Adriaan Koerbagh: Biblical criticism and Enlightenment', in W. van Bunge (ed.), *The early Enlightenment in the Dutch Republic 1650–1750* (Leiden, 2003), 61–80.

That, however, did not mean an end to press regulation.[3] Instead, creative use of libel legislation meant that authors and printers had to contend with a range of different unpredictable threats and restraints on what they could print. English copyright laws were tightened in 1710, so that publishers in effect could continue to control much of what went on sale (except illegal imports from Scotland and Ireland, not covered by English law). In practice that often meant predicting what might reliably make a profit in a society still very much on edge: ultimately, printers and publishers wanted to make money, and the publicity impact of libel prosecutions could cut both ways. The growth of newspapers presented a different kind of challenge, since continuity and reputation were crucial components of success. In practice, the imposition of a Stamp Duty in 1712 appears to have had only a temporary dampening effect on the insatiable demand for news. We should also note the potential political impact of theatre, a very popular form of entertainment with as much subversive potential as print. It was subjected to its own forms of control in the licensing legislation of 1735.

As the complexities and obstacles to effective print regulation became clearer, observers across literate Europe gradually became concerned not just about appropriate mechanisms for formal control of print, but also its fundamental purpose. The justifications for censorship and the prosecution of authors, publishers and booksellers were legal quagmires, beset by increasing confrontations, infringement, harassment and changes of policy aiming to restrict the ever-growing supply of print – especially of popular texts which might be deemed to undermine stability and deference. At the same time, censors were themselves routine readers, sometimes also authors and not infrequently closely associated with the printing industry they were supposed to regulate. Inevitably, therefore, censorship priorities, prosecutions and punishments were a matter of unstable compromise, based on interests and prejudices that to some extent reflected the preferences of those in power. Aberrations and inconsistencies aside, the kinds of text censors chose to repress can therefore tell us a great deal about the mental world they were supposed to represent.

---

[3] The significance of the lapse of the Licensing Act in 1695 should not be overstated. For the wider context, see G. C. Gibbs, 'Press and public opinion: prospective', in J. R. Jones (ed.), *Liberty secured? Britain before and after 1688* (Stanford, CA, 1992), 231–64; G. C. Gibbs, 'Government and the English press 1695 to the middle of the eighteenth century', in A. C. Duke and C. A. Tamse (eds.), *Too mighty to be free* (Zutphen, 1987), 87–105; W. St Clair, *The reading nation in the Romantic period* (Cambridge, 2004), 84–5.

Biblical Interpretation and the Power of Intolerance in Civil Society

The standard version of the Bible in western Europe before the Reformation, the vulgate version, attributed to St Jerome and fairly stable as a text since the fifth century, was itself a Latin translation from older Greek versions, which in turn were translations mostly from Hebrew and Aramaic.[4] Since Latin remained the language of the church in western Europe, vernacular translations of major sections of the Old or New Testament did not materialise for nearly a millennium. Renaissance interest in all classical texts, however, also affected the Bible, especially amongst critical readers who were concerned about discrepancies in liturgical practice. Close scrutiny of the Bible was always liable to raise accusations of heresy: major controversy had already surrounded the innovative approaches to translation and textual analysis adopted by John Wycliffe (died 1384) and John Huss (burnt at the stake in 1415). Much later, the great humanist scholar Desiderius Erasmus (1466–1536) had to follow a very cautious scholarly strategy in his enormous published output, keeping firmly to the middle ground in the confrontations over church reform erupting from 1517. Vernacular translation of the whole Bible was inevitable, but when it happened it had an irreversible impact on the whole Christian community: the German version by Martin Luther, compiled between 1522 and 1534, in effect made the Protestant-Catholic split permanent. On a practical level, Luther became the focal point for significant political alliances to ensure his demands for reform were not ignored. But on a theological level, detailed study of the Bible became fundamental to most of the Protestant churches that emerged during the sixteenth century. It took considerable time before vernacular translations into all the major western European languages were completed, but the process had become an essential component in virtually all forms of Protestantism, eventually creating several revised or alternative versions in any one language.

Translation is never straightforward – least of all for a 1000-year-old text which itself had been compiled from translations from several ancient languages, yet was regarded by many as an immutable cultural and religious icon. Inevitably, the search for 'accurate' translation not only initiated a new wave of religious disputes, pitching reformers and theologians into interminable controversy. It also guaranteed a lively interest in the classical languages, in dictionaries and in scholarly analysis that might

---

[4] On the complex history of the Bible, see J. Barton and J. Muddiman, *The Oxford Bible commentary* (Oxford, 2001); and E. Cameron (ed.), *The new Cambridge history of the Bible*, vol. III, from 1450 to 1750 (Cambridge, 2016).

clarify the precise meaning of difficult passages. But thorough textual exegesis also had the potential of raising doubts over the status of substantial sections not just of the apocrypha but also of the canonical texts at the heart of Christian (and in part Jewish) beliefs. Once discrepancies and contradictions within the Bible became clear, intelligent readers might also be more prone to question the power and control of a clergy already divided by Reformation disputes. Close reading of variant translations, and detailed study of the Bible itself, was almost certain to bring more doubts to even the most devout readers. This is not the place to discuss how far, in the century after the Reformation, scepticism, rational scrutiny and personal doubt was hidden below a necessary cover of ostensible outward religious conformity. But it is not difficult to understand why church authorities might well be alarmed at the thought of independent lay readers tackling such a difficult text unsupervised.

It is an oversimplification to say that textual analysis was resisted within the Catholic church, or successfully repressed for much longer in the Greek and Russian orthodox churches. Yet there is no doubt that those areas with a thriving printing industry had the most far-reaching challenges to text-based religious authority. In the west, the number of variant translations and interpretations offered to readers during the sixteenth century had (as we shall see) major long-term repercussions, but every significant European language had its own story, often reflecting the many dissenting groups into which western Christianity splintered. For many of the Protestant sects, the Bible alone (*sola scriptura*) was meant to be the foundation of their entire religious outlook, so translation of keywords became all-important. For Catholics, especially after the Council of Trent (1545–63), the translation process itself posed a threat, as scholars could not avoid following up the work of Erasmus in analysing and questioning texts that the church had traditionally regarded as immutable and sacred. Translating the Latin vulgate Bible at best necessitated full explanation to a lay audience, but also in effect opened up for scrutiny the authority of the church fathers and the prophets themselves. Inevitably, different parts of the Bible, the apocrypha and a range of patristic texts became unstable and disputable.

Most scholars agree that during the sixteenth century the primary focus was on theological interpretation, linguistics and semantics. It seems that the enthusiasm for producing new translations died down by the early seventeenth century, only to be replaced by a new phase of research which was at least as divisive. As long as the whole text had been considered sacrosanct and timeless, any critical analysis of particular sections, in terms of their value as historical records, was unacceptable. However, efforts to achieve meaningful translation led some commentators to start questioning both the chronology and reliability of particular narratives, and hence the historical authenticity and authorship of some parts of the Old and New Testament.[5] Such questioning had enormous philosophical, scientific and political consequences. Famously, the astronomical observations of Galileo landed him from 1610 in long-running and complex confrontations with established church doctrine and authority regarding issues ranging from Biblical time to theological interpretation of the shape of the universe – culminating in papal prosecution and a final trial in 1632. The punishment of Galileo has created much scholarly controversy and was evidently in part also a conflict of personalities and temperament, but it clearly also had implications for scientific research and for the application of empirical evidence.

Scholarly analysis of the Bible had major implications for core religious principles, including notions of predestination, free will and justification by faith, not to mention fundamental belief in the existence of God or the efficacy of prayer. But there were also practical questions of church governance, the mediating (or obstructing) role of the clergy, the authority of bishops, the legitimacy of church consistory courts, ecclesiastical control of education and poor relief, church funding and the rights of property, and a great number of other issues where church and lay community life intersected. Generally speaking, on theological issues Lutheran reformers adopted a relatively soft stance, while the Calvinist church followed a more rigorous logic. In the Netherlands, this had immediate political ramifications in the decades up to 1618: Remonstrants and Counter-Remonstrants became locked in battle over the degree of latitude permissible in individual and collective professions of faith within a well-ordered civic society – a controversy which split whole provinces and cities, and came close to breaking the United Provinces apart.

One of the key participants in the Dutch crisis of 1618, Hugo Grotius (1583–1645), is best known today for his 1625 tract on international law, *De jure belli ac pacis* (above, Chapter 2). But, during his long exile from the Netherlands, he also wrote extensively on matters of religion and textual interpretation. His writings against Calvinist fundamentalism, and in favour of reconciliation and compromise within Christianity, were more widely disseminated than his writings on law. His tract *On the truth of the Christian religion (De veritate religionis Christianiae)*, first published in 1627, was an uncritical affirmation of core Christian beliefs, set against paganism, Judaism and Islam. Grotius never openly questioned the

---

[5] R. H. Popkin, *The history of scepticism from Erasmus to Spinoza* (Berkeley, 1979); A. Matytsin, *The specter of skepticism in the age of Enlightenment* (Baltimore, 2016).

fundamental truth of the canonical texts and avoided the divisive theological problems generated by the Reformation; but he did try, through scholarship and historically informed translation, to offer cautious conciliatory explanation of some of those passages where analysis of either the language, the chronology or the historical context could help. His text, avoiding key points of contention and couched in quite general terms, clearly suited a wider readership: not only was it reprinted in Latin at least eleven times by 1715 (some in pocket-sized duodecimo format), but it had seven English printings, at least four in French and three in German. His *Discourses* on religious questions, and the various *Annotationes* of Biblical texts on which he was working in the last years of his life, had only a modest success in either Catholic or Protestant Europe.

From mid-seventeenth century onwards, a number of major studies of the Bible as a historical and narrative text led to some more startling conclusions with implications across the whole religious spectrum. Arguments for polygenism (the theory that humanity developed from several different origins), as presented in 1655 in the work of the seventeenth-century French millenarian writer Isaac La Peyrère (1596–1676), generated a long-lasting and very acrimonious controversy about the origins of mankind beyond the creation story in the Bible.[6] Far more serious, however, were the comprehensive and detailed analyses of the historical reliability of the Bible which appeared from 1650, first by Hobbes, soon pursued by other scholars including Baruch de Spinoza and Richard Simon. Spinoza had read La Peyrère and Simon knew him personally, so although their books were independent works coming from different perspectives, they can be seen as part of a new trend in Biblical scrutiny that could no longer be reserved for theologians and senior churchmen alone. Hobbes and Spinoza, in particular, tackled questions of scriptural historical reliability with such energy and clarity that the established churches had no alternative but to respond as best they could – by scholastic means, polemics and of course by direct censure and repression, justified on the basis of tradition and established authority. Inevitably, however, the dissemination of the controversial texts was liable to be enhanced whenever churchmen tried to suppress them – especially so in the case of Hobbes, because his was written in powerful and accessible English.

We noted earlier (see pp. 63–7 and 97–9) how Hobbes's *Leviathan* of 1651 took a very pessimistic view of human nature, arguing that a strong sovereign was essential for the preservation of an orderly and stable civil

---

[6] I. La Peyrère, *Prae-Adamitae* (1655); C. Kidd, *The forging of races: race and scripture in the Protestant Atlantic world 1600–2000* (Cambridge, 2006).

society. But Hobbes also went much further than any of his contemporaries in his discussion of Biblical texts. Chapter 12, 'Of Religion', opens with a statement that astounded many of his readers:

Seeing there are no signes, nor fruit of Religion, but in Man onely; there is no cause to doubt, but that the seed of Religion, is also onely in Man; and consisteth in some peculiar quality, or at least in some eminent degree therof, not to be found in other Living creatures. And first, it is peculiar to the nature of Man, to be inquisitive into the Causes of Events they see... Secondly, upon the sight of any thing that hath a Beginning, to think also it had a cause, which determined the same to begin... And when he cannot assure himselfe of the true causes of things, (for the causes of good and evill fortune for the most part are invisible,) he supposes causes for them, either such as his own fancy suggesteth; or trusteth to the Authority of other men...[7]

This was followed up in chapter 32, entitled 'Of the Principles of Christian Politiques', with a statement that much knowledge relies on supernatural revelations. But Hobbes then immediately states that 'we are not to renounce our Senses, and Experience; nor (that which is the undoubted Word of God) our naturall Reason': the power of reason has been given to us to use 'and therefore not to be folded up in the Napkin of an Implicite Faith, but employed in the purchase of Justice, Peace, and true Religion'. For although some aspects of belief are beyond rational demonstration or refutation, 'yet there is nothing [in religion] contrary to [reason]' if we exercise that reason properly. His confirmation that Christians agree that parts of the Bible are canonical may well have struck some readers as more than hinting the opposite. Hobbes at times questions the history and authorship of the Bible and notes that we may doubt how another person interprets a revelation which we ourselves did not have.[8] Inevitably, he also tackles the credibility of miracles (chapter 37) and the nature of the power of the church itself (chapter 42). His detailed commentary on selected passages from the Old and New Testament are framed to sustain what is really a political argument. Only belatedly do we reach an emollient statement that can hardly have pacified angry critics: 'I pretend not to advance any Position of my own, but onely to shew what are the Consequences that seem to me deducible from the Principles of Christian Politiques, (which are the holy Scriptures,) in confirmation of the Power of Civill Soveraigns, and the Duty of their Subjects.'[9] It is not difficult to see why passages such as these, written in accessible and powerful English prose, were soon regarded not just as heretical but also patently dangerous. Hobbes was engaging directly in a noisy and wide-reaching political argument in post-

---

[7] T. Hobbes, *Leviathan*, edited by N. Malcolm (Oxford, 2012), vol. II, 164.
[8] Hobbes, *Leviathan*, vol. III, 576–8.   [9] Hobbes, *Leviathan*, vol. III, 954.

civil-war England and did so in terms that went well beyond the limits of what most of his contemporaries regarded as acceptable.[10] It is no surprise that when accusations of heresy and blasphemy mounted against him, after 1664, the *Leviathan* was banned in England and elsewhere: Hobbes probably escaped severe punishment only by virtue of his age and his good connections (above, p. 65).

Almost concurrently, Spinoza was applying his detailed knowledge of Hebrew scholarship to a critical examination of the Hebrew Scripture (Old Testament), using his thorough understanding of Cartesian philosophy to sustain universal theories encompassing history, theology, politics and ethics. Spinoza knew Hobbes's Latin work, but may not have encountered the *Leviathan* until it was translated into Dutch or Latin (both versions printed in the Netherlands, 1667–8). As we noted earlier, Spinoza's *Tractatus theologico-politicus* (1670) and his unfinished *Tractatus politicus* (published posthumously in 1677 as part of the complete edition of his writings) were intended by the author to appear only in Latin, in order deliberately to minimise controversy and the risk of reprisals (above, p. 67). In all his works, Spinoza deployed a rigorous deductive process of reasoning that was more theoretical and intentionally less accessible than the forthright style of Hobbes. Nevertheless, we find some striking arguments that were bound to cause controversy even in Latin, as in chapter 18, where he makes clear:

1. How disastrous it is for both religion and the state to give ministers of religion any right to make decrees or to handle state affairs; and how greatly general political stability is increased if these ministers are not allowed to give responses except when asked, and at other times must only teach and practise what is received and hallowed by custom.
2. How dangerous it is to apply religious law to matters purely speculative, and to legislate concerning beliefs about which it is common or possible for men to dispute; for tyranny is at its worst where the opinions to which everyone has an inalienable right are regarded as criminal. In fact, where this happens, the supreme tyrant is usually the anger of the mob...[11]

---

[10] J. Parkin, *Taming the Leviathan: the reception of the political and religious ideas of Thomas Hobbes in England 1640–1700* (Cambridge, 2007), traces the very extensive reactions to Hobbes over the following decades. In particular, the fact that his analysis of the Bible was both scholarly and in English made it, in the eyes of some, a uniquely dangerous text because it could reach independent lay readers.

[11] B. Spinoza, *Tractatus theologico-politicus* ([Amsterdam], 1670), cited from the English translation in A. G. Wernham (ed.), *Benedict de Spinoza: the political works* (Oxford, 1958), 197–9. J. Israel, *Radical Enlightenment: philosophy and the making of modernity 1650–1750* (Oxford, 2001), 275–85, notes probably eight separate printings of the *Tractatus* during the 1670s, though it is of course impossible to establish how many actual copies were produced in each printing.

Spinoza not only wanted to exclude the clergy from interfering in politics, but also warned against excessive doctrinal regulation in areas where some degree of latitude was both unavoidable and conducive to peace and stability in civil society. No wonder the Dutch churches attacked his work as dangerous and heretical, leading to a formal ban in 1674. Not surprisingly, Spinoza held back publication of his other major work. Instead, a complete edition in Latin was published in great secrecy after his death in 1677, organised by his close friends including the experienced non-conformist publisher Jan Rieuwertsz.[12] The Dutch authorities, alarmed even more by the Dutch translation that was also launched, again prohibited the sale of any of Spinoza's writings in 1678. But the false imprint and underground trading network seems to have secured a wide dissemination: the complete edition is commonly found in many major libraries today and became an icon of heresy and subversion especially amongst those who went by hearsay rather than reading it thoroughly.

During the 1670s, at the other end of the religious spectrum, the Oratorian priest Richard Simon (1638–1712) adopted a more concilia-tory historical approach from within the Catholic church. The publica-tion of his *Histoire critique du vieux Testament* in 1678 nevertheless soon rightly earned him a reputation as one of the most independent-minded and controversial Catholic scholars. In the preface, he explicitly denounced Spinoza and made clear that only detailed historical and exegetical analysis could demonstrate current errors in interpretation and understanding. He noted that 'first of all, it is impossible to gain a perfect understanding of the sacred books unless one already knows the different circumstances of the text of these books, according to different times and different places'. He added that although it was dangerous to regard some sections as more divine than others, nevertheless the texts that survived were those intended for general use by the people and therefore did not necessarily constitute the complete story. The rest of his long and detailed book was neatly organised around a critical evalua-tion of the Hebrew text, a systematic discussion of existing translations and a number of specific problems arising from the translation of parti-cular passages.[13] Significantly, the book had initially been cleared by the

---

[12] B.d.S. [B. Spinoza], *Opera posthuma* (Hamburg [actually publ. by J. Rieuwertsz, Amsterdam], 1677).

[13] The citations are translated not from the original 1678 edition seized by the French authorities, but from a new edition published two years later: *Histoire critique du vieux Testament, par le R.P. Richard Simon, prestre de la congrégation de l'Oratoire* (Paris, 1680; 612 pages in quarto format, nearly a quarter of a million words, in a high-quality printing).

French censors but, once the implications of Simon's argument were fully understood, this decision was overturned and his book seized and banned. Various versions of the text, and sequels for the New Testament, appeared over the next two decades,[14] each analysing the historical dimensions of the Bible in terms that caused controversy both within his own Catholic order (which expelled him) and amongst Protestant theologians. Amongst those who engaged Simon in public disputation in print was the Calvinist-Remonstrant theologian Jean Le Clerc (1657–1736), whose *Sentimens de quelques théologiens de Hollande* (1685), and the subsequent rebuttals, indicate how far concerns about the nature of the Bible as a text now affected the whole spectrum of Christian churches.

The examples cited here are merely the best known from a growing output of theological polemical writings in the period 1685–1720. In France, the Netherlands, Scotland and the German lands, in particular, these polemics proved difficult to control. They created new ways of questioning not just core beliefs but also traditions of church governance, the self-reinforcing role of the clergy as mediators between God and ordinary worshippers, the nature and purpose of religious symbolism and art, the precise form of church services, the style and substance of preaching, and much else.[15] Bitter disagreements within Christianity were of course nothing new, but the presentation of the argument was. Most fundamentally, the reliance of previous generations on divine revelation, taking the Bible as God's word, had now been problematised. Historical analysis, demonstrating that the Bible was a composite text of variable accuracy, could not be dismissed, but had to be addressed in detail. Any such discussion, of course, merely served to alert lay readers to the specific problems, not least because a growing proportion of the texts were now written in the vernacular rather than being presented as Latin academic texts. With an apparently almost insatiable market for sermons, polemics and vitriolic counterarguments, print served to empower lay readers and certainly challenged the exclusive authority of the established churches. The aspiration to have a 'priesthood of all believers' seemed to

---

[14] Simon's main impact seems to have been explosive but fairly brief: after the first French printing of 1678, there were at least four further French printings of the commentary on the Old Testament (1680, 1681, 1685 and 1689), two in Latin and two in English (all in the 1680s); while works by him on the New Testament had six printings in French (1689–1702), with three in English and two in German.

[15] A. Raffe, *The culture of controversy: religious arguments in Scotland 1660–1714* (Woodbridge, 2012) analyses the religious controversies in Scotland. On the wider public debate, see K. Bowie, *Scottish public opinion and the Anglo-Scottish union 1699–1707* (Woodbridge, 2007).

be coming all too true, at the obvious expense of the authority of the clergy of the established churches themselves, Catholic as well as Protestant.

Assessing the dissemination and reception of any one individual text, however, can be difficult. The traditional approach by historians of ideas, locating evidence of influence by noting citations and refutations in the writings of subsequent authors, is problematised by the levels of deliberate ambiguity which authors invariably had to adopt just in order to survive. For the troubled last years of the late seventeenth century, it is more instructive to examine how writers experimented with unconventional forms of writing in order to reach a deliberately problematised conclusion. A prime example is the French Protestant in exile in Rotterdam, Pierre Bayle (1647–1706), who in his monumental *Dictionnaire historique et critique* (first published in Rotterdam, 1696–9, with a second edition in 1702) used the format of an encyclopedia to present persuasively objective information on a wide range of key individuals. He included an exceptionally long and notoriously ambiguous article on Spinoza, whom he describes as 'Jewish by birth, then deserter of Judaism, and finally atheist, but systematic atheism of an entirely novel kind'. Bayle explains in a very long footnote what he means by systematic atheism, sprinkling this footnote with additional marginal notes citing all kinds of scholars in various languages including Latin and Greek. Towards the end of the article, Bayle notes that:

It is not true that [Spinoza's followers] were numerous. Very few people are suspected of adhering to his doctrine; and amongst those who are under such suspicion, there are few who have studied it; and amongst these, there are few who have understood it, and have not been put off by the embarrassments and impenetrable abstractions which one finds there. [Inserted in a marginal note:] That is the reason why there are people who think that one should not refute him. See [Bayle's journal] *Les Nouvelles de la Rep des Lettres*, June 1684, art. 6, p. 388–9.[16]

Although it is very difficult to reproduce the famously laborious scholarly layout of Bayle's pages, it is worth noting that the main text was typically fairly brief, sometimes occupying just a few lines at the top of the large folio page, with elaborate footnotes, marginal notes – and marginal notes to the footnotes – occupying all the rest of the space. Bayle's material was laid out in articles under keywords (mostly personal names, all historic in the sense that no living person was included). But by making the text almost three-dimensional in this way, covering a vast selection of alternative viewpoints, citing scholarly references and (as here) even reviews in

---

[16] P. Bayle, *Dictionaire* [sic] *historique et critique* (Rotterdam, 1697), vol. II, part 2, 1083–1100 (this passage translated from p.1100).

a journal published twelve years earlier, he could disguise the most controversial arguments, and either totally confuse his readers about what his real opinions were, or force them to try to think about their own processes of reasoning.

Bayle's work quickly attained both notoriety and widespread acclaim, as much for its innovative presentation as for its careful scholarship. A few years earlier, in 1693, Bayle had been stripped of his professorship and salary at Rotterdam, following accusations from the consistory that his critical opinions were dangerous to the Calvinist church, so it is hardly surprising that he took particular care to disguise his theological and political views in the *Dictionnaire*. Despite the substantial cost of such a large-format and complex printing, his *Dictionnaire* became standard reading amongst the French-speaking elite across Europe, with at least ten separate printings. Its first English version appeared in 1710, followed by two further printings, while a German version of 1740–4 had an abridged reprint in 1779.[17] What clearly fascinated readers was the way ideas could be retrieved by circuitous use of footnotes and references (much like a modern online hypertext) – a technique that did not escape notice amongst his hostile critics, but made it more difficult to pin him down. The *Dictionnaire* became a versatile model for a number of major encyclopedias published during the eighteenth century.

Genuine religious toleration (accepting that there might be several different but equally valid systems of belief) was scarcely conceivable in any part of early modern Europe. More grudging concessions could take the form of civic tolerance (allowing unavoidable differences of belief, as long as they caused no disturbance) or theological tolerance (accepting specific variants of interpretation and liturgy, as ways towards salvation, provided these were not in direct conflict with stated articles of faith). But an additional argument could now also be made (on good empirical evidence) that civil society might function perfectly well – in some cases better – if matters of religious conviction were kept out of the public domain altogether and left to the discretion of the individual. Such full acceptance of a peaceful coexistence of a diversity of religious beliefs was, as we have already noted, totally at odds with seventeenth-century ways of thinking. In the German lands, specific and narrowly defined rights of religious self-determination had been devolved to princes and territorial governments in 1555, and had been further sanctioned in law in the Peace of Westphalia of 1648, but no-one assumed that individual freedom of

---

[17] On German interest in Bayle, see I. Dingel, 'Die Rezeption Pierre Bayles in Deutschland', in H. Duchhardt and C. Scharf (eds.), *Interdisziplinarität und Internationalität: Wege und Formen der Rezeption der französischen und der britischen Auklärung in Deutschland und Russland im 18. Jahrhudert* (Mainz, 2004), 51–63.

conscience was a personal right. Even the Electors of Brandenburg, keen to grant minimal civil liberties to members of certain religious minorities in order to attract useful and productive citizens, did not develop these policies into general principles of religious freedom, or grant legal civic equality to religious non-conformists. Right through to the late eighteenth century, European governments experimented with various limited policies of this kind, usually to gain economic and social advantage from the recurrent crises of religious refugees.[18] Louis XIV's revocation of the Edict of Nantes was merely the most blatant and misjudged manifestation of the kinds of religious intolerance that were still fundamental in most parts of Europe. Although Jewish communities were sometimes granted minimal civic rights in specific towns, in order to enhance commercial life, their position remained even more precarious, subject to all kinds of discrimination, with few genuine attempts at merely modest improvement until the mid-eighteenth century.[19]

Significantly, the phrase 'liberty [freedom] of speech' does not appear in normal English usage until the late sixteenth century, and the first occurrence of 'liberty of the press' noted in the Oxford English Dictionary dates from 1633, becoming more common from 1680. Even more controversial was any hint of toleration of religious dissent, essentially unacceptable according to seventeenth-century notions of commonwealth or monarchy: since it was assumed there could only be one will of God, deviance of any kind was heresy and connivance in the work of the Devil, something that a magistrate was entitled to confront and punish. In this context, we can perhaps understand why John Locke (1632–1704) continued after 1689 to publish most of his work anonymously, especially since it was designed to appeal to a much broader audience than for example Spinoza's. The full-length book by Locke on *The reasonableness of Christianity* (1695) was a characteristically moderate and scholarly defence of Protestant adherence to scriptural foundations. It achieved two reprints during his lifetime, two reprints in the complete editions collected after his death and a further four independent reprints later during the eighteenth century. Significantly, it also had five printings in French, two in German and one each in Swedish and Dutch. His *Epistola de tolerantia* (1689) was different in nature: a quite short tract of 61 pages, it presented a closely reasoned but readily accessible practical argument

---

[18] O. P. Grell and R. Porter (eds.), *Toleration in Enlightenment Europe* (Cambridge, 2000).
[19] One of the first serious attempts to consolidate Jewish civic rights, beyond Spinoza's general arguments, was John Toland's *Reasons for naturalizing the Jews* (London, 1714), a characteristically outspoken text which was not reprinted: see J. Champion, 'Toleration and citizenship in Enlightenment England: John Toland and the naturalization of the Jews, 1714–1753', in Grell and Porter (eds.), *Toleration in Enlightenment Europe*, 133–56.

for not using state power to enforce religious conformity – an argument that Locke had first begun to draft many years earlier, while he was in Germany and Holland, but which now in 1689 had immediate political relevance.[20] Apparently without the author's permission, the tract was quickly translated by William Popple and published in London as a (still anonymous) *Letter on toleration*. The English version had at least another seven reprintings during the eighteenth century, a French translation (published as part of Locke's complete works in 1710, reprinted in 1732), a separate French version in 1764, a German translation in 1710, two Dutch printings and a belated Swedish version in 1793.

Still without acknowledging his authorship, Locke immediately followed up with a *Second* and a *Third letter* (1690 and 92), this time in English, while a *Fourth letter* and a *Discourse on miracles* were published after his death. These texts had countless responses and citations amongst contemporaries across Protestant Europe, with its many smaller dissenting and radical groups (such as Anabaptists, Socinians and Unitarians). Locke's text on toleration was written from a pragmatic point of view to suit the specific English need for a separation of the authority of state and church, but he was also applying Spinoza's much more theoretical and universalist view that toleration itself created no inherent political problem, if society was able to live according to rational principles. If Spinoza was a visionary, Bayle wrapped his arguments in scholarly references and academic ambiguity, while Pufendorf suggested very limited toleration merely as part of a historical narrative. For Locke, however, the argument for toleration was based on non-negotiable political necessity and required all members of society to be loyal to the sovereign state (an argument which, in England in 1689, unavoidably excluded Catholics, whose primary loyalty was assumed to be to Rome). Locke was also making an unambiguous and explicit general case for the separation of ecclesiastical and civil power. This no doubt explains why he scrupulously retained anonymity in these texts and refused to acknowledge his authorship even when it became clear that there would be no resulting prosecution.

By the 1690s, therefore, the idea of equating the authority of princely power with God's kingdom on earth – even the idea of a hierarchical 'great chain of being' from God and king down to mankind and beyond – could no longer be taken for granted. Scrutiny of the Bible as a historical text had revealed major inconsistencies and problems of interpretation; and actual political experiences in different parts of Europe had created fertile ground both for popular misgivings and, even more, for detailed and

---

[20] [J. Locke], *Epistola de tolerantia* (London, 1689).

comprehensive analysis of faith-based ideologies, theories of power and political practice in civil society. In such a climate of uncertainty, some observers had difficulty forgetting either the English radical experiments with decentralised, even democratic, church governance in the 1640s and 1650s, or the practical failure of the Dutch Calvinists to impose coherent doctrinal control in the United Provinces. The writings of both Bayle and Simon indicate that Catholic Europe was also exposed to these difficulties; and the serious personal reprisals suffered by both men, at the instigation of religious traditionalists everywhere, merely increased public awareness. It is no surprise, therefore, that major efforts were made to reconsolidate traditional thinking about both the Bible and the nature of princely authority.

In France, divine-right monarchy was itself reshaped and presented on the basis of theology and selective Biblical quotation, as in the sermons and writings of the French court preacher for Louis XIV, Jacques-Bénigne Bossuet (1627–1704). In the Protestant parts of the German lands, major last-minute reconstruction was attempted by leading intellectuals such as the conservative philosopher-politician Gottfried Wilhelm Leibniz (1646–1716). Leibniz gained a great reputation as a mathematician, scientist, librarian and historian, and served as counsellor at the electoral court of Hannover for the last forty years of his life. He was a prolific writer (in Latin, French and German), but his only widely read published work was his *Essais de theodicée* of 1710, a spirited defence of traditional Christian unity, ecumenical re-unification and the inevitability of God's will (later lampooned by Voltaire). In the words of Patrick Riley, 'he struggled throughout his life to fuse Platonism, Cartesianism, Christian voluntarism, scholasticism, Hobbesian mechanism and a number of other doctrines into a plausible whole'.[21] Such a formidable agenda meant confronting the perceived threats also posed by Spinoza (whom Leibniz had met personally in 1676), Bayle and many more younger writers around the turn of the century. Leibniz also commented on Hobbes's analysis of the power of the sovereign over religious beliefs, questioning his use of scripture. Although Leibniz had some general impact on German thinking, he seems to have had fewer readers than for example the historian Samuel Pufendorf (1632–94) or the noted liberal and rationalist professor of law at the new Halle University, Christian Thomasius (1655–1728).[22]

---

[21] P. Riley (ed. and transl.), *Leibniz: political writings* (Cambridge, 1988), 2; M. R. Antognazza, *Leibniz: an intellectual biography* (Cambridge, 2009); F. Biederbeck, I. Dingel and W. Li (eds.), *Umwelt und Umweltgestaltung: Leibniz' politisches Denken* (Göttingen, 2015).

[22] G. W. Leibniz, *Theodicée* (Amsterdam, 1710) was reprinted three times over the next decade, in its original French, and by mid-eighteenth century had had one further French printing, at least four in German (1720–44) and one in Latin (1739). On the broader

Impact of Forbidden Reading

The texts discussed so far might well suggest that differences of opinion over godly governance were becoming irreconcilable: for some acute observers, religious guiding principles did not fit well with political pragmatism as foundations for good governance and a stable civil society. But were these merely academic debates, conducted amongst scholars, philosophers and the educated elite? The works of Hobbes, Simon, Locke and Bayle were cited by other writers, alongside published rebuttals, providing evidence of impact amongst intellectuals – but was that enough to reach a broad readership? How can the historian of ideas demonstrate whether innovative new texts had any significant impact beyond a narrow circle of dedicated readers? These questions are not easy to answer, but the circumstances of publication and dissemination of a given text, and the style of argument in the text itself, can give clues as to both intended and actual readership. Many of the books discussed so far were not immediately banned in the place they were published – perhaps because they had been written with an educated readership in mind, so as not to appeal too openly to a popular audience. Cautious writers on theology and politics still published in Latin: in context, the decision by Hobbes to switch to English in 1651 was itself a major watershed. By the 1680s, many more authors opted for their vernacular language as a matter of course, but, as we have seen in the case of Locke, not all without hesitation. Bayle and Simon both used French, their own language, yet aimed for a meticulous academic style of writing far removed from the popular market. So language and quality of production can provide us with obvious clues about the intended market. Most of the books discussed so far were in any case fairly high-quality printings probably intended by the publisher to be restricted to wealthier buyers.

To these indicators we can now also add patterns of translation, on the grounds that the republic of letters was by the later seventeenth century relying increasingly on the major native European languages, with French as the international norm. This is clearly reflected in the first experiments to create what was soon to become a major feature of Enlightenment publishing: the independent review journal disseminating summaries of major new books. Bayle's own journal, *Les Nouvelles de la république des lettres*, launched in 1684, became a model for others across Europe, providing a wonderful reflection of the kind of new work that editors thought their readers would want to know about. With French as the language of choice, a real international reputation could now be created,

German early Enlightenment, see also U. Goldenbaum (ed.), *Appell an das Publikum: die öffentliche Debatte in der deutschen Aufklärung 1687–1796* (2 vols., Berlin, 2004).

which in turn might lead to translation into other vernacular languages (as we have noted already in the case of Locke).

However, patterns of translation can also give us counter-indications – of texts that appear not to have crossed linguistic and cultural barriers particularly well. It is worth noting that some writers who may have been regarded as controversial or significant in one national context appear not to have gained much resonance, amongst either elite or popular readers, outside their own context. Particularly surprising in this context is the Dutch-born writer Bernhard Mandeville (1670–1733) whose satirical stories *The grumbling hive* (1705) and *The fable of the bees* (1714, with reprints, and Part 2 added in 1729) portrayed a form of social organisation based on self-interest rather than Christian morality. Though well-suited to their English readers, these stories were not translated into his own native language, and only reached French readers after his death (1740 and 1750 editions). Equally interesting is the apparent lack of success of the distinguished writer Henri de Boulainvilliers (1658–1722), translator for Spinoza's *Ethics* and author of several analyses of French history: his work seems to have gained only limited and belated circulation in French, and no success in other languages.

This raises more profound questions about the nature of shifts in consensus opinion. It is now clear that a number of issues remained highly contentious during the last decades of the seventeenth century: church–state relations, church governance, discussion of (very limited) religious toleration, the spiritual foundations of royal power, and hence far broader questions of legitimate political authority and order in civil society. These issues could rarely be discussed openly, at least in general terms: rather, they tended to become contentious and 'public' within specific and local power confrontations. Equally, further scrutiny of the language of the Bible itself, and hence interest in its translation, was most likely to generate disagreement when channelled through new styles of preaching amongst enthusiasts and sectarians, or when church authorities confronted popular adherence to superstitions and traditional forms of worship. Some non-conformist splinter groups turned inwards towards a more personalised and emotional religious response, as in the Pietist movement in Lutheran Germany from the 1690s onwards, amongst the Methodists in England from the 1730s, and elsewhere.[23] Many such revivalist movements met in 'conventicles' (unauthorised prayer

---

[23] J. Sheehan, *The Enlightenment Bible* (Princeton, 2005); S. J. Barnett, *The Enlightenment and religion: the myths of modernity* (Manchester, 2003); on Pietist initiatives to print cheap Bibles for universal access, see R. Gawthrop and G. Strauss, 'Protestantism and literacy in early modern Germany', *Past & Present*, 104 (1984), 31–55; for a very different, exceptionally outward-turning comparative global view of religion, see also L. Hunt,

meetings and scriptural study groups organised by laymen), inevitably causing recurrent concern amongst senior clergy alarmed at the prospect of losing control over popular beliefs and collective behaviour.

Clearly the full range of factors in what a historian once described as the 'crisis of the European mind'[24] cannot be discerned through print alone. Amongst intellectuals, there was a lively exchange of manuscript works, personal marginal annotations in printed works and voluminous comments and discussion in private correspondence (making up the 'republic of letters' and its peripheries). Amongst the broader urban population, there is ample evidence of 'subversive' talk, disrupted church services, feuding town councils and drink-fuelled arguments – mostly now beyond the reach of historians, except through witness statements (if the authorities intervened) and other reports. But even in accepting these limitations, do we have solid grounds for attributing at least some of the disputatious uncertainty to the impact of printed work? Was religious belief genuinely threatened by scepticism and scholarly questioning, or just made out to be so? Was there a real shortfall in persuasive responses from traditionalists, or are we looking at an array of chaotic and incoherent skirmishes between belligerent writers, using the opportunities of print when they could? Did the sense of urgency come from the perceived threats to religious dogmas and liturgy, or on the contrary from more worldly practical problems created by the political and ideological instability of the decades from 1685 up to 1721? Was politics in effect becoming more secular, in tacit recognition of Locke's argument that magistrates could not, and should not, try to impose an unattainable spiritual unanimity?

None of these questions can be answered simply by assuming that the new ideas offered in the 1680s and 90s were widely understood; nor, of course, can we assume that what we see in printed texts accurately reflects deeper underlying uncertainties, when these could only be expressed publicly in coded language or by means of indirect allusions. More recent research has pointed instead to the diversity of individuals developing new ways of arguing their points of view and the shifting networks across unlikely ideological battle lines. Ann Thomson has revealed that much was indeed about fundamental philosophical and religious positions, but that questions of free theological discussion and freedom of thought sometimes created unexpected alliances and agreements both in England and on the continent. She notes how as historians we need to

M. C. Jacob and W. Mijnhardt, *The book that changed Europe: Picart and Bernard's 'Religious ceremonies of the world'* (Cambridge, MA, 2010).

[24] P. Hazard, *La crise de la conscience européenne 1680–1715* (Paris, 1935), translated as *The crisis of the European mind* (London, 1953).

avoid falling into the trap of identifying with the churchmen and politically conservative propagandists of the decades around 1700 who believed there was 'a single coherent network with a coherent philosophy aimed at undermining the existing religious and political establishment': accepting their assumption 'that all expressions of heterodox thought were proofs of an atheistic conspiracy to undermine Christianity and even all religion and to promote republicanism' will merely blind us to the real tangle of viewpoints, and sometimes unlikely associations, that drove these discussions onwards.[25]

Understanding how these private and necessarily concealed networks could operate requires a great deal of groundwork. One of the best-known polemicists whose career and influence depended almost entirely on his wide-ranging contacts was John Toland (1670–1722). He was a student at the universities of Glasgow, Edinburgh, Leiden and Oxford, ended up publishing most of his work from London, but had very extensive connections right across the social scale from princely courts (including Electress Sophia of Hanover) to local coffee houses, and including wealthy friends (such as the third earl of Shaftesbury, Anthony Collins, the Quaker Benjamin Furly and Sir Robert Molesworth), especially those who owned large collections of illegal books. His first major publication was a short tract, *Christianity not mysterious* (1696). Even the title would have alarmed conservative churchmen and although the first edition was published anonymously, Toland added his name to a second printing within a few months. His simple argument poured scorn on those who were attached to mysteries, asserting that even 'the poor, who are not suppos'd to understand Philosophical Systems, soon apprehended the Difference between the plain convincing Instructions of Christ, and the intricate ineffectual Declamations of the Scribes'.[26] At just 176 octavo pages in generous typeface, sprinkled with biblical quotations but devoid of academic pretensions, the tract was clearly intended for the widest possible readership. It attracted many responses, some accusing him of being a Socinian (Unitarian) or a deist, but these merely gave Toland an opportunity to reply in print. In the present context, it is important to emphasise that not only did he readily engage with his critics at whatever level might stir up a good argument, but he also deliberately served as

---

[25] A. Thomson, 'Toland, Dodwell, Swift and the circulation of irreligious ideas in France: what does the study of international networks tell us about the "radical Enlightenment"?' (*SVEC* 2013: 12, Oxford, 2013), 159–75, quoting from p. 175; A. Thomson, *Bodies of thought: science, religion and the soul in the early enlightenment* (Oxford, 2008); A. Thomson, *L'âme des lumières: le débat sur l'être humain entre religion et science* (Seyssel, 2013).

[26] J. Toland, *Christianity not mysterious: or a treatise shewing, that there is nothing in the Gospel contrary to reason, nor above it* (London, 1696), Introduction, xxi.

a conduit for the popularisation of key philosophical ideas initiated by others. He certainly knew how to communicate with audiences and readers at all social levels, whether in conversation, in unpublished manuscripts, or printed texts. This made him an influential disseminator, but much of this impact is visible only indirectly.[27]

Christianity not mysterious stands in noticeable contrast to Locke' s much longer and more cautious *The reasonableness of Christianity* (published the year before, 1695). But what we also now know is that both had contacts within diffuse but lively intellectual underworlds only partly visible in print. Toland, like many others, thrived on private conversations, more or less formal disputes, and, not least, unpublished manuscripts copied and lent amongst thinkers who were prepared to explore the bounds of what was possible, with or without permission. Contacts between radical thinkers and writers were often made by personal introduction or even chance encounters in the thriving urban communities stretching from London across the Netherlands to the western parts of the Holy Roman Empire (eventually extending south to Basel, Neuchâtel and even Venice). By definition, such contacts are difficult to map, and the nature of the philosophical interests of the participants can be only partly determined from copies of manuscripts, private letters and other elusive evidence. Martin Mulsow has done richly rewarding forensic work on the German intellectual underground in the years 1680–1720, noting how this early philosophical radicalism requires us to modify the traditional view of the early German Enlightenment as moderate and limited in scope. Some of the important participants are not well known today – amongst them Samuel Crell (1660–1747), Nikolaus Hieronymus Grundling (1671–1729) and Johann Joachim Müller (1661–1733). Müller may have been the originator of one of the most notoriously provocative (and elusive) anti-religious tracts of the age, *De tribus impostoribus,* portraying Judaism, Christianity and Islam alike as the work of impostors.[28] It is clear from Mulsow's research that there are far more leads to be pursued before we can fully

---

[27] J. Champion, *The pillars of priestcraft shaken* (Cambridge, 1992); J. Champion, *Republican learning: John Toland and the crisis of Christian culture 1696–1722* (Manchester, 2003). For an example of how elusive some of the most radical texts could be, see M. Hunter, '*Pitcairneana*: an atheist text by Archibald Pitcairne', *The Historical Journal*, 59 (2016), 595–621.

[28] Also known as the *Traité des trois imposteurs,* or *Book of the three impostors* and a number of disguising variant titles, this work has puzzled historians for many years and its attribution remains in doubt. It appears to have been best known in manuscript form, although a clandestine printing took place around 1719. See J. Israel, *Radical Enlightenment: philosophy and the making of modernity 1650–1750* (Oxford, 2001), 302–6 and 694–700; and M. Mulsow, *Enlightenment underground: radical Germany 1680–1720* (Charlottesville, VA, 2015, translated and abridged from the German *Moderne aus dem Untergrund,* Hamburg, 2002).

understand this intellectual underworld; but already he has made clear that radicals and conservatives sometimes learnt more from each other than one might have expected on the basis of published texts, even if precise meanings are often concealed by satire, irony and provocation. He has also made clear that there were no obvious limits to how far some thinkers were prepared to go in challenging all accepted ideas – fragmentary and inconsistent though some of these attempts were.[29]

Many of these early Enlightenment exchanges focused on issues of personal access to (or loss of) faith, knowledge of God and forms of worship. Wider philosophical concerns were also affected in the decades before and after 1700, notably amongst those trying to align Cartesian rational philosophy with changing perceptions of matter and the soul, or amongst those searching for what was loosely called 'deism' or other forms of free thinking.[30] But in addition, there were immediate questions concerning the nature of civil society itself, raised by recurrent religious-political crises in different parts of Europe: the French Huguenot predicament after 1685; the Jacobite cause in Britain after 1689; the fiercely contested loyalties of sectarians, Covenanters, Presbyterians and Episcopalians in Scotland throughout these years; or the recurrent Jansenist crises in France seeking reform of the Catholic church in the last years of Louis XIV's reign and beyond – as well as the precarious and grudging toleration disputes relating to the religious dissenter or revivalist groups in the Netherlands and parts of the German lands which we have already noted. In all of these cases, opposing religious perspectives had the potential to create fundamental challenges to prevailing political authority (monarchical, republican or local). Dissenting religious justifications for the right of resistance or rebellion were enormously powerful, precisely because they could claim higher spiritual or moral authority.

Significantly, all of the areas affected by such confrontations also generated substantial quantities of printed polemics, newspaper reports and even ideologically tinged almanac stories.[31] In order to minimise the risk of prosecution, many of these texts relied on subtexts, motifs and symbols that were deliberately ambiguous or obscure. The impact both on oral communication and on print culture is therefore very difficult to

---

[29] Mulsow, *Enlightenment underground*; for a very controversial attempt to translate the Bible, see P. S. Spalding, *Seize the book, jail the author: Johann Lorenz Schmidt and censorship in eighteenth-century Germany* (Purdue, 1998).

[30] For detailed discussion of the religious and philosophical divisions amongst European intellectuals, see also Israel, *Radical Enlightenment;* and for a different perspective, M. C. Jacob, *The radical Enlightenment: pantheists, freemasons and republicans* (London, 1981).

[31] D. Parrish, *Jacobitism and anti-jacobitism in the British Atlantic world 1688–1727* (London, 2017), 66–88, points to different forms of dissemination across the Atlantic.

evaluate. It is likely that these publications were too context-specific to attract long-term relevance (as evidenced in citations, reprints or adaptations), yet they undoubtedly helped keep the underlying questions alive for years to come.[32] Jansenism in particular became a very strong focal point for political resistance, especially in France, even as its religious foundations changed over time.[33]

We may now be in a better position to trace the impact of subversive thinking in literate circles and the 'republic of letters': we can see clear evidence that outspoken printed texts were in demand amongst dissenters, religious splinter groups and their preachers, and even in coffee houses and other social spaces during these years of turbulence around the turn of the century. Politics and religious beliefs were of course never far apart: both had to do with power and control, and contemporaries took an alarmingly confrontational view of ecclesiastical politics, linking these intimately to questions of legitimate power and the use of authority in civil society. Fears of heresy and frequent resort to accusations of 'atheism' often clouded the argument, at a time when outright statements of disbelief were dangerous and hence extremely rare. Authors no doubt wrote for specific readers in narrowly defined contexts, and successful writers such as Locke, Bayle and Thomasius were acutely aware that they worked in an unstable environment. In effect they competed against, and were at times challenged by, some very creative, radical and subversively populist writers who were fully able to convey religious, philosophical and political ways of thinking to new readers. It is misleading to see the resulting tensions as simply binary, between writers and readers on one hand, and censors and political authorities on the other. Writers were themselves acutely aware of how difficult it was to attract or keep readers, remain relevant and yet avoid alienating traditionalists or censors. In the more buoyant cities, authors, publishers, readers, intellectuals and the authorities all faced new and uncertain challenges in matters of content, style, market distribution and intended impact.

---

[32] See for example D. Soulard, 'Les journalistes du Refuge et la diffusion de la pensée politique de John Locke auprès du public francophone dès la fin du dix-septième siècle', in A. Thomson, S. Burrows and E. Dziembowski (eds.), *Cultural transfers: France and Britain in the long eighteenth century* (*SVEC* 2010: 04, Oxford, 2010), 147–59; and R. Hammersley, 'The "Real Whig"-Huguenot network and the English republican tradition', in the same volume, 19–32.

[33] W. Doyle, *Jansenism: Catholic resistance to authority from the Reformation to the French Revolution* (Basingstoke, 2000); D. van Kley, *The religious origins of the French Revolution: from Calvin to the civil constitution, 1560–1791* (New Haven, CT, 1996).

Civil Society in Fact and Fiction in the Age of Locke, Toland, Fénelon and Montesquieu

The political troubles of the decades from around 1685 to 1715 were bound to focus attention on the use of power in civil society. There were no obvious answers to how to make international relations conform to rudimentary legal norms, or how to reconcile the fiscal demands of militarisation with the search for domestic stability and security: the combination of economic crises, the French quest for 'gloire' and political instability was bound to cause widespread social unrest across much of Europe. The close connection between religious, civil and political tensions, however, became particularly clear for all to see in 1685, in a blunt and arbitrary manifestation of royal power: the revocation by the French crown of the limited religious and civic rights which French Protestants had been granted in the Edict of Nantes of 1598, redefined in 1629. For some time, the distinct liturgical and ceremonial practices of the Huguenots had challenged domestic French ideals of religious unity, but the Revocation of the Edict in 1685 marked a turning point – denoting total rejection of pragmatic compromise, creating a dramatic increase in asylum seekers and giving the issue of civil rights an immediate international resonance. Systematic persecution of the Huguenot minority in France now became a truly international crisis.

Within the Huguenot communities in France there were endless grounds for concern, many predating 1685. Huguenots had faced extensive use of bribery and force to achieve conversions to Catholicism, the billeting of undisciplined soldiers on recalcitrant households, the weeding out of Protestants from offices (ranging from the *parlements* right down to low-level guilds), extensive confiscation of property, the splitting of families suspected of Huguenot allegiance, the repression of Huguenot baptisms, marriages or burials, the systematic destruction of actual Protestant church and school buildings, the dismantling of congregational organisation, the alarming confiscation of church records to identify individual adherents – all reinforcing the image of France as one of the most visibly intolerant countries in Europe. Very harsh penalties against those who tried to flee were reinforced by granting new powers of control to the Catholic clergy and encouraging community neighbours to denounce potential suspects. Not surprisingly, the often brutal but inconsistent enforcement of additional persecution policies after 1685 resulted in the emigration of several hundred thousand religious refugees in defiance of stringent prohibitions and punishments. The impact on civil society was noticeable both in the major cities and in the more remote and mountainous parts of eastern and southern France to which non-emigrating Huguenots fled. Specifically in Paris, the recurrent warfare from the 1680s forced several Protestant embassies and foreign chapels to close, sometimes for long periods, depriving Parisian Protestants of protected places of worship.[34]

Interpreting the effect of all this on public opinion is difficult. Within France itself, it was impossible to express dissenting viewpoints: most of the printed material to do with the Revocation, therefore, was formal state legislation or effusive commendation of the policies. It soon became clear that these losses had a very damaging impact on the French economy, yet only a few brave officials in France dared to speak up – notable amongst them the intendant Henri d'Aguesseau and the brilliant military engineer Sébastien le Prêtre de Vauban (1633–1707).[35] With an ageing and exceptionally obstinate monarch, any scope for mitigation (let alone change) was not immediately apparent. In any case, the vast majority of conformist Catholic opinion (including even Richard Simon, as well as the relatively liberal archbishop Fénelon) appear to have applauded the attempt to reunite France around a single religion, regardless of the human cost. Amongst France's Protestant neighbours, of course, there were equally good political reasons for making the most of French violent intolerance as a focal point for vigorous propaganda. Many of the refugees were skilled craftsmen and brought precise knowledge which could readily be disseminated in print. Hostile criticism of France no doubt attracted sympathetic readers, but was not always conducive to a nuanced analysis of the realities of political and civil society. The French Huguenot exile Pierre Jurieu (1637–1713) gained international notoriety by publicly urging his co-religionists to remain defiant, so much so that he probably endangered the position of those left behind. He was rebuked by Pierre Bayle, who was characteristically much more guarded in his comments. A number of Dutch, English and German Protestant polemicists joined the fray, accounting for a significant cluster of publications right after the Revocation in 1685 and at key points later. More was to follow in England before and after the flight of James VII/II in 1688,

---

[34] D. Garrioch, *The Huguenots of Paris and the coming of religious freedom 1685–1789* (Cambridge, 2014), especially 24–74; G. Adams, *The Huguenots and French opinion 1685–1787* (Waterloo/Ontario, 1991); J. Bergin, *The politics of religion in early modern France* (New Haven, CT, 2014), 252–98; on the 'refuge' (Huguenot diaspora), see also B. van Ruymbeke and R. J. Sparks (eds.), *Memory and identity: the Huguenots in France and the Atlantic diaspora* (Columbia, 2003).

[35] Vauban's *Projet d'une dixme royale* ([no place], 1707), written as an attempt to persuade the king to adopt a fairer universal tax where the rich elite would pay a bigger share, was published without authorisation: distributed illegally, it was soon banned, but Vauban died that year, before any prosecutions were launched. The text was reprinted several times.

paving the way for the dramatic consolidation of English and Dutch Protestant interests in the hands of William and Mary. The belated Camisard revolt in southern France after 1702 also figured in print, albeit more sporadically.

In spite of the bitterness, these events did encourage some writers to re-examine the nature of civil society and the role of both power and oppression in achieving national coherence. The best-known example is Locke's *Two Treatises of Government*, containing ideas which he had developed over a decade or more as a general response to current political controversies and as a specific answer to Robert Filmer's *Patriarcha* (a much older royalist text dating from before the civil wars, but published posthumously in 1680). Locke's *Treatises* appeared anonymously in 1689/90, and according to Laslett went through seventeen English reprints by 1800, with a further four in Dublin and one in Glasgow. The French translation of the second treatise had nine reprints over the same period, with several printings in 1795 alone – indicating that it was still deemed potentially relevant in addressing new questions raised so long after. Locke's second treatise also had translations into German (1718), Swedish (1726) and Italian (1773).[36] His younger contemporary John Toland, by contrast, was much less cautious in engaging directly in contemporary affairs. He produced new editions in the 1690s of the earlier republican works of Harrington, Algernon Sidney, Milton and others, as well as researching the questionable authorship of the *Eikon Basilike* (ghost-written for Charles I in 1649, above, p. 92). In the years up to 1714, Toland primarily wanted to strengthen the argument for a Hanoverian succession. But in more universal terms, he was also adapting and redeveloping older English republican thinking from half a century earlier.[37] Both Locke and Toland, of course, wanted to demonstrate how important it was to have both a moderate political–constitutional consensus and a church which served civil society within a rationally defined spiritual sphere.

Other writers used direct evidence from contemporary politics to underline that message. Robert Molesworth (1656–1725), for example, used his observations as English ambassador at the Danish court to write a famously withering critique of arbitrary government there, in *An account of Denmark as it was in 1692* (London, 1694). This work warned against

---

[36] J. Locke, *Two treatises of government*, edited by P. Laslett (1960, rev. 1963), Appendix A.
[37] Toland's output is vast, some of it of acknowledged authorship, some of it attributed to him on the basis of evidence of variable reliability. Champion, *Republican learning*, illuminates Toland's political engagement and his many networks and dissemination strategies, but some of Toland's output is elusive (much of it unpublished or in small private print runs).

the terrible long-term effects of arbitrary government, but did so very much from his own point of view, incorporating both his Irish perspectives and commonwealth ideals in his determinedly Whig vision of contemporary politics. The book was of sufficient interest to Huguenots that it sold well, notably in French editions published in the Netherlands, going through altogether twenty-two editions in various languages during the eighteenth century.[38] In the English context, given the government's need for public support, many other writers were equally committed to engage in public discussion regarding Catholic exclusion, high Tory anxieties about hereditary succession and the risk of constitutional crisis – fears which persisted when it became clear that neither William and Mary nor queen Anne would produce surviving heirs. These questions were also, from a different point of view, highly relevant to Dutch readers. The continental impact of English writings, however, was very uneven. All of Locke's major works continued to have European resonance for most of the eighteenth century, especially amongst intellectually inclined readers. As we noted, Molesworth's *Account* also continued to be read in several languages. By contrast, Toland's work was much less widely disseminated and rarely translated: significantly, he became best known for his edition of Harrington's *Oceana* – which had at least three reprints in English after his death and was reissued in French in a new edition as late as 1795.

There were many other ways of presenting political subject matter to readers, including history, travel accounts and fiction. Some works of history were obvious pieces of propaganda. In Sweden, for example, Olof Rudbeck relied on aristocratic sponsorship to compile his *Atland eller Mannheim,* published in Uppsala from 1679 in several volumes. This ruinously expensive work was printed in Swedish and Latin parallel texts and was meant to demonstrate that the Swedes were the founding nation on earth after Noah's flood – using scientific arguments which did not convince everyone at the time. All over Europe, however, historical overviews sold well, especially if they covered more recent times, as

---

[38] R. Molesworth, *An account of Denmark as it was in 1692* (London, 1694), was reprinted five times in English, as well as having several French, German and Dutch editions; it also generated significant rebuttals and of course strong disapproval from the Danish government. Molesworth also produced a new translated edition of Hotman's *Francogallia* (London, 1711) and was part of a circle that included Toland. See the editorial comments in J. Champion (ed.), *An account of Denmark, with Francogallia and [other texts]* (Indianapolis, 2011), xii–xlviii; D. W. Hayton, 'The personal and political context of Robert Molesworth's *Account of Denmark*', in K. Haakonssen and H. Horstbøll (eds.), *Northern antiquities and national identities* (Copenhagen, 2007), 41–67; and S. Olden-Jørgensen, 'Robert Molesworth's *An account of Denmark as it was in 1692*: a political scandal and its literary aftermath', in the same volume, 68–87.

readers naturally sought accounts and explanations of major developments. In his *Behemoth*, Hobbes himself turned to historical writing,
boldly tackling the recent English civil wars – but publication was delayed
until 1679, the year of his death, even though the book had largely been
completed ten years earlier. In the German-speaking world, Samuel
Pufendorf (1632–94) was able to build an entire career on the compilation of major university textbooks on jurisprudence and history, opting
for a sufficiently uncontroversial and cautiously descriptive approach to
ensure that he continued to be cited by commentators of quite different
persuasion at least down to the middle of the eighteenth century.
Amongst Pufendorf's most frequently reprinted and translated works
was *De jure naturae et gentium* (1672), translated into English as *Of the
law of nature and nations* (1691), soon also into French, with regular
reprints until the mid-eighteenth century. He presented similar material
in a shorter summary, *De officio hominis et civis* (1673), which was translated into English as *The whole duty of man* (1691) and into French
(1696). Pufendorf's more history-oriented works also came to be
regarded as standard texts, notably his *Introduction to the history of the
principal kingdoms and states of Europe*. It was written when he was histor-
iographer royal at the Swedish court, and originally appeared in Swedish
in 1680, followed by versions in German from 1682, as well as translations into French in 1685 and English in 1695. His texts had numerous
reprints over the next half-century, becoming standard reading for the
well-educated. His younger compatriot Christian Thomasius (1655–
1728) helped spread and integrate Pufendorf's ideas into later German
political and social thought, through his own teaching and publications.[39]

Altogether more approachable for lay readers, however, was an unlikely
bestseller by the archbishop of Cambrai, François Fénelon (1651–1715):
his novel *Les aventures de Télémaque* (1699) written as a fictional story to
fill a gap in Homer's *Odyssey*. In the style of its classical antecedent, it told
the story of the son of Ulysses, guided through a series of challenges of
leadership and judgment that gave him the qualities needed to become
a wise prince. The story was immediately taken as an allegorical critique
of the French monarchy, and although it had initially been cleared by the
censors was then officially suppressed.[40] But *Télémaque* never went out of

---

[39] L. Krieger, *The politics of discretion: Pufendorf and the acceptance of natural law* (Chicago, 1965) remains the best explanation of Pufendorf's authoritative status in the early Enlightenment, and his loss of status after the mid-eighteenth century. For more recent work, see also M. Seidler, '"Monstrous" Pufendorf: sovereignty and system in the dissertations', in C. Cuttica and G. Burgess (eds.), *Monarchism and absolutism in early modern Europe* (London, 2012), 159–75.

[40] See editorial introduction and textual notes in Francois de Salignac de la Mothe-Fénelon, *Oeuvres*, J. le Brun (ed.), (2 vols., Paris, 1983–97).

print in eighteenth-century France (with perhaps twenty-five reprints by 1798) and more remarkably had an equal success in Protestant Europe, with a record-breaking number of English printings (conservatively estimated at forty during the eighteenth century), as well as seven in Dutch, six in German, two in Swedish and one in Danish. This kind of pattern illustrates the full impact that an accessible, entertaining, suitably edifying and moral work of fiction was capable of having. It became a 'classic' text, readily acceptable across different religious cultures, yet conveying a clearly relevant message of political wisdom and moral leadership.

No less interesting in terms of political analysis of Louis XIV's kingship is another well-known text by Fénelon, his *Examen de conscience sur les devoirs de la royauté*. Written before April 1711 as an instructional catechism for the Duke of Burgundy, the king's grandson (then second in line to the succession), the text was manifestly not intended for publication. Manuscript copies indicate that it nevertheless had some readers during the last years of the reign, and an attempt at publication was made in 1734, nearly twenty years after Fénelon's death. The printed edition was seized, but not before some copies had been distributed, allowing publishers in the Netherlands and in London to launch further editions from 1747 (with reprints again indicating viable demand). The book remained illegal in France, and it is not difficult to see why. A concise and hard-hitting text, it raised a wide range of timeless questions concerning the duties and principles of a good monarch, grouped into thirty-eight sections. The text starts by tackling religious principles, emphasising how a monarch could follow the precepts of Christian doctrine, rejecting flattering courtiers and self-seeking advisers. But the text soon moves onto the wider responsibilities of the French monarch: absolute justice in peace time and scrupulously limited use of warfare solely for just causes, with due attention to natural rights and natural law (section 8):

Have you studied the fundamental laws, and those unchanging customs that have the force of law in the general governance of your particular nation? Have you sought to discover, without flattering yourself, what are the limits of your authority? Do you know ... how present conditions have come to be? – on what basis change has happened? – what anarchy is? – what arbitrary power is, and what constitutes monarchy governed by law?

The text also includes questions about morality at court, honesty and luxury, and how the monarch should set a good example in everything. It includes specific questions on whether foreign policy and diplomacy is conducted according to justice and international law and military conscription kept as low as possible. It asks whether the monarch has chosen the best and most honest advisers, without regard for flattery and self-interest, and has gathered accurate information as the basis for policy decisions. Excessive and unjustified impositions by the state are a recurrent theme, as in section 18:

Have you sought means to relieve the people and only take from them that which the true needs of the state force you to take for their own best interest? ... You know that formerly the king never took anything from his people solely by his own authority. It was the Parlement, that is, the assembly of the nation [as it was then], that granted him the funds necessary for the extraordinary needs of the state ... Have you ever imposed new charges on the people to sustain your superfluous expenditures, the luxury of your table, your stable and your furniture, the embellishment of your gardens and houses, the excessive rewards lavished to your favourites?[41]

In short, Fénelon's *Examen de conscience* was a substantive critique of the misuse of power by Louis XIV. The text was ostensibly intended as a didactic piece, to ensure that the person who was expected soon to become crown prince would question his own role and distance himself from his predecessor's view of kingship, becoming more aware of the moral obligations of power and the needs of a peaceful civil society. But the text could be equally effective in providing any political reader not just with a generic framework for political accountability but also for a new moral order based on natural law and a sense of shared responsibilities. It is obvious why the *Examen* was unpublishable in France: it was manifestly more outspoken and critical of the king than *The adventures of Telemachus* and very different from Fénelon's more conventional devotional texts (such as his conservative *Instructions for the education of a daughter,* which also had a large number of editions across Europe, including eight in English between 1707 and 1797). Not surprisingly, Fénelon, despite his quietist beliefs, became a focal point for liberal critics of the régime during the last years of Louis XIV.

These few examples do not demonstrate a trend, but do suggest that the political challenges of 1685–1715 had wider resonance. Clearly, authors were willing to deploy considerable ingenuity to get political ideas into the public domain in imaginative and lower-risk ways, not just in England and the Netherlands, but also in France itself (albeit usually via Dutch printing presses) and in the more decentralised German lands. However, the risks of forcible suppression remained very considerable, and in any case conservative market demand continued to force authors to exercise enormous self-restraint in respect of both the religious conventions of their intended

---

[41] Fénelon, *Examen de conscience sur les devoirs de la royauté,* in Le Brun (ed.), *Oeuvres,* vol. II, 973–1009. The extracts cited here are translated from this edition, but see also the English version published in 1747, entitled *Proper heads of self-examination for a king.*

readers and the political system within which they operated. Again we note that print was not necessarily the most appropriate method of dissemination: making manuscript copies evidently remained a more flexible way of disseminating texts amongst a small number of reliable friends, at less risk, and with the added possibility that the text itself could easily be modified to suit the individual intended reader. That said, we now have substantial evidence that ideas and texts in printed form did travel relatively freely between France, the Netherlands and England during this period, either in translation, or through direct contacts between publishers, journalists, authors, reviewers and readers across this highly literate north-western area of Europe.

The French Huguenot exiles settling in the Netherlands and in England, and English exiles who maintained their cross-cultural contacts after returning home in 1689, had an obvious interest in nourishing this communication network both in print and through personal correspondence. Pierre Desmaizeaux (?1666–1745) was one of these Huguenot exiles and settled in Britain in 1699 thanks to contacts with the third Lord Shaftesbury and with Anthony Collins. He translated the writings of Pierre Bayle, edited those of John Locke and many others, and in effect helped readers on both sides of the Channel acquire mutual understanding and new conceptual vocabularies. Another independent-minded Huguenot refugee, Michel de la Roche, settled in London around the turn of the century and later made his mark as editor of the French-language journals *Bibliothèque angloise* and *Mémoires littéraires del la Grande-Bretagne*, which disseminated predominantly English controversies on politics, science and religious toleration of interest to French readers across the Channel.[42] As Rachel Hammersley has also recently demonstrated, Huguenot journals and writings created bridges between English commonwealth and liberal political writers, their Dutch and Huguenot counterparts, and readers who shared similar concerns about contemporary religious and political challenges.[43] In northern Germany,

---

[42] A. Thomson, 'Des Maizeaux, Collins and the translators: the case of Collins' Philosophical inquiry concerning human liberty', in Thomson et al. (eds.), *Cultural transfers* (*SVEC* 2010: 04), 219–31; A. Thomson, 'In defence of toleration: La Roche's Bibliothèque angloise and Mémoires littéraires del la Grande-Bretagne', in the same volume, 161–74; E. Grist, 'Pierre des Maizeaux and the Royal Society', in the same volume, 33–42.

[43] R. Hammersley, *The English republican tradition and eighteenth-century France: between the ancients and the moderns* (Manchester, 2010), 53–98, identifies a number of other writers, journal editors and translators connected to this cross-channel network, including Jean Le Clerc, Jacques Bernard, Pierre Auguste Samson and others, who made Milton, Algernon Sidney and other English writers familiar to continental readers, whilst providing those Englishmen who had been in exile until 1689 with updates of continental writings and further mutual Anglo-French connections. Jacobite exiles from England

readers were on the whole more conservative, but even there radical writings appear to have been disseminated privately in universities and in the independent cities, albeit mostly amongst avid readers.[44] Outside the areas of lively printing and vigorous urban cultural life, it was more difficult to foster active political consciousness. Even there, however, print could help disseminate historical accounts, official (state-sponsored) peace and anniversary celebrations, and other material that in certain contexts could make readers more aware of the structure of power in their community.

In those parts of Europe where print culture was less highly developed, particular events were still capable of triggering significant changes in political perceptions. A striking example is the reaction in Sweden after Charles XII was killed in the trenches in December 1718. Resentment had built up around the huge costs of his ill-considered military adventures, exacerbated by his pronounced leanings towards an even more autocratic form of monarchy than what the Swedish Estates (Riksdag) had agreed in the 1680s. The king's sudden death created the perfect opportunity for a substantial change in political direction, guided by the aristocratic leadership in the noble Estate within the Swedish Riksdag. A new parliamentary constitution was compiled through successive legislation, culminating in a final *Riksdags-ordning* published in 1723, reprinted in 1740 and 1757, and remaining in force until 1772. Not surprisingly, the broadly representative nature of the Swedish Estates made print an essential component of political life. The years 1719–20 saw at least twice the normal average output of new titles in print, including texts on both historical and current political issues. This in effect started a trend of lively engagement in print which continued to correlate visibly with the regular meetings of the full Estates General every two or three years[45] and which by mid-century led to a remarkably active and wide-ranging public discussion nourished by significant political pamphleteering (below, Chapter 5).

In England, the frequent discussion of politics in print was clear for all to see and remarked on by foreign visitors browsing London bookshops. Compared with other European states, the English monarchy during the 1680s was weak, and traditional loyalties divided both by religious

---

also found inspiration in Fénelon for their visions of a more balanced restored Stuart monarchy: see A. Mansfield, *Ideas of monarchical reform: Fénelon, Jacobitism and political works of the chevalier Ramsay* (Manchester, 2015).

[44] Mulsow, *Enlightenment underground*.

[45] Quantification based on *Svensk bibliografi 1700–1829*, and the catalogues of the Royal Library in Stockholm. For a general account critical of the flaws of Swedish parliamentarian government, see M. Roberts, *The age of liberty: Sweden 1719–1772* (Cambridge, 1986).

disputes and by open political partisanship. The deployment and dissemination of news-sheets, polemics, sermons, visual imagery and other forms of communication from the late 1670s to the Hanoverian succession of 1714 (and its aftermath) were less controllable than anywhere else.[46] Mark Knights has noted how parliamentary elections, political crises of various kinds, as well as the changing expectations of an increasingly commercialised society, made public engagement an unpredictable but important variable in politics. He also notes how restrictions on collective petitions were essentially unenforceable, especially when they were shaped as addresses of loyalty and directly linked to current affairs as presented in newspapers and pamphlets.[47] A closer look at the contours of printed texts yields some interesting insights. We noted earlier that the total output of London printers averaged around 1000 items in the 1670s, rising to nearly double in years of political turmoil 1679–85 (with over 2000 items in 1680 and 1681) and even higher in the years 1688–90 (exceeding 2400 items in 1689). For most of the 1690s the output was in the range 1400–1550 titles per annum. The temporary spike around 1695–6 could be attributed to the lapse of the Licensing Act, but since it did not last, other political explanations are equally plausible. During the first decade of the eighteenth century, London production averaged 1800 titles per annum, with a predictable spike in the years 1714–15 (with 2200 and 2342 items respectively). These fluctuations fit the patterns of political uncertainty quite well, considering that a fairly continuous output of other types of reading material would cushion the market and the sector.

When we search the ESTC data by means of title keywords, some interesting trends come to light. There was a predictable continuity in religious focus throughout this period, but in the 1680s there was a noticeable increase in the number of titles including words such as 'superstition' and 'fanatic', variants of 'papist' and 'popery', as well as 'heretic', 'atheist' and 'presbyterian'. In the 1680s, we also find clusterings of more overtly political words, notably 'libel' and 'liberty'. Variants of 'free' and 'freedom' continue to figure prominently in the 1690s and beyond, as does 'right' (not counting purely formal use of the word, as in 'right honourable'). The word 'king' occurs frequently, but the use of 'remonstrance', 'petition' or 'grievance' is more uneven. Other words with strong political associations remain prominent in the early years of the eighteenth century, including variants of 'power', 'authority', 'parliament' and 'nation'. But we also note

---

[46] See notably T. Harris, *London crowds in the reign of Charles II: propaganda and politics from the Restoration until the exclusion crisis* (Cambridge, 1987).

[47] M. Knights, *Representation and misrepresentation in later Stuart Britain: partisanship and political culture* (Oxford, 2005), 109–62.

frequent use of 'commons' and 'people' in printed titles throughout these years.[48]

The ESTC lists a wide variety of works likely to have been of interest to the highly politicised reading public in London. We find that some older titles were reprinted during the critical years from 1685, including for example an English translation of the old republican tract *Vindiciae contra tyrannos: a defence of liberty against tyrants* (1689), which had already been reissued in 1648 but originally dated from the 1580s (above, p. 14). An English translation of Pieter de la Court's *The true interest and political maxims of the Republick of Holland* was issued in 1702, and reprinted in 1712, although the Dutch original was decades old (above, p. 118). Naturally, a number of new texts tackled the flight of James VII/II, some of them by authors who were otherwise little known: thus Edmund Bohun in 1689 published *The history of the desertion, or an account of the publick affairs in England,* which went to a second edition. Publications referring in their title to the 'present government' were predictably numerous in the period 1689–95 (as they had been in the years 1649–60) and now focused very much on obligations of loyalty either to the traditional royal succession or to the new constitutional settlement.

The term 'vox populi' (voice of the people), used sporadically in 1620 and in the 1640s, was deployed more often in titles from 1681 as a way of highlighting various causes where popular demand could be extrapolated, whether in a conservative or a subversive sense. A text published in 1681 carried the title *Vox populi, or the peoples claim to their Parliaments sitting, to redress grievances, and provide for the common safety, by the known laws and constitutions of the nation.* John Nalson responded soon after with *Vox populi, fax populi; or a discovery of an impudent cheat and forgery put upon the people of England* – a short polemic attacking the seditious and subversive intent of the first text and warning against returning to the populism of 1641 or 1648. A number of further publications continued using the catchphrase 'vox populi' right up to 1714 (and more rarely afterwards). These contested what the 'voice of the people' might really be, bringing up an impressive range of core political issues, including the royal prerogative(s), the nature of government and the traditional rights of subjects going back to the time of the Anglo-Saxons. Other writers, such as Charles Povey, focused on the role of parliament, whilst some tackled the freedom of the press itself in providing wide-ranging political reading material. Typically for this period, few of these texts were more than polemic contributions to current concerns and they rarely contained

---

[48] All data is from the ESTC: see above, p. 36.

any substantive theoretical or analytical reflections. That much of what came out of the printing presses may with hindsight appear to be ephemeral, however, should not lead us to underestimate the significance of a politically conscious reading public: reprinting was not the sole indicator of impact, and particular texts may well have been influential at the right moment, even if they were not reprinted and were not explicitly cited by others. John Toland is a clear example of how this kind of vigorous and rapidly moving argument could work, much of it conducted by word of mouth or in manuscript, rather than openly in print. Emerging polemical writers such as Daniel Defoe would have found plenty of stimulus from such contacts.

As in the Netherlands, variations between cities in the British Isles were significant. If we select just the publications produced in Edinburgh, we predictably find a huge increase in printed items whose titles contained variants of 'covenant', 'presbyterian' and 'episcopacy', culminating at the turn of the century. Words relating to 'royal', 'popish' and 'papist' are frequent in the 1680s, and 'indulgence' (for Episcopalians) in the years 1703–5. Disputes over ecclesiastical politics covered the entire spectrum from Quakers at one extreme, through more traditional congregational and presbyterian variants, to episcopalian and high-church Catholic tendencies, all competing for control or at least civic recognition. But there were also polemics with more overtly economic or patriotic political orientation, ranging from disputed loyalties after the 1689 Revolution to fundamental disagreements leading up to the Treaty of Union of 1707. We might have expected the Darien adventure to have figured explicitly in titles – both when the speculative expedition was proposed and launched (1695–9) and after its catastrophic failure in 1700 – but in fact the word 'Darien' is found in only nine distinct titles (in the years 1699–1700). By contrast, trade, the Indies and other commercial terms appear far more frequently in titles in these years. Equally, it is no surprise that references to the union, the English and the 'nation' were common in Edinburgh publications in the years immediately before 1707 than they had been previously. Recall of the General Assembly of the church in 1690, for the first time since 1649, naturally also encouraged much discussion in print. Explicit references to 'parliament' doubled in frequency, cumulatively, for every decade from 1670 to 1710, heading texts which were often in effect petitions, even though that contentious word was used sparingly. Some of these texts reflected the kind of popular political concerns also seen in the crowd disturbances and riots of 1706–7. Interestingly, we even find the word 'right' (in the sense of political right) occurring regularly from the late 1680s, for example in a short tract entitled *The proceedings of the present parliament justified by the opinion of . . . Grotius* (Edinburgh,

1689). Overall, public discussion around political and economic issues was clearly reflected in print alongside the ongoing (and related) religious confrontations.[49]

Alternative visions and imaginary worlds created through fiction may well have reached an even wider readership. Protected by a cloak of light-hearted entertainment, both author and reader could give free rein to their creativity. A fictional setting, as in the case of Mandeville and Fénelon already noted, was a convenient way of engaging in critical analysis of the structures of civil society and was by now also a well-established technique to reduce the risk of rejection by readers and the authorities. Descriptions both of utopia (Atlantis, long lost idealised worlds) and of other civilisations and cultures (travel literature, whether real or manifestly imaginary) were common literary forms throughout the early modern period, which of course also served to highlight the peculiarities of European cultural-political traditions through a deliberately distorting lens.

The end of the disruptive European wars of the last years of Louis XIV, and the sigh of relief at the peace settlements of 1715–21, created fertile ground for new forms of fictional portrayals of civil society. Amongst the most popular was Montesquieu's *Lettres persanes* (*Persian Letters*) written during the last years of the reign but held back for publication until 1721. Disguised as an epistolary novel featuring two complete outsiders visiting France for the first time, the book was not just accessible and entertaining, but full of controversial questions and comparisons disguised with so much irony that a censor might well be disarmed. In letter 24, for example, Montesquieu has one of his two Persian observers note:

The king of France . . . is a great magician: he exercises his dominion even over the minds of his subjects; he makes them think the way he wants to . . . If he has a difficult war to sustain, and has no money, he only has to put into their heads that a piece of paper is money, and they are immediately convinced . . . What I say about this prince should not surprise you: there is another magician stronger than him . . . called the pope. He makes the king believe that three are merely one, that the bread one eats is not bread, or that the wine one drinks is not wine, and a thousand other things of this kind.[50]

Montesquieu continues by criticising the Papal Bull *Unigenitus* of 1713 (condemning a long list of Jansenist propositions), questioning its discriminatory restrictions on lay reading of the Bible especially amongst women. A central theme throughout Montesquieu's book, not least in its

---

[49] For a full discussion of this period, including the relationship to actual riots, and more active government promotion of certain political causes, see Bowie, *Scottish public opinion*.

[50] [Montesquieu], *Lettres persanes* ('Amsterdam', 1721), letter 24.

dramatic conclusion, is the use and abuses of power across a range of social and gendered contexts. Although initially published anonymously, its authorship was not a well-kept secret, and was acknowledged by Montesquieu as soon as he was confident that the book would not be suppressed. The text was reprinted several times already in its first year and then again two or three times every decade, attaining at least twenty-two reprintings in French between 1730 and 1795. It was published in an English translation already in 1722 and reprinted at least six times in London before 1800, with further reprints in Dublin, Glasgow and Edinburgh. However, it seems to have been too controversial for other European publishers to take on: there was only one German version (1759) and, apart from excerpts of the Troglodytes, none either in Danish or in Swedish, where its highly relevant but very outspoken core political message may have been considered too dangerous. Surprisingly, no Dutch translation appears to have been published either.

We should of course remind ourselves that political texts with too much contemporary relevance (fictional or not) were likely to be counterproductive. Even in Britain, political fiction had to be sufficiently remote from reality to escape prosecution for libel and such a tactic was always difficult to bring off (both for the author and the printer). We have already noted that Bernard Mandeville's *Fable of the Bees* (1714) caused a scandal for its rejection of traditional moral values in economic thought[51] and was prosecuted, but had limited market success even in the Netherlands. By contrast, the overwhelming popularity of Jonathan Swift's anonymously published satire *Gulliver's Travels* (1726) probably protected it against serious penalties, despite its obvious political relevance. The more oblique and simpler politics of Daniel Defoe's *Robinson Crusoe* (1719) were readily acceptable. Both books not only had immediate success in Britain, but also won widespread admiration and imitation on the continent for decades to come. Travel stories, whether realistic enough to appear initially plausible (such as the *Persian Letters*) or manifestly counterfactual (such as *Gulliver's Travels*), became hugely popular precisely because they could be used to throw fresh comparative light both on the real world and on utopian alternatives, while at the same time allowing the author to hide behind the mask of fiction.

Across Europe, we find many other examples of fictional travel-writing. In Denmark Ludvig Holberg (1684–1754) is universally regarded as the first enlightened cosmopolitan, gaining wide recognition with the *Subterranean journey of Niels Klim*. First published in Latin in 1741, it

---

[51] J. M. Stafford, *Private vices, publick benefits? The contemporary reception of Bernard Mandeville* (Solihull, 1997).

was translated almost immediately into German, Dutch, French and Danish. The genre remained popular throughout the century. Voltaire's *Candide* (1759) became a bestseller in France (where it was rarely out of print if we include the complete editions of his works launched after his death in 1778) and had recurrent editions in English and German, as well as one in Swedish in 1783 (translated from English). It clearly outsold Louis-Sébastien Mercier's *L'an 2440, rêve s'il en fût jamais* (1771), which had six further editions in French before the Revolution, was quickly translated into English as *Memoirs of the year 2500* and rendered in German in 1782, but had few subsequent foreign-language versions even after Mercier acquired a new role in the French Revolution. More difficult to track, but perhaps of greater potential impact, were the published versions of theatre plays and opera librettos. Historians are now alert to all of these as vehicles for the dissemination of ideas, fuelling controversies or even commenting on political shifts. As always, the forms of sponsorship involved can be difficult to trace accurately, especially when individuals with significant power or social standing were involved.

Such a growing diversity of texts, styles and public communication strategies makes the task of the cultural historian more complex. Ideally, quantitative and qualitative analysis needs to be combined with a close awareness of the finer nuances of styles of discourse and attentiveness to oblique contemporary references where the meaning is no longer obvious. Most polemics relied heavily on topical relevance and tended to be thin on theoretical and analytical content, so contextualising them fully is almost impossible. At the same time, we need to be aware how far patronage and sponsorship determined what both pamphleteers and journalists could write – not to mention the commercial interests of all the participants in the print trade and the numerous technical challenges faced by early modern printers and publishers (in everything from paper supply to guild regulations, as noted in Chapter 1). Taken in conjunction with the elusive pressures of censorship, self-censorship and threats of legal prosecution or blackmail, we can see how complicated the strategies of both printers and readers might be. Flexibility and adaptability were essential, and changes were neither linear nor always readily visible.

Newspapers, Journals and Periodicals around the Turn of the Century

News became big business across Europe in the later years of Louis XIV, no doubt in part because governments themselves began to recognise the value of releasing carefully selected information to the reading public in an age of very tense religious and military–diplomatic confrontations. In most centralising monarchies, not least France until 1715, newspapers were very tightly regulated through privileged editors operating under licence – their role restricted to publishing authorised news without editorial comment. Yet such monopolies did not go unchallenged. As far as France was concerned, refugee publishers across the north-eastern and eastern borders had ready access to alternative news networks, in effect making the Netherlands and the Rhineland area an information hub for international news for publishers across Europe (and by extension, the Atlantic world). Because of the universally tight restrictions on domestic reporting, however, most newspapers adhered to strictly factual (and often derivative) summaries of news. The general lack of independent political analysis or commentary makes it more difficult to identify editorial policies, intended readership or evidence of impact. That, however, did not deter readers: from the last years of the seventeenth century onwards, the increase in demand for newspapers in prosperous urban societies is indisputable. A proliferation of new titles and formats reflects the willingness of printers and editors to experiment in search of more effective dissemination. A reputation either for reliability or for controversial partisanship might pay off, but in general we lack sufficient evidence to understand why some newspapers had much greater success than others.

Historians of the early eighteenth-century press now typically sort serial publications, periodicals and newspapers into a number of distinct categories. Such categorisation is often based on hindsight, as most ventures of this kind were short-lived and overlapping. Nonetheless, in addition to news-sheets, newspapers and 'intelligencer' sheets (now often appearing several times a week, sometimes becoming dailies), it is useful to distinguish advertisers (carrying mostly uncontroversial commercial and trade news), almanacs (usually annual, often with blank spaces for user annotations), calendars, literary and scientific review journals, and emerging special-interest serials (medical, religious, musical).[52] All of these might carry information with political potential, but generally played safe by concentrating on matters that were less likely to attract the attention of censors, state licensing authorities, theological controllers, or local vigilantes.

Commercial information itself could serve the interests both of local markets and of long-distance international traders, so dissemination naturally followed existing maritime trade routes and navigable rivers.

---

[52] E. Fischer, W. Haefs and Y.-G. Mix (eds.), *Von Almanach bis Zeitung: ein Handbuch der Medien in Deutschland 1700–1800* (Munich, 1999).

The rapidly developing postal networks, especially in the Holy Roman Empire, also carried printed material and news-sheets, allowing publishers in hubs such as Hamburg or Amsterdam to reprint news material from correspondents all over Europe.[53] Many new periodicals made extensive use of material translated, summarised or plagiarised from other publications: it was often cheaper and more effective to reissue such material in a new format for local distribution, rather than to import multiple copies of the original publication. Such copying provided an easy way of filling space on the page, once local or regional interests had been covered. In providing useful or interesting information, local papers also created a focal point for a sense of community amongst their readers, even if in reality they had no more than a few hundred subscribers or a few thousand readers. In the process, periodicals and newspapers undoubtedly also contributed to the standardisation of language and vocabularies, albeit with local variation.

The best opportunities for a commercially growing and lively newspaper industry arose in the dense urban network across the Netherlands, the Rhine valley and into north-western Germany. This whole area was directly and visibly affected by the Huguenot asylum-seekers from France after 1685, and since some of the refugees ended up as skilled workers (including printers) in their new homes, much news reporting naturally tended to take a critical view of French politics. The *Gazette de Leyde* had been founded already in 1677 by an early French Huguenot exile, Alexandre de la Font. Appearing in French, it was able to secure viable distribution along the main trade routes and even sold in France itself despite successive attempts by the French government to ban it (not to mention repeated diplomatic pressure on the Leiden authorities to suppress the publication altogether). Although the paper did not gain its real reputation for quality reporting until it was taken over by Etienne Luzac (another Huguenot) in 1739, its full variant title, *Nouvelles extraordinaires de divers endroits,* accurately reflected its aspiration to provide detailed and reliable chronicling of events.[54] A number of other

---

[53] On overall changes in communication, see W. Behringer, 'Communications revolutions: a historiographical concept', *German History,* 24 (2006), 333–74. For a particular case study relating to the later years of Louis XIV, see E. Schnakenbourg, 'Les chemins de l'information: la circulation des nouvelles depuis la périphérie européenne jusqu'au gouvernment française au début du xviiie siècle', *Revue historique,* 308 (2006), 291–310.

[54] J. D. Popkin, *News and politics in the age of revolution: Jean-Luzac's Gazette de Leyde* (Ithaca, NY, 1989); C.-H. Depezay, 'Between the French Gazette and Dutch French-language newspapers', in Dooley (ed.), *The dissemination of news,* 179–92. On the slightly later developments in northern Germany, see S. Doering-Manteuffel, J. Mancal and W. Wüst (eds.), *Pressewesen der Aufklärung: periodischen Schriften im alten Reich* (Berlin, 2001).

newspapers thrived in the relatively deregulated and prosperous Netherlands, including the long-lasting *Gazette d'Amsterdam* and the Dutch-language *Amsterdamsche Courant*, both dating from the last decades of the seventeenth century.

In England, the succession of dramatic political developments in the 1680s naturally generated a huge demand for news – and hence new titles trying to compete against the older official *London Gazette* of 1665. Roger L'Estrange (1616–1704), Surveyor and Licenser of the Press until 1679 and a ferocious conservative polemicist, launched a periodical in the 1680s, *The Observator*, which appeared four times a week until 1687. Given his position, the political purpose of this serial publication was plain for all to see, and it is hardly surprising that other publishers eager to get access to the news market experimented with more independent approaches. Given the controlled monopoly on domestic news, however, they had to make the most of foreign news reports, combined with any marketable secondhand reporting of official domestic news released by government. By the turn of the century there were dailies such as the *Daily Courant* (published by Elizabeth Mallet from 1702 and ostensibly carrying only foreign news) and the *Evening Post* (from 1710). North of the border, too, attempts were made to establish regular newspapers, such as the *Edinburgh Gazette* of 1699 or the *Edinburgh Courant* of 1705. It is likely that London newspapers benefited particularly from the lapse of the Licensing Act, temporarily for a few years from 1679, then permanently in 1695: the essential periodicity of newspapers meant they had always been particularly susceptible to such controls. But the dramatic events of 1688–9 were in any case bound to make controls on domestic reporting unenforceable, and the wars against France could only fuel public demand further. Londoners came to expect reporting of major domestic events, as well as extensive pamphleteering, whenever there was something newsworthy. The riots and protests which followed a three-year ban on preaching imposed on the high-church anti-Whig clergyman Sacheverell in 1710, and the general election that took place shortly afterwards, were accompanied by outpourings in print. The imposition of a stamp duty in 1712 appears to have had only a modest and temporary dampening effect. The long-standing conflicts of loyalty inherent in the Hanoverian succession of 1714 sparked renewed polemics, pamphleteering and partisan newsprint.[55]

---

[55] For the general background, see notably B. Harris, *Politics and the rise of the press: Britain and France 1620–1800* (London, 1996); H. Barker, *Newspapers, politics and English society 1695–1855* (London, 2000); and J. Sutherland, *The Restoration newspaper and its development* (Cambridge, 1986). Particularly relevant in this context is J. Raymond, 'The newspaper, public opinion and the public sphere in the seventeenth century', in J. Raymond

Growing demand led to experiments with different types and genres. We noted (above, p. 49) how in April 1709 Richard Steele anonymously launched the *Tatler*, thereby creating a new trend in lighthearted, entertaining and ostensibly impartial observer-journalism commenting on social mores, civil society and its economic foundations. The *Tatler* ran for just under two years, after which Steele and Addison replaced it with the *Spectator,* a periodical carrying even less actual news but referring to current issues of social and general interest. This new title was also of limited duration (March 1711 to December 1712), but set the tone for innumerable imitations in England and across Europe,[56] often categorised as 'moral weeklies' (appearing once or several times a week, but not daily). In format and layout such publications were usually indistinguishable from other short printed texts, but some acquired easily distinguished visual emblematic titles at the top of the front page.

Without ever appearing provocative, both the *Tatler* and the *Spectator* were genuinely intended for all kinds of readers in comfortable urban society. Although carrying actual news only incidentally (through the device of reported conversations in coffee houses and other spaces of sociability), they regularly commented on the role of newspapers and other forms of print:

There is no Humour in my Countrymen, which I am more enclined to wonder at, than their general Thirst after News. There are about half a Dozen Ingenious Men, who live very plentifully upon this Curiosity of their Fellow-Subjects. They all of them receive the same Advices [*avisi*, or news-sheets] from abroad, and very often in the same Words; but their way of Cooking it is so different, that there is no Citizen, who has an Eye to the Publick Good, that can leave the Coffee-house with Peace of Mind, before he has given one of them a Reading ... This general Curiosity has been raised and inflamed by our late Wars, and, if rightly directed, might be of good use to a Person who has such a Thirst awakened in him. Why should not a Man, who takes Delight in reading every thing that is new, apply himself to History, Travels, and other Writings of the same kind, where he will find perpetual Fuel for his Curiosity, and meet with much more Pleasure and Improvement, than in these Papers of the Week?[57]

At face value, of course, this is a didactic piece meant to direct readers to better material. But it highlights the insatiable interest in news amongst the general public and notes the social space in which such reading of a shared newspaper would take place.

(ed.), *News, newspapers and society in early modern Britain* (London and Portland, OR, 1999), 109–40.

[56] A. Lévrier, 'Justus van Effen, "passeur" entre les presses anglais et francaise', in *Intellectual journeys* (*SVEC* 2013: 12, Oxford, 2013), 233–46.

[57] The *Spectator,* no. 452, Friday, 8 August 1712, attributed to Joseph Addison.

If the precise impact of such newspapers is difficult to analyse, there can be little doubt that they reflected, and responded to, substantial public interest. We have noted how, in particularly unstable political contexts such as the Netherlands in 1672 or England at various stages in the 1680s, pamphlets, flysheets and news could provide information at critical points. Similarly, international events such as the failed peace negotiations in 1709, when France seemed on the verge of economic and military collapse, also generated a huge demand for news. But given the context, it is hardly surprising that most newspapers trying to stay in business had to remain very cautious – and with no expectation of editorial commentary, readers had to make do with short factual summaries. Even in the lively environment of the many small and often fairly autonomous principalities and cities of the Rhineland and western German-speaking lands, there is little evidence that newspapers aimed to pursue independent political lines.[58] Yet newspapers increasingly reported political change and occasional unrest in sufficient detail to interact with public opinion, especially in combination with other forms of print (such as pamphlets and flysheets). Readers would find further information in print regarding core grievances and might be able to locate narratives, the texts of earlier formal privileges, declarations or any other material that might throw light on the legitimacy of contested political arguments. We find examples of this for example in Basel in 1691, in Frankfurt and Hamburg from the 1690s onwards, and in Scotland in the run-up to the Union in 1707. In each of these cases apparently simple printed news reporting, in flysheets as well as regular serial newspapers, clearly contributed to greater public discussion by publicising the factual basis for alternative interpretations of existing narratives.[59] It is worth noting that the biggest surge in the newspaper market appears to have been in the western German-speaking lands, building up a larger range of durable titles there than anywhere else in Europe.[60]

---

[58] A. Gestrich, *Absolutismus und Öffentlichkeit: politische Kommunikation in Deutschland zu Beginn des 18.Jhrh.* (Göttingen, 1994), 130–4.

[59] For a full analysis, see K. Bowie, *Scottish public opinion and the Anglo-Scottish Union*; D. Bellingradt, *Flugpublizistik und Öffentlichkeit um 1700: Dynamiken, Akteure und Strukturen im urbanen Raum des Alten Reiches*, especially the analysis of impact and instability in Hamburg, 131–257; A. Würgler, *Unruhen und Öffentlichkeit: Städtische und ländliche Protestbewegungen im 18.Jahrhundert* (Tübingen, 1995), particularly 202–26; and M. Lindemann, *The merchant republics: Amsterdam, Antwerp and Hamburg 1648–1790* (Cambridge, 2015).

[60] Würgler, *Unruhen*, 203, notes around fifty-eight different papers available simultaneously in the western parts of the German lands around 1701, nearly doubling by mid-century – though such numbers have to be treated with caution, given the instability of many newspaper ventures.

In those parts of Europe nearer the periphery of active newspaper printing, the restrictions on what information could be circulated were much tighter. Both Stockholm and Copenhagen acquired a newspaper by the middle of the seventeenth century, invariably closely based on material derived from Hamburg or other north-German sources – and sometimes initially even published in German. These early papers were censored and supervised under the terms of royal grants of exclusive privilege. Additional restraints on content and distribution could be enforced through the crown-controlled postal system itself. It goes without saying that no paper in either Sweden or Denmark could publish anything that might have a bearing on domestic policy, or might in any way imply criticism of the state and its allies: the papers were initially in effect official state-sponsored news monopolies, emphasising formal and ceremonial events much like the *Gazette de France*. In Denmark in 1672, however, a second publisher was allowed to launch a rival, the *Extraordinarie Relation*, thereby breaking the monopoly. The resulting competition provided an incentive to improve the amount of detail offered to readers, who also benefited from the long-standing close contacts with Hamburg through the adjacent Danish settlement of Altona.[61] Further competing papers appeared in Copenhagen during the period 1680–1721, including a French-language derivative of the *Nouvelles de divers endroits* (using the same title). Nevertheless, recurrent wartime restrictions and an unstable market demand meant that none of the Copenhagen papers during this period could offer any real independent news. As we would expect, therefore, readers gained little more than superficial summary information in respect of the political upheavals in England, the Netherlands, or France. Yet here as elsewhere in Europe, the newspaper, starting from a tentative and sporadic medium in the seventeenth century, with little more than summary accounts from correspondents in various cities, had by the eighteenth century become an essential component of the urbanised sociability spreading across Europe. The coffee house became a focal point for collective discussion of newspaper material, enhanced by pamphlets and flysheets. The relative significance and impact of newspapers compared with pamphlets or even books is impossible to measure, but the combination of all forms of print certainly allowed more of the reading public to engage directly with political issues.

---

[61] P. Ries, 'The politics of information in seventeenth-century Scandinavia', in Dooley and Baron (eds.), *The politics of information*, 237–72; J. D. Søllinge and N. Thomsen, *De danske aviser 1634–1989*, vol. I (Odense, 1988).

Public Opinion and the Public Sphere 1685–1721

Since the publication in 1989 of the English translation of a short but seminal book by the German sociologist Jürgen Habermas, his theory regarding the emergence of the 'public sphere' has become an indispensable component of any discussion of public opinion at the turn of the seventeenth into the eighteenth century.[62] Many historians have challenged the empirical evidence for his theory, criticising both the chronological framework he deployed and the way he defined the social groups activating a more autonomous 'public sphere' in theatres, coffee houses and urban spaces outside the control of the exclusive noble and patrician power elites of *ancien-régime* Europe.[63] There is broad agreement that social structures and networks in the early modern period were much more complicated than either early modern categorisation of the three (or four) Estates, or nineteenth-century notions of class, rank and status might suggest. In any case there was no shared social cohesiveness in the 'public sphere', and the emergence of a 'public' collective self-awareness was much slower in some parts of Europe than in others.

Crucially, notions of 'public' and 'private' did not correspond to modern definitions of those words, and property rights were themselves conditional on social status and social relationships. If the 'public sphere' had been in the process of becoming genuinely independent, there would inevitably have been far more conflicts of interest regarding offices which carried what might now be regarded as 'public' or collective responsibilities (paid or honorific): in central or local administration, the law courts, town councils, municipal health and poor relief, in local guild and parish organisations, as town waits and night watchmen, in the many corporations of merchants and professionals, or even in 'private'

---

[62] J. Habermas, *The structural transformation of the public sphere: an enquiry into a category of bourgeois society* (Boston, MA, and Oxford, 1989; first published as *Strukturwandel der Öffentlichkeit*, Neuwied, 1962); see also R. Koselleck, *Critique and crisis: Enlightenment and the pathogenesis of modern society* (Oxford, 1988).

[63] Major scholarly contributions to this debate include K. Baker, 'Public opinion as political invention' in his *Inventing the French Revolution* (New York, 1990); A. J. de la Vopa, 'Conceiving a public: ideas and society in 18thC Europe', *Journal of Modern History*, 64 (1992), 79–116; J. Brewer, 'This, that and the other: public, social and private in the 17th and 18th centuries', in D. Castiglione and L. Sharpe (eds.), *Shifting the boundaries: transformation of the languages of public and private in the eighteenth century* (Exeter, 1995); Raymond, 'The newspaper, public opinion and the public sphere', in Raymond (ed.), *News, newspapers and society*, 109–40; J. Van Horn Melton, *The rise of the public in enlightenment Europe* (Cambridge, 2001); A. Gestrich, 'The public sphere and the Habermas debate', *German History*, 24 (2006), 413–29; P. Lake and S. Pincus (eds.), *The politics of the public sphere in early modern England* (Manchester, 2007), and a follow-up discussion in the *Journal of British Studies*, 56 (2017), 709–854; M. Rospocher (ed.), *Beyond the public sphere: opinions, publics, spaces, in early modern Europe* (Bologna and Berlin, 2012).

institutions such as masonic orders, convivial clubs or reading societies. Offices were of course in part status-giving, but might also be financially rewarding, and in some contexts might be the venal or even hereditary 'property' of the incumbent. Some positions, notably as representatives in Assemblies, Estates or parliaments, were nominally elective, but rarely democratically so. Any attempt, therefore, to impose a notional separation between 'public' and 'private' before 1789 is doomed to failure, or at best liable to anachronistic misunderstanding.[64] Contemporaries did not use these words in ways consistent with more recent practice and had no difficulty understanding special interests, privileges and corporations, patronage relationships, or the innumerable personal or family interests that affected relationships within highly deferential and status-conscious communities.

The Habermas theory, despite its empirical weaknesses, has nevertheless led to a vigorous discussion amongst historians regarding the role of 'public opinion' – a term which, as we saw in Chapter 2, was occasionally used by early modern writers themselves. But if the word 'public' needs careful historical contextualisation, so does 'opinion'. As we have seen in this chapter, the shared norms of religious beliefs had been prone to bitter dispute ever since the Reformation and were now further undermined by the critical evaluation of the Bible itself as a flawed historical narrative. The autonomy of individual conscience had to some extent been acknowledged in most versions of Christianity, but in theological terms the existence of free will and personal choice (as opposed to predestination and the doctrine of the elect) was hotly contested between and within even the major Protestant churches such as Lutheranism and Calvinism. Not surprisingly, this had a profound impact on contemporary notions of what 'public opinion' might amount to and above all on questions of who was entitled to provide the core ideals around which much messier individual opinions might converge. It is of course absurd to postulate that a general consensus on religious or political issues might ever have existed: the difficulty was always defining who was entitled to make their opinions generally known, in what contexts and within what strict bounds of decorum, tradition, beliefs and power structures. On a rational and ethical level, Locke was clearly right in arguing that the civil magistrate should leave decisions of conscientious belief to the individual and should seek to guarantee religious toleration as the only workable basis for the reconstruction of a peaceful civil society; but his message was itself deeply

[64] The word 'public' was, however, in common use in the major languages: see for example G. Baldwin, 'The "public" as a rhetorical community in early modern England', in A. Shepard and P. Withington (eds.), *Communities in early modern England* (Manchester, 2000), 199–215.

controversial, as the published responses to his *Letter on toleration* demonstrated.

In secular matters, and not least in terms of the exercise of power at all levels, the rights of the individual were not always clearly acknowledged. Even where elections were held, the choice by the individual voter was both restricted and very public: the idea of a secret ballot would have gone against accepted notions of community and transparency. In short, the individual interest was invariably subject to the supposed collective interests of the community as a whole. It is therefore not difficult to understand why in effect two mutually excluding concepts of public opinion were well established by the early eighteenth century: on the one hand, an idealised and abstract consensus, as outlined for example in Hobbes's *Leviathan* and later developed by Rousseau in his 'general will'; on the other, the much grubbier, potentially corrupt or divisive opinions of individuals promoting 'factions', or even risking rabble-rousing polemics and public disturbance in pursuit of divergent opinions at odds with the consensus. The second of these types of opinion could easily be deemed contrary to the 'public interest' and in some eyes might appear literally intolerable.

Political, social and religious disagreements exist in every society which has the appropriate conceptual language and means of communication. During the period 1640–1721, however, such disagreements became more visible because of several distinctive developments. First, the profound ideological and religious disputes already made irreconcilable by the Reformation were now given detailed rational and scholarly substance, with major and inescapable implications for perceptions of authority and power in civil society as a whole. Second, a rapidly growing experimentation and freedom in the use of language itself allowed a more refined expression of key concepts in the vernacular and potentially wider dissemination outside the exclusive educated elite. And third, the rapid growth in the use of print made these redrawn and exceptionally polarised opinions accessible to a much broader range of readers. In terms both of location and time, these changes were uneven and often dependent on the recurrent instabilities in politics and power during these decades – making inescapable but contradictory interpretations relevant for all. The virtual community of readers in some languages (but not in all) clearly grew rapidly from the late 1630s and again during the political-religious crises of the 1680s onwards. The innovative vocabulary, styles and format of some writings facilitated a socially more diverse engagement in politics at all levels of society, and particularly in urban communities. It is also clear that many readers were propelled forward as first-time authors – visibly democratising and energising the market for print during periods of critical instability, first in England and the Netherlands, but soon also in France, parts of the German lands and Italy. The process was not all-pervasive: the growth in reading skills was largely urban, in social terms mostly encompassing the lower middling sorts upwards, with male authors remaining strongly predominant. We also need to remember that 'public opinion' was never monolithic or even coherent, did not take similar form in different parts of Europe during the later seventeenth century and did not follow similar patterns amongst different kinds of readers or in different places. The decades around 1700 therefore cannot be portrayed as a 'turning point' in the emergence of a new 'public sphere' or some kind of 'modernity'. But public opinion, however we define it, was becoming a more obviously recognisable component in politics.

In matters of authority and power, different forms of communication served distinct purposes. Verbal and manuscript communication was used in much the same ways as always; visual material, as we saw in Chapter 2, developed in new directions and for new purposes, with woodcut and more nuanced copper-plate engraving making wider dissemination possible. At a basic level, the printing of texts allowed cheaper and much wider distribution. But this was not merely incremental change: as English evidence in the 1640s demonstrated, a printed text was capable of serving a manifestly different purpose in terms of intent and impact. Printed texts signalled an intent to 'go public': compared with manuscript, they not only made possible a more consistent projection across time and space, but also openly broke the implicit assumption inherent in manuscript, that the communicated text was private to the writer and the recipient. Even where censorship could be made to work, a printed text provided potential access for any reader, effectively beyond the direct control of either the author or the authorities. Readers were able to join something akin to an imagined community – independent, dispersed individuals who mostly did not know each other personally but nonetheless could feel part of a like-minded group. This reading public was in some respects similar to the older 'republic of letters', but without the obvious limitations of status, education and social background, and without the need for any letters of introduction – a more democratic virtual community, far less controllable, ultimately accessible to anyone with the leisure to read or listen.

In towns where printing was available, not only did the kinds and formats of texts rapidly diversify, but – as the English civil wars and political crises elsewhere had already demonstrated conclusively – hitherto passive and marginal readers were more likely to become directly engaged. As with the modern internet, the use of print became self-reinforcing, and manifestly had the potential of politicising spaces and arenas outside the confines of princely courts and the political elite. This dissemination is not adequately summed up in an ill-defined phrase such as 'public sphere'. Rather, the role of print made discussion potentially accessible to all, both those in positions of authority and those who were not – a revolution in communication, dissemination and political engagement, which happened first in the Netherlands and England, more tentatively in France until boosted by the misjudged policies of 1685, then spreading more widely. Because of the profound instabilities in European politics, a lively public and private discussion was bound to develop wherever a wider reading community could access a range of texts.

Historians of print have so far made only limited progress in determining who the new readers really were and how their reading may have affected their sense of agency. But we do have a much clearer idea of the kinds of backgrounds from which the new army of authors came; and we know much more about the complexities of the industries and markets that made decentralised printing possible. Crucially, that brings us to the content itself: what these texts themselves can now do, better than other historical source material, is to provide extensive information on the issues which were most prominent in public debate – not just matters of religion (including both the finer details of theology as well as issues of church governance and restraints on latitudinarian tendencies) but also increasingly rational analysis of civil society and governance, and even the imaginary alternative worlds conjured up in fiction.

Most observers at all levels of society remained very uncomfortable questioning their own loyalty to a traditional form of government and its impersonation (or, in the case notably of England in 1689 and 1714–15, and in Sweden in 1718, bluntly discarding the senior line within a ruling family). Remembering the uncertainty of the 1640s and 50s, many feared a fundamental breakdown of civil authority altogether, if heredity and rank were questioned. On the other hand, tradition in some cases offered no convincing prospect of security at all: even if radical visionaries such as the Quakers or John Toland went to extremes, more limited fresh political thinking now made practical sense. Analytical re-evaluation of the very idea of monarchy – rule by one person or body (whether by divine right or by notional contract) – may have led to a number of different conclusions, but certainly did not lack depth.[65] We have noted a number of texts that tackled this core issue in fundamentally different ways – from Hobbes's *Leviathan* of 1651, through Spinoza and Locke, to Fénelon's use of a story from the classics in his

---

[65] For recent work in this field, see notably R. Asch, *Sacral kingship between disenchantment and re-enchantment: the French and English monarchies 1587–1688* (New York, 2014).

Adventures of Telemachus, or Montesquieu's brilliant satire in his 1721 bestseller *Persian Letters*, and many more. But in addition we also need to recognise a much wider body of printed material – some of it anonymous, some circulated illegally – which may well have been just as important to contemporary readers. The challenges were profound, and in context it is hardly surprising that arguments both for religious toleration and for slightly more freedom of expression remained extremely contentious. It is also understandable that cautious writers such as Locke adhered to strict anonymity for some of their publications.

4   Translation and Transmission across Cultural Borders

Anyone who has ever undertaken translation for publication knows that a perfect rendition is unattainable, and that accuracy is a matter of interpretation and judgment. The basic vocabulary may be relatively straightforward, but once we venture into more complex texts there are many choices to be made: at one end of the spectrum is a fairly mechanical translation conveying the sentence structure and vocabulary in a functional way, while staying close to the original; as opposed to a more creative 'cultural translation' that may attempt to transmit the conceptual and cultural resonances of the text by means of a more sophisticated choice of words aspiring to link the mental worlds of the author and the new reader. All readers (including a potential translator) have imagery and cultural constructs of their own, with which a translation somehow has to connect. Poetry is therefore almost impossible to translate in a way that stays close to the original, and more prosaic literary texts can present huge challenges too. Should the translator be primarily a native speaker of the target language, or is a more balanced bilingual fluency preferable? How familiar should the translator be with the subject matter, before starting? If the original author is still available, is contact or even consultation desirable, let alone formal approval of the new version? If the original text includes quotations from, or indirect references to, another language (even to the new target language itself), should the translator revert to that version rather than (re)translate the text at hand? How does the translator deal with passages or references that may have been clear in the original language, but may not make sense to new readers in a different cultural environment? If there is already an existing translation – or more challenging still, the translator is using an intermediary translation (rather than the original) as the basis for work – who decides between alternative interpretations?

Many more questions and problems could be added, but for now it may be as well merely to note that some of the best early modern translators recognised all these problems, sometimes even making their choices clear in a translator's preface, or (by the later eighteenth century) in the discussions that sometimes arose in the more enterprising review jour-nals. Others, however, undertook a translation with scant concern for the integrity of the original, in effect rewriting the text to suit their own purposes. As we shall see in this chapter, the finer detail of 'cultural translation' – how far translators should act as cultural intermediaries – was not lost on those contemporary readers who were sensitive to the difficulties of locating precise meanings across language barriers. The difficulties were exacerbated by the havoc that various forms of censor-ship and print regulation could wreak even on apparently innocuous texts: controversy might be good for sales, but an outright ban, if enforced, might destroy any financial or reputational gains from the whole translation enterprise.

For the historian of print, however, these difficulties are a real and positive asset. First, the very fact that a translation was attempted, when it was undertaken and whether it led to publication gives us clear evidence that the original text was considered to be of interest in the target-language community, specifically for readers not sufficiently educated to read it in its original language. Translation therefore makes geographic dissemination much easier to map out. An early modern text in a standard language accessible to the educated elite across Europe (usually Latin, but by the eighteenth century more often French) can be difficult to locate in cultural or geographic terms, precisely because the language was in common international use, and such texts were often distributed across Europe. By contrast, a text newly translated into any other language immediately allows us to see that either the publisher or the translator thought that there was a wider market for it amongst readers who had no access to the original language.

Translations also raise interesting questions of timing. A text such as Milton's *Defence of the English people* of 1651, originally published solely in Latin, for an international audience, had its first English translation 41 years after publication (in 1692) and appeared in French 138 years later (in 1789). In both cases the reasons for renewed interest are obvious, in context, but still provide us with clear evidence of impact amongst readers other than those for whom the work had originally been intended. That said, we have to recognise that the timing of translations (or indeed sometimes their failure to get into print) could also be either accidental or the result of personal factors: the baron d'Holbach, one of the leading Paris intellectuals of the later eighteenth century, and the host of one of the most important salons, not only wrote a number of extremely subversive texts which he published anonymously, but also organised and paid for transla-tions of a number of 'dangerous' books from abroad (some old) that he wanted the French to read.[1] He had the resources and hidden networks to bring many of these projects to fruition, but his selection was somewhat arbitrary and idiosyncratic. Similarly, we should not ignore texts that failed to make an impact in translation primarily because the translator had done a poor job. Accident, personal factors and market unpredictability are all part of the historical evidence we can use in mapping cross-border dissemination. Most of the texts discussed in this chapter have complicated 'life stories' of their own, with clear implications for the international exchange of ideas.

There is an even better reason why, as historians, we might want to pay close attention to translations. Given that any translator should try to understand the text properly, we in effect get a reader's interpretation every time we see a new translation – an interpretation which is of course sensitive to the cultural context as well as the specific political moment in which it was produced. Every translation therefore becomes a (possibly slightly distorting) mirror reflecting the way a text might have been understood at the time: in other words, we can use the new version to help us analyse how the translator interpreted the source text in a particular time and place. Moreover, if reviews of the translation were also published, we can see disputed interpretations and disagreements regarding the degree of cultural adaptation which every translator necessarily has to undertake. And of course if the translation is not based on the originating language, but rather on an intermediary language, the result is likely to be substantially further removed from the original – as we shall see later in this chapter with well-known examples such as Beccaria's *On crimes and punishments* of 1764.

Dictionaries and Encyclopedias

It is difficult to imagine how exploration, travel and international trade could be conducted in an age before pocket dictionaries or phrase books were readily available. Dictionaries were first compiled as manuscript

---

[1] Baron d'Holbach was particularly keen to secure French versions of older English radicals, which he knew would otherwise be forgotten. By having these texts rendered in the dominant transnational language of the day, he gave them much wider impact, but also reminded readers of the long tradition of materialist philosophy. See M. Kozul, *Les lumières imaginaires: Holbach et la traduction* (Oxford University Studies in the Eighteenth Century, 2016: 05, Oxford 2016); N. Treuberz, 'The diffusion and impact of Baron d'Holbach's texts in Great Britain, 1765–1800', in L. Curelly and N. Smith (eds.), *Radical voices, radical ways: articulating and disseminating radicalism in seventeenth- and eighteenth-century Britain* (Manchester, 2016), 125–47; M. Schmeisser, 'Baron d'Holbach in Deutschland: Reaktionen in deutschen Zeitschriften der Aufklärung', in C. Haug, F. Mayer and W. Schröder (eds.), *Geheimliteratur und Geheimbuchhandel in Europa im 18. Jahrhundert* (Wiesbaden, 2011), 85–108.

glossaries, for use in the study either of the ancient classics or theology. Amongst Protestant reformers and theologians, the rapidly expanding demand for new vernacular Bibles and commentaries made printed dictionaries indispensable and economically viable. A *Dictionarium trilingue* was published by Sebastian Münster in Basel in 1530, covering the main languages needed for Biblical studies (Hebrew, Greek and Latin). The following year the well-established Paris scholar and printer Robert Estienne (1503–59), who had a particular interest both in theology and in Cicero, launched a substantial two-volume folio Latin dictionary and thesaurus with French translations, which over the next decades went through several revised editions and fostered competitors. In 1572 Robert's son, Henri Estienne, completed a huge Greek dictionary covering 64,000 words in over 4000 folio pages. By then, a wide array of dictionaries was available, some of them monolingual (giving definitions, or synonyms as in a thesaurus), some bilingual with Latin as the referencepoint. Multilingual dictionaries were also compiled, such as Christophe Plantin's *Dictionarium tetraglotton* of 1562 (with 20,000 entries covering Latin, Greek, French and Dutch).

By the early seventeenth century, in response partly to demands for translations of Luther's German Bible and other religious texts, most important European languages had acquired substantial bilingual dictionaries to and from the bridging language, Latin – ranging from Thomas Elyot's 424-page English–Latin dictionary of 1538 to more modest Danish (1626) and Swedish (1640) dictionaries for school use. Bilingual dictionaries linking two vernacular languages also appeared, no doubt intended in the first instance for use in everyday international exchange. Coverage of older languages followed, such as the *Dictionarium saxonico-latino-anglicum* of 1659, as well as glossaries for non-European languages. Yet for some small language groups there was a much longer wait, for example until 1741 for the first Gaelic dictionary (published by the Scottish Society for Promoting Christian Knowledge, for school use).[2] Basic grammars and word lists also became readily available during the eighteenth century, alongside short stories and parallel-text translations for instructional purposes.

Compact dictionaries for portable or educational use, however, could not meet the needs of translators of more complex texts. We do not know as much as we should about these often hidden literary entrepreneurs: foreign books were often published without the name of the translator, unless he (more rarely she) had made a real reputation. We may therefore

---

[2] A helpful overview is found in J. Considine, *Dictionaries in early modern Europe: lexicography and the making of heritage* (Cambridge, 2008).

have to assume that the translator could have been either an enthusiastic reader with time to spare, or (as in the case of for example d'Holbach's secret network) a would-be author acting as translator to secure a modest living in the 'grub street' cultural life of Paris or another city. Judging from contemporary comment (to which we will return), not all translators were fully proficient in the languages from which they translated, so the demand for substantial and scholarly dictionaries was bound to rise in step with the growing market for translated texts.

From the late seventeenth century, as French became the dominant international language replacing Latin, a more substantial academic lexicography was deemed necessary. César-Pierre Richelet's *Dictionnaire françois* of 1680 tried to meet that demand, with Antoine Furetière's a decade later (posthumous, published in the Netherlands in defiance of the French authorities), followed by the long-delayed launch in 1694 of what was meant as a 'definitive' reference work, the *Dictionnaire* compiled under the auspices of the Académie Française. The aim was to standardise good usage, but in the opinion of some, the work of the Académie in particular was part of the cultural absolutism of Louis XIV's advisers. Rival dictionaries continued to appear, such as the *Dictionnaire de Trévoux* (1704), and by the end of the eighteenth century the dominance of the Académie was challenged on several fronts. As we shall see below, the French Revolution had a dramatic impact on the French language, noted all over Europe.[3]

Other major languages were slow to follow French leads. Samuel Johnson's monumental *Dictionary of the English language* (London, 1755), compiled over seven years and published by a consortium backed by benefactors and subscribers, was a much more detailed compilation which also included many examples of older usage. It was a huge success despite its very large format and high cost: first issued in two folio volumes, it covered over 40,000 keywords, with definitions, quotations to explain specific usage, synonyms and other invaluable information. It was indisputably the most thorough guide to any language, to date, and remained definitive until work started on the Oxford English Dictionary a century later. Significantly, Johnson's *Dictionary* earned him a substantial fee of 1500 guineas, but took a long time (and editions in more practical formats) to become fully profitable. Despite having significantly smaller vocabularies than English or French, other European languages struggled to produce anything remotely equivalent. A large

---

[3] Richelet's dictionary had at least twenty-two reprints and revisions over the next century, despite competing against a number of later arrivals. See R. Reichardt and E. Schmitt, *Handbuch politisch-sozialer Grundbegriffe in Frankreich 1680–1820* (Munich, 1985), vol. I, 86–107.

Dutch dictionary was compiled by Pieter Wieland (1799–1811), but was not regarded as definitive. It took the Danish Academy of Sciences so long to complete their full dictionary (launched with a first volume in 1793) that scholars such as Christian Molbech chose to produce more manageable reference works from the 1820s.

Meantime, for some of these smaller language groups, bi- or trilingual dictionaries may have served a useful bridging purpose. A good example of how this could work is the Swedish–English–Latin dictionary by Jacob Serenius (first published in Hamburg in 1734, followed by new editions in Stockholm 1741 and Nyköping in 1757). This work was no doubt aimed primarily at those Swedes who wanted to learn English, but as a very large quarto volume with around 400 pages printed in double columns, and sold by subscription, it would not have been accessible to users on a limited budget. What is interesting in this context is that it included a preface in both English and Swedish, emphasising the importance of accuracy and context (with, in the 1757 edition, explicit reference to Johnson's Dictionary – though Serenius's was much shorter). The dictionary used Latin as a bridging language in order to explain the complex usage of certain English words to the Swedish reader. For example, the English word 'common' is broken down into distinct meanings, each with a Latin keyword, so that its use in phrases such as 'common thing', 'common prayer' and 'common people', each with a Swedish equivalent phrase, could be distinguished from more politically oriented use as in 'common council', 'common law', or 'common-wealth'. Revealingly, 'commonwealth' is defined as 'res publica', that is, a state or regime with a republican government, as opposed to a monarchy – a distinction that would have been disputed by Hobbes, but was highly relevant to Sweden in this period of severely limited constitutional monarchy.[4]

By the eighteenth century, however, readers with less technical but more wide-ranging interests in language could increasingly look elsewhere. Encyclopedias were not a new invention, nor was the desire to try to represent universal knowledge in a single compendium, normally organised thematically in some grand system of knowledge. Publishing one in a language other than Latin, however, could be a response to changing markets, or might signal a desire to reach different kinds of readers; and the use of articles based on keywords, sorted alphabetically, made it much easier to construct large serialised compilations that could be published over a period of years (spreading costs) and could even add

---

[4] Jacobus Serenius, *Dictionarium Anglo-Svethico-Latinum* (Hamburg,1734), revised as Jacob Serenius, *An English and Swedish dictionary wherein the generality of words and various significations are rendered into Swedish and Latin* (Nyköping, 1757).

new entries and ideas as work progressed. The encyclopedias of the eighteenth century thus offered a more accessible and entertaining route to better understanding, and their editors could (as we have already seen in the case of Bayle's biographical dictionary) use the alphabet sequence to construct more complex reference works (thus also helping to confuse censors and critics by including ideas and contradictions in unexpected places).

A number of general and specialist reference works appeared from the 1690s onwards: Thomas Corneille's *Dictionnaire des arts et des métiers* of 1694; John Harris's *Lexicum technicum or an universal English dictionary of arts and sciences* (1704); as well as works focusing on science, economy and trade. In London, the two-volume *Cyclopædia or an universal dictionary of arts and sciences* published by Ephraim Chambers in 1728 was a particular commercial success, going through at least twelve printings before 1789, and thereby becoming a natural target both for translation and for pirated Dublin editions. A much larger *Universal Lexicon* was launched by Johann Heinrich Zedler in Leipzig/Halle in 1732, but took so long to complete (1754) and was so large and expensive (sixty-eight volumes) that it would have been inaccessible to most users. A different path was taken by the Paris publisher André-François Le Breton, who in 1745 secured royal privilege (copyright) for a proposed French translation of Chambers' *Cyclopædia* in 1745, but the plan failed. Two years later, a new consortium of publishers (including Le Breton) agreed on an editorial team consisting of Denis Diderot and Jean le Rond d'Alembert: starting with the idea of an augmented translation, they turned the project into something much more innovative and at times polemical.[5]

The first volume of this new *Encyclopédie, ou dictionnaire raisonné* appeared in 1751, launching what quickly turned into one of the most ambitious and controversial publishing initiatives of the eighteenth century. Originally projected to be complete in ten volumes, it ended up having seventeen volumes of around 1000 pages each, printed in double columns in a generous folio format, running to around 20 million words of text clustered around 72,000 keywords. As the volumes came out sequentially, there was ample publicity and controversy surrounding the project, which helped in raising the total number of subscribers from an initial 1400 to over 4000. The director of the book trade, Malesherbes, played a key role in protecting the

[5] R. Yeo, 'Encyclopaedism and Enlightenment', in M. Fitzpatrick, P. Jones, C. Knellwolf and I. McCalman (eds.), *The Enlightenment world* (London, 2004), 350–65; P. Swiggers, 'Préhistoire et histoire de l'*Encyclopédie*', *Revue historique*, 271 (1984), 83–92.

work from early censure, but the panic following the attempted assassination of Louis XV in 1757 strengthened its critics so much that the *Encyclopédie* was banned (stalling publication following volume 7). Yet Malesherbes continued to protect Diderot's work, and the final ten volumes appeared in 1765 under a false imprint (with some articles toned down or truncated by Le Breton, to avoid further trouble). The accompanying eleven volumes of superb plates were completed by 1772.

In 1979, Robert Darnton set new standards for book history with the publication of his magisterial study of the afterlife of the *Encyclopédie*. Thanks to his research, and that of other scholars including John Lough, we know more about the history of the *Encyclopédie* than about any other publishing initiative of the Enlightenment. Darnton established that, although the whole set originally cost subscribers a hefty 980 livres, smaller reprints (and some pirated adaptations) brought the price down to 240 livres by 1781. By 1789, the *Encyclopédie* had gone through six editions, so that an estimated 25,000 copies were in circulation in France and abroad – a truly staggering diffusion considering that the price was by then still equivalent to half the annual wage of a labourer. As Darnton made clear, we cannot be entirely sure who the readers were, but these numbers suggest that the work had already acquired an unrivalled reputation as the standard reference work of the French Enlightenment. It even enticed Le Breton's successor, the entrepreneurial publisher Panckoucke, to launch a new and still more ambitious updated *Encyclopédie méthodique* in 1782, which took half a century to complete and eventually ran to 160 volumes.[6]

The success of the *Encyclopédie* can be attributed to several factors: the impressive array of at least 140 contributing authors (many of the articles had no identifier); the enticing range of articles, intended to cover all human knowledge but with a clear emphasis on practical and scientific material; and (despite uneven quality) the sheer detail. Just as important in the present context were its internal self-contradictions – some of them accidental or arising from the lapse of time, some deliberate (as in larger articles with multiple authors, where ambiguity and contradiction was plain for all to see). Some contradictions were quite unexpected – one notes how the articles 'Intolérance' and 'Tolérance' in no way match, either in style or content, even though both were published in 1765. We cannot be sure whether this was to confuse the censors, or to allow a free hand for the contributors, chosen as they were from across the intellectual

---

[6] R. Darnton, *The business of Enlightenment: a publishing history of the Encyclopédie, 1775–1800* (Cambridge, MA, 1979); and J. Lough, *The Encyclopédie* (London, 1971).

spectrum in eighteenth-century France.[7] But the inclusion of some very conservative viewpoints was no doubt deliberate, to ensure the whole work was acceptable to as many readers as possible. In that sense the *Encyclopédie* was a true reflection of the rich complexity, changeability and lack of coherence of the French Enlightenment.

Not surprisingly, Diderot himself was overworked and at times exhausted, and he had recurrent doubts about both the work as a whole and the quality of articles from individual contributors. His indefatigable and unpaid assistant, Louis de Jaucourt (1704–79), who took on an ever-greater part in managing the project, and was by far the most prolific contributor overall, was less openly belligerent in tone than some of the more famous contributors. D'Alembert never fully settled in his role as co-editor and left altogether in 1758. Rousseau was a major contributor (with nearly 400 articles), but just as his paranoia damaged many of his other friendships, so he fell out with Diderot even while work on the *Encyclopédie* was still progressing. Other prominent contributors, such as Voltaire, were uncomfortable with the radical tone of some of the articles, privately distancing themselves from the whole enterprise whilst remaining supportive in public in order not to be seen to support conservative critics. Voltaire's own approach is more clearly discerned in his own bestselling *Dictionnaire philosophique portatif* of 1764. However, Paul Thiry, baron d'Holbach (1723–89) remained one of Diderot's most consistent supporters and benefactors, contributing a large number of acknowledged pieces on geology and minerals. But as we know from the way he handled his later (more controversial) publications, d'Holbach often hid behind anonymity or pseudonymity, so it seems likely that he may have had a hand in other more politically subversive sections and no doubt discussed overall strategy with Diderot.

For these and other reasons, the *Encyclopédie* remains to this day a richly unpredictable and sometimes frustrating work to use, just as it was for its first readers. However, in line with many other major reference works over the previous decades, the *Encyclopédie* did from the outset provide guidance towards a systematisation of knowledge. Already in volume 1, readers found a grand if not entirely convincing schema of all branches of knowledge (the *Système figuré des connoissances humaines* attached to d'Alembert's 'Preliminary Discourse'). The real point of the *Encyclopédie*, however, was to challenge and potentially change the

---

[7] F. A. Kafker and S. L. Kafker, *The Encyclopedists as individuals: a biographical dictionary of the authors of the Encyclopédie* (*SVEC* 257, Oxford, 1988); F. A. Kafker, *The Encyclopedists as a group: a collective biography of the authors of the Encyclopédie* (*SVEC* 345, Oxford, 1996).

knowledge and reasoning of its readers. Diderot, who wrote some of the most subversive articles, used his long entry under the keyword 'Encyclopédie' to encourage readers to use the work interactively as a hypertext: explicit cross-references (*renvois*) and unexpected connections took readers off on tangents and even to creative self-contradictions. Using keywords was a brilliant way of leading readers astray and not infrequently confusing them.[8]

As we would expect, the *Encyclopédie* contained articles on language itself, and on translation, which rarely resolved the conceptual and philosophical difficulties caused by its eclecticism.[9] The words used as headings at the start of most articles were in themselves revealing, even though they represented a smaller vocabulary than big dictionaries such as Johnson's. For example, the article headed 'Enthousiasme' made clear that the word was difficult to define, but was normally to be taken to mean a kind of fury which captures the spirit, inflames the imagination but also makes us say or do extraordinary things driven by emotion rather than reason. The anonymous article on 'Miracle' was more circumspect, defining the concept formally as an event or effect that does not match any known laws of nature, but noting differences of opinion: it mentioned that Spinoza had argued that it was not rationally possible for the laws of nature to be broken, but also cited authors who believed this conclusion to be incorrect and discussed a number of examples which might point either way. A later, very short article, 'Superstition', allowed Jaucourt to take a philosophical view of excessive religious credulity, without going into detail. It is also interesting to observe that part of Spinoza's work ('Spinosa, philosophie de') was discussed in greater detail than 'Newtonianisme', and was quite unlike the presentation of most of the more traditional thinkers.[10]

---

[8] An interesting case study of how this might work is J. Vanpée, 'La femme mode d'emploi: how to read the article FEMME in the *Encyclopédie*', in D. Brewer and J. C. Hayes (eds.), *Using the Encyclopédie: ways of knowing, ways of reading* (*SVEC* 2002: 05, Oxford, 2002), 229–45.

[9] J. C. Hayes, 'Translation (in)version and the encyclopedic network', in *Using the Encyclopédie* (*SVEC* 2002: 05), 99–118.

[10] Diderot's own article on 'Hobbisme', however, is extensive and was clearly based on Diderot's own reading of Hobbes's work, including *De cive* and the Latin (not the English) version of *Leviathan*. Diderot emphasises that it was the experience of civil war that pushed Hobbes to argue for unconditional sovereign control and includes a long list of single-sentence summaries of key points from his politics. Diderot notes Hobbes's inclinations towards materialism, but does not deal with the analysis of Biblical authority found in the *Leviathan*. All articles in the *Encyclopédie* cited here are located by means of the keyword itself, either in the original printed edition or using the digitised version prepared by ARTFL (online digital resource managed by The Project for American and French Research on the Treasury of the French Language).

Civil society in general, the natural social orders and people ('Peuple') are all discussed in substantial detail, with a great deal of information on nobility and privilege, the clergy as a social order, citizens, bourgeois (as an inhabitant of a town), lawyers, financiers, skilled craftsmen (and their crafts), those who work the land, the poor and beggars. Social inequality is noted, but despite occasional references to the natural equality of man (for example in 'Société') there is rarely any hint of a wish to change the existing order. A fairly long article on 'Economie' was written by Rousseau for vol. V (published 1755) and heralds some of his later ideas: for example, it has recurrent statements of the need for government in conformity with both the law and the best interests of the people, and notes the need for consent and respect for what he (and other contributors) already call the 'general will' – a concept which is explored more precisely in Diderot's article on natural law ('Droit naturel'). Surprisingly for an article on economy, Rousseau has only vague ideas on fiscal policies[11] and does not press the need for change or reform, except to encourage more opportunity and better public education. There is no hint of the sharp economic analysis provided by the great minds of the French Revolution.

A number of other articles tackled political topics head on, for example Diderot's own article in the first volume, under 'Autorité' – which stated bluntly that no man has received from nature the authority or right to command others, and that liberty is a right which belongs to everyone. The article on power ('Pouvoir') reiterates the need for consent and argues that the purpose of all government is the greater good of society; yet its sub-article 'Pouvoir paternel' takes a more traditional patriarchal view of authority within the family, as a natural responsibility, without seriously questioning the subordination of women. Other articles, such as Jaucourt's discussion of 'Monarchie', give an impression of moderate political views in line with the work of Montesquieu, paying no attention for example to the radical republicanism of 1650s England. Yet in an article published earlier, in volume 4 (1754), Diderot had cited Montesquieu as the authority for a biting critique of a court which:

conceals ambition in idleness, baseness within pride, desire for enrichment without work, aversion to truth, flattery, treason, perfidy, abandonment of all commitment, contempt for the responsibilities of the citizen, fear of the virtue of the prince and hopes for his weakness...[12]

---

[11] A very thorough discussion of taxation was added to the very end of the last volume, out of alphabetical order, under 'Vingtième', covering much more of the detailed fiscal debate that was taking place in France at this time; see also Jaucourt on 'Impot', and for a wider discussion of *laissez-faire* economics, Turgot's article on 'Fondation'.

[12] Diderot, 'Cour', p. 355. As John Lough noted a long time ago, there is more explicit political material to be found elsewhere: Lough, *The Encyclopédie*, 271–326.

In short, the *Encyclopédie* was an extraordinary work, containing many different polemics and counter-polemics all within one set of volumes. It probably represents French political and scientific thinking in mid-eighteenth century better than any other work – but as Diderot himself explicitly recognised, the cultural identities of France were composite and constantly changing, so no reference work such as his would stand the test of time. He also noted that the language in which such identities might be expressed required constant redefinition: enlightenment was, in short, work in progress.[13] Diderot's was neither the first nor the last great reference work published during the Enlightenment, and certainly not the most accurate or consistent, but it was the most significant in its use of language and in overall impact, and the boldest in terms of exploring the limits of what censors and the state could tolerate. By comparison, *Encyclopaedia Britannica*, first published in three volumes in Edinburgh in 1768–71, or the German *Conversations-Lexicon* published in Leipzig in six volumes from 1796 to 1808, were much more modest functional productions: as such they had a longer (indeed continuing) afterlife, but lacked the startling unpredictability and imagination of the *Encyclopédie*.

Theories of Language and the Tower of Babel

In the early modern period, the normative explanation for the great diversity and disconnected groupings of languages was the Biblical story of the tower of Babel (Genesis, 11: 1–9): the descendants of Noah, in trying to build a huge tower to reach heaven, were thwarted by divine intervention that made them unable to understand each other, so they gave up and dispersed across the world. The whole narrative in Genesis, however, created a number of related intellectual challenges, not least the theory of polygenesis raised by La Peyrère in 1655, problematising issues of identity, ethnicity and race,[14] as well as a range of other questions regarding divine action and historical time (see Chapter 3). When Diderot wrote his short entry on 'Babel' in volume 2 of the *Encyclopédie*, he was therefore able to insert alternative explanations – a now characteristic way of casting doubt on established dogma. He even suggested that the archaeological remains attributed to the tower of Babel, near the Euphrates, were unconvincing.

Theories about the origin of communication through signs, symbols and vocalisations had already been examined by philosophers for some time, inconclusively. The Protestant insistence that 'in the beginning was the

---

[13] For a full discussion, see R. Morrissey, 'The *Encyclopédie*: monument for a nation', in *Using the Encyclopédie* (*SVEC* 2002: 05, Oxford, 2002), 143–61.

[14] Brilliantly discussed by Colin Kidd, *The forging of races: race and scripture in the Protestant Atlantic world 1600–2000* (Cambridge, 2006).

word' created more problems than it resolved. If Christian theology assumed that Adam and Eve spoke fluently, rational analysis called for alternative theories of the origins of speech. In reaction to Descartes, Hobbes considered disagreement over words and language one of the fundamental sources of tension and conflict in society, and a major problem. Philosophers also struggled with the relationship between cognitive processes, rational abstract understanding and the changing nature of language. For Locke, language was one of the core systems of knowledge we learn, but which itself evolves – constantly redefined in use and from experience, without reference to some pre-ordained or universal system. Leibniz disagreed, and since the issue was fundamental to any understanding of reason, meaning and communication, a succession of Enlightenment thinkers confronted the issue. Significant amongst them was Etienne de Condillac, whose *Essai sur l'origine des connoissances humaines* (1746) took an empirical approach, seeing language as something evolving in harness with knowledge itself, from basic prehistoric gestures to classical antiquity and beyond (entirely without divine origins or plan). La Mettrie pursued this line of argument even further, in his materialist tract *L'homme-machine* (1747), which denied there was any difference between humanity and animals. Philosophers wondered whether words are necessary for cognition and conceptual analysis: can we reason without language?

Argument around these major theoretical problems intensified in the 1750s, notably in the revived Berlin Academy of Sciences and Belles Lettres led by Maupertuis. In 1757, the Academy set, as the heading for their next prize essay competition, the question 'What is the reciprocal influence of the opinion of a people on the language, and of the language on the opinion?' The winning entry, by Johann David Michaelis (1717–91), argued that language formation was truly democratic, the outcome of collective decisions and usages adopted by everyone in a language community, which no one person or authority could regulate or control. Scholars (and by extension institutions such as the Académie Française, not to mention church authorities) were despotic if they tried to impose pedantic rules, or wanted to suppress more popular and naturalistic usage. Such a radical argument, and indeed the whole competition, led to wider discussion, including journal reviews and responses by Moses Mendelssohn, Johann Georg Hamann and even by the conservative-minded Huguenot secretary of the Berlin Academy itself, Jean-Henri-Samuel Formey.[15] To these we should add a number of other authors

---

[15] Michaelis's prize essay was particularly appreciated in its French translation (1760), but also appeared in English in 1769. However, his scholarly work on history and antiquity was of longer-lasting influence. See A. Lifschitz, *Language and Enlightenment: the Berlin debates of the eighteenth century* (Oxford, 2012); and for a wider context, M. Lauzon, *Signs*

including Rousseau and, slightly later, an essay by Johann Gottfried Herder on the origin of language (1772), all hugely important in terms of intellectual and philosophical analysis amongst fellow intellectuals. In Scotland, James Burnet (Lord Monboddo) joined the discussion with the first of six volumes of his *Of the origin and progress of language* (1773). But the core philosophical issue – trying to establish whether language was a set of fundamental symbols representing rationally determined universal concepts, or whether on the contrary it was a malleable and constantly changing form of communication subject to individual creativity and imagination – remained unresolved. While these texts were significant landmarks in the theory of language, few of them attracted a wide readership either in their original language or in translation: and we may be entitled to ask whether they had much impact in the real world of writing, polemics and political discourse.

In the *Encyclopédie* itself, an exceptionally long article on 'Langue' (language) investigated cultural identity, linguistic structures, and the origins and development of vernacular languages. A number of early texts were cited, with further cross references, to throw light on the evolution of languages over time. The (unidentified) author of this article also made some significant observations, noting that:

when a language is spoken by a nation composed of several equal and independent peoples, as were the Greeks formerly, and as are now the Italians and the Germans, accepting general use of the same words and the same syntax, each people can have inflections of their own as regards pronunciation and endings of shared words: these subordinate usages, equally legitimate, constitute the dialects of the national language. When, as in ancient Rome and as in the France of today, the nation is one in respect to government, there can only be one legitimate usage in its way of speaking: any other usage which deviates from this in pronunciation, endings, syntax, or in any other way, is neither a distinct language nor a dialect of the national language. Rather, it is a *patois* given over to the ordinary people of the provinces, and each province has its own.[16]

This kind of statement certainly recognises the reality that linguistic identity and governmental sovereignty did not match very well, but it also seems to search unsuccessfully for ways of classifying dialects and idioms in relation to 'national' identity. Eighteenth-century France, like most other national conglomerates under one government, manifestly lacked the linguistic unity postulated here. Some commentators before 1789 recognised that language was an important component of national identity, and perhaps even a means of generating rational

---

of light: French and British theories of linguistic communication 1648–1789 (Ithaca, NY, 2010).
[16] The *Encyclopédie*, 'Langue', vol. IX, 249.

consensus, but readers of the *Encyclopédie* were left without full analysis of the implications.

At a more practical level, the politics of dialects and variant usages mattered, both as objects of cultural study in their own right and as a subjective aspect of functional communication and co-ordination within a group of individuals. If reasoning itself was directly dependent on the use of symbols and language, it might be shaped accordingly, as many reformers noted already during the Reformation and Counter-Reformation period, particularly in regard to religious education. By the eighteenth century, the linguistic agenda had become much broader. In 1757, for example, the Berlin Academy set, as the subject for its prize-winning essay competition, the question of whether language and public opinion are mutually dependent, perhaps even decisively so. By extension language was now recognised as potentially a key component of power, identity and even critical public awareness – conservative, affirmative or subversive. Early modern Europe was far more diverse in terms of languages and dialects than it is now and, given the surprisingly high levels of geographic mobility, language borders were fluid and permeable. But dialects could both strengthen and shape those who belong, as well as excluding outsiders – culturally, socially (vertically) and geographically (horizontally). Even simple exchanges might identify the speaker (voluntarily or not) in terms of social status, family or tribal identities. The power of language in creating a shared identity is enormous, but exploiting that power can be regarded as both negative and positive, depending on your point of view and on prevailing concepts of local, national, cultural and other identities. This potential was recognised in early modern Europe from the time of the Reformation onwards. By the later eighteenth century, and in particular (as we shall see) during the 1790s, politicians learnt to exploit language much more effectively for very specific purposes – a technique which has been firmly embedded ever since. Crucially, print almost inevitably served the purpose of standardisation and centralisation, simply because its wide dissemination created norms of expression and vocabulary, as well as normative concepts and ideas. In short, language in general, and its dissemination in print in particular, can never be a neutral medium: efforts to standardise language could be seen as a form of cultural imperialism, but could also serve to bridge dialects and create more inclusive identities – or even do both at the same time.[17]

---

[17] P. Burke, *Languages and communities in early modern Europe* (Cambridge, 2004); N. Furrer, *Die vierzigsprachige Schweiz: Sprachkontakte und Mehrsprachigkeit in der vorindustriellen Gesellschaft, 15.-19. Jahrhundert*, 2 vols. (Zurich, 2002) offers a very detailed analysis of dialects, languages and usage in one of the most multilingual regions of Europe.

From the 1990s onwards, a number of historians, notably Peter Burke, have focused attention more closely on 'cultural translation' in the early modern period – how far translators deliberately deviated from a technically 'straight' translation in order to meet the cultural norms and expectations of the intended new readers, sometimes even openly acknowledging they were doing so. In 2007, Burke argued that whilst literary scholars had done a great deal of work on translation practices in relation to individual works of fiction, collaboration with cultural historians had made less progress, especially as regards non-fiction. He noted how the Jesuit order (at the forefront of cultural translation from their founding in 1540) had recognised that the further you moved from the family of European languages, the more creative the translator had to be in order to make sense to the new audience. Missionaries in China, for example, had to borrow local cultural concepts (and the specific words in which they were expressed) in order to make sure their new hosts engaged with what they were saying: they changed the way they expressed even fundamental concepts like 'god' and 'heaven', in order to approximate to what Confucians might find intelligible. Such cultural adaptation did not meet with approval back in Rome, where such language looked like potentially heretical mistranslation. Similar problems arose in Japan, and (very differently) amongst the native tribes in north America, where the scope for ultimately fatal misunderstandings had to be weighed against more literal adherence to the original agreed Latin-defined concepts. In other words, the scope for conflict between literal and cultural translation was enormous, and, since there was a finely shaded scale in between the two, virtually every translation was bound to raise doubts and criticism. This of course explains why translation of the Bible itself, even within the main European languages, remained extremely contentious. But it also forces us to realise that the politics of translation was (and is) inescapable: translation was an absolutely essential component in any inter-cultural exchange, but relied on a string of difficult choices made by many different translators, all influenced by their personal interests in relation to sponsors and authorities, the choice of texts, and not least the intended readers and their cultural expectations. Only genuinely bi- or multilingual translators can attempt to understand both the original and the recipient culture sufficiently to make a difficult translation work really well – and the requirements for different forms of fiction and non-fiction vary substantially.[18]

[18] P. Burke, 'Cultures of translation in early modern Europe', in P. Burke and R. Po-Chia Hsia (eds.), *Cultural translation in early modern Europe* (Cambridge, 2007), 7–38; and other papers in this volume; F. Oz-Salzberger, *Translating the Enlightenment: Scottish civic discourse in eighteenth-century Germany* (Oxford, 1995), 77–85 and *passim*; from a different

Latin remained a standard language in some subjects such as medicine, botany and law; but native languages took over (at varying rates in different parts of Europe) for religious polemics, history, the emerging 'social sciences' (such as political economy), political discussion more generally, and of course most forms of fiction and poetry. As Latin lost its role of *lingua franca,* even amongst the republic of letters, and as markets for more accessible vernacular texts expanded rapidly from the later seventeenth century onwards, translation itself came under closer scrutiny. We have already seen that authors themselves increasingly faced critical decisions in their choice of language: Milton made a conscious choice of language for certain texts, using English for the domestic audience and Latin to address a wider European readership, while Spinoza chose Latin in order to deliberately reduce the risk of his writings getting into the popular domain. Hobbes had gone one big step further, writing *Leviathan* in English, then many years later producing a Latin version deliberately modified to suit his intended new readers – perhaps the first case of a free 'cultural translation' of a major work by the author himself. We will investigate this and other examples, below, to see how cultural translation might work in different contexts. But it is worth emphasising that increasing reliance on vernaculars and translation had a number of very important consequences: not only was a text in a vernacular language likely to be more clearly located in time and place than a Latin text, and not only was it accessible to a different kind of readership, but it also unavoidably became much more culture specific. Vernacular languages were more context-sensitive than the rather artificial post-Renaissance Latin still in use in traditional academic circles. If well adapted to their new cultural setting, good translations could acquire a life of their own and a much wider readership.

A number of contemporary writers and translators reflected openly on both the theory and practice of translation. Whereas Cartesian philosophy assumed a single origin for everything (including language), some eighteenth-century philosophers questioned whether all languages had the same fundamental structures and the same capacity to express ideas. Diderot's co-editor at the start of the *Encyclopédie,* d'Alembert, was amongst those who raised doubts, while some professional translators noted the logical consequence, namely that a literal translation was not always the best when bridging the gap between two different cultural environments. John Dryden had noted as much already in 1680 in his

perspective, see also J. G. A. Pocock, 'The concept of language and the *métier d'historien*: some considerations on practice', in A. Pagden (ed.), *The languages of political theory in early modern Europe* (Cambridge, 1987), 19–38.

translation of Ovid, while Anne Marie Dacier called for a more creative translation in her introduction to her French version of the *Iliad* in 1699. Montesquieu, in his *De l'esprit des loix* (1748), book 14, even attempted to give scientific justification for cultural differences on the basis of climate and environment. Many eighteenth-century translators took this much further, explaining their approach in their prefaces. Paraphrasing the original seemed to have no limits: eventually some French translators made a virtue of 'improving' their source texts by much more substantive adaptation, justifying their rewriting and reorganisation of the original by arguing that French readers expected something better. Such transmission through translation and adaptation became a major industry during the eighteenth century, especially as English and German began to catch up with French as the dominant literary languages. As Laszlo Kontler and others have observed, translation was a two-way process, potentially affecting the interpretation of the original text amongst its readers, sometimes even leading to its modification and certainly creating mutual cultural influences across linguistic borders.[19]

All kinds of texts could be treated this way, fiction as well as non-fiction. The most popular genres, especially novels, were particularly prone to creative adaptation (sometimes bordering on unacknowledged plagiarism), whereby a story could go through so many successive stages of free translation and cultural adaptation that it would no longer be clearly recognisable to the originator. Plays for the theatre often had an even more unpredictable afterlife and might end up in several substantially different forms even in the same language and under the same title: thus Beaumarchais's extremely successful play *Le mariage de Figaro* (first performed in 1784) had significantly different concurrent versions both in French and in English translation, partly as a result of censorship of certain very subversive passages and the effects of theatre licensing, partly no doubt as a result of accident or rivalry between publishers: even the English versions published in London and Dublin almost simultaneously in 1785, all crediting Thomas Holcroft as translator, differed substantially, for example in Act 5 in the variant versions of the subversive soliloquy by Figaro. The enthusiasm for translations clearly helped

---

[19] L. Kontler, *Translations, histories, enlightenments: William Robertson in Germany 1760–1795* (Basingstoke, 2014); F. Oz-Salzberger, 'The Enlightenment in translation: regional and European aspects', *European Review of History/Revue européenne d'histoire*, 13 (2006), 385–409; and her earlier shorter article on 'Translation', in A. C. Kors (ed.), *Encyclopedia of the Enlightenment* (Oxford, 2003); see also L. Asfour, 'Theories of translation and the English novel in France, 1740-1790' (*SVEC* 2001: 04, Oxford, 2001), 269–78; L. Andries, F. Ogée, J. Dunkley and D. Sanfey (eds.), *Intellectual journeys: the translation of ideas in Enlightenment England, France and Ireland* (*SVEC* 2013: 12, Oxford, 2013).

make the Enlightenment genuinely cosmopolitan, and created a huge publishing and dissemination industry – but also sometimes makes it difficult to locate variant texts precisely in their cultural context.

Translators themselves therefore need to be recognised and studied as independently creative links in the increasingly complex cultural transmission processes of eighteenth-century Europe. They were frequently not even named in printed editions and very few gained reputations remotely matching that of the original authors. If the name of the translator is indicated at all, we often still struggle to place them in their own context, or clarify the networks they relied on to earn a living from such work.[20] A few escaped anonymity, such as Thomas Nugent (c. 1700–72), best known as the translator of Montesquieu's *The spirit of laws* and many other major texts. Although he was an author is his own right, when translating he often adopted a deliberately subservient role as mere facilitators of cultural transfer, so much so that we still lack core biographical information about him.[21] Others may deliberately have posed as mere translators, when they were in fact much more than that. The most famous case of cultural fabrication was James Macpherson's *Fragments of ancient poetry* (1760) and *The works of Ossian* (1765): they purported to be translations of old Gaelic poetry collected from oral tradition and fragments, when in fact they were in part inventions of his own, in part highly creative adaptations of genuine older Gaelic stories. Although disputes over the status of Macpherson's texts erupted almost immediately, Ossian had a huge impact on early romantic tendencies in European literature, admired and imitated by many, and translated across the continent.[22]

It seems likely that many translators worked part-time, as a secondary employment, or even as a leisure activity. Translation was considered suitable work for women with aspirations to work on the fringes of intellectual life or in the publishing industry, but very few of them (probably the least typical) can be named: for example Emilie Marquise du Châtelet (1706–49), an eminent mathematician and physicist who translated Newton, or Mary Wollstonecraft (1759–97), who worked as translator and editor for the radical London publisher Joseph Johnson while also gaining a reputation as an author. We have already noted that the wealthy intellectual d'Holbach commissioned translations, but since he had to operate secretively we have few clues as to the identity of those

---

[20] A. Thomson, S. Burrows and E. Dziembowski (eds.), *Cultural transfers: France and Britain in the long eighteenth century* (*SVEC* 2010: 04, Oxford, 2010).

[21] S. P. Donlan, '"If my labour hath been of service": translating Thomas Nugent, c.1700–1772', in *Intellectual journeys* (*SVEC* 2013: 12), 45–54.

[22] H. Gaskill (ed.), *The reception of Ossian in Europe* (London, 2004).

working for him. One of the great literary entrepreneurs of the later eighteenth century, Friedrich Nicolai (1733–1811), was an enthusiastic Anglophile, book-trader, writer, publisher and translator, while also editing one of the leading long-running German-language review journals, the *Allgemeine deutsche Bibliothek*. Publishers of his stature had a real professional interest in analysing the international book market: Nicolai knew what he was doing and kept his business going very successfully for more than thirty years, into the revolutionary period. But we cannot be sure how much of the actual translation work he would have found time to do himself, how far he commissioned others.[23] Regrettably, most translators have remained elusive, their crucial role in the international print industry taken for granted, unacknowledged.

Books and Reputations across Frontiers: Case Studies

Although much more research is needed on the cross-cultural translation and dissemination of particular texts, it is already abundantly clear that the transmission process was complicated and fragile, both in space and time. For texts with non-fictional content, an appropriate social and political context was essential to securing a positive reception, but so were a number of other factors: publicity (intended or not), possible censorship, personal (if necessary underground) networks, accident and of course the quality of the translation itself. It is generally recognised that French was the crucial bridging language across Europe throughout the eighteenth century, delivering fast and elegant translations of texts in other languages. But as the London market expanded rapidly, English translation grew in importance and by mid-eighteenth century the German-language book market was also well served. By contrast, texts originally written in Italian appear to have had difficulty gaining recognition further north. The Dutch were very active in the international book trade and printing network, but did not so often translate their own texts. Danish authors had to rely heavily on German transmission, while very few Swedish texts gained any international recognition further afield. Such imbalances are even more striking in languages with smaller print markets.[24]

---

[23] P. E. Selwyn, *Everyday life in the German book trade: Friedrich Nicolai as bookseller and publisher in the age of Enlightenment* (University Park, PA, 2000); Möller, *Aufklärung in Preussen: der Verleger und Geschichtsschreiber Friedrich Nicolai* (Berlin, 1974).

[24] Burke, *Languages and communities;* N. Ó'Ciosáin, 'The print cultures of the Celtic languages 1700–1900', *Cultural and social history*, 10 (2013), 347–67; C. Madi, 'Pour une étude des choix de langue en milieu plurilingue: représentations et pratiques en Bohême à l'époque des lumières', *Revue historique*, 315 (2013), 637–59.

The major disruptions of the post-Reformation period clearly created enormous opportunities for printers and booksellers and, despite the fluctuations noted in Chapter 1, there is no shortage of case studies from the mid-seventeenth century onwards. Hobbes himself provided some crucial insights into the opportunities and risks of trans-cultural dissemination. It is very clear (p. 65 and p. 98f) that the original English version of *Leviathan* faced strong criticism, which intensified in the reactionary mood of the Restoration, culminating in a serious threat of prosecution after 1666. The Dutch translation of 1667 was circulated cautiously and when it was reprinted in 1672 even the Dutch authorities took fright, banning the book in 1674 (alongside the works of Spinoza) in the aftermath of the political crisis in the United Provinces. However, the Latin version (published in Amsterdam in 1668, reprinted 1670, before the troubles) deserves separate discussion here. That Hobbes had decided he needed to use Latin, the old scholarly language, to reach a wider international audience is itself significant. But since the translation was done by Hobbes himself, his own take on a text he had written many years earlier, at a time when he was now singled out by a parliamentary commission investigating blasphemy, is remarkable both for its content and for the insights it gives us into the author's own thinking. As Noel Malcolm has made clear, Hobbes did what comes naturally to most multilingual authors: he rewrote his own text fairly freely in the new language, deviating from direct translation when he saw fit. This gave him the opportunity to modify (and often condense) his argument, either removing sections that he deemed redundant for foreign readers, or even adjusting the argument slightly in response both to criticisms and to the substantially changed political climate. Significantly, Hobbes made no concessions regarding religion and scripture: on the contrary, he replaced his original (English) Review and Conclusion with a new lengthy (Latin) Appendix, in which he openly confronted, point by point in dialogue form, those who had accused him of heresy and atheism.[25] In short, Hobbes was undertaking a real cultural translation, far more authoritative than what any other translator could have done, offering us fresh insights into his thinking later in life. He was now willing to adjust his political language slightly, to make his text more clearly supportive of the monarchy, but he was not prepared to moderate his views on the interpretation of scripture and flatly denied that his work contained anything contrary to the faith of the church. He also vigorously

---

[25] T. Hobbes, *Leviathan*, edited by N. Malcolm (Oxford, 2012), vol. I, editorial introduction, especially pp. 146–95, and on the questions surrounding the dating and purpose of the Latin translation; see also Malcolm's translation of, and notes on, the Appendix, vol. III, 1142–243. On the German translation, see below, p. 315.

maintained his stand that there were no good theological grounds for arguing that temporal power should ever be restricted by the authority of theologians – some of whose interpretations and teachings he clearly continued to regard as perniciously wrong.

Much more research is needed on the complex dissemination, reception and longevity of some of the most influential books of the eighteenth century. The works of John Locke appear to have been widely appreciated in a number of languages, notably on education, religion, limited toleration and government. The dissemination of his work throughout the eighteenth century suggests his cautious and moderate views continued to attract readers, encountering less criticism than he himself had perhaps expected. In the last years of Louis XIV, French authors ranging from Fénelon and Vauban to Montesquieu also gained international recognition despite (or because of) fears of suppression within France itself. Fiction was a good way of concealing the true purpose of a book, protecting the author and allowing the reader more freedom of interpretation. A number of English-language authors chose this route with great success: thus Daniel Defoe's *Robinson Crusoe* (1719) was translated almost immediately into French, German and Dutch, with Danish and Swedish translations following twenty years later. Adopting a more overtly political tone, Jonathan Swift's *Gulliver's Travels* (1726) had a huge success in modified translations and imitations across much of Europe, but often lacked the satirical and subversive edge.[26]

Some authors of non-fiction faced different kinds of obstacles. David Hume, for example, was best known (both at home and abroad) for his historical writings. He had difficulty getting any reception (even at home) for his *Treatise of human understanding* (1739–40). He had more success with his essays (on philosophical, political, moral and other subjects), but they were re-edited and republished so much in the 1740s and 50s that their precise evolution in his own lifetime remains unclear, and we cannot yet be sure which were the most widely read, nor which versions were used for competing French editions. The four-volume compilation of Hume's essays published in German in 1754–6 appears to be closely based on the *Essays and treatises on several subjects* released in London in 1753, but his essay on superstition included in that collection was naturally toned down in the German translation, while his essays on suicide and on miracles were disseminated far more selectively. Of all his

---

[26] H.J. Real (ed.), *The reception of Jonathan Swift in Europe* (London, 2005) maps out the wide range of translations, adaptations, imitations and abridgements across most of Europe, starting with French and German versions within a year, Italian (1729), Swedish (1744–5) and Russian (1772–3), all of them adapted or rewritten for their new readers. Shorter sections also found their way into Danish (1768) and Polish (1784).

writings, it was Hume's *Political discourses* (1752) that appeared to travel best: widely disseminated both in English and in French, they also had at least one Dutch and one German version soon after, lots of journal reviews and a belated Swedish selection in 1791.[27]

Dissemination to and from Scandinavia was much less consistent. The best-known contributor to the earlier Enlightenment in Denmark, and the only one with a significant international reputation, was Ludvig Holberg (1684–1754). As professor (from 1717) at the tradition-bound University of Copenhagen, he had to use Latin for much of his academic output. Throughout his life, however, Holberg was at best an occasional conformist to tradition and anything but a conventionally pedantic professor – perhaps because, as a native Norwegian, he could see Copenhagen and Danish society from the outside. He published across a very wide range of genres and subjects, including history and topography (in Latin and Danish), church history, law, moral philosophy, comic and mock-epic satires in prose and verse (many of them published anonymously or under a pseudonym), selections of autobiographical letters and, not least, comedies for the theatre (thirty-seven of them, all in Danish – the first durably popular stage works in that language). In his student days, Holberg had travelled widely across Europe and so acquired an eclectic taste as well as an impressive command of other languages.

Amongst Holberg's most widely disseminated texts is his Danish mock-epic poem *Peder Paars* (1719–20) and his Latin prose novel *Nicolai Klimii iter subterraneum* (*Niels Klim's journey to the world underground*, 1741). Both were ostensibly fictional stories with hints of classical influence, but *Niels Klim* was directly inspired by Swift's *Gulliver's Travels* (1726), and both really served to parody and reflect on contemporary social structure, tackling questions of self-discovery and identity. While *Peder Paars* had some reprints in its original Danish and two German translations (1750 and 1764), the story was too firmly located in its Scandinavian context to travel well. By contrast, *Niels Klim*, already accessible across Europe in the Latin, was translated immediately into German, Dutch and French (1741), followed by Danish and English (1742) and even Swedish in 1756 (two years after Holberg's death). The book enjoyed a number of reprints in each of these languages over the following decades, indicating some degree of sustained interest even after his death. By comparison, Holberg's comedies had more limited international transmission in French, German and Dutch, while his

---

[27] M. Malherbe, 'Hume en France: la traduction des Political Discourses', in Thomson et al. (eds.), *Cultural transfers* (*SVEC* 2010: 04), 243–56.

substantial narrative *History of Denmark* (1732–5) had two German translations and one Russian (1765–6).[28]

Overall, Holberg's cross-cultural success was exceptional in an age
where those working within small language communities and in a small
market often made little or no European-wide impression. The domestic
market both in Danish and in Swedish was bound to be limited:
Copenhagen and Stockholm, as capital cities, were approaching
100,000 inhabitants each, while the overall population of Denmark-
Norway (with the north-German territories) was close to that of
Sweden (with Finland).[29] Why then did Holberg gain a significant international reputation, while the substantial and innovative work published
in Sweden in the middle years of the eighteenth century did not? Close
connections between the Danish and German social and intellectual elites
may offer some explanation, but perhaps we also need to examine the
question of international receptiveness. Foreign literary review journals
tended to ignore publications in languages with which they were unfamiliar, so translation into German or French was often a necessary precondition for wider cross-cultural recognition.

Was French an assured means of reaching the widest possible readership, at least after 1715? Rousseau, as a native of Geneva, wrote in
French, but that did not ensure a consistent reception. He seems to
have earned his international reputation in two stages. His *Discours sur
l'origine et les fondements de l'inégalité parmi les hommes* (1755, usually
rendered as *Discourse on inequality*) was available in English in 1761, but
had only limited or delayed dissemination in other languages. Both *Julie*
and *Émile* were translated quickly into English and German, but had to
wait until the 1790s before reaching Dutch and Scandinavian readers, no
doubt because the author's name was now attracting attention in connection with the French Revolution. The book for which Rousseau is best
known today, *Du contrat social* (1762, translated as *The social contract*), did
not gain German, Dutch or Scandinavian readers until the 1790s either,
except through a German version which appeared in a complete edition of
his works issued from 1779. During his lifetime, Rousseau feared that his
works were the target of a conspiracy to have them completely destroyed –
an explanation he seems to have genuinely believed, not just adopted as
a publicity stunt. His extraordinary *Confessions* were not published in full

---

[28] K. Haakonssen and S. Olden-Jørgensen (eds.), *Ludvig Holberg (1684–1754): learning and
literature in the Nordic Enlightenment* (London, 2017).

[29] Denmark had a population of around 786,000 in the first official census of 1769, Norway
much the same, with the German-speaking subjects of the Danish crown around
Schleswig-Holstein amounting to another half million. Sweden (with Finland) had
a population of 2.2 million, according to their census of 1749.

until 1782, four years after his death, adding greatly to his growing reputation as a paranoid but entertaining eccentric.

Amongst major books with clear implications for politics and the use of power in society, the large work published by Guillaume-Thomas, abbé Raynal (1713–96), illustrates a different aspect of the eighteenth-century dissemination process. The *Histoire philosophique et politique des établissements et du commerce des Européens dans les deux Indes* (usually shortened to *History of the two Indies*) first appeared anonymously in 1770, ostensibly in Amsterdam and without any kind of permission. It sold slowly at first (partly because of its size and cost), but then gained beneficial publicity when it was condemned by the crown in 1772 and may have had ten reprints in 1773 alone. A revised and extended second edition (1774) went through sixteen reprints, and became the basis for both an English translation (1776) and a possibly unauthorised abridgement (1777) which named Raynal as the author. An even bigger and revised 'third' edition appeared in 1780, which ran to seventeen reprints in various formats (from several misleading places of publication). Although the work at first glance seemed just a rambling narrative global history, its potential for making political comparisons was highly subversive and its increasingly sharpened attacks on the European hypocrisy of the slave trade even more so. We now know that the most outspoken sections were written by Diderot, so it seems Raynal was in part just a protective frontman for a collective enterprise. But Raynal was not in France by the time the authorities, having identified him as the author but failed to suppress the book, tried to arrest him. The work had at least ten English translations between 1776 and 1798, three in Dutch from 1775, several in German and even a belated one in Danish in 1804, perhaps marketed in the wake of the early Danish ban on their own slave trade.[30] Few texts anywhere could rival such a rapid and wide dissemination.

Translating and Rewriting Beccaria's *On Crimes and Punishments*

By the eighteenth century, Italian appeared to have lost its prominence as a language of international cultural communication, and surprisingly few Italian writers of the Enlightenment acquired a substantial international audience by means of translation. Vico (1668–1744) was not widely

---

[30] There is an extensive literature on Raynal: see G. Bancarel and G. Goggi (eds.), *Raynal: de la polémique à l'histoire* (*SVEC* 2000: 12, Oxford, 2000). It includes a paper by P. Jimack, 'La traduction anglaise de l'*Histoire des deux Indes*, et Raynal en Ecosse', 323–32, noting that the English translations were mostly close to the original, except for slightly toning down some of its critical comments on Christianity.

recognised during his lifetime, except in Naples, and his friend Antonio Genovesi (1713–69) did not reach much further with his work in economics. The historical and antiquarian writings of Muratori (1672–1750) had slightly wider appeal and the controversial historical writings of Pietro Giannone (1676–1748) appeared in French, English and German. However, none of these works had anything remotely like the international impact of the single short work by Cesare Beccaria (1738–94), his *Dei delitti e delle pene* (*On crimes and punishments*) published anonymously in 1764. A substantially reworked and edited French version by Morellet (late 1765) had to be reprinted repeatedly within the first year, attaining at least ten printings in French before the end of the century, many of them with false imprints. Translations into German and English (1766–7) confirmed its status as an international bestseller, and by the end of the century the book had been printed five times in German and no less than fifteen times in English. A Dutch version appeared in 1668, a Swedish one in 1770 and a Danish one somewhat later (1796–8). Meantime, by 1796 the Italian version had run to an astonishing twenty-seven reprints including several revised and extended editions – some of the earlier ones (up to at least the fifth Italian edition of 1766) remaining anonymous but overseen by the author, others clearly pirated.[31]

This extraordinarily wide interest is not surprising. Beccaria's book contained exceptionally subversive ideas on social rank, poverty and the purpose of criminal punishment – and being very concise, was cheap to buy in its small-format versions. The original Italian text bears all the hallmarks of having been compiled as discussion pieces for a circle of Beccaria's friends (the 'Academy of Fisticuffs', including his collaborator Pietro Verri), and the additions made in later Italian editions naturally followed the same pattern: this was clearly never meant as an academic book, but rather as part of a lively and evolving public debate. Beccaria's own revisions suggest that the Italian text never fully stabilised, so it is not surprising that editors and translators were also keen to take liberties with the text. The adaptable nature of the text was confirmed already in December 1765, with the first French translation prepared by Morellet, who (with Voltaire's explicit approval) substantially reorganised and edited the whole work. In his preface, Morellet explained what he had

---

[31] Details of the Italian editions are based on L. Firpo (ed.), *Edizione nazionale delle opere di Cesare Beccaria*, vol. I (Milan, 1984); editions in other languages have been identified through the relevant library catalogues. See also D. Medlin, 'Catalogue of Morellet's works', in J. Merrick and D. Medlin (eds.), *André Morellet (1727–1819) in the republic of letters and the French Revolution* (New York, 1995), 185–232; D. Medlin and J. Merrick, *André Morellet: texts and contexts* (*SVEC* 2003: 10, Oxford, 2010); R. Loretellli, 'The first English translation of Cesare Beccaria's *On Crimes and Punishments*', in *Diciottesimo Secolo*, 2 (2017), 1–22.

done, suggesting that a book with such a universal message belonged to everyone and deserved to be adapted to suit all readers. Others, including Diderot, strongly disagreed, fearing Morellet had destroyed the character of the book. The English translator himself noted (in the preface to the English edition of 1767) that:

> the French translator hath gone much farther; he hath not only transposed every chapter, but every paragraph in the whole book. But in this, I conceive, he hath assumed a right which belongs not to any translator, and which cannot be justified. His disposition may be more systematical, but certainly that author hath as undoubted a right to the arrangement of his own ideas, as to the ideas themselves, and therefore to destroy that arrangement is to pervert his meaning.[32]

Beccaria himself politely commended Morellet's reordering of the argument, but pointedly did not adopt it for his own later revised editions in Italian. The first German translation (Hamburg, 1766) was clearly based on the French version (noting the difficulties of translating from Italian), the second (Ulm, 1767) claimed to be based on the Italian original with as yet unpublished corrections by the author, while the third (Breslau, 1778) was a fresh translation from the Italian accompanied by both annotations and a disproportionately long 51-page introduction by a Leipzig lawyer.

Because of the impact made by the first French reorganised translation, and Voltaire's added commentary, readers across Europe in effect had two substantially different core texts to choose from, each with an increasing number of variants and emendations by successive translators – some proclaiming loyalty to the original Italian, others aiming to improve the text (with or without explanation). Not surprisingly, review journals all over Europe soon became aware of these issues, alerting their readers to the difficulties of 'accurate' translation. As Beccaria's text was structured around very short and only loosely connected thematic chapters, it seemed almost to invite active engagement. Many sections worked well as short stand-alone essays, and different readers would see different connections or thematic strands.

Morellet may well have had the best of intentions in trying to make the work more elegant. He explained in his own preface what he had done, justifying it in terms of what he assumed French readers would expect. Such editorial intervention, however, carried real risks. The Danish

---

[32] C. Beccaria, *An essay on crimes and punishments, translated from the Italian; with a commentary, attributed to Mons de Voltaire, translated from the French* (London, 1767), Preface v–vi, by the anonymous English translator. As noted by Franco Venturi, cited in Firpo (ed.), *Edizione nazionale*, I, 305–6, the German literary critic and journalist Friedrich M. Grimm was even more scathing, describing Morellet's editorial intrusions as 'impertinent and reprehensible ... [resulting in] a work of marquetry, where there is no longer either proportion or harmony'.

translator Christian Alstrup, going into print from 1796 and therefore working well after the international community had identified the discrepancies in various other translations, chose to follow Morellet's French version, but without alerting his readers to the difficulties. His version was therefore greeted with understandable hostility, even in the normally balanced and moderate review journal *Kjøbenhavnske lærde Efterretninger*. It noted the enormous significance of Beccaria's work, the value of which would be challenged only by 'monks, inquisitors and other advocates of prejudice and tools of self-interest'. But the Danish translation was described as exceedingly bad, characterised by gross sloppiness and ignorance. The anonymous reviewer cited a number of specific examples where the translator had failed to understand the terminology he himself had used, sometimes even failing to make any sense at all. The second (companion) volume of 1798 was described in the same journal as in every way a match for the first – 'in wretchedness'.[33]

So how severe were the alterations in the many variant translations? Was the core meaning and intent of the text distorted? Can we ever, in such cases, be certain which text should be considered 'authentic' or definitive? Would Morellet's work, and the strongly worded disagreements, all in fact serve to enhance the book's bestseller status? With so many different translations and variants, none of these questions are easy to answer. We may start by assuming that one of the later editions overseen by Beccaria himself must represent the final version as he intended it to be. But when we compare translations, we realise that three distinct processes of adaptation were at work, all creating the potential for altering the tone of the work. First, the actual translation was bound to be a matter of subjective judgment, open to potential criticism: after all, no translation can be totally faithful to the original. Yet generally speaking, translators seem to have done their best to convey what they thought was the intent of the original, and the criticisms of the Danish version may be unduly harsh. Secondly, the addition of footnotes and extensive commentaries or introductions, as in the later German versions and in the Danish two-volume set, might well affect the reader's response. In Morellet's version, the lengthy commentary attributed to Voltaire, roughly two-thirds the length of the original book, was to a considerable extent tangential to the text itself, focusing for example on matters of religious belief, which Beccaria himself had almost completely avoided.

---

[33] The review appeared in two stages, following the publication of each volume of the translation: *Kjøbenhavnske lærde Efterretninger*, 1797, 613–25, with an ineffective response by the translator, 685–8, and *Kjøbenhavnske lærde Efterretninger*, 1798, 281–6.

Most commentaries and responses were far less powerful and compact than Beccaria's original.

A third and more problematic way of changing the impact of a text was to reorganise and adapt it. In the case of Morellet, as the English translator had noted, this involved much more than minor revision. Out of the forty-six chapters available to Morellet, only the first five were left in the original position and even these had additions and revisions based on sections taken from other chapters. The rest of the text was totally re-arranged into three new thematic blocks focusing on procedure, penalties and the typology of crimes. Sometimes Morellet just moved existing chapters into a new sequence, leaving the original chapter title. But some of his chapters were completely reconstituted from paragraphs taken from a number of different chapters of the original. Thus for example a new chapter dealt solely with the crime of *lèse-majesté*, which in the original was discussed as part of an overview of types of crimes: to readers of a more royalist disposition, highlighting this subject in a distinct chapter would no doubt have seemed pleasingly appropriate. Significantly, the reverse happened with a chapter on 'Punishment of the nobility', which Beccaria added to the third Italian edition, but which Morellet tucked into a longer chapter on 'Crimes against the security of individuals'. In a short and pithy text without explicit historical examples, such changes were bound to shift the emphasis, even when the wording of the translation itself was well enough chosen. Morellet's last chapter, on 'Means of preventing crimes', was an amalgamation of five very short final chapters in the original, enabling him also to halve the length of the conclusion into a single more bland paragraph. In effect, Morellet's version substantially changed the relative emphasis on some of Beccaria's key ideas. Contemporary readers themselves could not agree whether such changes were an enhancement or not. Yet Voltaire's endorsement, and access through the French language, no doubt ensured that the book acquired more readers than might otherwise have been the case. We know that both Frederick II and Catherine II read this version, while some elite readers elsewhere (including in the American colonies) owned copies in more than one language. We are left with a work achieving bestseller status through substantially variant texts, many of which could claim a kind of 'authenticity' on their own, and which were clearly read and interpreted in different ways.

Review Journals and the Imagined Republic of Readers

Beccaria was an extreme case of wilful editing by the first French translator, compounded by subsequent translations into other languages. That particular example reminds us that cultural translation could have a major impact on the reception of a text amongst its new readers. But detailed study of variant translations, and the processes involved, is itself extremely labour-intensive, and for the great majority of even the major works circulating across enlightened Europe the groundwork has not been done.[34] Not many contemporary readers would have been able to make such comparisons, either – except if they were reviewers writing for the growing number of literary journals. They became increasingly keen to provide their eighteenth-century readers with critical assessments of translation practices, in terms that often serve also the needs of modern cultural historians. The intended readers of these reviews, after all, were precisely the kind of interested but non-specialist 'public' whom authors themselves were keen to address.

The market for general review journals became ever stronger during the eighteenth century.[35] We noted in Chapters 1 and 3 the appearance of newspapers as essentially printed newsletters, in formats similar to fly-sheets or pamphlets: it was just another step for such papers to add news (or advertisements) about intellectual discoveries and major books. After 1660, more systematic reporting of philosophical and scientific work ensured sustained interest in the published transactions of learned societies such as the Royal Society in London founded in 1662 or the French Académie des Sciences of 1666. The state-sponsored French *Journal des Sçavans* from 1665, the Leipzig-based *Acta Eruditorum* from 1682 and the trendsetting but short-lived French-language *Nouvelles de la république des lettres* (launched in the Netherlands in 1684 by Pierre Bayle) all set new standards for intellectual exchange across Europe. This was still an experimental phase, and even French-language publications such as those launched by members of the refugee communities might have only limited success. Thus Jean Le Clerc's *Bibliothèque universelle et historique*, launched in 1686, included both reviews and original essays, but the intervals between issues gradually lengthened, and it ceased publication in 1693. Better conditions followed the conclusion of peace in many parts of Europe in the years 1715–21, enabling independently published,

---

[34] Richly informative but different ways of examining the translation history of individual works are found in N. Malcolm's edition of Hobbes's *Leviathan* already cited; Oz-Salzberger, *Translating the enlightenment*; S. A. Reinert, *Translating empire: emulation and the origins of political economy* (Cambridge, MA, 2011); L. Kontler, *Translations, histories, enlightenments: William Robertson in Germany 1760–95* (Basingstoke, 2014); and other studies cited in this chapter.

[35] T. Habel, *Gelehrte Journale und Zeitungen der Aufklärung: zur Entstehung, Entwicklung und Erschliessung deutschsprachiger Rezensionszeitschriften des 18. Jahrhunderts* (Bremen, 2007); H. Böning, *Periodische Presse: Kommunikation und Aufklärung, Hamburg und Altona als Beispeil* (Bremen, 2002).

general-access literary and scholarly review journals to proliferate. Those serving commercially viable markets could now secure regular periodicity and thereby earn a reputation as efficient means of disseminating information about new work.[36] Such journals had the capacity to go beyond the old 'republic of letters' (which still relied on personal contacts and letters of introduction), creating instead a much more open and accessible imagined community of readers, the notionally broader but abstract 'public' (*Publikum*).

The new literary, scientific[37] and specialist review journals were not all viable, so it is tempting to focus on those reviews that survived for longer periods and served major centres in the book and print trade. During the eighteenth century, most languages with major or at least viable reading communities acquired some form of literary review, and in major centres several journals might even compete long-term for readers. While French remained the dominant educated language within the elite republic of letters, periodicals and journals could serve more diverse language communities and a wider range of readers. Some newspapers even issued weekly supplements providing short reviews of new books, as in the *Gazette de Leyde* (published from 1677, but substantially improved from 1738) and in the *Hamburgische Correspondent* (1721, also consolidated after 1730). Far more substantive, however, were the dedicated review journals designed as commercial ventures for as broad a readership as they could muster. Some of these explicitly aimed to report systematically on as many major new books and intellectual developments across Europe as they could.

Amongst the most durable and prestigious of these ventures was the Copenhagen *Lærde Efterretninger* (from 1720, briefly switching to Latin in 1721, but then reverting to Danish and running continuously to 1810) and the elite *Göttingische Anzeigen von gelehrten Sachen* (from 1739) – both of them subsequently challenged within their respective language communities by other more adventurous journals. As with newspapers, the north-German market for reviews and other specialist journals was particularly fertile. Hamburg had an early experimental version from 1732 and a number of other commercial centres followed later, including Leipzig and Frankfurt. Moses Mendelssohn and Friedrich Nicolai launched the

---

[36] Even so, there were many journals that had a significant readership yet did not last more than a few years: see for example the efforts by Michel de la Roche to keep a French-language journal alive from London (1717–24), discussed by A. Thomson, 'In defence of toleration: La Roche's Bibliothèque angloise and Mémoires littéraires de la Grande-Bretagne', in Thomson et al. (eds.), *Cultural transfers* (*SVEC* 2010: 04), 161–74.

[37] More research is needed on specialist scientific (including medical) journals, but these tended to avoid political discussion except to promote public policies of improvement.

literary *Bibliothek der schönen Wissenschaften und der freyen Kunsten* in Leipzig in 1757. In 1765 Nicolai established what became arguably the most influential and systematic German review journal of them all, the *Allgemeine deutsche Bibliothek*, which, with a print run eventually reaching 2500 copies, amounted by 1792 to 106 volumes of around 600 pages each, not counting 19 supplementary volumes.[38]

Sweden acquired its first dedicated review journal in 1745, the *Lärda Tidningar*, launched by Lars Salvius, and in 1755 the enterprising publisher Carl Chr. Gjörwell set up a wider-ranging rival, *Den Swenska Mercurius*. In England, *The Gentleman's Magazine* (from 1731) carried occasional comments on some general-interest publications, but regular literary reviews did not emerge until mid-century, with the *Monthly Review* (from 1749) and the more conservative *Critical Review* from 1756. In 1788 the enterprising London publisher Joseph Johnson launched his much more lively and radical *Analytical Review*, but it failed after Johnson was arrested in November 1798 on a charge of selling seditious texts. Surprisingly, Edinburgh did not have a durable review journal even at the height of the Scottish Enlightenment: attempts invariably failed within a very short time span, perhaps because the market was too small, or because many Scots active in publishing preferred to operate through, or even move to, London.[39]

Dutch readers, despite their lively international market for print, had at first also struggled to sustain a durable journal: *De Boekzaal van Europe*, launched by Pieter Rabus in 1692, lasted until 1701, and attempts at revival under variant titles fared no better. Much more successful was the *Vaderlandsche Letteroefeningen* of 1761, its tone – set by its Mennonite and dissenting editors – remaining very moderate and dependable: running to well over 1000 pages of text per annum, it became an essential tool for Dutch readers and indeed remained influential for more than a century. But as we would expect, the Dutch printing industry also facilitated wider international exchange. As Ann Thomson has shown, a number of Huguenot refugees in London were active in the transmission of religious and political discussion across cultural and linguistic frontiers. Thus Michel de la Roche published both in London (in English) and in Holland (in French), using his review journal

---

[38] T. Munck, 'Eighteenth-century review journals and the internationalization of the European book market', *The International History Review*, 32 (2010), 415–35.

[39] D. Roper, *Reviewing before the Edinburgh, 1788–1802* (London, 1978); F. Donoghue, *The fame machine: book reviewing and eighteenth-century literary careers* (Los Angeles, 1996); A. Forster, 'Review journals and the reading public', in I. Rivers (ed.), *Books and their readers in eighteenth-century England* (London, 2001); R. B. Sher, *The Enlightenment and the book: Scottish authors and their publishers in eighteenth-century Britain, Ireland and America* (Chicago, 2006).

Bibliothèque angloise and its continuation (1717–24) to provide French readers with detailed summaries of the much more open religious controversies in England at that time, consistently arguing for religious toleration and a more rational approach to theology and scientific knowledge generally.[40]

Where possible, religious groups were not averse to using review journals to shore up particular beliefs against perceived external threats. In France, for example, the *Nouvelles ecclésiastiques* was launched by a group of Jansenists in 1728, gradually acquiring a considerable reputation and large circulation through its subversive discussions and polemics against the Jesuits – at first mostly through testimonies and reports, but increasingly also through reviews of publications and polemical discussion of religious, philosophical and political questions. Officially banned, this journal maintained such secretive production and distribution systems that the French authorities never succeeded in closing it down and, although it started losing momentum before the Revolution, it ceased publication only in 1803. Other French-language journals adopted substantially different editorial perspectives commensurate with the composite and factionalised French Enlightenment. Fréron's *L'année littéraire* (1754–76) was highly critical of the French *philosophes* and their radical Enlightenment views, in contrast to Pierre Rousseau's *Journal encyclopédique* (1755–94), which was more sympathetic to critical and potentially subversive work. Linguet's *Annales politiques, civiles et littéraires* (1777–92), on the other hand, was sufficiently conservative to be acceptable reading even at the French court.[41]

These are just a few examples in a genre which could evidently generate sufficient profits to entice many publishers during the later eighteenth century. Although at first sight seemingly quite elitist and very selective, the market for review journals clearly grew as much as any other sector of the printing industry. Journals that thrived did so either because they gained a reputation on the grounds of high scientific standards, or on the contrary because they broadened their remit to include fiction, general essays and other material intended for an inclusive readership. Already at the outset in 1720, the Copenhagen *Lærde Efterretninger* indicated that it would review 'all books that are useful', but excluded 'unusable' legal texts and foreign poetical and rhetorical works, intending instead to concentrate on theology, philosophy, history, philology, politics, travel accounts and memoirs. In practice, however, its remit broadened

---

[40] Thomson, 'In defence of toleration', in Thomson et al. (eds.), *Cultural transfers* (*SVEC* 2010: 04), 161–74.

[41] *Dictionnaire des journaux (1600–1789): édition électronique revue, corrigée et augmentée*, ed. J. Sgard (originally Oxford, 1991; revised version online at (http://dictionnaire-journaux.gazettes18e.fr).

appreciably over the next decades to cover the interests of all potential readers. So although we might simply gauge the likely significance and impact of these journals on the basis of their longevity or alleged numbers of readers, a better approach may be to examine how each journal actually engaged with its readers in the way it handled its material. All of the journals were prone to summarising or even citing lengthy extracts from the texts they were reviewing, but the best publishers attracted more lively teams of reviewers capable of exploiting opportunities to engage in real contemporary discussion.

One recurrent theme in several of these journals was language and cultural transfer itself. In 1760 the *Lærde Efterretninger* carried a supplement welcoming the growth in Danish-language writing, but also noting the need for a proper grammar and dictionary to match those of the major European languages. In 1767 it returned to this theme, suggesting that Danish authors still lacked confidence and experience because of the minority status of the language itself. By 1770, its detailed reviews of translations from English of works by Fielding and Fordyce included lengthy quotations to illustrate the quality of writing. Since its launch, the journal had routinely covered new work from France and Germany (whether translated or not), but now welcomed the growing availability of works translated direct from English. The discussion, however, soon took a very different turn: from late 1770 into 1771, the rapid rise to power of the German-speaking Johann Friedrich Struensee, not just as royal physician but also reformist head of government, created huge tensions between the traditional elite and those wanting reform and improvement, and these tensions focused on patriotic identity. In 1771 the *Lærde Efterretninger* carried a lengthy commentary on a series of polemics provoked by Jacob Bie's pamphlet *Philopatrejas*. The ostensible focus of attention was economic improvement, the role of the clergy and other questions of reform, but with the abolition of censorship (1771) a number of texts responded in more satirical tones. Although freedom of expression was substantively undermined after Struensee's fall, a long-running discussion of national identity and traditional patriotism nevertheless continued, often aligned with supporters or opponents of north-German cameralist reforms and improvement.[42]

---

[42] The *Lærde Efterretninger* of 1771 (then under a variant title of *Kiøbenhavnske Efterretninger om lærde Sager*) was extremely cautious in this discussion, unsure of the political ramifications. When Struensee was deposed in 1772, tried for *lèse majesté* and executed, a narrow Danish reaction set in, which limited serious discussion of transnational influences until 1784. On the disputed Danish concepts of national identity, see T. Munck, 'The northern periphery: German cultural influences on the Danish-Norwegian kingdom during the Enlightenment', in R. J. W. Evans and P. H. Wilson (eds.), *The Holy Roman Empire: a European perspective* (Leiden, 2012), 293–312.

Discussions of translation practices were common in many journals serving small language communities, including the *Vaderlandsche Letteroefeningen*. But discussion of linguistic identity also appeared in the German review journals. The editor of the *Allgemeine deutsche Bibliothek*, Friedrich Nicolai was particularly conscious of the importance of effective translation. His reviewers for texts of French origin regularly commented explicitly on this, and he also printed discussions on the qualities of German dictionaries and on matters of style. A substantial review of Bodmer's *Die Grundsätze der deutschen Sprache* (1768), by the young radical philosopher Johann Gottfried Herder (1744–1803), went into some detail about dialects, word usage and other details.[43] Successive translations of major works such as Montesquieu's *De l'esprit des loix* merited separate reviews, as did commentaries on such works by German scholars. A German translation of David Hume's posthumously published *Dialogues concerning natural religion* (1779) resulted in a discussion of important enlightenment keywords and concepts, including Hume's use of 'nature' and 'natural'.[44] However, we also find in-depth comparisons of competing translations. In 1779, two German versions of part of Raynal's *Histoire des deux Indes* were compared in some depth, focusing entirely on the quality of the translations so that potential readers (expected already to know of the French original) could make the right choice. Some years later the journal compared two German translations of Locke's now almost century-old *Thoughts concerning education*, citing both German versions alongside the much older English original.[45]

The 1793 German translation of Wollstonecraft's *Vindication of the rights of woman* (1792), published with a German preface and annotations by Christian Gotthilff Salzmann, was given a substantial (but as usual anonymous) review in the *Allgemeine deutsche Bibliothek*. The text itself was warmly welcomed for its rational and clearly presented arguments. Wollstonecraft's critique of the traditional kind of upbringing of daughters recommended by Fordyce and others was summarised and her call for sound education for women noted with approval. The review then turned to the quality of the translation itself, which was seen as generally true to the original. However, the reviewer disapproved of the

---

[43] *Allgemeine deutsche Bibliothek*, 9, 1 (1769), 193–205. Herder was clearly anticipating some of the patriotic ideals he developed more fully in his *Treatise on the origin of language* (1772).

[44] On Montesquieu, see for example *Allgemeine deutsche Bibliothek*, 11, 2 (1770), 264–5, and 61, 2 (1785), 381–2; on Hume, *Allgemeine deutsche Bibliothek*, 49, 1 (1782), 131–6.

[45] *Allgemeine deutsche Bibliothek*, vol. 39, 1 (1779), 276–81, on Raynal; and *Anhang* 53–86, vol. IV (1791), 2291–6, on Locke.

wordiness of the German translation, quoting a number of passages where the clear and accessible English original was printed (in double-column parallel text) with what are visibly much more convoluted and long-winded German renderings. The reviewer also notes Salzmann's elaborate introductory summary and extensive notes – so lengthy indeed that the German translation ran to 730 pages and was being published in two volumes, which were therefore reviewed separately.[46]

Reviewing new books was also an effective way of disseminating their content. Just as censors could not avoid actually attracting attention to the texts they wanted to suppress – often turning otherwise relatively weak texts into bestsellers – so the process of reviewing (even if hostile) was effective publicity. One of the most independent French review journals, the *Journal encyclopédique* (1756–93), published first from Liège and then in Bouillon under the auspices of the Duc de Bouillon (in the southern Netherlands), and therefore just outside the direct jurisdiction of the French crown. Edited by Pierre Rousseau, assisted as usual by a circle of mostly anonymous independent reviewers, the journal was particularly effective in reporting on what it considered major works of the (mostly French) Enlightenment, including new publications on history, politics and government. Starting in August 1766, it carried a major series of reviews and commentaries on the recently published final volumes of text of the *Encyclopédie*, praising it as an 'immortal work, which is such an honour to the French, and to the *philosophes*, scientists, literary writers and artists who are its authors – a more durable monument than the famous constructions of which Egypt can boast'.[47] But the journal also noted that there were many weaknesses, mistakes and major flaws, and proceeded over the next months to publish detailed discussion of a selection of articles chosen by keyword (entry heading word) – including 'heresy', 'Hobbism', the now notorious Hume–Rousseau quarrel and a number of other contentious topics. The journal was in effect creating a reader's digest of current intellectual developments and controversies and, although it frequently expressed more conservative criticisms, the detailed discussions provided what was probably the most substantial overview of the most contentious entries in the later volumes.[48]

Review journals were useful in disseminating summaries of new texts, highlighting what was most important and where relevant evaluating the quality of translations. But it is also clear that the best journals

---

[46] *Neue allgemeine deutsche Bibliothek*, 9, 1 (1794), 126–32, and 17, 1 (1795), 66–71.
[47] *Journal encyclopédique*, issue dated 15 August 1766, 3–22.
[48] For a full range of reviews and responses to the *Encyclopédie*, see Lough, *The Encyclopédie*, 98–136.

could go further: in choosing which translated foreign works to review, they could in effect take a lead in prioritising key issues and strengthening the conceptual framework for discussion in print. It is also interesting to observe how the longer-running journals could help consolidate new vocabularies appropriate for a creative discussion of religious, social and political issues. We need to remember that journals such as the Danish *Lærde Efterretninger* or the Dutch *Vaderlandsche Letteroefeningen* soon became by far the largest coherent body of printed text in their respective languages, with each running to well over 10,000 pages per decade. Now that some of these huge bodies of text are becoming digitised, we can measure aggregate changes in word usage and map out the appearance of key terms over time. For example, we note that variant words derived from the root term 'republic' were well established in German journals in discussions of states such as Venice, the Swiss confederation and the United Provinces, and gradually emerged in Scandinavian texts as well. As we will see in Chapter 5, an increasingly pointed discussion of censorship and freedom of expression also emerged, notably in connection with the Swedish and Danish legislative reforms of 1766 and 1771 respectively, in turn feeding into reports in the German review journals. By contrast, 'toleration' did not become a clear focus of attention until the 1780s: it was hardly an issue in Scandinavia, nor (it seems) amongst the journal-readers of northern Germany, until a wider controversy about 'natural religion' created new challenges. It took even longer for the concepts of 'democracy' and 'despotism' to gain full currency in central and northern Europe, but when that happened, in relation to reports on France after 1789, their relevance in discussions of domestic politics soon became apparent.

There were also more general discussions, no doubt triggered by an increasing awareness of patriotic and proto-national identities. In 1798 *Der neue Teutsche Merkur* in Weimar published an article (in German) on the nature and development of the Swedish language, noting the close similarities to Danish despite the differences in nuance and cultural significance attached to words shared across both languages. German readers were expected to be much more familiar with Danish, so Swedish was contrasted in terms of pronunciation and a greater tonal range and clarity. Significantly, the author of this article noted how much less text had been printed in Swedish compared with German, but also observed the efforts of contemporary Swedish writers and the Swedish Academy to broaden and enrich the style and conceptual framework of the language. French influences had been particularly strong, notably in the development of Swedish theatre through translations, directly encouraged by Gustavus III.[49] Given the close proximity, it is not surprising that German journals had a much longer track record of in-depth discussion of Danish authors and publications, but it is nonetheless interesting to find that *Der neue Teutsche Merkur* had already in 1798 also published a descriptive article on the Danish language, praising the library resources available in Copenhagen in both the Royal Library and the University Library.[50] No doubt such discussions took place in response to a growing practical awareness of linguistic identities and the power of language in shaping cultural identities. For those with stronger analytical and philosophical awareness, however, these discussions would have been a reminder of the bigger questions going back to Descartes and Locke, concerning the nature of human reasoning, understanding and linguistic representation.

Revolution and Neology

It is no surprise that the biggest battles over language occurred in France. As we noted earlier, the compilation of French-language dictionaries became something of a power struggle in the later eighteenth century, when the extremely slow work of the crown-sponsored Académie Française in compiling and revising its voluminous *Dictionnaire* was challenged by other, less traditionalist, lexicographers. One of these was Jean-François Féraud, whose more personalised and colourful *Dictionnaire critique de la langue française* appeared in three volumes (Paris, 1787–8). After the Revolution, Louis-Sébastien Mercier, already a popular author before 1789 and directly involved in the politics of the 1790s, published his *Néologie* (Paris, 1801), a much more idiosyncratic overview of changes to the French language. In between these two, we have the fifth edition of the *Dictionnaire de l'Académie Française* of 1798 – mostly compiled before the Revolution and closely based on the fourth edition of 1762, but adding a twelve-page Supplement 'containing the new words coming into use since the Revolution'.

The dictionaries edited by the Academy and by Féraud were very closely related, using very similar (or even identical) core definitions of many words, with Féraud merely adding some variants and a few more common usages. Mercier, however, set out to do something very different. In a lengthy introduction to his work, he argued that the French language should be freed from the constraints of Academy control and

---

[49] D. Ekman, 'Ueber die Schwedische Sprache', in *Der neue Teutsche Merkur*, 2, 1798, 119–29.

[50] G. H. Merkel, 'Ueber die dänische Sprache und die Bibliotheken zu Kopenhagen', in *Der neue Teutsche Merkur*, 1 (1798), 435–46.

that French authors should adopt foreign and new words as freely as, he argued, the English and the Germans already did. He poured scorn on the Academy's insistence on narrowly defined traditional usage, and the reductionist definitions that went with it, citing a number of examples of how significant new meaning could easily be added through the creation of new words. He noted how women were particularly creative, since unlike men they were less bound by (and felt no need to demonstrate adherence to) the conservatism of scholarly knowledge. He also emphasised that neology and neologism were fundamentally worlds apart: neology (and to 'neologise') was an intellectual pursuit of new ideas through an inventive way of expressing them, while neologism was a form of fanaticism which, by imposing lexicographical rules and system, merely destroyed creativity. In short, Mercier wanted to revolutionise the French language without creating a new straitjacket.[51] Interestingly, he made no attempt to define the word 'revolution' itself, for which he did not even have an entry.

The term 'revolution' was given entirely conventional and generalised definitions not only in Féraud but also by the Academy (even in the Supplement of new usage in the 1798 edition). Curiously, Féraud merely added that 'nothing is as frightening as the Revolution which has taken place amongst women, in the way they think and act' – without providing any detail. Although occasionally observing changing usage over time, all three dictionaries were sparing in terms of citations that might illustrate the complexities of associations and contexts in which a word might have been used. Mercier, however, deliberately set out to undermine conventional usage. His *Néologie* is not really a dictionary at all (and certainly not a substitute for Féraud's): he included only a modest selection of keywords, and rather than explaining normal usage, he deliberately subverted it by using ironic aphorisms, unexpected quotations, irony and contradiction. He did reflect new revolutionary usage, but in a manifestly partisan way (most clearly revealed in a well-timed but misleading rehabilitation of his former faction, in his entry on 'Girondisme'). As we would expect for a work published in 1801, his political stance was otherwise evasive. He had no nostalgia for the pre-revolutionary world: under 'Régime (ancien)', we find a short but blunt statement that 'everyone knows what it is. France, bowed for centuries under the iron sceptre of kings, at last began to pick itself up, despite the huge burden crushing it.' But his entry under 'Proletaire', a last-minute addition in the Supplement, is characteristically rhetorical and unfocused:

---

[51] Louis-Sébastien Mercier, *Néologie, ou vocabulaire de mots nouveaux* (2 vols., Paris, 1801), Introduction, vi–lxxvi.

[a proletarian] is someone who owns no property. Good heavens! Get born! And have no place on the globe for his own cradle! Oh human laws! In order for every republic to thrive, it is essential that every citizen own something, and shows he is careful of the obligations and rights that such right of ownership assumes ... Unhappy the nation that is divided into two classes that are necessarily enemies, that of proprietors and that of proletarians! Proletarian is the most repulsive word in the language ... J.J. Rousseau did not have even a cabbage-patch as property, but his head was easily worth as much as a cabbage-patch...[52]

Mercier's *Néologie*, as its title suggested, was updating the imaginative explorations of language and street culture that he had started before the Revolution. In effect, he directly contradicted the article on language in the *Encyclopédie*, from forty years earlier (above, p. 193). Thus he noted (under 'néologier') that a lexicographer should merely be a 'secretary of usage', not a legislator. In his comments on hundreds of words, in alphabetical order in the 670 pages of his work, he constantly challenged the idea that language could or should be controlled centrally. It would have been self-contradictory for him to have offered new 'standard' definitions: instead, his word list is clearly designed to undermine fixity in language. By forcing the reader to go outside the normal framework of a standardised language, he sought to convey the underexplored territory of cultural change and the relativity of cultural meanings. He praised the practice of ostracism ('ostraciser') in ancient Greece. Equally provoca-tively, he noted ('naturalisme') that the fundamental rapport between early christianity (with a lower-case initial letter) and naturalism 'disap-peared later under a great many monastic inventions'. He did list the guillotine ('guillotage'), but claimed that he wanted to remove the perso-nal associations of that word, so added a new alternative of his own invention, 'decaput'. He also has a word for people who change opinions to suit the context: 'caméléoniser'.

There are many other entries in this work which would have enter-tained or surprised the reader. Mercier seems to have nothing but scorn and contempt for Newtonian science ('newtonianisme'), which is dis-missed as contrary to simple common sense. He also cited two authors, including the *ancien-régime* critic Linguet, to suggest that 'Encyclopédisme' is a cold and fruitless pursuit (see also 'nihiliste'). But he then adopted a typical technique from the original *Encyclopédie* by using head words to tackle entirely unexpected issues: the verb 'energiser', for example, is used to praise the incisive and spirited thinking of the Jansenists (while giving no other variant usages of the word). Mercier often cited other authors for

---

[52] Mercier, *Néologie*, vol. II, Supplément, 380. Other words cited here are all located in the alphabetical sequence of the work, except where otherwise stated.

extra effect, but unlike in his Introduction did not provide precise references or footnotes. He cited Napoleon in enthusiastic support of a republic based on true liberty and national representation ('représentation nationale'). He described 'patriotisme' as a 'sublime fever which in its convulsions triumphs over nature', but then seems to regard 'fraternisation' as a word that needs no definition: 'the fatherland (*patrie*) is the shared mother [!] of all the French: there is no-one who does not carry in his heart a definition of the word fraternisation, if he is a patriot; and if he is not, I would provide it in vain, since it would be like showing a painting by Greuze to a blind person, or singing an air from Gluck to someone who is deaf'. By contrast, 'liberticide' is given a short and blunt entry that would have fitted the mood of 1793 perfectly: 'this is the word one uses for all the ways employed by the enemies of the republic to kill liberty, whether they make use of the pen, the sword or the crucifix'.

What do we make of this work? Was Mercier simply trying to revive his literary career, late in life, by attracting attention to himself? Was he serious in his efforts to destabilise language, or merely (as so often in his earlier writings) exploiting his ear for popular forms of speech, overlaid with irony? Was he trying to shape political thinking back towards the middle ground, or using irony to exploit the many contradictions of the previous decade? All of these questions are difficult to answer, but there can be no doubt that Mercier was an acute observer of the ambivalence of language, keen to demonstrate how unstable it could be and sincere in his attempt to alert his readers to the scope for manipulation and misrepresentation. His choice of entry headings rarely matched those of Féraud or the Academy and he liked to convert common words into new abstract nouns or verbs, as well as actually inventing genuinely new words. He would fit well in a postmodernist theory of language.[53]

Speaking, Writing, Translating: Texts and Concepts

The universal but unpredictable restraints on freedom of opinion in early modern Europe affected all forms of expression, but to different degrees. By the early eighteenth century, the French government was institutionalising efforts to monitor conversation in public spaces,[54] and by 1793 had normalised citizen vigilantism, but, as elsewhere in Europe, the task

---

[53] The context and purpose of Mercier's *Néologie* is discussed more fully in D. Rosenberg, 'Louis-Sébastien Mercier's new words', *Eighteenth-century Studies*, 36 (2003), 367–86; and in the introduction to J.-C. Bonnet, (ed.), *Louis Sébastien Mercier: Néologie* (Paris, 2009).

[54] A. Farge, *Subversive words: public opinion in eighteenth-century France* (Cambridge, 1994).

appeared overwhelming and counterproductive. Accusations of insubordination or 'dangerous talk' were liable to disrupt social relationships in a community and might well simply attract unwanted attention. It is apparent from surviving private letters and clandestine manuscripts that subversive or free-thinking conversation could thrive in urban environments where there were long-running religious and political divisions, within some universities, or within other active enclaves of interested individuals. We have already noted that the links between conversation, manuscripts and printed texts are closer than historians used to assume, yet what little documentation we have suggests that the relationships between oral communication and print are far from straightforward. We need to take full account of both context, the material form and the content of the many kinds of 'text', and what they represented – not only in their original version but also as disseminated in print, in translation and through summary reviews.

Post-modernists and post-structuralists have tended to portray the Enlightenment as an age which expected a rational system of truth and knowledge to be attainable through observation and reason – the Enlightenment as a stage towards a structured modernity, expressed in progressively refined and reliable language structures. That view of the Enlightenment is not one that would readily have been accepted by anyone reading the *Encyclopédie*, even superficially, at the time of its publication. 'Reason', whether applied to beliefs, knowledge or the machinery of state, meant fundamentally different things to different people and could manifestly serve incompatible ends. Few of the best writers in the French Enlightenment can be fitted comfortably into either the linguistic structuralism that literary theorists have used, or into any one coherent 'modernising' agenda with an agreed set of aims. Equally, no eighteenth-century readers of Beccaria, for example, would have retained the illusion that print 'fixed' a text – or that translations were accurate – at least not once they realised how the variant versions had been reshaped by French and other translators. This is not the place to undertake a thorough discussion of linguistic and cultural symbolism in general. But it will be clear from the works examined in this chapter that post-modernist and post-structuralist theory is liable either to ignore the historical context in which eighteenth-century texts were written, or at best unwittingly follow in the very footsteps of those they targeted – reading meta-narratives or notions of progress into texts which consciously exploited the ambiguity of words and rebelled against programmes of any kind. Mercier was merely an extreme example of how verbal innovation could enhance or subvert rational intellectual life during the Enlightenment. A few writers may have followed Rousseau in trying to visualise a new coherent democratic world vision based on an ideal collective consciousness. But you would not have to read much Voltaire or Diderot before realising that such an ideal world did not exist and that there was no prospect of consensus either on what it might look like or how to get there.[55]

What, then, would contemporary readers have made of the texts they read? How did they respond to such texts, discuss them verbally, or interpret them in the privacy of their personal reading? How significant for their pattern of reading was the tone and style of what they read, or even the physical appearance and presentation of the text? And even as we ask such questions, are we oversimplifying the changeable environment in which texts worked?[56] Can translations produced before 1800 tell us how readers might have interpreted what they read? Much more work needs to be done on these questions. Equally, there is still a great deal of work to be done on the nature of reading and on the significance of texts as material objects, whose appearance, layout and mystique could have more impact on the reader than he or she might ever have consciously recognised.

In terms of trying to understand the layers of meaning in some of the more complex texts considered so far, we have in effect already used tools provided by several distinct groups of historians working in what is now called 'conceptual history' (*Begriffsgeschichte*). German cultural historians led by Reinhart Koselleck and Rolf Reichardt examined the use and development over time of significant key terms, not just as individual words but in semantic groups (for example, power, sovereign, authority) – the aim being to clarify and potentially define semantic usage over time.[57] By contrast, English-language historians have tended to follow the different approach of John Pocock and Quentin Skinner, in which political theory, and language itself, was firmly anchored in historical context in an effort to study concepts diachronically (across time) rather than as fixed philosophical abstracts.[58] Their approach allowed cultural historians to

---

[55] There is a large body of literature on post-modernism, but an excellent starting point with specific reference to this period is D. Gordon, 'On the supposed obsolescence of the French Enlightenment', in D. Gordon (ed.), *Postmodernism and the Enlightenment: new perspectives on eighteenth-century French intellectual history* (New York and London, 2001), 201–21; and his entry on 'Post-modernism', in A. C. Kors (ed.), *Encyclopedia of the Enlightenment* (Oxford, 2003); for a broader overview, see also A. Green, *Cultural history* (Basingstoke, 2008).

[56] B. Stock, *Listening for the text: on the uses of the past* (Baltimore, 1990).

[57] O. Brunner, W. Conze and R. Koselleck (eds.), *Geschichtliche Grundbegriffe: historisches Lexikon zur politisch-sozialen Sprache in Deutschland* (8 vols., Stuttgart, 1972–97); R. Reichardt, H.-J. Lüsebrink and J. Leonhard (eds.), *Handbuch politisch-sozialer Grundbegriffe in Frankreich 1680–1820* (Munich, 1985–); M. Richter, *The history of political and social concepts* (Oxford, 1995).

[58] J. G. A. Pocock, *The Machiavellian moment: Florentine political thought and the Atlantic rebublican tradition* (Princeton, 1975); Q. Skinner, *The foundations of modern political thought*

emphasise the diversity of meanings and connections deployed (consciously or not) by different writers in their distinct environments, recognising individuality and inconsistencies in usage (such as differences arising synchronically between writers from different social, educational and regional/cultural backgrounds). Their work had a major impact on the actual selection of texts to be studied, confirming a trend (already strongly sustained by Robert Darnton) towards deliberately discarding the notion that there was a 'canon' of supposedly major Enlightenment texts. Skinner also alerted historians to the significance of the 'speech act': the potential of a text (whether spoken or written) to have 'agency' (to do something) – whether that was intended by the speaker/author or not.[59]

Most of the pre-1800 texts that have been examined here were meant to achieve a change of mind, trigger action, or at least persuade the reader that something could be done. How such possibilities were put into words was of critical importance: in that sense, conceptual history, and especially the work of Pocock and Skinner, is fundamental to any thorough exploration of the history of print and the nature of any written or spoken text in the early modern period. Since the 1980s, historians have made substantive and increasingly explicit use of the many strands of this 'linguistic turn', in order to frame their study of dissemination, reception and impact. To that, we need to add more research on translation, the tools used by translators (including dictionaries), and the theories of translation explored by eighteenth-century writers aware of these problems.

But as everyone acknowledges, the evidence which we can use is elusive. Reading-diaries (diary annotations indicating significant reading) are rare and socially self-selective; book inventories after death, or related sales catalogues, tell us very little about what was read, or how; actual reader's annotations and marginalia offer rich pickings, but only sporadically and more rarely in popular types of reading material such as pamphlets and periodicals. In examining the texts that we have from the early modern period, we obviously also need to remind ourselves of the extent to which authors had to self-censor or disguise the layers of meaning that could be regarded as subversive or dangerous. The very nature of the controlling or repressing mechanisms manifestly militated against meaningful recording of the reactions of individual readers.

(2 vols., Cambridge, 1978); W. Steinmetz, M. Freeden and J. Fernandez-Sebastián (eds.), *Conceptual history in the European space* (New York and Oxford, 2017).
[59] I. Hampsher-Monk, 'Speech acts, languages or conceptual history?', in I. Hampsher-Monk (ed.), *History of concepts: comparative perspectives* (Amsterdam, 1998), 37–50, and other valuable chapters in this volume.

The many forms of expression relevant to our understanding of early modern political culture clearly all need to be read 'across the grain', locating them accurately in their particular time and place, while analysing both the explicit meanings and their underlying implications. For spoken words (including speeches later edited for publication), the form in which they survive clearly limits what we can do. But for manuscripts and printed texts we have far more scope. The intended audience/readership can be gauged in part from the stated intentions of the author and the style of writing, but may also be judged on the basis of the material quality, format, length (and hence likely price) of the text – its physical characteristics as a material object. We can then scrutinise its vocabulary more closely, with an eye to the variant forms of conceptual history outlined above. This chapter has added one further dimension: a transnational perspective, combining conceptual history with detailed study of actual translations (and summaries in foreign review journals) as a way of seeing how a text *might have been understood* by readers in different cultural contexts across Europe. The next two chapters will examine the evidence of how texts might have been deliberately designed to encourage the kinds of multiple understandings and practical engagement which became so central a feature of late Enlightenment thinking.

5   High Enlightenment, Political Texts and Reform 1748–89

The wars of 1740–63 not only brought an end to two decades of relative stability and economic prosperity, but also greatly extended the global impact of European colonial rivalry and exploitation in both human and economic terms. The precarious peace of Aix-la-Chapelle in 1748 led to some fundamental shifts in the balance of power in Europe and world-wide. The Seven Years War (1756–63) was even more bitter and destructive, aggravating major fiscal and administrative problems for the main belligerents and their alliance partners. The peace treaties of Paris and Hubertusberg (1763) created new overseas tensions and left nearly all the European participants dissatisfied and politically troubled: France was reluctant to recognise its considerable loss of status as a major colonial power and as the once-dominant land power in continental Europe, but it had no sustained political leadership capable of achieving substantive reform; Prussia could have collapsed had it not been for the succession of tsarina Elizabeth and consequent Russian withdrawal; the Austrian Habsburg conglomerate under Maria Theresa failed to recover Silesia, had to review its imperial priorities and faced major difficulties in some of its provinces over the next decades; Sweden remained destabilised by fiscal problems and alleged diplomatic interference from the great powers; and Poland faced another royal election in an increasingly dysfunctional republican monarchy. Even the British government of George III, which appeared to have come out of the peace settlement well, was troubled by factional instability, provocative domestic criticism from John Wilkes and others, increasingly virulent political satire in cartoons and newspapers, and – once the revolt of the American colonies became serious – significant popular unrest which put the whole British political nation under further strain. There were tensions even in smaller states, as illustrated in revolts in Corsica (culminating in 1767) and in Geneva (1781–2), mounting unrest and violence against government inertia in the United Provinces from 1781, and mounting tensions in the Habsburg Austrian Netherlands and in Hungary in the late 1780s. Nearly all European governments faced huge fiscal problems resulting from wartime overspends and administrative disarray. The return of wide-spread economic instability in the years 1770–4 and in the later 1780s made effective reform even more challenging.

Patriotism and jingoism may have dampened outright political criticism in wartime, but peace brought explicit recognition of the need for change within many of the governments and political establishments across Europe and, just as important, challenged the imagination of authors and publishers in terms of how to use print effectively. There were obvious risks attached to the use of print to scrutinise royal patronage and factions, the law courts, or the institutional weaknesses of the established churches. But in the deeply divided and hierarchical societies of eighteenth-century Europe, concerns about good governance and stability also affected readers in major capital cities, ports and some regional administrative centres. Given the tense context, it is hardly surprising to find a seemingly insatiable demand for newsprint, a growing interest in economic reform and improvement (when presented as well-meant projects), and an increasingly vigorous pamphlet discussion about everything from poor relief to international trade. Fiction (especially novels) continued to play a major part in alerting readers to social problems, moral questions and the potential difficulties arising from misused power at all levels of society and across the conventions of gender relations. Theatre and opera provided even more extraordinary means of highlighting social issues: we need only look at the extraordinary success of plays such as Beaumarchais's *The marriage of Figaro* (1783), controversy over its initial ban and subsequent release, and adaptation for Mozart's opera (1786) to realise just how controversial and effective the stage could be as a means of communicating with a very large and socially mixed audience – an impact made even greater by the printed collections of successful stage works which continued to sell extremely well throughout the eighteenth century.

Where there were active parliaments (notably in Britain and Sweden), we naturally find more sharply focused political discussion in print. The return of hope for prosperity and stability may also have generated fresh interest in international news and political economy, as well as in more abstract political questions such as sovereignty, representation and ultimately the relationship between the state and the rights of individuals. It is interesting to observe a more analytical approach even in the writing of history itself: Voltaire, Hume, Catherine Macaulay, Raynal, Gibbon and other successful writers were able to attract readers by providing much more than just 'official' histories. This, combined with the revolt of the American colonies and some challenging political crises within Europe, generated fresh interest in the principles of representation and political rights. Analysts even came to recognise that, since effective control of print was very difficult, governments might achieve more by trying to influence public opinion through proactive sponsorship of supportive texts and state propaganda.

The aim of this chapter is to examine how certain types of print, published in the context of major political events in the second half of the eighteenth century, might enhance public awareness of political issues and the bounds of legitimate authority. With the notable exception of visual satire and cartoons in Britain from the 1760s and in France from the late 1780s onwards, no major new types of printed material came into widespread use in the second half of the eighteenth century. However, newspapers and periodicals acquired much more outreach and range, and pamphleteering as always lent itself to rapid polemical response. That in turn changed the way in which power was discussed and satirised, opened up more topics of public interest and forced governments themselves to become visibly more proactive in terms of domestic and social responsibilities. Government initiatives often continued to focus primarily on political economy and improvement, but even within these conventional bounds new standards were set for the collation and publication of reliable information to help inform a widening public consensus.

Quantifying these changes in print in the eighteenth century is even more difficult than for earlier periods. Less progress has been made on the comprehensive short-title cataloguing necessary for systematic analysis, so for many European languages we are forced to rely on sampling and keyword searches in the catalogues of major libraries. As we will see later in this chapter, such searches can yield significant qualitative results, but given the growing complexity of the book trade cannot yet provide reliable quantification. The main exception is once again the English-language Short Title Catalogue (ESTC). The overall quantitative conclusions that one might draw from the ESTC, as we noted in Chapter 1, indicate a substantial but gradual increase in the total number of titles in the later eighteenth century, with little sign of sudden changes in print reflecting significant political changes such as the conclusion of peace in 1763. Even the city of Dublin, surpassing Edinburgh during the 1780s in terms of the number of printed items, did not experience significant overall spikes in new titles until the rebellion of 1798 (when the annual average of outputs suddenly doubled). Across the Atlantic, it is no surprise to find clearly marked but uneven fluctuations in print output, with Philadelphia on average ahead of Boston and New York. In particular, Philadelphia printers seem to have reinforced their lead in the 1790s, consistently surpassing even the total output of Edinburgh from 1794. In the context of American independence such data is unsurprising, but because

American printers operated under entirely different political and regulatory practices, these trends do not help to explain fluctuations back in London. It is unfortunate that we have no means of comparing English-language data with reliable aggregate information for revolutionary France or for the German lands. Nevertheless, there is no doubt that significant developments, such as the widespread economic difficulties of the early 1770s and the American struggle for independence, triggered substantial public interest and significant publishing initiatives.

By then, a remarkable cluster of new analytical publications had appeared, from around mid-century, most of them in French and most of them soon translated. At the end of 1747, La Mettrie had produced a hugely controversial short materialist tract, his *L'homme machine* (translated into English in 1749).[1] Burlamaqui published his *Principes du droit naturel* in 1747 and his *Principes du droit politique* in 1751 (both of them quickly acquiring the reputation of standard texts in the field, translated into English, Latin and other languages, and reprinted regularly before 1789). Even more durable amongst books on law, politics and civil society was Montesquieu's *De l'esprit des loix*, which appeared under a Geneva imprint in 1748 and rapidly went to several reprints (with the author publishing a *Defence* of his book two years later, when facing controversy, censorship and censure from church authorities). Thomas Nugent translated *The spirit of laws* almost immediately (1750), with six further London editions, as many in Edinburgh, three in Dublin and one each in Aberdeen and Glasgow (but surprisingly no identifiable American printings); German editions appeared in 1753 and 1782, a Danish version in two volumes in 1770–1 and a Dutch version that same year. In 1749 the first volume of Buffon's monumental *Histoire naturelle* appeared, with a further thirty-five volumes added by the time he died in 1788; it too was disseminated in English and German translations and abridgements, paving the way for a complete rethinking of the natural world and man's relationship to other animals. As we noted in Chapter 4, the enormously ambitious French *Encyclopédie* started appearing in 1751, with seven volumes in print by 1757 despite repeated efforts to have it stopped.

The extraordinary flow of major new books did not stop there. In Britain, David Hume had notable success with his *Philosophical Essays* of 1748 (later revised as his *Enquiry concerning human understanding*). Hume responded directly to the precarious international peace treaties of 1748 by publishing his concise and brilliantly accessible *Political discourses* of 1752, and immediately turned to his multi-volume *History of*

---

[1] Julien Offray de la Mettrie, *Machine man and other writings*, edited by A. Thomson (Cambridge, 1996).

Great Britain which began appearing in 1754, followed by his *History of England* a few years later.[2] Condillac, although in holy orders and a member of the Académie française, used Locke as a starting point for increasingly innovative studies of the psychology of sense perception (and a denial of innate ideas), culminating in his *Traité des sensations* of 1754. In 1755 Rousseau had his first major success with a prize essay entitled *Discours sur l'origine et les fondements de l'inégalité parmi les hommes* (commonly known in English as his *Discourse on inequality* and also appearing in German translation in 1756). Voltaire published his highly controversial poem on the Lisbon earthquake in 1756, questioning the nature of divine intervention on earth – to which he added his light-hearted bestseller *Candide* in 1759. Helvétius published another materialist tract, *De l'esprit,* in 1758, which appeared in English the following year under the title *Essays on the mind* and in German in 1760. Following the lead from the almost impenetrable *Tableau économique* disseminated by Quesnay in 1758, writers all over Europe also turned their attention to political economy. In philosophy, 1759 saw Adam Smith's first major work, his *Theory of moral sentiments,* which was regularly reprinted in English, had a French translation in 1764 and a German one in 1770.

This deluge of new books with political implications hardly seemed to slow down after the predicted outbreak of war in 1756 and continued in the 1760s with an impressive array of major works from Rousseau, Beccaria, the baron d'Holbach, Adam Ferguson, Lessing, Moses Mendelssohn and many others.[3] In France in particular, the market for subversive, irreligious and irreverent reading clearly continued to develop during the 1760s and 1770s – so much so that Robert Darnton has been able to challenge fundamentally the whole concept of Enlightenment bestsellers.[4] Even though Darnton's research has not taken full account

---

[2] Mapping out the development of Hume's political and philosophical ideas in print, in the period after the unsuccessful *Treatise of human nature* of 1739–40, is not yet complete, but there is no doubt that his short essays were accessible to a much wider British and international readership. There were a number of reprints and a four-volume collection in his *Essays and treatises on several subjects* (1753). This new version was itself reprinted regularly in various formats, both in Edinburgh and in London, continuing after his death in 1777, and also translated into French, German and other languages. His histories were even more successful, giving Hume a very substantial income. See J. A. Harris, *Hume: an intellectual biography* (Cambridge, 2015), notably 265–304.

[3] S. A. Reinert, *Translating empire: emulation and the origins of political economy* (Cambridge, MA, 2011), 38–72 and *passim,* not only demonstrates that around 1750 there was a marked increase in the rate of translation and dissemination of texts relating to political economy, across the major European languages, but also confirms (as we noted in the previous chapter) that the translation process often involved major modification and rewriting of the original text, to suit the new readership and context.

[4] Robert Darnton 'The forbidden books of pre-revolutionary France', in C. Lucas (ed.), *Rewriting the French Revolution* (Oxford, 1991), 1–32; R. Darnton, *Edition et sédition:*

of more popular and polemical texts published by smaller printers within France,[5] and does not take account of the growing importance of journals and reviewers (not least those printed outside the jurisdiction of the French crown), there can now be no doubt that an evaluation of public discussion in print needs to include a much wider range of material than that which was the focus of earlier research on the Enlightenment, both in France and for other parts of Europe. Print remained the most effective means of gaining a reputation, broadcasting ideas and even engaging in transnational analysis of human society – but the style and types of text, as well as the mechanisms of dissemination, were ever more diverse and imaginative. Print could serve the interests both of new authors trying to make a living and of highly successful ones who had attained financial independence, such as Hume and Voltaire. Many writers cut their teeth as reviewers and journalists, or by circulating manuscripts amongst friends and in discussion groups. Fiction, poetry and the theatre had even greater potential for experimentation. Some writers explored fictional travel writing for the more popular market, including futuristic utopias as in Mercier's *The Year 2440* (1771), which gained immediate publicity when it was banned by the French government in view of the looming Maupeou crisis. As we shall see in this chapter, innovation both in style and thematic content was a precondition of success, especially in France.

However, highlighting these well-known texts risks reinforcing the notion that there was a 'canon' of 'great' Enlightenment works recognisable even to contemporary readers. It is important to remember that financial security eluded almost all who tried to be freelance writers: many struggled for years to try to gain independence from patrons, sponsors and friends, often having to survive, in the words of Robert Darnton, in 'grub street' or on the margins of fashionable society. In any case market success was achieved at great risk – the risks of financial failure (when publications did not sell well), the threats of piracy (which stemmed from inadequate copyright protection across most of Europe except England), as well as the risk (and constant fear) of prosecution and censorship – not to mention the humiliation of simple lack of interest, sluggish demand or rejection by

l'univers de la littérature clandestine au xviiie siècle (Paris, 1991); R. Darnton, *The forbidden best-sellers of pre-revolutionary France* (London, 1996); and H.T. Mason, *The Darnton debate: books and revolution in the eighteenth century (SVEC* 359, Oxford, 1998).

[5] The trading network and methods of operation of the Société Typographique de Neuchâtel, first studied by Darnton, have now revealed more of the intricacies of a book trade operating on the margins of legality: M. Curran, 'Beyond the forbidden best-sellers of pre-revolutionary France' *Historical Journal,* 56 (2013), 89–112; L. Seaward, 'The Société Typographique de Neuchâtel (STN) and the politics of the book trade in late eighteenth-century Europe, 1769–1789', *European History Quarterly,* 44 (2014), 439–57.

readers. The print industry remained very volatile, deeply affected by an unpredictable market. It was also extremely labour-intensive at all stages of production – from writing, typesetting and proofreading, to paper supplies, physical manpower in printing, not to mention the substantial risks of distribution in the face of ever-vigilant but totally unpredictable police checks, prosecution and imprisonment.

Censorship, Libel and Illegal Books

As the printing industry grew during the eighteenth century, regulation of print became both more difficult and more openly contested. As we observed earlier, the idea of freedom of expression (in words, writing or print) was scarcely considered, even as an abstract ideal, in seventeenth-century Europe. In those states where censorship was weakening, for example the Netherlands, it was because of the lack of effective authority, not out of choice. In England, Milton's call for greater freedom (1644) was not acted on, even when he himself held government office after 1649. The regulatory role of the Stationers Company, though formally weakened with the lapse of legislation in 1695, retained some significance through the principle of perpetual copyright (claimed on the basis of new legislation in 1710, legally overturned only in 1774). But both copyright and regulation became easier to evade by means of illegal printing under false imprints, or more often, the use of satellite printers in a different jurisdiction. This commonly happened in Scotland or in Dublin in the case of English-language printing; in Dutch, Swiss or Rhineland cities in the case of French texts; and in neighbouring jurisdictions or free cities in the case of German texts. Such tactics, however, should not lead us to assume that the risks were substantially lowered: as most authors knew, all over Europe there were many ways books could be penalised or even systematically confiscated and destroyed if the text was arbitrarily deemed to transgress either the religious and moral standards of church and local vigilante authorities, appeared to question anything relating to the authority of the state, or caused offence to powerful factions or individuals. Publishing anonymously was no real protection, since penalties could be imposed on publishers, booksellers or readers instead.

Most of the active authors that we noted above had personal experience of prosecution, public outcry, temporary exile or even imprisonment. La Mettrie used foreign or false imprints and intermittent anonymity, and both he and Helvétius left France to find some kind of interim protection at the court of Frederick II in Potsdam. Voltaire was a salaried office-holder at Frederick's court from 1750 to 1752, then settled in a property on the Swiss border so that he could easily seek refuge in Geneva in case of threats from the French authorities. Many major authors, including both Diderot and Hume, deliberately kept back some of their more provocative writings, to be published after their death. Diderot, with experience of imprisonment for an earlier work, struggled to exhaustion to keep the *Encyclopédie* going in the face of several serious threats and the formal condemnation of the work by the Parlement de Paris (1758–9). Rousseau, always willing to create a sensation out of his substantive troubles with French censors in the 1760s, earned substantial author's fees while remaining paranoid about plots to suppress and destroy his work. We will see many other instances of such troubles. But the key point to bear in mind is that the fear of harsh censorship could work just as effectively as any real enforcement mechanisms. For publishers, hitting a balance was of critical importance: the publicity value of having a book banned might increase demand and raise prices, even cover the cost of fines and the impounding of stock, but if you pushed your luck too far you risked your entire business and livelihood. This kind of unpredictable and inconsistent threat was more than enough to ensure caution by everyone in the book trade. Thus the publisher of the *Enclyclopédie*, Le Breton, pre-empted further trouble by self-censoring the last ten volumes without even informing Diderot. The use of false imprints was so commonplace that it is often difficult to follow the real trajectory of many texts. In short, knowing how the system *might* work was a precondition of success.

The complicated and self-contradictory methods of control used in eighteenth-century France have been studied in greater detail than their equivalents elsewhere in Europe.[6] Contemporaries, not surprisingly, were increasingly concerned that the French system of pre-publication censorship was hopelessly inconsistent. Those in favour of more freedom complained of the unpredictable hazards of post-publication prosecution, which might hit authors, publishers, booksellers and even readers who were in possession of illegal books. The system appeared so arbitrary and unreasonable that even some of those in charge of making it work expressed ambivalence about their own role. The printing industry was supposed to be controlled by a separate section of the Chancery, headed by a Directeur de la Librairie (director of the book trade) who co-ordinated more than 100 unpaid royal censors. From 1750 to 1763, the

---

[6] R. Birn, *Royal censorship of books in eighteenth-century France* (Stanford, CA, 2012); R. Chartier, *The cultural uses of print in early modern France* (Princeton, 1987); Darnton, *Edition et sédition;* W. Hanley, 'The policing of thought: censorship in eighteenth-century France' (*SVEC* 183, Oxford, 1980), 265–95; C. Hesse, *Publishing and cultural politics in revolutionary Paris, 1789–1810* (Berkeley, 1991); R. L. Dawson, *Confiscation at customs: banned books and the French booktrade during the last years of the ancien régime* (*SVEC* 2006: 07, Oxford, 2006); J. McLeod, 'Provincial book trade inspectors in eighteenth-century France', *French History*, 12 (1998), 127–48.

Directeur was Lamoignon de Malesherbes. As the precocious and well-educated son of Lamoignon de Blancmesnil, Chancellor of France, Malesherbes was well-connected at court, but also had many friends in the circle of radical thinkers around Diderot and the Encyclopedists. He clearly saw the need for reform of the complicated system of which he was in charge, not only recognising that pre-publication censorship was increasingly unworkable and counterproductive, but also aware that both the cultural and the economic interests of France were being undermined when authors had to go abroad to get their books printed. Yet with a very weak monarch and competing court factions, Malesherbes had no effective means of achieving reform of the law (which consisted of an accumulation of regulations, revised in 1723, 1744 and again in a draconian but imprecise declaration of 1757 which followed the attempt by Damiens to assassinate Louis XV). Instead, he made routine use of a whole scale of dispensations. A book which failed to achieve the standards required for an official royal *privilège* (formal pre-publication authorisation with copyright protection) might instead be given a *permission tacite* (registered permission to publish, but without official notification of approval or public naming of the censor, and of course lacking legal protection), or a *tolérance* (unwritten and usually indirect verbal notification that printing could proceed, without any assurances of what would happen). Sometimes the publisher might be encouraged to circulate a limited number of copies, to see whether there would be a serious reaction – in effect making the publisher take all the risks in case a public outcry made prosecution necessary.

Individual case studies can serve to illustrate how openly contentious all this had become by the 1750s, not least in the tense atmosphere after the assassination attempt in January 1757. The Parlement de Paris had become more active since 1748, reviving what it saw as its historic role counterbalancing the legal authority of the crown. During the 1750s it also laid claim to more direct regulation of the book trade, independently of (and sometimes directly contradicting) the crown's appointed officials. Since much of the printed material appearing in the 1750s met with disapproval amongst the very conservative or Jansenist lawyers of the Parlement, confrontations were unavoidable. One of the most high-profile cases was Helvétius's materialist tract *De l'esprit* (*Essays on the mind*), analysing human cognition and self-interest in relation to civic society and the exercise of power, illustrated mostly with examples from the classics and from notional oriental despotism. The book had been submitted to the censor Jean-Pierre Tercier, who was cajoled into reading sections of the book in reverse order (ostensibly to suit deadlines imposed by the publisher). Not surprisingly, he missed a number of controversial arguments in the book, and unexpectedly gave it full royal approval after minor changes. As soon as it was published in 1758 it caused a scandal: the Parlement immediately reviewed its contents and formally condemned it, as did the Sorbonne theologians. Helvétius had to retract several times and was compelled to issue a printed public apology. Tercier had to appear before the Parlement and was demoted from the list of censors.[7] Serious though it was for them, the case was also symptomatic of a much more fundamental structural conflict within the machinery of government.

Malesherbes's position as director of the book trade was of course the real target for the conservative critics, both because he was a well-placed yet subordinate senior crown official and because his willingness to circumvent existing laws had become increasingly obvious. During the Helvétius crisis Malesherbes submitted several memoranda on the printing trade, where he explained his points of view more clearly. Essentially he wanted to simplify and minimise legislation on the printing trade, invalidate the claims of overall control by the Parlement and in general create a more liberal policy towards texts which were intended in good faith to serve the public interest. Ultimately, Malesherbes argued, public opinion should be the final judge of what was permissible, and freedom of expression should be extended to all works, including those aiming at political reform and enlightenment, provided they did not directly threaten public peace. Malesherbes, also an exponent of economic deregulation, advocated the removal of guild privileges and exclusive rights within all aspects of the printing industry and the book market, hoping thereby to encourage domestic high-skills trades.[8]

[7] [Claude Adrien Helvétius], *De l'esprit*, published anonymously (Paris, 1758). Some extant copies of the original edition (for example, two copies in Glasgow University Library) include, within their eighteenth-century binding, the printed cancellation of the original royal privilege and the texts of the resounding condemnations by the Parlement of Paris and the Faculty of Theologians. One of the Glasgow copies (Glasgow University Library, Special Collections, BC33-x.13) also has bound-in extracts from the notorious underground Jansenist journal, the *Nouvelles ecclésiastiques*, dated 12 November 1758 through to 13 February 1759, where part of the blame is attributed to the Jesuits in senior church positions, and where Helvétius's materialism is described as 'decrying all religion, openly mocking the true Religion, its Morality and its Mysteries'. The *Nouvelles ecclésiastiques* quotes sections from the book, but also on occasion breaks off such quotations out of 'decency'. Presumably the first owner of this copy found such documentation sufficiently interesting and significant to have it included in the binding, perhaps even expecting such material to increase the value of the book itself as it was now illegal. Demand for the book may well have increased as a result: over the next twenty years there were at least six reprints in French (various imprints) and an English translation in 1759.

[8] R. Birn, 'Malesherbes and the call for a free press', in R. Darnton and D. Roche (eds.), *Revolution in print* (Berkeley, 1989), 50–66; R. Birn, 'Book censorship in eighteenth-century France and Rousseau's response' (*SVEC* 2005: 01, Oxford, 2005), 223–45;

Needless to say, none of his proposals were put into practice. The war between factions in the Parlement and various branches of the royal administration continued, and in particular the Parlement persisted in scrutinising and condemning not just new texts, but also ones that had already been cleared by the censors. The Parlement suspended the *Encyclopédie* in 1759, even demanding that the first seven volumes, though already published with formal approval, be re-examined by a team of nine censors. This created enormous difficulties for Diderot: although disagreements within his team had surfaced early on, he now lost the support of a number of key authors, including his co-editor d'Alembert, Voltaire, Morellet and Turgot, some of whom withdrew already completed articles intended for the later volumes. Rousseau also made his final break with Diderot at this time, though this was part of his idiosyncratic behaviour towards all his friends. Various offers were made to Diderot to move the *Encyclopédie* abroad, but he refused, rightly fearing that he would lose what editorial control he still had. With the protection of Malesherbes, he continued working on the remaining volumes, assisted by a smaller circle of trusted friends and supporters, including d'Holbach, Jaucourt and Saint-Lambert. The publisher Le Breton also kept going, in the hope of rescuing his investment in the work (though as we noted above, he took the precaution of censoring some of the later articles without informing Diderot). The remaining ten volumes of text appeared all in one go, in 1765, without permission and under a false imprint (ostensibly Neuchâtel, but actually Paris itself).

Not surprisingly, discussions surrounding both the efficacy and the need for censorship resurfaced regularly. In 1764, André Morellet had written a tract on the practical benefits of freedom to discuss political and economic state policy, but chose not to try to get it published until after the Maupeou crisis (1771–4). Now, with the powerful support of Turgot (installed in 1774 as reform-minded Controller-general of French state finances), Morellet obtained a *permission tacite,* and the text appeared under a false London imprint.[9] In 1776 Condorcet spoke against the need for any kind of pre-publication censorship whatever. Others argued in favour of voluntary pre-publication censorship for those who wanted to have a guarantee that their work would not be prosecuted. Malesherbes himself drafted another memorandum, as late as 1788, but it was not published until after the Revolution.[10] In the event, nothing changed

E. P. Shaw, *Problems and policies of Malesherbes as Directeur de la Librairie* (New York, 1966); P. Grosclaude, *Malesherbes, témoin et interprète de son temps* (Paris, 1961), 63–186.

[9] A. Morellet, *Réflexions sur les avantages de la liberté d'écrire et d'imprimer sur les matières de l'administration* (London [Paris], 1775).

[10] For these and many other texts, see Birn, *Royal censorship,* 73–98.

until *ancien-régime* government itself collapsed: in practice, attempts to suppress controversial books were probably counterproductive both inside France and further afield. We have already noted, for example, that Raynal's *History of the two Indies* had substantially increased sales after it was banned: in the later 1770s and 1780s the book turned into a bestseller, with regular reprints as well as extended and revised editions, commentaries and even rebuttals. It seems as if the continuing attempts by the French government to suppress it merely gave it enhanced publicity and strengthened its message.[11]

Right up until 1789, therefore, the French censorship system remained unstable, based on unworkable legislation and buffeted by the rival claims and actual influence of conservatives and reformers, Jansenists, lawyers and court factions. With no single authority in effective control of any final decision, we need to recognise that acceptance or rejection depended not just on technical legality (whether the work had been passed by censors and not challenged in law), but also on the extent to which the intellectual elite itself, and those with political and literary influence within government, were prepared to tolerate new work. In the theatre, for example, a playwright could obtain formal approval from a censor and yet encounter resistance from those who might blacklist works that did not conform to the unspoken rules and conventions of theatre directors, patrons and even audiences.[12] With no consensus on what should be censored, it is clear that many within the political elite in France recognised the advantages of relative freedom of expression at least amongst responsible readers. It is also clear that censorship really no longer stifled innovative thinking – indeed Paris easily remained the undisputed centre for the more extreme and subversive publications of the European Enlightenment. The system did continue to create many *causes célèbres* amongst victimised authors and ideological martyrs, and censorship often served merely to attract attention to books and plays that otherwise might not have had much commercial success. Inconsistent censorship and ineffectual bans added substantial overhead costs to the printing and

---

[11] Dawson, *Confiscation at customs*, 86–93, details the impact of bans and confiscations on many other books (whether already established bestsellers or not), including Beaumarchais's very ambitious complete edition of the works of Voltaire (the Kehl edition, 1784–9); see also P. Benhamou, 'The diffusion of forbidden books: four case studies' (*SVEC* 2005: 12, Oxford, 2005), 259–81, highlighting the role of *cabinets de lecture* (rental libraries).

[12] G. S. Brown, 'Reconsidering the censorship of writers in eighteenth-century France: civility, state power and the public theater in the Enlightenment', *Journal of Modern History*, 75 (2003), 235–68, makes a clear distinction between legality and legitimacy on the Paris stage, noting the important mediating role of for example Jean-Baptiste Antoine Suard (1732–1817) as theatre censor from 1774 to 1790.

bookselling trade in France, but the attendant scandals and publicity also ensured that the profits to be made in the trade in illegal books might well outweigh the risks and fines. But this was not just a game. We need to remember that the real incarceration of authors and publishers continued right up to the Revolution: the Bastille alone, for example, continued to hold a significant number of offenders against printing laws, with an average of around fifty authors and as many distributors incarcerated every decade in the period 1750–80.[13] In short, French censorship did genuinely serve its purpose as a deterrent and in that respect its unpredictability and inconsistency was an advantage. Yet at the same time the scandals and mistakes in the system provoked precisely the kind of awareness and publicity that censorship was meant to avoid.[14]

Several further conclusions can be drawn from recent research on French censorship. The fascinating range of reports produced by the more active royal censors themselves are ample testimony to the sheer richness and diversity of intellectual life that managed to exist in the grey areas between conflicting jurisdictions.[15] With censors themselves often being active writers, they reflected the huge range of conflicting opinions characteristic of the late Enlightenment in France. In practice, however, their reports also demonstrate an acute awareness of the need for a flexible understanding of the public mood: *permissions tacites* were often granted to works that, despite reprehensible content, were deemed unlikely to stir any significant public trouble. Thus Dom Devienne's *Administration générale et particulière de la France* (published anonymously, ostensibly in Amsterdam but actually Paris, in 1774) provided an overview of a comprehensively reorganised government, much of it pre-empting the Revolution – but it was deemed so visionary and impracticable that the censors thought it harmless, and no scandal resulted.[16] The records of the French book trade demonstrate very clearly that many of the censors were sympathetic to, and participants in, new ways of thinking and often sought a compromise acceptable to public opinion. In other words, French censorship was not primarily a system of state control,

---

[13] D. Roche, 'Censorship and the publishing industry', in Darnton and Roche (eds.), *Revolution in print*, 24.

[14] See also S. Rosenfeld, 'Writing the history of censorship in the age of Enlightenment', in D. Gordon (ed.), *Postmodernism and the Enlightenment*, 117–45.

[15] W. Hanley, *A biographical dictionary of French censors*, so far 2 vols. (Ferney-Voltaire, 2005–16), gives detailed summaries and citations from those censors whose reports survive. One of these, Cadet de Sainville (vol. 2, 1–75), was active from 1761 right through to 1789, and the more than 100 reports of his that survive provide a rich kaleidoscope of comments not just on the individual books that he censored, but also on the changing intellectual framework in which he worked.

[16] Birn, *Royal censorship*, 70f.

more a matter of power brokerage within the many literary, intellectual and political factions in Versailles and in Paris.

The source material both on censorship and on the illegal book trade demonstrates how deep the divisions and quarrels could be even within the more liberal circles of French intellectual and political life after 1750.[17] Voltaire himself is a clear example. He continued to claim leadership of the *philosophes* right up until his death, despite his manifest conservatism and political caution. But even his admirers also had to admit that he never succeeded in uniting even just the moderates, let alone presenting a united front with his more politically adventurous former allies. His hostility to Rousseau was plain for all to see, but he was also instinctively unable to accept, let alone participate in, the kind of discussion pursued by Diderot, d'Holbach and other more controversial writers. This was no doubt partly because of differences of temperament, but was also a consequence of the unpredictable divisiveness of the censorship system, where each writer had to protect his own work as best he could. Many of them, Voltaire included, did not want to risk their own reputation by directly attacking the political establishment – and for Voltaire this worked, since the state recognised that any significant attempt to restrict or suppress his work would be counterproductive.

The French system of state censorship is so important because it was by far the biggest operation in Europe and was trying to control the widest range of radical and subversive texts. In comparison, censorship decisions by the Catholic church itself were of much less practical significance: the Papal Index of prohibited books had unchallenged legal standing only in some of the Italian states and, heavily qualified, in the Spanish peninsula. It had no legal force in France and was increasingly regarded as advisory in most other Catholic states in Europe. Even in France itself, theological censorship (notably by the Sorbonne), while continuing to carry some weight in particular cases, was often ignored: substantive discussion of ways of regulating print increasingly focused on texts with more immediate implications for political, social and economic reform. Malesherbes was broadly representative of enlightened contemporary French opinion in leaving the finer points of religious beliefs and the protection of orthodoxy to theologians and the self-appointed guardians of tradition. Significantly, his moderate and practical viewpoint may have been similar to that of many readers and members of central and local government

---

[17] For a systematic analysis, see in particular O. Ferret, *La fureur de nuire: échanges pamphlétaires entre philosophes et anti-philosophes 1750–1770* (*SVEC* 2007: 03, Oxford, 2007).

throughout Europe, who did not want to enforce strict censorship on those books that were essentially well meant and respectable.

Even so, the only two states willing to attempt deliberate abolition of pre-publication censorship were on the fringe of the European Enlightenment. Sweden adopted an astonishingly liberated censorship law in 1766, and Denmark-Norway abolished pre-publication censorship altogether in 1771. The context and impact of these two initiatives, however, had nothing in common. The Danish reform was implemented by executive decree, without any discussion at all – the brainchild of the German reformer Johann Friedrich Struensee, who had acquired much of the power of a regent through his position as royal physician to the severely mentally disturbed monarch Christian VII. Although the decree was not formally rescinded after his fall from power in 1772, it was in effect suspended. Significant public discussion emerged only in the late 1780s, in circumstances to which we will return later in this chapter.[18]

Far more significant in the present context is the reform of censorship in Sweden. Its printing industry was extremely small, even compared with that of other small languages such as Dutch. But during the period of limited constitutional monarchy (1719–72) Sweden did have a strong national parliament (*Riksdag*) with two major active political parties. By the mid-1750s its deputies had begun to exercise their right to publish free from censorship, and a number of other reformers tried to exploit a gradual relaxation of the regulations. In 1759, Peter Forsskål published a short tract, *Thoughts on civil liberty*, consisting of a series of statements which amount to a declaration of rights. Paragraph 7 states that 'the life and strength of civil liberty consist in limited government and unlimited freedom of the written word, as long as serious punishment follows all writing which is indisputably indecent, contains blasphemy ..., insults individuals and incites apparent vices'.[19] Public opinion shifted over the next few years, as a number of other pamphlets added further detail. The one (and only) state censor, Niclas von Oelreich, gradually came round to

---

[18] Detailed analysis of the impact of the Danish press reforms is found in H. Horstbøll, 'Trykkefrihedens bogtrykkere og skribenter 1770–1773', *Grafiana*, (2001), 9–25; Horstbøll, 'Bolle Luxdorphs samling af trykkefrihedens skrifter 1770–1773', *Fund og forskning i det Kongelige Biblioteks samlinger*, 44 (2005), 371–412; and his shorter overview, 'The politics of publishing: freedom of the press in Denmark, 1770–73', in P. Ihalainen, M. Bregnsbo, K. Sennefelt and P. Winton (eds.), *Scandinavia in the age of revolution: Nordic political cultures 1740–1820* (Farnham, 2011), 145–56; see also K. L. Berge, 'Developing a new political culture in Denmark-Norway 1770-1799', in E. Krefting, A. Nøding and M. Ringvej (eds.), *Eighteenth-century periodicals as agents of change: Perspectives on northern Enlightenment* (Leiden, 2015), 172–84.

[19] P. Forsskål, *Thoughts on civil liberty*, edited by D. Goldberg and others (Stockholm, 2009), which includes a full modern translation of the text, from which this quote is taken.

a practical and liberal point of view similar to that of Malesherbes, recognising that pre-publication censorship was restricting constructive political and economic discussion. He too began to tolerate certain kinds of moderate pamphleteering, including texts published in anticipation of a full session of the Riksdag.

The Swedish parliament eventually approved an Ordinance for the Liberty of Printing on 2 December 1766 (with the three lower Estates outvoting the nobility). The legislation retained pre-publication censorship of theological texts, but removed it for everything else. Criticism of the constitution, the Riksdag, the church and officers of state remained subject to strict libel laws. Nonetheless the decision was hugely significant, creating a climate in which a number of major political issues could be discussed openly, in print – including press regulation itself and access to information. As we will see later in this chapter, Sweden's pamphlet controversies now became more open and comprehensive, covering many aspects of public policy including corruption in political life and other issues of public concern. The reading public could now, for example, gain insights into the balance of power between the well-entrenched noble elite, the crown, central and local officeholders (persons of rank), and commoners (townsmen, clergy and the rural population). But other major issues could be raised: concerns over communication and information itself, and even accusations of corruption, bribery and political manipulation by influential lobbyists including foreign embassies.[20]

These differences help to explain why press freedom did not last: after the bloodless political coup by Gustavus III in 1772, the crown pursued a determined policy of centralisation, part of which involved a systematic prosecution of authors, booksellers and publishers, such as Carl C. Gjörwell and his newspaper *Allmänna Tidningar*. The precise impact of this retrenchment has not yet been examined in full.[21] The king continued to argue that the 1766 ordinance was being maintained, but, as an enthusiastic follower of the more conservative part of the French Enlightenment, he centralised power systematically and clearly aimed to

---

[20] M.-C. Skuncke, 'Freedom of the press and social equality in Sweden, 1766-1772', in Ihalainen et al. (eds.), *Scandinavia in the age of revolution*, 133–43; M.-C. Skuncke, 'Press and political culture in Sweden at the end of the age of liberty' (*SVEC* 2004: 06, Oxford, 2004), 81–101; M.-C. Skuncke and H. Tandefelt (eds.), *Riksdag, kaffehus och predikestol: Frihetstidens politiska kultur 1766–1772* (Stockholm, 2003).

[21] S. Boberg, *Gustav III och tryckfriheten 1774–1787* (Göteborg, 1951); J. Eriksson, *Carl Christoffer Gjörwell som aktör på den svenska bokmarknaden 1769–1771* (Uppsala dissertation, 2003). Significantly, German review journals also took note of the Swedish difficulties from 1772 onwards: for example, the *Allgemeine deutsche Bibliothek*, 39 (1779), 300–2, reviewed a German translation of a Swedish study of press freedom covering the early years of royal retrenchment in the 1770s.

suppress independent political views expressed in print. Further restrictions were added for the theatre and for newspapers (1785), and the reporting of news from revolutionary France was severely curtailed already in 1790, before most other governments reacted.

Sweden therefore seems to confirm the general experience of later eighteenth-century Europe: that centralised states could not easily tolerate freedom of expression – and conversely that genuine political discussion was best served by the somewhat chaotic politics found in states with strong parliaments or other institutional frameworks that allowed press regulations to become lax or unenforceable. Ending pre-publication censorship, or shifting responsibility to the law courts to determine the boundaries of libel, could make a significant difference only where the political context also changed: after all, most courts of law were staffed by men who were already members of the political elite. Print prosecutions had as much to do with power relationships as with the actual text, and in such cases the English courts, the French *parlements* and the Swedish supreme court were all willing to take their cue from a hostile prosecutor wanting to punish those responsible. But everywhere, and especially in the smaller devolved jurisdictions of central Europe and northern Italy, enforcement of print regulations and the prosecution of authors were uneven, and the transmission and trade in illegal books could never be stopped. At best, sporadic prosecution, police raids and customs confiscations could only impede the illegal market, try to avoid creating too much counterproductive publicity, and in effect increase the risks and hence the costs of carrying illegal books.[22]

In the wake of increasing public discussion of the framework of civil society (many strands of which will be examined below), and the major constitutional questions fuelled by the American Revolution, it is hardly surprising that censorship itself became a prominent subject of discussion in the 1780s. An informative example of such debate, within the confines of monarchical government, is that which took place in the Mittwochsgesellschaft in Berlin in the last years of the reign of Frederick II. Diderot had already noted the hypocrisy of Frederick's enlightenment: his willingness to exploit the publicity value of his correspondence with Voltaire and his demonstrative toleration of religious and philosophical dissent, seemingly at odds with his autocratic style of personalised government and his demand for civil obedience in

---

[22] In addition to the Darnton debate already cited, see also C. Haug, F. Mayer and W. Schröder (eds.), *Geheimliteratur und Geheimbuchhandel in Europa im 18. Jahrhundert* (Wiesbaden, 2011).

public affairs.[23] Such an apparent contradiction, however, may have been illusory, at least if judged by the published response to the Prussian Academy competition in 1780 on the question 'Is it advisable to deceive the masses?' and the equally fundamental question raised in an Academy lecture in 1783, 'What is enlightening [or Enlightenment]?' As Eckhart Hellmuth has pointed out, and some cautious essays published in the *Berlinische Monatsschrift* and elsewhere tend to confirm, only a few of the Berlin intellectuals (notably Moses Mendelssohn and Friedrich Nicolai) were willing to argue for substantial freedom of information and better education to ensure that all citizens could understand and share the values of an open society. We do not know exactly how the arguments on both sides were presented in the exclusive and secret Mittwochsgesellschaft itself, but from what was cautiously printed many continued to voice the kind of hesitation also expressed by Kant: that careful public regulation was necessary. In effect, the views of Carl Gottlieb Svarez prevailed, in line with the consensus amongst officeholders of the Prussian state, that consensus-based 'popular' enlightenment was appropriate for everyone, but that censorship remained necessary, since only the intellectual elite had the full rational powers and understanding necessary to analyse more complex issues.[24] This was a discussion which continued across much of Europe in the 1790s, with frequent comparisons made between different regulatory regimes. Under the impact of French revolutionary radicalism, caution invariably prevailed in favour of stronger and more repressive censorship.

In England the discussion took a different direction but ended with comparable repressive policies. Since 1695, reliance on libel law did have the advantage of allowing the government to avoid direct responsibility for controversial decisions – now devolved to judges, juries and prosecutors – while continuing to deploy various forms of bribery and harassment of authors and publishers, too, as was normal all over Europe. The English use of libel prosecutions to control print has not yet been

---

[23] Denis Diderot, *Pages contre un tyran*. Unpublished manuscript from around 1771 written in response to a critique by Frederick II of a work by d'Holbach. Diderot's short essay was first published in 1937 in an edition by Franco Venturi and is now available in P. Vernier (ed.), *Diderot: Oeuvres politiques* (Paris, 1963), 135–48.

[24] E. Hellmuth, 'Enlightenment and freedom of the press: the debate in the Berlin Mittwochsgesellschaft, 1783-1784', *History [The Historical Association]*, 83 (1998), 420–44; G. Birtsch, 'Die Berliner Mittwochsgesellschaft', in P. Albrecht, H. E. Bödeker and E. Hinrichs (eds.), *Formen der Geselligkeit in Nordwestdeutschland 1750–1820* (Tübingen, 2003), 423–39; J. Schmidt, 'The question of Enlightenment: Kant, Mendelssohn and the Mittwochsgesellschaft', *Journal of the History of Ideas*, 50 (1989), 269–91; J. Schmidt (ed.), *What is Enlightenment? Eighteenth-century answers and twentieth-century questions* (Berkeley, CA, 1996), citing further examples from amongst the many articles and pamphlets on the subject published before 1789.

examined systematically, but judging from some well-known cases it seems that the formal nature of such prosecutions provided plenty of material for public controversy and partisan political polemics. Libel prosecutions had been relatively infrequent in the earlier eighteenth century,[25] perhaps because of the uncertainty of securing a conviction. But after the succession of the relatively benign George III (1760–1820), and especially with the peace settlement of 1763, political controversies were pursued with increasing vigour in newspapers, pamphlets and innovative personalised satirical cartoons, leading to more prosecutions. Charges of libel or seditious libel, however, could easily raise issues of principle, notably regarding the relative powers of judges and juries in deciding whether there was sufficient evidence of 'malicious intent' on the part of the person responsible for publication. Defence lawyers could respond by making grand rhetorical references to ancient constitutional rights and the hallowed liberty of Englishmen.[26]

A turning point in this respect was the series of confrontations following publication of the notorious number 45 (1763) of John Wilkes's journal *The North Briton*. Wilkes was an exceptionally gifted self-publicist, promoting himself as an outsider struggling against the corrupt use of power. His repeated attacks on government policy before and after the conclusion of peace in 1763 ensured that he had enthusiastic support amongst his London readers. Over the next ten years, his disputed re-elections to parliament, the prosecutions launched against him and those assisting him, and the 'Wilkes and Liberty' disturbances in effect kept on raising questions around both ministerial powers and the authority of the House of Commons itself. His imprisonment in 1768 enhanced his populist reputation and provided a core cause for the Society of Supporters of the Bill of Rights, which he founded in 1769, but which quickly acquired momentum beyond his control.[27] Wilkes became Lord Mayor of London in 1774 and over the next two years assisted both the American colonists

---

[25] G. C. Gibbs, 'Government and the English press, 1695 to the middle of the eighteenth century', in A. C. Duke and C. A. Tamse (eds.), *Too mighty to be free: censorship and the press in Britain and the Netherlands* (Zutphen, 1987), 87–105, who notes that Nathaniel Mist's *Weekly Journal* was prosecuted for libel no less than fifteen times, and sometimes fined, but that sales tended to improve as a result of this kind of publicity. Mist paid a number of writers, including Daniel Defoe, even though Defoe was also a propagandist in the pay of the government. The Old Bailey (one of the courts handling cases of seditious libel) heard a few cases before 1763, and print-related offences became more common in the later 1780s and 1790s.

[26] T. A. Green, *Verdict according to conscience: perspectives on the English criminal trial jury 1200–1800* (Chicago, 1985), 318–85; R. R. Rea, *The English press in politics 1760–1774* (Lincoln, NE, 1963). See also F. O'Gorman, *The long eighteenth century: British political and social history 1688–1832* (London, 1997), 221–32.

[27] P. D. G. Thomas, *John Wilkes* (Oxford, 1996).

and the demands for parliamentary electoral reform. But by then his popular appeal was on the wane and others were taking the lead in the use of journals, pamphlets, demonstrations and petitions in support of a range of broad political causes, and in particular pushing the boundaries of what could be said in print.

Partly as a result of the tactical manoeuvres of Wilkes, the traditionally enforced ban on publishing reports of the House of Commons debates was itself tested in court in 1771. Although the continued prohibition was upheld in law, it quickly became unenforceable: publishers already knew that they might make enough profit from publication to cover the risks of prosecution and fines. British government policies towards the American colonies (and by 1779 the visible British failure to recover control) created sustained interest in fundamental constitutional issues of sovereignty and representation, as well as questions of property rights and freedom of expression.[28] These issues created the basis for associations and societies calling for substantive constitutional and parliamentary reform, including notably Christopher Wyvill's Yorkshire Association (1779), John Cartwright's Society for Constitutional Information (1780) and soon other organisations using a combination of meetings, pamphleteering and newspaper reporting to promote moderate ideals of political change. Naturally, there were substantial differences of viewpoint, ranging from moderate demands for 'economical reform' to more traditional loyalist counterclaims.[29] There were also substantial developments in the range of political questions discussed in print, the level of criticism of the policies of successive ministries and underlying concern for the claimed 'rights of Englishmen', ancient freedoms, parliamentary franchise, parliamentary privilege and royal prerogatives.

Printing in London may well have been less effectively controlled than in many other parts of Europe, but it was certainly neither deregulated nor risk-free. London newspapers and pamphleteers, especially those tending towards a more radical position, all had to take great care not to provoke libel prosecution or other challenges.[30] Similarly, some of the more far-

---

[28] On the connection between Wilkes and the radical and commonwealth legacy, see R. Hammersley, *The English republican tradition and eighteenth-century France: between the ancients and the moderns* (Manchester, 2010), 100–9; on the wider context, E. Hellmuth, '"The palladium of all other English liberties": reflections on the liberty of the press in England during the 1760s and 1770s', in his *The transformation of political culture: England and Germany in the later eighteenth century* (Oxford, 1990), 467–501.

[29] R. Duthille, *Le discours radical en Grande-Bretagne, 1768–1789 (SVEC 2017: 11*, Oxford, 2017).

[30] W. St Clair, *The reading nation in the Romantic period* (Cambridge, 2004), 84–102 and 480–8; and K. Temple, *Scandal nation: law and authorship in Britain, 1750–1832* (Ithaca, NY, 2003).

sighted reformers such as the scientist Joseph Priestley, the influential dissenting preachers Richard Price and the hugely important London publisher Joseph Johnson carefully linked current issues to the political legacy of earlier mainstream writers such as John Locke, as well as to more recent texts including James Burgh's *Political disquisitions* (1774). The centenary of the 1688–9 Revolution provided an ideal context in which to review the British constitution and the condition of representative government. For example, the Revolution Society acquired a more visible profile by adopting a set of radical principles including a right of resistance against the abuse of power, specifically in respect of liberty of conscience and freedom of the press. A sermon delivered by Price in November 1789 called for a cohesive civic society where the government would genuinely serve the public interest and the people: the text was deemed so important that it was reissued as a pamphlet, *A discourse on the love of our country*, which became a bestseller.[31] As we will see in the next chapter, such principles quickly became controversial in the early 1790s: already by 1791 some of those demanding reform risked violence and government harassment of a kind that would certainly have inhibited cautious authors.

Major legal cases, not least those focusing on seditious libel and the visible challenges to government, created sensational material in print: both in Britain and in France,[32] defence lawyers increasingly used publication of legal memoranda or judicial summaries as a means of highlighting not only the particular details of major cases but also the repressive use of the law against what could tentatively be described as cases of 'public interest'. In practice, efforts to control what was published might well challenge the inventiveness of publicists to find new means of evasion. In short, questions surrounding censorship, freedom of opinion and the ambiguities of what could be said in public were fiercely contested but essentially unresolved in most of Europe before 1789. No governments really wanted freedom of the press, but opinions differed widely on what could be tolerated and why. This uncertainty persisted through the 1790s: successive French governments hailed public opinion but backtracked on free discussion, and once war broke out in 1792 both France and its European opponents could claim the need for emergency restrictions on freedom of information. No-one knew how to reach the unattainable balance between allowing 'responsible' public debate while avoiding divisive criticism of domestic politics – and this applied as much to pamphlets as to newspapers (the two remaining virtually

---

[31] Richard Price, *A discourse on the love of our country* (London, 1789). This 60-page tract had nine printed editions in English and three in French over the next year.

[32] S. Maza, *Private lives and public affairs: the causes célèbres of prerevolutionary France* (Berkeley, 1993).

indistinguishable except for the fact that pamphlets were usually stand-alone, whilst newspapers were serialised and so had to be more cautious in order to stay in business).

News and Political Periodicals

The growth in demand for news continued unabated in the later eighteenth century. In the more prosperous parts of Europe so many new titles appeared that urban readers could hardly avoid being aware of current events. In the major cities the competition became so severe that some titles had only a short duration, appeared irregularly, or were abandoned by the publisher.[33] Amsterdam, Leiden and other Dutch cities continued to support long-running quality newspapers, both in Dutch/Flemish and in French, with for example the *Gazette d'Amsterdam* (founded 1691) surviving the turbulent revolutionary years until 1796. Similarly, the number of durable French-language journals and serials increased five-fold during the period 1745–85, if we also include those produced across its borders (beyond the reach of France's censors and therefore containing more reliable political information).[34] The first daily French newspaper, the *Journal de Paris*, ran from 1777, but had to remain fairly bland in order to comply with the censors. By the 1780s, however, press regulation in France was no longer up to the challenge of a rapidly expanding industry responding to huge reader demand. By then a mixed-content literary and political journal such as the weekly *Mercure de France* could sell upwards of 20,000 copies.[35]

London sustained a rapid growth in the newspaper industry from the early years of the century, fuelled by interest in factional and personal power struggles, commercial opportunities and any political news that could be printed without too great a risk of prosecution. By the 1780s, London is estimated to have had at least ten regular daily newspapers (including a Sunday paper from 1779) and as many appearing twice or three times a week, with far more local papers appearing in provincial towns.[36] In Habsburg Italy in the 1760s and 1770s, archduke Leopold supported the publication of the *Notizie del mondo* and the *Gazetta universale*, both under state censorship but intended to foster informed

---

[33] J. Sgard (ed.), *Dictionnaire des journaux (1600–1789): édition électronique revue, corrigée et augmentée* (online at http://dictionnaire-journaux.gazettes18e.fr).

[34] J. Censer, *The French press in the age of Enlightenment* (London, 1994), 6–12.

[35] *Dictionnaire des journaux 1600–1789*.

[36] J. Black, *The English press in the eighteenth century* (London, 1987); R. Harris, *A patriot press: national politics and the London press in the 1740s* (Oxford, 1993); H. Barker, *Newspapers, politics and public opinion in late eighteenth-century England* (Oxford, 1998).

political engagement. Copenhagen could not yet support a daily newspaper, but had very successful weeklies and bi-weeklies. Stockholm acquired two daily papers during the period of substantially reduced print regulation (1766–72).[37] Many smaller market towns in the more prosperous parts of Europe also acquired their own local papers ('intelligencers', *affiches*), typically serving both as advertisers and news digests.

The most successful papers anywhere, however, were found in northern Germany. One of the most reliable was Hamburg's great newspaper, its variant titles often simplified to *Der Hamburgische Correpondent* (*The Hamburg Correspondent*). It dated from 1721, was on a permanent footing from 1730 and acquired such a reputation for independence that by the 1780s, with four issues per week and various supplements, it needed up to twelve printing presses operating in parallel in order to meet public demand of upwards of 30,000 copies: there was no other way of overcoming the limits of the existing technology, where a team of two strong men on one press (with others setting the type and doing ancillary tasks) could at best print upwards of 2000 to 2500 sheets (one-sided) per ten-hour day.[38] *The Hamburg Correspondent* had such a full coverage of international and commercial news that many other newspapers used it for reference. It regularly reported on the proceedings of the British parliament and gave details of the recurrent reform proposals which the French government struggled with in the last two decades before 1789. It had regular literary supplements and reports of learned societies, as well as occasional advertisements for new books (including French books available from a specialist bookseller and printer in Hamburg). It also included local news, as when (in January 1784) citizens there were required to clear snow and ice from their houses as a public safety measure. The first January issue of every year often had a broader overview. Thus, in January 1785, we find a tally of the size of land armies in all the major states of Europe, including Russia with 470,000 men under arms, the Ottoman Empire with 210,000, Britain with 58,000 ranking below Denmark's 67,000 and Poland with a mere 15,000.[39]

Newspapers usually printed the name of its publisher, or an editorial address, in order to receive advertisements and secure subscriptions.

---

[37] M.-C. Skuncke, 'Medier, mutor och nätverk,' in Skuncke and Tandefelt (eds.), *Riksdag, kaffehus och predikstol*, 255–86.

[38] B. Tolkemitt, *Der Hamburgische Correspondent: zur öffentlichen Verbreitung der Aufklärung in Deutschland* (Tübingen, 1995). The paper had a circulation of around 13,000 by 1789 and twice that by 1800, unrivalled by any other newspaper anywhere. Its normal full title was *Staats- und Gelehrte Zeitung des Hamburgischen unpartheyischen Correspondenten*.

[39] Issue 1 (1 January 1785). By the 1780s the paper usually had 208 numbered issues per year, often around 24 pages per week, in a standardised format which continued through the 1790s and beyond.

Accordingly, they had to be more cautious than pamphleteers in complying with prevailing print regulations. This no doubt explains why so many papers continued to report merely supposedly factual news and authorised government information, rather than attempt editorial analysis. French-language papers such as the *Gazette de Leyde*, published outside French jurisdiction, could therefore thrive by providing more analytical reporting with a reputation for sober reliability. Their high cost of subscription within France allowed the authorities to turn a blind eye to their illegal import, since they were in effect beyond the reach of the less well-off Parisian readers whose volatility the French government feared. The French government itself even allowed leaked information to reach these French-language papers abroad to test public reaction amongst their more exclusive readership. The French foreign minister could then lodge a formal complaint to the relevant urban magistrates in the Netherlands, in the certain knowledge that the publisher would be reprimanded but would not effectively be silenced.[40] Increasingly, in the later eighteenth century, newspapers thus could become part of the network of communication used in (and changing the rules of) international diplomacy.

Some journalists rebelled sensationally against the expectations of their times. Simon-Nicolas Linguet's extremely outspoken, idiosyncratic and personalised serial *Annales politiques* (1777–92) was published much of the time in London, appeared very irregularly, but nevertheless had many enthusiastic readers – perhaps because it combined aggressive independence with a hostile rejection of most of the French Enlightenment. The *Annales* landed Linguet in prison in 1780, but despite gaps in publication it had a large readership, no doubt attracted by his extremely unconventional style. Other publishers tried to meet the demand for more sober news-based political analysis, adopting the type of general overview already sustaining many specialist journals (literary, philosophical and scientific reviews) and *Spectator*-type journals. Monthly or weekly political review journals lent themselves particularly well to thematic summaries, without competing directly with daily newspapers. Significant political developments, such as the Maupeou crisis in France (1771–4), the open revolt of the American colonies from 1775 and the growing disturbances in the Austrian Netherlands in the 1780s, created new opportunities for the release of information and discreet comment in ways (and in locations) that might minimise problems with the censors. Quality newspapers such as the *Gazette de Leyde* or the *Hamburg Correspondent* had already led the

---

[40] J. D. Popkin, *News and politics in the age of revolution: Jean Luzac's Gazette de Leyde* (Ithaca, NY, 1989), 68–98 and *passim*.

way in substantive international journalism, printing recurrent full reports on all major developments, including for example full summaries of the proceedings of the British Parliament and details of French efforts to stabilise its fiscal system.

Across Europe, news of the revolt of the American colonies made sensational newspaper material in the 1770s – not least in the light of the many other major political news items across Europe in 1772, including the Stuensee crisis in Denmark in January, the seizure of absolute power by Gustavus III in Sweden, the Maupeou crisis in France and the first partition of Poland in August 1772.[41] British public reaction to the American crisis was predictably mixed, ranging from sympathy amongst religious dissenters and merchants, or cautious interest in the legal and constitutional questions, to patriotic support for government policies (often expressed in loyal petitions and addresses denouncing the rebels).[42] A significant number of pamphlets published in Britain referred to American grievances in order to highlight arguments for or against comprehensive constitutional reform,[43] or to engage directly in partisan politics – often providing yet more material for the growing range of newspapers. Fearing government reprisals, some newspapers refrained from editorial comment, providing little more than essentially factual summaries. But some journals covered the colonial revolt in more detail, especially once arguments for independence came to the fore. Although the Declaration of Independence was not formally signed in Philadelphia until July 1776, the preparatory discussions in the colonial Continental Congress were reported in Britain already from the start of the year. The *London Magazine or Gentleman's monthly Intelligencer,* which by the mid-1770s printed lengthy monthly summaries of parliamentary debates, naturally reported the difficult discussions that took place in the House of Commons. From March 1776, the *Scots Magazine* provided its readers with accounts which were dismissively critical of the colonists, as did the *Westminster Magazine.* In June 1776, the Dublin *Hibernian Magazine* reprinted lengthy extracts from Paine's *Common sense* (published anonymously in January 1776 in Philadelphia), and although the magazine was

---

[41] On the response of one quality newspaper to all this, see Popkin, *News and politics,* 137–57.

[42] J. E. Bradley, 'The British public and the American Revolution', in H. T. Dickinson (ed.), *Britain and the American Revolution* (London, 1998), 124–55.

[43] H. T. Dickinson (ed.), *British pamphlets on the American Revolution 1763–1785,* vol. I (London, 2007), lxvi, estimates that around 1000 pamphlets published in Britain during this period focused on American issues, including over seventy originally published in the colonies; on the British engagement, see E. Macleod, *British visions of America 1775–1820* (London, 2013).

unable to identify the author, it suggested collective authorship was likely since the pamphlet appeared to reflect a broad consensus in the colonies.

Review journals were able to discuss the key arguments in greater depth. Already in March 1776 the *London Review of English and Foreign Literature* wrote that:

The contest between Great Britain and her Colonies has produced, among other evils, a deluge of speculative publications, calculated to bewilder the weak, and impose upon the ignorant. Several Writers, either biassed by party or swayed by vanity, have enlisted themselves under the banners of rebellion; and, with a strange perversion of argument, attempt to justify the conduct of the Colonists, upon the principles of reason and civil liberty. Having formed, in their distempered imaginations, some wild theories of polity, they presume to judge of the degree of freedom in government, in proportion to its departure from their own inadmissible maxims. Of these fanciful abettors of American resistance, the latest and the most violent is Dr Price, who has given the Public a Pamphlet, which he calls 'Observations on the Nature of Civil Liberty... [44]

Richard Price was quoted, summarised or criticised in a number of other publications, and his tract was extensively reprinted and over the next year translated into French, Dutch and German, indicating that his text was widely disseminated.[45]

By November 1776, the *Monthly Review* could declare that:

Every attentive and dispassionate reader of the Declaration [of Independence] must have observed that many of the articles of Impeachment there exhibited against his Majesty's administration ... have more the appearance of frivolous council, and peevish invective, than of the manly resentment of a people suffering under the iron hand of oppression.

As was typical of journalism in this period, the *Scots Magazine* reproduced this denunciation word for word, a month later.[46] Clearly, book reviews could lend themselves readily to direct engagement in the discussion of current political affairs, and the (often anonymous) reviewers did not spare their readers from the kind of invective that might in itself have seemed libellous. But over the next years the British press continued to report the American conflict, by means of news, commentary and review of publications and speeches. They gave predictably varied reactions to the peace settlement of 1783, with the kind of partisan and at times

---

[44] The *London Review of English and Foreign Literature*, 3 (March 1776), 241.

[45] D. O. Thomas, J. Stephens and P. A. L. Jones, *A bibliography of the works of Richard Price* (Aldershot, 1993), lists no fewer than thirty-two reprints of, and several additions to, the *Observations*. Its bestseller status is clear from the fact that, since its first publication early in February 1776, it had reached the seventh printing already by 6 May, each print run by then no doubt running to several thousand copies.

[46] *The Monthly Review*, 55 (Nov 1776), 345–54; *the Scots Magazine*, 38 (1776), 652–55.

thoroughly misleading information that is typical of some forms of social media today.

During the 1780s, some journals opted not to compete with daily or weekly news reporting as such, concentrating instead on political overviews and long-term issues. This type of news dissemination could include more editorial commentary, often organised by theme and contemporary historical context. Such an approach helped to create an impression of reliability and impartiality, even when in practice such journals relied as much on second- or third-hand information, not to mention the kind of plagiarised reporting common across the newspaper industry from the start. Several dedicated political reviews also quickly learnt how to adapt their coverage to suit the interests and assumptions of their readers. One of these was the quarterly *Stats-Anzeigen* launched in 1782 by August Ludwig von Schlözer (1735–1809), professor at the University of Göttingen and a productive published historian. Schlözer was politically conservative, but was keen to develop an empirical and quantitative approach to recent history and to analyse German and east European political and constitutional history in some depth. He had prior experience of editing journals on current affairs, and the *Stats-Anzeigen* soon became a recognised leader amongst political serials. It had run to seventy-two issues by the time it was suppressed in 1793, and Schlözer claimed that it acquired upwards of 4000 subscribers, though this has not been verified. Only a few of the contributors to his journal are known, but it is clear that Schlözer developed a wide correspondence network and a robust sense of journalistic independence.[47]

At least as influential was the *Politische Journal*, launched slightly earlier, in 1781. It was a regular monthly focusing on current affairs under set headings, with regular reports from correspondents in other cities. It also carried lengthy articles that provided an overview of events over the previous month, with in-depth editorial comment on what was regarded as the most important political and economic developments. The only named editor, Gottlob Benedikt von Schirach (1743–1804), had left an academic post at the minor university in Helmstedt, tried to make a career as a journalist and eventually settled just outside Hamburg, in Altona, in the pay of the Danish crown. From the start, the *Politische Journal* concentrated on north-German and Danish politics, with occasional dismissive discussion of the unrest in the Netherlands (from 1781) which he

---

[47] H. Duchhardt and M. Espenhorst, *August Ludwig (von) Schlözer in Europa* (Göttingen, 2012); and for his observations on Sweden, M. Persson, 'Transferring propaganda: Gustavian politics in two Göttingen journals', in Krefting et al. (eds.), *Eighteenth-century periodicals as agents of change*, 93–109.

regarded as irresponsible and damaging to public peace.[48] Schirach became an influential voice advocating traditional patriotic loyalty to the established order, often in such extravagant and sycophantic terms that he could be sure of a good reception even by the most traditional German princes. This may help explain the success of this journal, which at its height achieved a circulation estimated at upwards of 8000 across much of Germany. Schirach clearly intended it to be bound and kept as a work of reference, much like literary and other specialist reviews: each monthly issue was organised in a set pattern, and every six months he issued an index to make up one neat octavo volume.

The *Politische Journal* became a consistent advocate of German cameralism and conservative-enlightened centralised government. He covered events in the major European powers, including throughout the 1780s the efforts of French ministers to achieve fiscal reforms. Generally, he was against innovation in politics and regarded the experiment in republican government in America as dangerous. Yet his report on the *coup d'état* in Denmark in 1784 (where a team around the crown prince seized power from the ultra-conservative regency that had been in place since 1772) demonstrated his ability to adapt his journal to political change when necessary. He noted in July 1784 (a few months after the coup) that other papers had called it a revolution, but denied that this was the case: the crown prince had merely re-established traditional enlightened autocracy in Denmark, preserving the constitution and replacing only a few individuals within the existing system.

His reporting covered some significant ground. In March 1785 he noted reports of the arrest of Beaumarchais in Paris, whilst carefully avoiding any judgments on why or with what justification. In September of that year he wrote approvingly of the tightening of censorship in Augsburg, noting that freedom of expression could be disruptive. Early in 1786 he observed the troubles in the Austrian Netherlands and the United Provinces, explaining that too much freedom of the press had inflamed public opinion. In a report on the Leipzig book fair (June 1786) Schirach gave a detailed breakdown of the range of printed material available, estimated at around 5000 titles across a wide range of subjects and genres, some of which he disliked. He consoled himself that the French book trade had an even larger proportion of dangerous books. Not surprisingly, the *Politische Journal* reacted strongly against events in France in 1789 and nourished German self-satisfaction that enlightened

---

[48] J. D. Popkin, 'The German press and the Dutch patriot movement, 1781–1787', *Lessing Yearbook*, 22 (1990), 97–111.

princely government ensured that such populist violence would be unnecessary in the Holy Roman Empire.[49]

Events in other countries provided fairly safe subject matter for political journals before 1789. But one further journal deserves mention, since it also cautiously began to cover domestic politics: the *Minerva*, a monthly launched in Copenhagen in 1785, one year after the establishment of the new reform-oriented regency in 1784, and lasting until 1807. From the start, *Minerva* was written and edited by a small group of liberal intellectuals closely linked to (but technically independent of) the new government. It was edited by the Danish-Norwegian government official Christen Henriksen Pram and the literary critic and translator Knud Lyhne Rahbek, and its contributors included many other Copenhagen intellectuals. As one would expect for a high-level journal in a small language community, it probably never achieved a print run beyond a few hundred copies, in monthly issues of usually just over 100 pages in small octavo. Nevertheless, it became a powerful platform for new cultural and political discussion amongst the Danish-Norwegian elite. Laid out in a regular format suitable for binding in book form, it was clearly intended as a durable work of reference.

To cater for all its intended readers, each issue of *Minerva* included book reviews, thematic articles and a summary of national and international news over the last month, with historical context. Significantly (given that it was unclear whether the new government would review censorship regulations), the journal included detailed discussion of domestic politics and cautiously welcomed the efforts made towards more open government. Not surprisingly, *Minerva* rapidly came out in strong support of the rural reform programme launched in 1786, but although it rarely discussed oppositional points of view, it nevertheless allowed some degree of freedom of discussion within liberal and moderate bounds. As evidence of the kind of political and cultural ideas that prevailed amongst the reading elite in Copenhagen, it is invaluable; but it also indicates the extent to which the press could help to promote reform agendas by providing detailed information and commentary. Given that the government remained reluctant to reimpose censorship in the 1790s, *Minerva* and other new journals also continued cautiously reporting on events in revolutionary France itself.[50]

---

[49] These comments are based on the print run of the *Politische Journal* in the Herzog August Bibliothek in Wolfenbüttel. See also J. D. Popkin, 'Political communication in the German Enlightenment: Gottlob Benedikt von Schirach's *Politische Journal*', *Eighteenth-century Life*, 20 (1996), 24–41.

[50] Complete print runs of *Minerva* are found in the Danish Royal Library and Copenhagen University Library.

It is difficult to assess the impact that such political journals may have had, and how far they may have supplemented and balanced the dissemination of news in daily or weekly newspapers and advertisers. Their readership may have been similar to that of the literary and philosophical reviews: compared with daily newspapers, intelligencers and advertisers, most political journals perhaps reached a smaller audience, yet one closer to power and with considerably more influence. But such speculation may be misleading, given that public engagement in politics varied enormously in line with cultural norms, levels of freedom of print and the nature of the government in each area of dissemination. In the German lands, especially in prosperous and fairly independent imperial cities such as Hamburg, or smaller trading centres such as Flensburg, patriotic societies set up to discuss practical social reform certainly fluctuated, but the trend towards intensive newspaper reading and very strong public interest was unmistakeable from the early eighteenth century through the 1790s and beyond.[51] In the sprawling and overgrown administrative system of later eighteenth-century France, regulatory practices were increasingly overwhelmed both by the sheer mass of material that would need to be checked and by growing public demand for more accurate information and analysis.[52]

Patriotic Societies, 'Improvement' and the Use of Data

Public opinion could be constructed in a number of different ways. During the eighteenth century, academies and other societies were set up all over Europe designed to promote discussion and general knowledge. The London Royal Society of 1662 and the crown-sponsored French Academy of Sciences of 1666 had set new standards for accessible scientific research and collective intellectual leadership, later imitated by other national institutions. Not all worked well: the Berlin Academy of Sciences, set up in 1700 with Leibniz as its first president, was turned into

---

[51] H. Böning and E. Moepps, 'Die vorrevolutionäre Presse in Norddeutschland. Mit einer Bibliographie norddeutscher Zeitungen und Zeitschriften zwischen 1770 und 1790', in A. Herzog (ed.), *Sie und nicht wir: die französische Revolution und ihre Wirkung auf Norddeutschland* (Hamburg, 1989), 15–36; M. Lindemann, *Patriots and paupers: Hamburg 1712–1830* (Oxford, 1990); U. Möllney, *Norddeutsche Presse um 1800: Zeitschriften und Zeitungen in Flensburg, Braunschweig, Hannover und Shaumberg-Lippe im Zeitalter der französichen Revolution* (Bielefeld, 1996); H. Böning, 'Publizistik und Geselligkeit – zu zwei Hamburger Versuchen einer überregionalen patriotischen Verbindung', in P. Albrecht, H. E. Bödeker and E. Hinrichs (eds.), *Formen der Geselligkeit in Nordwestdeutschland 1750–1820* (Tübingen, 2003), 455–79; J. Frimmel and M. Wögerbauer (eds.), *Kommunikation und Information im 18.Jhrh: das Beispiel der Habsburgermonarchie* (Wiesbaden, 2009); all with further references to earlier research on the north-German press.

[52] Censer, *The French press* (1994); Popkin, *News and politics* (1989).

a court jest under the philistine Frederick William I (1713–40). After 1740, with direct support from Frederick II, it needed a complete overhaul and change of personnel before it could claim academic credibility. A number of foreigners were invited to provide new leadership and prestige for the Academy, including the Swiss mathematician Leonhard Euler (from 1741), leading French scientists Maupertuis and d'Alembert, as well as the publicist Samuel Formey (born in Berlin but of Huguenot extraction). Voltaire also contributed when he visited Potsdam in the early 1750s, by which time the Academy (now French-dominated, and known as the Académie Royale des Sciences et Belles-Lettres) had become a significant European centre of scientific excellence and philosophical discussion. Although the Francophile orientation met with some hostility from German scholars, the Academy became part of the network of major academies across Europe and its newly created prize essay competitions attracted international interest.[53]

Many other intellectual societies and academies were established during the eighteenth century, especially during its second half. A focus on improvement and economic reform was common, but there was also growing support for more specialised organisations focusing on particular fields such as medicine, music, literature or the fine arts. In France, in the last years before the Revolution, there were more than thirty cities with formally constituted royal academies, typically with a respectable membership composed mostly of elderly all-male professionals (lawyers, medics, civil servants and clergy) and titled nobility. As so often, other monarchies followed the French model of formal and strongly hierarchical institutions. But state sponsorship could be restrictive, so in the less centralised political structures of the Netherlands, western Germany and Italy academies often relied instead on corporate patronage or even on the support of a group of wealthy patricians and benefactors. Hamburg set up its Patriotic Society in 1724 to achieve civic and economic improvement and even had an influential 'moral weekly' (*Spectator*-type journal) under the title *Der Patriot* (1724–6, later reissued in book form). By the second half of the eighteenth century, privately or locally organised patriotic societies were the norm in even smaller towns all over Europe. They were typically constituted on the basis of nominally egalitarian procedural rules and constitutions but restricted to the respectable middling sorts, and were fundamentally loyal in their aim to raise awareness of good causes and improvement through constructive debate, publications, modest reform and self-education. The costs could be covered by

---

[53] A. Lifschitz, *Language and Enlightenment: the Berlin debates of the eighteenth century* (Oxford, 2012).

a variety of means, ranging from self-financing membership fees to more entrepreneurial funding models, such as those adopted by commercial debating societies (or *lycées*) charging a small fee at the door. Even masonic lodges could serve as a kind of self-consciously sociable network of committed individuals, but Freemasonry was by definition an exclusive movement whose secrecy ensured it had almost no explicit impact in print and (despite rumours to the contrary) probably not much practical impact except on networking within a community.

Being a 'patriot' could mean a number of things. The Dutch Patriot reform movement from 1781 was not only a loose alliance of critics of the House of Orange, but also formed citizen militias and urban activist groups demanding more democratic government.[54] More often, however, being a 'patriot' meant membership of a local civic group, a society for reform, or even a formal academy working within the norms of existing power structures. But other forms of sociability, including that of commercial coffee houses, private salons and clubs, could lead to equally enthusiastic discussion. Even if their activity is often poorly documented, we should not underestimate the significance of all these forms of sociability in encouraging reading, raising awareness and providing a forum for would-be authors to try out ideas and secure more readers. Local history and antiquarian archaeology, schemes for public investment and economic improvement, projects for better education and improved literacy, the creation of communal libraries and reading societies, and many other community-based initiatives, created enough interest to sustain a market for all kinds of printed texts and polemics. In such discussions, the concept of 'patriot' acquired many connotations: it might signify a focus on the good of your community (however you defined it), love of the 'patrie', awareness of how to be a good citizen and the importance of civic development and public benefit. The label 'patriot' might even have negative connotations, when used in factional power struggles where loyalty to ostensibly collective interests might be questioned. However, most patriots emphatically operated within the confines of hierarchical social conventions and a constant focus on morality, stability and loyalty. Those were also key themes in the very exclusive Mittwochsgesellschaft (Wednesday Society) noted earlier, operating in Berlin under the protection of Frederick II, but constrained by the king's insistence that its discussions take place behind closed doors and never formally recognised in print: its members could publish cautious general essays in the

---

[54] The Dutch political tensions of the 1780s do not compare easily with those in other parts of Europe: see A. Jourdan, 'The Netherlands in the constellation of the eighteenth-century Western revolutions', *European Review of History* 18, (2011), 190–225.

Berlinische Monatschrift or in pamphlets, but were not allowed to publicise the activities of the Society itself.

Patriots were rarely what we might now call 'nationalist' or even proto-nationalist: on the contrary, their concerns readily crossed state frontiers and often aimed at some form of universality, sometimes based on ancient constitutions and rights. Indeed, any analysis of patriot ideals leads into problematic and ambiguous semantic territory: some patriots sought inspiration in the past (even in classical republicanism), others found it in dissenting religious tendencies or in the Jansenist movement within Catholicism, while yet others were provoked into action by local power disputes (as in Geneva in the 1760s or the Netherlands in the 1780s). The word 'radical' (in the sense of seeking to return to fundamentals) could now be applied in so many different ways that it was liable to lose any precise meaning. Patriots might claim to be opposed to aristocracy, but were often themselves so much part of the patrician elite that they would never consider a truly democratic form of governance. There was rarely any hint of 'revolutionary' intent, and if there was, it was more often the kind of revolution seeking to recover a mythological past than one trying to create genuinely new power structures. Predictably, women could participate only within strict limits of propriety: as patrons or supporters, but rarely as dynamic contributors. Equally, despite the ostensible egalitarianism of many societies and their insistence on some degree of freedom of speech, democratic rights were strictly limited by the conventions of what might later be called 'bourgeois' values and civic or intellectual utilitarianism.[55]

Without access to spoken words, we have an unavoidably incomplete picture, so we may legitimately question how far later eighteenth-century printed texts constitute reliable evidence of actual public opinion. Authors of polemics and pamphlets increasingly adopted the convention of addressing a preface to 'the public', but their readers could only ever be an 'imagined community'. Nevertheless, some types of publication can be placed in a clearer public context. Most obvious amongst these might

---

[55] K. Stapelbroek and J. Marjanen (eds.), *The rise of economic societies in the eighteenth century: patriotic reform in Europe and North America* (Basingstoke, 2012); on patriotic societies and concepts of patriotism, see notably J. Engelhardt, 'Borgerskab og fællesskab: de patriotiske selskaber i den danske helstat 1769–1814', *Historisk Tidsskrift*, 106 (2006), 33–63, based on a study of sixty-three patriotic societies established across Denmark-Norway in the later eighteenth century; on the much narrower vision and rapidly shifting reputation of the French *parlements* and their oppositional language, see P. R. Campbell, 'The politics of patriotism in France (1770–1788)', *French History*, 24 (2010), 550–75; and J. H. Shennan, 'The rise of patriotism in eighteenth-century Europe', *History of European Ideas*, 13 (1991), 689–710; see also D. K Van Kley, 'Religion and the age of "patriot" reform', *Journal of Modern History*, 80 (2008), 252–95.

be the texts submitted in response to prize essay competitions. Such competitions became increasingly frequent during the eighteenth century, often instituted by academies but sometimes even by governments themselves. For example, in Denmark in 1755 a royal anniversary was marked with a public competition for general (non-scholarly) essays on economics, natural history and useful knowledge. The winning essays were published in a serial, *Danmarks og Norges Oeconomiske Magazin* (1757–64), edited by the prolific writer and bishop Erik Pontoppidan.

All over Europe, academies (and some local societies) adopted sponsored essay competitions by way of encouraging public interest. Daniel Roche noted that there was a huge increase in the number of such prize essay competitions offered by academies and learned societies in Paris and other French cities, increasing tenfold in the course of the eighteenth century to reach nearly 500 prizes in the 1780s (not counting artisanal competitions or societies focusing on practical skills such as agriculture). We cannot determine how many individuals entered these competitions, but we do know that women could compete and might win. The subject matter ranged very widely, from poetry to music, history to civil society, science and technology to social medicine. Entries were normally anonymised and ranked by a committee or jury. Winning authors gained not only publicity and the prize money, but also usually secured guaranteed funded publication.[56] With hindsight, it may be fair to say that very few prize-winning essays made a distinctive or durable contribution to intellectual life: Rousseau's *Discourse on inequality* (Dijon, 1755) is a well-known exception. Nevertheless it is worth remembering that he was not the only writer to gain his reputation initially on the basis of prize essays. In other words, sponsoring academies and societies were creating genuinely new opportunities for widening – even to some extent democratising – public discussion beyond the traditional reading elite. Because essay competitions encouraged accessibility and brevity, winning entries could also readily be reported in journals across Europe, well beyond the old personalised republic of letters. The step from composing competition essays to writing independent pamphlets was not big. Equally, an interest in improvement and reform might lead the reading public to other sources of information, reference works, or even substantive scientific texts such as those published by the learned academies in their transactions.

Inevitably, authors adopting an empirical and rational approach to everyday problems would want reliable statistical information. Published

---

[56] D. Roche, *Le siècle des lumières en province: académies et académiciens provinciaux, 1680–1789* (Paris, 1978), vol. I, 323–55; J. L. Caradonna, *The Enlightenment in practice: academic prize contests and intellectual culture in France 1670–1794* (Ithaca, NY, 2012).

work on political economy, commerce and industry was rarely deemed sufficiently controversial to be censored. Accordingly, there were few publishing restraints on the kinds of speculative economic analysis which became common across Europe, whether from old-school mercantilists, German cameralists, French physiocrats, Scottish economic philosophers, or others. Some governments even came to accept that systematic collation of data was not only desirable, but also a necessary part of 'good police' (in the original sense of the proper formulation and implementation of effective domestic policy in areas such as trade, markets, state sponsorship of key manufactures, fiscal policy and poor relief). Anyone familiar with the nature of government records from before 1800 will have noticed how the filing of government data seems to occupy exponentially more physical space on the shelves of national archives from the later seventeenth century onwards, and especially after mid-eighteenth century. Although the word 'statistic' did not come into general use in the major European languages until the later eighteenth century, the concept was certainly not new. Publications devoted to 'political arithmetic', physical and natural observation, or 'accounts' of productive labour, manufactures and trade reflect this trend.

Governments gathering consistent data made practical sense; but releasing such information was quite another story and would require a fundamental change in political mindset. Governments have of course always been reluctant to recognise that even controlled public access to data could potentially bring more benefits than risks. Most seventeenth-century states kept what impressionistic information they had under a cloak of secrecy. Exceptions are instructive, and it is no surprise that general data on public health was the first to be released for its informative value. Thus bills of mortality had been printed in England already in the late Elizabethan period, and after 1660 John Graunt publish his *Natural and political observations . . . upon the bills of mortality* (1662, with several reprints up to 1676). Other tracts on 'political arithmetic' were published by William Petty and, around the turn of the century, by Charles Davenant, but the wider-ranging demographic data collated by observers such as Gregory King before and after 1688 remained confined to manuscript. Even great merchant republics kept most information secret: it is worth noting that the associates of the open regime in the Netherlands up to 1672 were reluctant to publish much detail, and it became dangerous to do so after 1672.

For years, preserving state secrecy in fiscal and economic matters was considered an essential prerogative of government. Colbert, in his key role as finance minister in the early decades of Louis XIV's reign, was insatiable in the range and detail of information he collated, which he summarised in confidential personal notebooks for the king to carry in his pocket.[57] In 1695 the fiscal reformer Boisguilbert published *Le détail de la France*, a critique of French financial and economic policies, printed without permission, and reprinted many times both before and after it was belatedly censored. Few others risked publishing specific proposals. The most notable exception came in 1707, when Louis's disastrous policies had taken such a heavy toll that the outstanding military engineer Vauban had his *Projet d'une dixme [dîme] royal* printed without permission: it, too, was extensively reprinted even though it was banned immediately. Both authors were clearly so alarmed by the social suffering and impoverishment caused by economic and fiscal mismanagement that they felt they could not remain silent. But while Boisguilbert argued for a rationalised economic system based on *laissez-faire* (he was the first to use the term), Vauban emphasised the disastrous impoverishment of the kingdom, making a case for a completely new fiscal system with far more limited exemptions for the elite and managed through substantial administrative intervention.[58] In Britain, because of the existence of the national Bank of England and an accountable national debt, slightly more information became accessible to the political elite. By 1759, Postlethwayt was able to publish a 350-page long critical analysis of British state finance, which was regarded as significant (though it was not reprinted).[59]

Across many states in Europe, the interest in solid information was increasingly reflected in the work of councils, government colleges of commerce and other new advisory bodies. In Denmark, a huge land-tax evaluation was carried out in the period 1682–8, visible to all, and intended to measure the entire agrarian foundation of the national economy, but the data was kept in the state archives, firmly out of reach of the public.[60] In the late 1690s, the English Board of Trade began to gather more data in response to the needs of state, but only some of this information reached members of Parliament, and in any case the prohibition against publishing even summaries of parliamentary proceedings remained firmly in place for another century.

It is instructive to observe how far attitudes to information were changing by the second half of the eighteenth century – both in terms of the

[57] J. Soll, *The information master: Jean-Baptiste Colbert's secret state intelligence system* (Ann Arbor, 2009).

[58] Pierre le Pesant de Boisguilbert, *Le détail de la France* ([no place], 1695); Sébastien le Prêtre, marquis de Vauban, *Projet d'une dixme royal* ([no place], 1695); and see M. Kwass, *Privilege and the politics of taxation in eighteenth-century France: liberté, égalité, fiscalité* (Cambridge, 2000), 222–31.

[59] J. Postlethwayt, *The history of the public revenue, from the Revolution in 1688* (London, 1759).

[60] Stored in the Danish Rigsarkiv (Public Record Office), Rentekammer.

accuracy and detail of quantitative data itself and of what was published. In England, the work of Joseph Massie from the late 1750s onwards focused on fiscal burdens, food prices and maritime trade. From the mid-1770s there was an obvious shift towards greater interest in the Atlantic trade, so relevant to the very powerful merchant community.[61] Lars Behrisch has recently emphasised how systematic quantitative data also became an essential component of enlightened government elsewhere after 1763, as the economic damage of war across much of Europe ensured growing interest in political economy, trade and the economic structures of the state.[62] The French *économistes* (physiocrats), led by François Quesnay, used his schematic *Tableau économique* (published 1758) as a framework for analysis in which all components of the state economy could be taken into account. Quesnay's own work was not widely disseminated, but his core ideas were influential in government circles and were soon developed by others, including Turgot (finance minister to Louis XVI, 1774–6, and noted for his major reform initiatives in poor relief and public works schemes, simplification of internal customs and trade barriers, and of course fiscal policy). Both Quesnay and Turgot had also contributed to the *Encyclopédie*.

Quantitative and mathematical methods were used in much more complicated political contexts, for example to devise accurate modelling of graduated and proportional taxation. Such calculations were promoted by a number of reformers from Boisguilbert (1702), through Rousseau (1755 and in his *Encyclopédie* article on 'Économie', with Jaucourt's on 'Impôt'), to the more sophisticated progressive tax proposals of Jean-Louis Graslin (1766–7), which became feasible (but were not fully implemented) after 1789.[63] Condorcet made his reputation in several distinct fields, ranging from abstract integral calculus (1765) to his more practical work as Turgot's assistant in areas such as the grain trade, public works projects and the royal mint. But in the 1780s he developed highly innovative theories of probability to analyse the reliability of voting systems within defined electorates[64] – work of a very technical nature which was nonetheless directly relevant to the proper functioning of the new

---

[61] P. Mathias, 'The social structure in the eighteenth century: a calculation by Joseph Massie', in his *The transformation of England* (London, 1979), 171–89; J. Hoppitt, 'Political arithmetic in eighteenth-century England', *Economic History Review*, 49 (1996), 516–40.

[62] L. Behrisch, *Die Berechnung der Glückseligkeit: Statistik und Politik in Deutschland und Frankreich im späten Ancien Régime* (Ostfildern, 2016).

[63] J.-P. Gross, 'Progressive taxation and social justice in eighteenth-century France', *Past & Present*, 140 (1993), 79–126.

[64] Jean-Antoine-Nicolas de Caritat, marquis de Condorcet, *Essai sur l'application de l'analyse à la probabilité des décisions rendues à la pluralité des voix* (Paris, 1785).

provincial representative assemblies being piloted across France. Condorcet and other scientists, such as the chemist Lavoisier, remained active as public intellectuals well into the French Revolution, until their untimely deaths in 1794 (both aged 51). Their efforts exemplify a common problem throughout the eighteenth century (and later): the reluctance of political leaders to pay attention to, or even fully understand, the detailed advice offered by experts, especially when such analysis did not fit with the particular prejudices and assumptions of the political moment.

Much detailed work might therefore remain unpublished, or unnoticed, or would appear in very generalised format to suit the intended audience and the political context. This seems to be the case with regard to the most fundamental form of data analysis in any state: core demographics. Enumerations of the entire population were compiled in some of the smaller European states from mid-century onwards, at first typically through church officers, but from the late 1760s more systematically by local officials acting on behalf of central government. In 1787, the Danish government carried out a full national census according to detailed instructions, accounting for every inhabitant, the household they lived in and the occupation of the head of household, using printed pro-formas. But it goes without saying that this data was meant solely for administrative purposes and no substantive summaries were published. In Britain, proposals in 1753 to undertake a national census were abandoned, and the type of work represented in John Sinclair's *Statistical account for Scotland* (belatedly published in 1791) was not extended across Britain until much later. Bigger states such as France struggled to compile even rudimentary census summaries both before and during the Revolution.

Not all quantitative or descriptive data was well understood, or as effectively analysed as one might have expected. Typical of the kind of superficial comparative summaries which would have been of limited use to any reader was the 1791 *Publicistical survey of the different forms of government of all states and communities in the world* by Thomas Brooke Clarke. By then, more detailed and informative surveys were available for those who were interested. For example, in 1790 Adam Christian Gaspari produced a volume of comparative data on the land area, economy, population (summarising actual censuses, or relying on estimates where there were none), forms of government, armed forces and finance of the major European states, including the Ottoman Empire, complete with comparative analysis.[65] A more comprehensive large-format tabulated

[65] Adam Christian Gaspari, *Versuch ueber das politische Gleichgewicht der Europäischen Staaten* (Hamburg, 1790).

summary was compiled by a Prussian government official, Adolph Friedrich Randel, in 1786 and revised in 1792 (no doubt with a view to the confrontations looming across Europe). While focusing on the German lands, it provided directly comparable data from across Europe, organised thematically and covering not just the main categories of political economy and regional government already noted, but also social composition, legal framework, languages and dialects. It even listed major intellectual and cultural institutions and provided data on the book trade and on leading writers in a range of academic fields including human rights (*Menschenrecht*), as they were conceived at the time.[66]

One of the most extraordinary published works raising public awareness of social issues was John Howard's *The state of the prisons in England and Wales* (1777) and his follow-up on medical-related institutions, *An account of the principal lazarettos in Europe* (1789). John Howard (1726–90) became a tireless and persistent self-appointed inspector of prisons and workhouses all over Europe, his books providing graphic detail of the inhumanity and brutality of punitive regimes everywhere. *The state of the prisons* was dedicated to the members of the House of Commons and provided a huge amount of data on prisons all over Europe. At the very start, he pointed out that:

there are prisons, into which whoever looks will, at first sight of the people confined, be convinced that there is some great error in the management of them ... Many who went in healthy, are in a few months changed to emaciated dejected objects. Some are seen pining under diseases ... expiring on the floors, in loathsome cells, of pestilential fevers, and the confluent small pox.[67]

This book had four subsequent revised editions, while the *Principal lazarettos* had two, including the collected edition of his works issued in 1792 after his untimely death from prison fever. This would seem a surprising success for what could never be described as popular writing: detailed descriptions of all the grim institutions that Howard managed to visit, complete with a great deal of tabulated quantitative material and analysis. Howard was very clear and outspoken in his condemnation of the appalling conditions he found everywhere and on the extent to which many lazarettos and hospitals in effect doubled as prisons. But he also made

---

[66] Adolph Friedrich Randel, *Annalen der Staatskräfte von Europa ... in tabellarischen übersichten* (Berlin, 1792).

[67] J. Howard, *The state of the prisons in England and Wales, with preliminary observations and an account of some foreign prisons and hospitals* (Warrington and London, 2nd edn, 1780), 5; his *An account of the principal lazarettos in Europe* (Warrington, 1789) is a more composite book, addressing a number of distinct issues. It included a reprint of a very large table quantifying capital convictions at the Old Bailey from 1749–71, by types of crime, noting that around 60 per cent of death sentences were carried out.

detailed proposals for their improvement, called for adequate ventilation and exercise regimes, demanded clean water and a basic but adequate diet, and proposed laws to impose minimum legal physical and moral standards on all the institutions. Both books were upmarket works, very well printed with ground plans and engravings to ensure no detail was missed. His work was widely noted across Europe, discussed, and translated into French and German.

Pamphleteering and Political Lobbying

Pamphlets (defined as short texts, typically in octavo format, often between 8 and 48 pages or longer, printed on cheap paper and sold unbound) had been a significant but somewhat unpredictable part of the daily work of printers, at least from the time of Luther onwards. The fast production schedules of some print workshops could be impressive. So was the ease with which clandestine printers might physically relocate small presses to evade regulatory authority and the scope in bigger cities for organising surreptitious distribution networks for modest print runs. Such flexibility made pamphlets a versatile tool of public communication and hence a valuable resource for historians of popular political culture. Individual pamphlets were rarely significant in their own right, but if we treat them the way readers might have done at the time – as outspoken material reflecting rapid responses to changes in public mood – then the flow and intent of a larger number of texts becomes significant. As in earlier periods of political uncertainty, pamphlets were the perfect medium for occasional authors, patriots and troublemakers: cheap to produce and distribute, sometimes effective, quickly forgotten.

Sweden experienced its own difficulties in the middle decades of the eighteenth century, in the wake of two unsuccessful wars (against Russia 1740–3, then Prussia 1757–62 as part of the wider European conflict). Since the death of Charles XII in 1718, undivided sovereignty had resided in parliament (or in its committees, when parliament was not in session), but the system was neither transparent nor accountable. The great aristocratic families controlled the key parliamentary committees and in particular the Secret Committee (which had no representatives from the fourth estate). Every noble family was entitled to have a representative and a vote in the House of Nobles, which was by far the biggest of the four Estates in the Riksdag (parliament), its ostentatious meeting hall (*Riddarhuset*) strategically placed in central Stockholm right next to the government buildings. In short, the Swedish parliamentary 'commonwealth' had the hallmarks of an oligarchy and adhered rigidly to a Form of Government (constitution) of 1719–20 which left little scope for change.

This inflexibility became seriously problematic from the 1740s, as severe monetary instability took its toll, compounded by problems in overseas trade and signs of overall economic stagnation. The apparent exposure of the parliamentary factions to manipulation by the major European powers, through endemic corruption, ensured growing public receptiveness to open discussion. As Karin Sennefelt has pointed out, the squares and streets of Stockholm already provided significant public spaces where interaction between representatives of all four parliamentary Estates was possible and where otherwise unrepresented groups could gain some awareness of generic political and social issues.[68] By mid-century, this politicisation became visible in print, first in pamphlets, then more slowly in the cautious newspapers. Swedish political openness reached a watershed in 1765–6, when (as we noted earlier) a shift in the power balance in parliament away from the noble-dominated Hats enabled the more liberal Cap party to secure legislation substantially curtailing censorship: all forms of print now helped to articulate and disseminate public information relating to key points of political disagreement.[69]

Once again, quantification can never be more than approximate in this period. It is nonetheless striking that the total number of printed texts published in Sweden, averaging 60–70 items per annum in the first two decades of the eighteenth century, increased significantly from 1738 onwards, often exceeding 200 items in the 1740s and 1750s, and exceeding 400 items in 1765 and 1766 – precisely coinciding with the most controversial and politically significant meeting of the Swedish parliament for decades. The total number of items doubled again, to over 900, in 1769 and 1771. Then after the coup of 1772, as parliament was sidelined (meeting much less frequently and for shorter sessions), public debate visibly subsided: until the late 1780s, the total number of titles rarely exceeding 300 in any one year.[70]

We should of course not assume that these fluctuations in print output were driven solely by political lobbyists trying to influence political debate: almanacks, devotional literature and sermons, ephemeral and celebratory publications, plays, fables and popular fiction, as well as

---

[68] K. Sennefelt, 'Citizenship and the political landscape of libelling in Stockholm, c.1720-70', *Social History*, 33 (2008), 145–63; K. Sennefelt, 'The politics of hanging around and tagging along: everyday practices in eighteenth-century politics', in M. J. Braddick (ed.), *The politics of gesture: historical perspectives* (*Past & Present* Supplement 4, 2009), 172–90.

[69] M.-C. Skuncke, 'Medier, mutor och nätverk', in Skuncke and Tandefelt (eds.), *Riksdag, kaffehus och predikstol*, 255–86; M.-C. Skuncke, 'Press and political culture in Sweden at the end of the age of liberty' (*SVEC* 2004: 06, Oxford, 2004), 81–101.

[70] These totals are based on the digitised version of Svensk Bibliografi 1700–1829 (Swedish Royal Library, Regina).

scientific and historical writings remained common. Nevertheless, it is striking how many authors genuinely took up the challenge of trying to raise public awareness of the urgent needs for change, or even published transcripts of actual parliamentary speeches, committee agendas and reports. Some pamphleteers seemed inexhaustible. For example, Anders Nordencrantz (1697–1772), a commoner ennobled in 1743, published a few book-length works on history, law and political economy, but became far better known for his numerous shorter pamphlets and vigorous polemics, often criticising government policy. He ranged from law reform, monetary policy and state finance, to demands for deregulation of guilds and manufactures, scrutiny of corrupt banking and merchant practices, and measures to boost exports. Until 1766, he also campaigned imaginatively for free speech and removal of censorship restrictions, no doubt because his own argumentative and provocative style had led to restrictions on what he could publish.[71]

It is no great surprise that many of the eighteenth-century Swedish polemicists were traditionalists, demonstrating patriotism, loyalty to religious and social norms, and support for strong government. These characteristics certainly fit Anders Chydenius (1729–1803), a university-trained Lutheran clergyman from Finland who acquired a reputation for his scientific work (notably on land usage and demography) but also gained prominence in the turbulent parliamentary politics in Stockholm of the 1760s. He was strongly influenced by French physiocratic thinking and campaigned vigorously for *laissez-faire* economic policies even in international trade. Once elected to the Swedish parliament of 1765–6, he became a central figure in achieving the censorship reforms of that session, while continuing to cause controversy. Significantly, his concern for 'natural liberty' did not make him an unconditional supporter of partisan parliamentary politics: he lived through and welcomed the return to royal absolutism under Gustavus III from 1772 and continued to serve both as a clergyman and occasional pamphleteer until the end of his life.

Recent research has given us a clear impression of the range and scope of the writings of Chydenius. His first major output was an essay on emigration which won the 1763 prize competition of the Royal Swedish Academy of Sciences. During 1765 alone, he published seven texts on political economy and free speech, all intended as contributions to parliamentary discussions, but some of them clearly also aimed at a wider readership. Another four publications followed in 1766, three of which were short pamphlets. His output then became more sporadic, but did

---

[71] See for example Anon [A. Nordencrantz], *Bewis at frihet i tal och skrifter är obillig, straffbar och skadelig* (Stockholm, 1762).

not cease. In a short publication from 1779, simply entitled *Memorandum on freedom of religion*, he asked whether it would not be worthy of the clergy if:

precisely in an auspicious era, when the Estates of the Realm have been able to transfer the weight of the administration of the realm onto the shoulders of their gracious and wise King, it were able to persuade the whole world of the zeal with which the clergy of Sweden mildly and patiently desire to follow the elevated and holy example of their head, the Saviour of the whole world?

He proposed a guarantee of civic protection and freedom of worship to immigrant Jews and Catholics (as well as dissident Protestants), provided they did not attempt to proselytise amongst native Swedes. Chydenius was in this case trying to persuade particularly his own clerical Estate in parliament to support existing crown policy: as elsewhere in Europe, there was fierce resistance by the church establishment to any relaxation of the requirements of strict religious conformity.[72] Overall, although Swedish readers in the 1760s had had access to more diverse texts than ever before, after 1772 they seemed to accept a return to a more traditional range of reading. The overall trend remained Francophile, but favouring the conservative tastes promoted by Gustavus III and his advisers.

During this period, in France itself, pamphleteering was becoming far more complex, subject to a more diverse public opinion but at the same time restrained by the threat of unpredictable censorship. The higher law courts in general, and the Parlement of Paris in particular, were exempt from pre-publication censorship. They used this privilege to great effect during major confrontations with the crown, such as the Jansenist controversy of the 1720s and 30s, the eruptions of 1748 and in particular during the Maupeou crisis (1771–4). The publication of remonstrances (official legal objections to crown policy) was important in each of these, but from 1770 was used much more systematically as a way of directly engaging public opinion. René Nicolas de Maupeou, Chancellor and first minister of France in the last years of Louis XV, set out to apply the full authority of the crown in imposing fundamental reform on the French judicial system, ultimately to replace the superior courts. When in January 1771 all members of the Parlement de Paris were confronted by

---

[72] M. Jonasson and P. Hyttinen (eds.), *Anticipating the Wealth of Nations: the selected works of Anders Chydenius, 1729–1803*, (London, 2012); the quoted extract is from the translation from the original Swedish into English, by P. C. Hogg, in this volume, 317–22. For the wider context, see also Skuncke and Tandefelt (eds.), *Riksdag, kaffehus och predikstol;* P. Winton, *Frihetstidens politiska praktik: nätverk och offentlighet 1746–1766* (Uppsala, 2006); and C. Wolff, *Vänskap och makt: den svenska politiska eliten och upplysningstidens Frankrike* (Helsinki, 2005).

a demand that they sign individual acceptances of the reforms, the proposals were branded as illegal and the crown accused of despotic action. The confrontation pitched Jansenist and *parlementaire* traditionalism openly against the autocratic demands of a powerful court faction. Since both sides could publish without reference to the censorship system, polemicists and printers could operate with unprecedented freedom across the political divide, creating a torrent of propaganda, much of it in pamphlet form.

Voltaire was the most distinguished recruit for the Maupeou reforms, while the higher ranks of lawyers argued a conservative (and often self-promoting) case based on the balance of power in a theoretical (unwritten) 'constitution'. General freedom of expression was never part of this dispute, nor did anyone question social privilege and exclusivity; but both sides deployed elaborate legal arguments in ways designed to court public opinion. Others used the opportunity to promote different points of view: for example the lawyer and journalist Simon-Nicolas Linguet, although he favoured 'legal despotism', disagreed fundamentally both with Voltaire and with physiocratic ideas of reform and spent most of his considerable energy deconstructing both sides of the argument. In the end, although the *parlementaires* were essentially defeated by Maupeou, it made no real political difference. On his succession to the throne in 1774, Louis XVI recalled the Parlement as a gesture of goodwill – a decision he would have cause to regret later. However, in the process, public opinion had been let loose in ways that could not easily be reversed.[73]

Other forms of high-level disputes attracted pamphleteers in later eighteenth-century France. Lawyers had extensive experience in writing *mémoires judiciaires* (judicial memoranda, or lawyers' briefs), but only gradually did they realise the potential of circulating these in print. In 1757, the trial and punishment of Damiens, the would-be regicide, created a flurry of polemics, and in 1762 Voltaire gave the genre even greater prominence when he used the Calas Affair to condemn intolerance and the miscarriage of justice in a corrupt system.[74] As Sarah Maza has demonstrated, in the 1770s and 1780s polemical *mémoires judiciaires* became almost an artform in their own right, good for generating business for the lawyers themselves, but also inherently profitable because of

---

[73] D. Echeverria, *The Maupeou revolution: a study in the history of libertarianism, France 1770–74* (Baton Rouge, 1985); D. Hudson, 'In defense of reform: French government propaganda during the Maupeou crisis', *French Historical Studies*, 8 (1973), 51–76; on the language deployed in the *mémoires*, see J. Merrick, 'Subjects and citizens in the remonstrances of the Parlement of Paris in the eighteenth century', *Journal of the History of Ideas*, 51 (1990), 453–60.

[74] Voltaire, *Traité sur la tolérance* (Geneva, 1763).

public interest in the scandals of celebrity lawsuits. Recognising this potential, lawyers adopted more dramatic and partisan language in print to secure momentary publicity. Marital breakdown and sexual misconduct could always be counted on to attract public attention, but all kinds of social discord, alleged legal miscarriage, court scandal or abuse of power might lend itself to sensationalist pamphleteering. In the 1770s, some *mémoires judiciaires* had print runs in the range of 3000 to 6000 copies, well above the norm for most books and newspapers.[75] Sensationalised reports of lawsuits implicating the elite could easily have wider implications. Thus the Diamond Necklace affair of 1785, dragging Marie-Antoinette unwittingly into a case of fraud, inflicted considerable damage to aristocratic credibility generally. Pamphlets on such topics became a widely read counterpart to the more durable literary achievements of pre-revolutionary France, such as the epistolary novel *Dangerous Liaisons* by Choderlos de Laclos (1782), or the hugely successful play by Beaumarchais, *The marriage of Figaro* (first performed in public in 1784, after difficulties with the censors).

There were so many other areas of confrontation in France in the later 1770s and 1780s that historians of print have not yet secured a systematic overview. Because of the restrictions of censorship and state monopolies on information, it was almost impossible to make either independent newspapers or subversive pamphlets self-financing. One-off pamphlets and *libelles* were easier to publish illegally, but nevertheless had to rely on the backing of wealthy patrons, so they were the print of choice in the factional political battles of high politics right until 1788. What has become abundantly clear in recent years is that even then hardly anyone used a language of revolution, or even of consistent opposition to the crown: we clearly are not entitled to assume that writers were anticipating what was to come, let alone leading the way in any significant sense.[76] Pamphlets can tell us a great deal about what kinds of issues captured public imagination at the time of publication, but it is fair to say that there was no common agenda. This is particularly noticeable in several key areas of politics. As we noted earlier, fiscal issues had been the subject of some sophisticated analysis in print already in the last disastrous years of Louis XIV's reign. A 31-page pamphlet by the *parlementaire* Roussel de la Tour, published anonymously in 1763 as *La richesse de l'état,* called for a drastic simplification of the tax system and the removal of exemptions – inevitably generating oppositional responses. Successive ministerial fiscal

[75] S. Maza, *Private lives and public affairs: the causes célèbres of prerevolutionary France* (Berkeley, 1993), 122–3 and *passim*.
[76] J. Popkin, 'Pamphlet journalism at the end of the old régime', *Eighteenth-century Studies*, 22 (1989), 351–67.

policies created almost continuous public polemics, sometimes fuelled by more substantial publications with wider political implications, such as Victor Riquetti de Mirabeau's *Théorie de l'impôt* (1760) or the many long articles in *Encyclopédie*.

The publication in 1781 of Necker's *Compte rendu au roi* (intended as a brief summary of state finances) attracted much attention, as did his more comprehensive work on the *Administration des finances de la France* (1784). The *Compte rendu* is reputed to have sold unexpectedly well, in seventeen reprints and possibly 100,000 copies, but it did not prevent Necker losing his job as finance minister. Previous finance ministers had produced summaries for the monarch, some even published, but Necker's appeared to give an impression of careful fiscal planning and deliberate transparency, while giving away very little accurate detail. Public interest in the *Compte rendu* therefore soon turned on his credibility, rather than on finding solutions to those underlying fiscal problems that were gradually coming to light. Itself a short work of just over 100 pages, the *Compte rendu* created such a flood of discussion that printers could produce large compilations of pamphlet responses, such as the very successful three-volume *Collection complète de tous les ouvrages pour et contre M. Necker* nominally printed in Utrecht in 1781, which included a contribution by a previous finance minister and distinguished physiocrat, Turgot. Such astonishing public interest in state finance created an additional challenge for subsequent finance ministers, notably Calonne. In 1786, he had to challenge Necker's arguments before he could convince others of the need to implement new reforms. French fiscal policy remained a battleground for factional disputes for years to come.[77] From 1788 this developed into the flood of pamphlets that offered suggestions regarding the calling of the Estates General and how the king could use his authority to rebuild political leadership in the interest of patriotic unity. These developments were followed across Europe with even more intense interest than had events in America a few years earlier.

Pamphleteering naturally worked best in particular moments and places of tension, public engagement and divisive controversy. Since pamphlets were printed in much the same formats as books, journals and other texts, it was easy for printers to switch between genres, in

---

[77] J. Félix, 'The problem with Necker's *Compte rendu au roi* (1781)', in J. Swann and J. Félix (eds.), *The crisis of the absolute monarchy: France from old regime to revolution* (*Proceedings of the British Academy*, 184, Oxford, 2013), 107–25; J. Félix, 'The financial origins of the French Revolution', in P.R. Campbell (ed.), *The origins of the French Revolution* (Basingstoke, 2006), 35–62; Kwass, *Privilege and the politics of taxation in eighteenth-century France*, 238–52.

response to market demand. The exceptionally decentralised and entre-preneurial print industry in the Netherlands was as flexible as any. The rapidly escalating confrontation between patriots and Orangists in the 1780s relied both on an exceptionally independent local newspaper pro-duction and on pamphlet polemics, including a seminal text by the experienced translator and polemicist Van der Capellen, entitled *To the people of the Netherlands* (1781).[78] But not all those parts of Europe which experienced significant political instability also had a sufficiently diverse and consumer-oriented urban market to sustain such a lively printing industry. This may explain why for example in Poland-Lithuania from the 1760s onwards, despite recurrent constitutional and political crises, pub-lic discussion in print never acquired a momentum in any way compar-able to that in Sweden, let alone the west.[79] The failure and dismemberment of Poland-Lithuania, leading to its disappearance as an independent state 1793–5, was of course conveyed to newspaper readers in other parts of Europe, but did not attract as much interest, let alone analysis, as did political developments in America and in France.

It would appear that in the German-speaking lands there was less scope for the kind of political lobbying and pamphleteering typically associated with political crises in other parts of Europe. There was certainly no shortage of political economists (cameralists), reformers and men of learning publishing substantial work on a broad range of contemporary themes, even when they also held administrative or university posts. Their texts traded vigorously in the thriving Frankfurt and Leipzig book fairs, or through hugely enterprising and literary-minded booksellers and journal editors such as Friedrich Nicolai. As we have noted, there was no shortage of high-quality newspapers, specialist journals, patriotic societies and other forms of activity that might strengthen civic cohesion. One might even imagine that, with so many small and fairly autonomous jurisdic-tions within the Holy Roman Empire, questions of authority and political

---

[78] Joan Derk Van der Capellen, *Aan het volk van Nederland* (Ostende, 1781), recognising American political ideas (Capellen had also translated Richard Price), but turning back to early Dutch republicanism; see also A. Jourdan, 'The Netherlands in the constellation of the eighteenth-century Western revolutions', *European Review of History*, 18 (2011), 190–225.

[79] It is significant that Rousseau's *Considérations sur le gouvernement de Pologne*, written on commission in 1772, was not published until 1782 (in French, with a false London imprint) and not widely disseminated. But the nobleman Michael Wielhorski, who had commissioned both Rousseau and Mably to comment on the Polish constitution, took Rousseau more to heart in his own work on Polish reforms, published in 1775: J. Lukowski, *Disorderly liberty: the political culture of the Polish-Lithuanian Commonwealth in the eighteenth century* (London, 2010), 121–47 and *passim*; and his article, 'Recasting Utopia: Montesquieu, Rousseau and the Polish constitution of 3 May 1791', *The Historical Journal*, 37 (1994), 65–87.

direction could be resolved more readily by other means, for example through petitioning and the law. The traditional conservatism and political respectfulness associated with both the Lutheran and the Catholic established churches may also have remained a factor, even if that does not help to explain the relative political quietism that seems to have been the norm even in areas dominated by Calvinist and dissenting religious affiliations. With so many small principalities and independent cities in the western part of the Empire, there may well have been genuine scope (as many German writers claimed) for more responsive and flexible policymaking appropriate to the varying needs and interests of each community.[80]

We cannot yet be sure whether such explanations are sufficient to account for the absence in Germany of real outbursts of political controversy comparable to the Wilkes or Maupeou crises, or approximating the rich public discussion and reform activism in Sweden during the 1760s and in Denmark from 1786. Political journals and learned reviews had the obvious advantage of allowing selective reporting of political upheavals and controversies at some distance, without making relevance to the local situation too obvious. But it is also interesting to observe that for the German reading public the great discussions in print tended to focus more on moral, philosophical and religious subjects – as reflected in the criticisms of rationalism by the religious writer Johann Georg Hamann (1730–88), the literary and philosophical essays of the scholar, translator and bookseller Christian Garve (1742–98), or the much more unconventional and often controversial writings by Carl Friedrich Bahrdt (1740–92). The 'pantheism' controversy initiated in 1785 by Friedrich Heinrich Jacobi (1743–1819) focused on his denunciation of the late Lessing as a Spinozist: Jacobi distorted (in print) conversations he had had (but failed to fully understand) with Lessing's great friend, the philosopher Moses Mendelssohn. This high-profile dispute became even more bitter when it appeared that Mendelssohn caught a fatal bout of pneumonia while trying to deliver a text to his printer, urgently, in order to put the record straight. This dispute was hugely important and engaged a number of writers and thinkers; but it only indirectly affected the exercise of authority and the stability of civic society in so far as it questioned the deeper religious loyalties of some of the greatest literary figures of the age.

---

[80] A good example is that of Justus Möser. For his extensive writings and newspaper editing, alongside his administrative responsibilities in Osnabrück, see J. B. Knudsen, *Justus Möser and the German Enlightenment* (Cambridge, 1986); for a wide selection of German authors and writings, see J. Schmidt (ed.), *What is Enlightenment: eighteenth-century answers and twentieth-century questions* (Berkeley, 1996).

Other writers tackled more political subjects, but rarely in a form or language that might appear polemical or populist. There were reprintings of, and commentaries on, the prolific but uncontentious works of the rationalist and educationalist Christian Wolff (continuing after his death in 1754). Even in the 1780s, tracts, textbooks and studies of public policy were mostly written in a tone intended to avoid confrontation, even when dealing with highly practical and relevant issues such as the reform of censorship, or the emancipation of serfs in the Austrian Habsburg lands from 1781. Friedrich C.J. Fischer's promising-sounding *History of despotism in Germany, with source-material* (Halle, 1780) was quite brief and factual. Garve contributed a characteristically cautious *Essay on the connection between moral philosophy and politics* (1788) which, at 156 pages in octavo format, was not an expensive or scholarly publication, but neither was it polemical. Amongst the more widely appreciated writings were those of Moses Mendelssohn: his *Jerusalem* (1783) was a concise and eminently readable essay exploring the relationship between religion and the state, in which he referred explicitly to both Hobbes and Locke. But he had bigger sales for his less political exploration of the existence of the soul, his *Phaedon* of 1767, also translated into a number of other languages. As we shall see in the next chapter, it took some time before even the French Revolution seriously destabilised moderate consensus opinion amongst the German reading public.

Government-sponsored Print

Monarchs, patrician republican governments, local authorities and other power brokers had a long tradition of sponsoring celebratory writings, pageantry, staged performances and other ways of representing or demonstrating their authority. The ostentatious projection of power is of course as old as power itself and has attracted a great deal of talent, ingenuity and innovation throughout history. Urban planning and grand building projects were the most visible components of such projection strategies, used to great effect by all kinds of governments, often in combination with patronage of the other arts. Prime examples are found all over Renaissance Europe, from the early Venetian republic to the personalised buildings of northern monarchs such as Christian IV of Denmark. Printing merely added another tool for wider dissemination. But printing carried the obvious risk that, being relatively cheap, it could be used by individuals of modest means, might reach a much wider audience and so was more difficult to control. Governments gradually had to learn that, since control was difficult, a more effective response might be to use print to project narratives of cohesion, stability and benevolence – and where necessary to attack opponents or neutralise foreign propaganda. As we have seen, printed visual imagery was used with extraordinary imagination by Sweden in the Thirty Years War to give an extra edge to the kind of formal textual propaganda, speeches and proclamations routinely deployed by all governments in the early modern period.

Writers and pamphleteers could be hired or encouraged to help. We have already noted how Charles I ensured that his version of the struggle with Parliament was published immediately after his execution, in the shape of the *Eikon Basilike*; and how Milton was charged with writing a formal response on behalf of the Commonwealth government. Many of the pamphlets, petitions and addresses of loyalty printed during the French Fronde 1648–53 were polemics sponsored by the most powerful participants in that conflict. It is not difficult to identify other writers willing to accept payment, status or favour in return for promoting a clear political message. In post-1689 England, possibly some of the publications of John Locke, and clearly some of those by Daniel Defoe, fall into this category, as do many of the writings by Bolingbroke (Henry St John, Viscount Bolingbroke, 1678–1751). In France later on, Voltaire and many of the other participants in the political battles of the 1770s and 1780s took it for granted that writing on behalf of political factions could be both lucrative and self-promotional. It is impossible to know how many of the texts mentioned throughout this chapter were commissioned or part-sponsored by politically minded patrons, but we do know that very few writers could survive on their independent earnings alone. This of course does not mean pamphleteers and polemicists were mere mercenaries: no doubt then as now, all writers engaged in political campaigning for a mixture of reasons.

Print could also be used officially by the state. An obvious example is the two great law codes compiled and published by the government in Copenhagen for the benefit of all subjects of the crown: *Danske Lov* in 1683 and *Norske Lov* in 1687. Both discarded Latin in favour of a clear and concise Danish text, compiled by committees of experts and explicitly intended to be accessible to all. Substantive work to standardise and modernise legal systems became common practice in the later eighteenth century, as in the civil and criminal law reforms ordered by Maria Theresa and Joseph II in the Habsburg lands, or in the comprehensive standardisation and clarification of the law commissioned in the 1740s by Frederick II of Prussia and culminating after his death in the *Allgemeines Landrecht* of 1794. Such reforms were intended to make the law comprehensible and accessible to intelligent lay readers. But they also clarified institutional functions and procedures, including the separation of judicial and executive responsibilities of government in line with accepted Enlightenment principles and the recommendations of Montesquieu.

The *Instruction* (*Nakaz*) compiled by Catherine the Great for her new Legislative Commission of 1767 may rank as the most ambitious political agenda published by any head of state before 1789. The fact that the Commission proved very unwieldy (with 564 elected delegates, a large number of sub-committees and a substantial clerical staff), and that Catherine was soon distracted by the Turkish declaration of war in 1768, does not diminish the significance of her initiative. Her *Instruction* consisted of an array of legal and political maxims, many of them derived selectively from the works of Montesquieu, Beccaria and others. The context in which Catherine worked, and the use she made both of the writings of the western Enlightenment and of advice from a few of her collaborators, has been analysed by several historians, as has the quality of her original drafts (in French). An official printed version in Russian soon followed, signed off by Catherine, and in 1770 a four-language version in parallel Russian, Latin, German and French texts. There were more than twenty other editions during the remaining thirty years of Catherine's reign.[81] Her own motivations were no doubt complex: her text could help stamp her authority on the Russian elite, project her international reputation as an enlightened ruler and could also initiate long-overdue civil and criminal law reform. Although a comprehensive law code never emerged from this work, subsidiary legislation did. No less significant for Catherine was the fact that her text generated huge interest across Europe, acclaimed by celebrities such as Frederick II and Voltaire. Diderot remained critical (but did not say so in print). Perhaps the French government response was the most illuminating of all: it banned the *Nakaz* as a dangerous book.

Catherine's text was never intended as a comprehensive political statement, merely a statement of key principles to guide the Commission. From a Russian perspective it was an innovative text, but it was not radical by the standards of European Enlightenment. It made clear, at the outset, that Russia could only be governed adequately by a ruler with absolute power (clause 10). It aimed to ensure everything worked for the greater good of all, within what was manifestly intended to be a traditional hierarchical society. It stated that the object of government was to secure order without infringing the natural liberty of the people, yet natural rights were not discussed. All citizens were notionally to be subject to

---

[81] P. Dukes, *Catherine the Great's Instruction (Nakaz) to the Legislative Commission, 1767* (Newtonville, MA, 1977); I. de Madariaga, *Russia in the age of Catherine the Great* (London, 1981), 139–83; S. Dixon, *The modernisation of Russia 1676–1825* (Cambridge, 1999), 144–5.

the same laws (clauses 33–4), but at the same time there was no hint of the accountability of government to civil society. The Commission itself was meant to work systematically through her *Instruction*, but discussion was to be confined solely to legal changes that the Commission might wish to recommend to the sovereign. To remove any doubt, clause 29 noted that:

These Instructions [as provided by sanctioned laws] restrain the People under penalties from contemning the Edicts of the Sovereign, and at the same time preserve them from their own headstrong desires and stubborn inclinations.[82]

Catherine gradually accepted that a less regulated press would be invaluable for the modernisation of Russia and by a decree of 15 January 1783 formally allowed printers to undertake commercial and private work outside direct state control. This deregulation significantly accelerated the growth of printing and publishing in Russia, boosting both translation of imported works and original publications including history, religious texts and fiction. As Gary Marker noted some years ago, the annual output of Russian-language printing reached 400 titles (books and journals) by the mid-1780s, and peaked in the year 1788. However, texts were still subject to an arbitrary form of censorship which depended essentially on the empress herself and some of her advisers. Without even nominally independent legislative processes, publishing in Russia remained risky.[83] The strong reactions to events in France in the 1790s brought disaster for some intellectual leaders, including the very enterprising publisher Nikolai Novikov (who had been active in the Legislative Commission of 1767 and the University of Moscow, but was imprisoned in 1792 and his stock destroyed) and the political writer Alexander Radishchev, whose *Journey from St Petersburg to Moscow* (1790) was sufficiently critical of contemporary Russia that Catherine had him exiled to Siberia and ordered the book to be destroyed. In 1796, Catherine even rescinded her decree of 1783, although by then no publisher would have dared printing anything that might have politically independent implications.

Perhaps the outstanding example before 1789 of a government using print to generate significant public support is found in the Rural Reform Commission established in Copenhagen in 1786. Initiating a wide range of social and economic reforms was common across most European governments in the later eighteenth century, driven by the kind of practical reform ideas put forward by many different groups inside and outside governments, including the French physiocrats, the Scottish political economists and the German cameralists. Ideas on how to standardise

---

[82] Dukes, *Instruction*, 45.
[83] G. Marker, *Publishing, printing and the origins of intellectual life in Russia 1700–1800* (Princeton, NJ, 1985).

poor relief, establish public works programmes, improve public health, achieve fundamental school reforms, modernise the criminal code and penal codes, achieve better-distributed tax burdens, and much else, were now routinely published in journals, as prize essays, or as pamphlets and books. In Denmark, such publications became common under the new liberal regency government of 1784, lasting right through to the late 1790s.[84] The primary remit of the Danish Rural Reform Commission of 1786 was to review and reform the legal status of tenancy contracts between peasants and landowners, but all aspects of peasant–seigneur relations came under scrutiny, including the valuation of holdings, labour services, rents, tithes, military conscription, social discipline, and much else. The unusual circumstances surrounding the establishment of the Commission, the moderate but wide-ranging reform programme of which it was a key component and the enlightened team of ministers who held power in Denmark from 1784 to 1797 have been discussed at length by Danish historians, as have the substantial legislative results emerging directly from the Commission's work.[85] More important in the present context is the Commission's use of print and public dissemination to help achieve durable change.

The Commission worked with considerable energy from September 1786 and by June 1791 had held eighty-seven minuted meetings (despite a gap for the whole of 1789). It received 145 formal written submissions in the first two years of operation, both from its own members and from a wide range of government bodies and private individuals.[86] Some of these submissions were quite brief, but some long enough to be published separately as substantial pamphlets or books in their own right. It is worth noting that the government not only allowed, but in some cases actively encouraged, the publication of tracts and proposals by private individuals: altogether sixty-seven publications relevant to the work of the Commission had been reviewed by late 1787 in the Copenhagen literary review *Lærde Efterretninger*.[87] Even more extraordinary was the unprecedented decision taken early on to publish the Commission's own minutes, two hefty volumes

---

[84] T. Munck, 'Public debate, politics and print: the late Enlightenment in Copenhagen during the years of the French Revolution 1786–1800', *Historisk Tidsskrift*,114 (2014), 323–52.

[85] T. Munck, 'The Danish reformers', in H. M. Scott (ed.), *Enlightened absolutism: reform and reformers in later eighteenth-century Europe* (Basingstoke, 1990), 245–63.

[86] The Commission's extensive archive is found in Rigsarkivet, Rentekammer Rtk.434.1 to Rtk.434.8. It resumed regular meetings in 1795–7, and again in 1804, by which time it had received more than 200 further submissions, but it was not active after May 1805.

[87] T. Munck, 'Absolute monarchy in later eighteenth-century Denmark: centralized reform, public expectations and the Copenhagen press', *Historical Journal*, 41 (1998), 201–24.

of which appeared (1788–9) while the legislative work was still in progress.[88] This publication, laying bare the inner workings of a government committee – and in effect publicising the initiatives by an absolute monarchy to review and reform the most fundamental social and economic relationships sustaining the kingdom – demonstrates an unprecedented confidence in the advantages of public transparency within what was still a very hierarchical and centralised state. Part of the explanation may be found in the almost naive enlightened idealism of the head of the Treasury, Count Christian Ditlev Reventlow, and the political shrewdness of its energetic clerk, the Norwegian lawyer Christian Colbiørnsen, both of whom managed to keep most of the fourteen other Commission members engaged despite fundamental differences of viewpoint. Perhaps just as important was the government strategy of ensuring public awareness of the reforms to counterbalance the inevitable resistance from certain quarters – a resistance which led to two high-level resignations from the Privy Council itself in 1788, as well as a number of other protests culminating in a mass petition from landowners in 1790.

Until March 1794, it appears that all attending members formally signed the Commission's official minute-book (Protocol) at the end of each actual meeting to indicate their approval of the minutes as recorded longhand by the clerk. The published text (two substantial volumes covering the period up to May 1788) mirror almost exactly the handwritten minute-protocol, recording the individual participation and opinions of each Commissioner. The publication also included, or referred in detail to, the written submissions received by the Commission. Such transparency was not achieved without objections: the War Commissariat, for example, pointed out on 7 January 1788 that it was uncomfortable about presenting detailed arguments against the proposed legislation, knowing that these would in due course be read by the public. Later, on 19 May, the War Commissariat asked that an additional text which they had submitted too late to influence the Commission's discussion should nevertheless be published with the rest – a request which the Commission refused, noting that the Commissariat could publish the text on their own if they so wished. We now know that the minutes and submissions for meetings after May 1788 never did appear in print, but this was not the result of a deliberate change of policy: on 25 October 1790, for example, the Commission took the trouble to finalise a text specifically in order for it to be ready for publication. We can only assume that the government decided to discontinue publication plans in the light of growing public controversy, mounting peasant

---

[88] *Den for lanboevæsenet nedsatte commissions forhandlinger*, 2 vols. (Copenhagen, 1788–9).

expectations concerning reform of labour services and the manifest hostility of a number of landowners which came into the open in a formal protest in 1790. Sensitivity to the news from France from 1789 onwards may also have played a part.

From the start, the new Commission was presented as a major government initiative, and no contemporary observer could have missed its significance. The remit was substantially wider than the rural reform initiatives attempted elsewhere in Europe and significantly included a fundamental review of the entire peasant–seigneurial relationship including the traditionally unrestricted rights of landowners to use the labour of their tenants as an entitlement inherent in the ownership of the land and hence in whatever way they thought fit. Even a review of this fundamental issue was controversial, let alone any attempt at regulation. Commensurate with this task, in terms of actual composition the Commission was therefore one of the most high-powered for generations. Yet the membership itself clearly signalled that there could be no foregone conclusions. Not only were some traditionally minded landowners unwilling to concede the argument that liberal economic policies might be to their advantage, but there were substantive challenges concerning the legality of some of the reforms, especially those that appeared to circumscribe the property rights of landowners, or might jeopardise rural manpower and military conscription. Given the context, it is hardly surprising that the actual legislation drafted by the Commission was moderate and consensus-driven, establishing a clear regulatory framework for a wide range of issues: binding tenancy contracts, freedom of movement for tenants, prescribed labour services (with mediation services if necessary), the break-up of communal farming, and much else. Equally, it is not surprising that a number of concessions had to be made to the landowning interests, in particular at the expense of smallholders and rural labourers. Despite such reservations concerning both the legislation and its implementation, however, we can recognise the work of the Commission as a unique example in pre-1789 Europe of an autocratic government engaging directly with public opinion through print, with the explicit purpose of achieving sufficient consensus to secure fundamental and lasting change.

Public Opinion and Political Discourse in the European Context

Once again we have noticed that the role of print in relation to public opinion and political culture changed unevenly across different parts of

Europe. Active discussion of politics (power, authority, relationships in civil society, economic power, institutional reform, constitutional law) was undoubtedly becoming more common in urban Europe in the 1760s and 1770s, both in print and by other means. It was almost as if ending the mid-century European and global wars had unleashed a flood of questions for which new answers might now be attempted. At the same time, public discussion was bound to come into conflict with prevailing restrictions on freedom of expression, especially regarding domestic politics. In those areas with a viable print and newspaper industry, authors and publishers found techniques of evasion and ambiguity that tested (almost to destruction) both the traditional mechanisms of censorship and the scope for effective post-publication legal prosecution.

Engagement in public discourse could take many forms – including fiction and the theatre, pamphleteering and earnest reform proposals – and could range from critically innovative scrutiny to traditional or conservative reinforcement. But as we have also seen, the processes for monitoring and regulating print manifestly failed to keep up: not only was the sheer quantity of print liable to overwhelm regulatory mechanisms, but many new texts were designed to made judgment more difficult, while at the same time attracting readers from across a wider and more volatile urban market. Significantly, after 1763, there was clear recognition in many political systems across Europe that regulation of print was liable to be counterproductive. Accordingly, some governments eventually recognised that more might be achieved by trying to influence public opinion directly through new forms of publicity of their own, or even by allowing individuals within government to engage directly with the reading public. Frederick II of Prussia was exceptional in his willingness to go personally into print,[89] but other governments were proactive in other ways.

No-one expected individual books or newspapers on their own to make much difference, but when we consider the whole spectrum of printed material it is difficult not to think of the period from around 1750 as one of huge growth in political engagement through print, especially amongst the professional, middling or industrious sorts across

---

[89] Frederick II used print far more than any other ruler in the eighteenth century, clearly recognising the value of publication to project his own political vision. He published essays on politics, forms of government and the duties of rulers; a history of his own time (a history of Brandenburg appearing already in 1751 and further volumes later); *Letters on the love of the fatherland* (1779); and much else. He clearly also used his extensive correspondence with leading intellectuals across Europe, especially Voltaire, to enhance his reputation as a progressive and well-read intellectual. See T. Schieder, *Frederick the Great* (ed. and transl. by S. Berkeley and H. M Scott, London, 2000), 233–67.

most of urban Europe from northern Italy to Stockholm, or Edinburgh to Vienna. What evidence we have on dissemination, impact, reviewing, reprinting, imitation and translation admittedly provides only patchy data on how texts were actually read, understood and possibly discussed. The texts themselves provide some clues, but are perhaps only a muffled echo of what might have been heard in conversations amongst friends, in the street, or in the rapidly spreading sociable venues ranging from coffee houses to salons and learned societies. Nevertheless, print remained the only medium through which a wider public could reliably be reached, and had now become the obvious tool for public political discussion, a vehicle for all kinds of ideas (enlightening or otherwise) and a means of speedy communication and dissemination of material on every conceivable topic. The very fact that governments continued to monitor print very carefully, and prosecute where necessary, suggests that everyone regarded print as important.

Although we need to be careful about drawing conclusions from problematic data, we may also observe shifts in thematic content. Matters of faith, religious beliefs and associated devotional practices were still important to many readers. Yet some markets and certain contexts created strong demand for texts which focused more on social rank and moral authority, political economy, history and the fabric of civil society. Practical and patriotic discourse could reinforce community coherence, but could also generate interest in accurate information and factual knowledge. The great *Encyclopédie* – the last ten volumes of which could at last be released (without permission) in 1765 – tried to reshape a complete system of European knowledge. But short essays could also find a surprisingly wide readership, as demonstrated by authors adopting such totally different topics and styles of writing as Hume, Rousseau, Mendelssohn and his friend Lessing. For those particularly concerned with the practicalities of good government, there were other thought-provoking texts. Beccaria's extremely brief analysis of crime and punishment reached far more readers than, say, John Howard's analysis of the failings of workhouses and prisons, yet both demonstrated the persistent short-comings of institutions across Europe and the abject failures and social complacency everywhere.

We may also now be in a position to draw some wider conclusions about the Enlightenment itself. It no longer makes sense to look for patterns of 'enlightenment in national context' – at least not if, by using such a phrase, we expect to identify trends particular to a part of Europe governed as a 'nation-state'. We also need to be wary of assuming that a word such as 'patriotic' might have roughly the same connotations as 'national' had for later generations.[90] And we are liable to misread our texts if we use them to identify characteristics shared by everyone speaking the same language. French, in particular, was a vehicle for so many contradictory and incompatible ways of thinking that the idea of a single 'French Enlightenment' is patently absurd. The types of writing we associate with the Scottish Enlightenment may be less diverse than the French, but were firmly comparative rather than 'national' in intent, aiming at improving civic society anywhere. Enlightened thinking in German-speaking central Europe was far more decentralised than in any other language community: with so many universities, courts, thriving cities and cultural institutions, there was a huge variety of cultural parameters and styles which shared little beyond the language itself and a general interest in civil society.

Contemporary readers, however, could hardly have failed to notice that both Paris and London sustained an extraordinarily lively market for scurrilous, subversive and divisive polemics, nurtured by political factions, enterprising patrons and proactive publishers, greatly diversified by what may have seemed like hordes of aspiring pamphleteers or inveterate polemicists meeting the demands of a very volatile market. As historians, we may even feel tempted to compare, say, the polemics of the Wilkes disturbances with those of the Maupeou crisis – if only to examine the linguistic turns, range and conceptual frameworks of public opinion in each. We may on that basis conclude that writers in these confrontations were considerably more outspoken and subversive than anything observed in their own hinterland (for example in other major cities in France and Britain), let alone other parts of Europe. By comparison, the Struensee period in Denmark revealed an unexpected polemical and populist streak from 1770 to early 1772, but one that turned out to be a short aberration followed by twelve years of stagnating print culture, before a new and more durable outburst after 1784. We find a much more responsible, constructive and wide-ranging public engagement in Stockholm in the 1750s and 60s, but its frame of reference was specifically Swedish and hardly any of the texts were translated or disseminated outside that language community. We may conclude that the real achievement of the high Enlightenment was to challenge all monolithic authority and make a whole range of contrasting ideas and implacable

---

[90] See notably Richard Price, *A discourse on the love of our country* (London, 1789), a text based on a sermon delivered in 1789 to commemorate the 1689 revolution, explaining the conditions for creating a cohesive civic society, while highlighting the need for a government that genuinely sees itself as a servant of the public interest and the people. This 60-page tract had nine printed editions in English and three in French over the next year.

disagreements visible and accessible to a broader reading public, whatever their political inclinations.

If the extreme forms of political discourse in Paris and London in fact stand out as exceptional, some further explanation may be in order. No doubt political writers there were making the most of the dangerous mix of political incompetence and manifest corruption – in court politics, in the self-serving parliaments or *parlements* and within some of the political elite (but far from all). But if that was the case, why were critics in London and Paris more outspoken than, say, in Stockholm, where factional struggles and ineffective leadership seemed just as obvious in the 1760s? And why might writers in the Scottish Enlightenment seem to prefer to keep their distance from London politics, even though they were keen to gain recognition in the London (and Paris) book markets? Was Dutch political life so decentralised that its political writers struggled to see any coherent patterns at all, or did they prefer (as did many German writers) to focus on broader moral and historical issues? More generally, why were so few prepared to speak up about the role of women in public life, or to challenge the many prevailing prejudices and the abusive authority of patriarchy, social inequality or racial discrimination? This chapter has at best sketched some potential answers to these questions, and we need to look far beyond print itself to understand whether late *ancien-régime* society was as innovative and exciting as the texts may suggest, or just overheating in the face of multiple pressures. Ultimately, the extraordinary sequence of upheavals in France from 1789 onwards suggest that, as in the 1640s and 50s, print and public discussion was impossible to moderate and difficult to harness during periods of political crisis.

6   Revolution: Democracy and Loyalism in Print 1789–95

The 1790s did not bring major changes in the technology of printing or its ancillary industries, nor were there major innovations in terms of presentation or the mechanisms of distribution. The most significant change was in the content, as some authors and printers adopted more imaginative or provocative forms of discourse to represent rapidly shifting political realities or seek further change. The violence of events in France, and successive major shifts in the location of power there, visibly changed what could be said in print. As in England in the 1640s, the style, imagery and words deployed in newspapers, posters, pamphlets and printed speeches reflected a more polarised political culture. Some texts were marketed specifically to attract a wider readership, notably amongst skilled and semi-skilled workers in the poorer districts of large restless cities such as Paris and London. In Paris in particular, some newspaper editors adopted colourful (if sometimes contrived) populist styles of discourse aimed at radicalising their readers with increasingly violent metaphors, while trying to outdo each other to attract attention. Meanwhile, major social groups hitherto on the fringes of political culture – or offstage altogether – sought to engage in political life in ways that had never been possible before. In Paris this happened not only for urban semi-skilled and skilled workers, soldiers and lesser officeholders, but also for professional groups such as lawyers, hitherto on the fringe of political life. Even more striking was the scope for women of middling and lower status to make their voices heard in innovative and tangible ways – most clearly in the powerful events of 5–6 October 1789 and subsequently by their participation in political organisations.

Because of administrative change and instability in the 1790s, there are more gaps or weaknesses in the empirical evidence regarding print than for earlier decades, especially for France. Bibliographical data, as we have seen, is problematic even for the stable years of the eighteenth century, but much worse for the 1790s, in part because of the collapse and formal abolition of censorship and print regulation in France in 1789, the abolition of guilds, and the multiple divisions of effective central and local authority through the 1790s. As before, most newspapers and serials had to continue indicating their date and the location of their editorial office, in order to function properly. But it becomes more difficult to quantify pamphlets, tracts, reprints of earlier works and other French-language publications, some of which appeared without indication of year or place of publication, printer, or even author. Although printers and authors were never free from the threat of prosecution for libel, and some pamphleteers still had to resort to secret publication, there was a brief period of increasingly outspoken public discussion in print – on politics as on many other issues – from the autumn of 1789 until Terror policies effectively destroyed free speech in 1793. Legal disputes over intellectual rights and copyright, as we will see at the end of this chapter, may also have made commercial publication of larger works in France less viable. In other parts of Europe in the 1790s the printing industry did not become quite so anarchic, yet the impact of French revolutionary thinking everywhere led to major controversies and certainly gave some authors and publishers continuing good reason to seek cover in anonymity or underground publication.

The years from 1786 encouraged growing interest in new ideas regarding civic society, public accountability, legitimate authority and political representation. Although there were political confrontations and minor revolts elsewhere in Europe in the 1780s, events in France quickly took on both a scale and a seemingly irreversible momentum that was without precedent, watched in fascination (or revulsion) by observers everywhere. Critical discussion of constitutional law, in the early eighteenth century undertaken only by specialists, gained new momentum and relevance as a result of the revolt of the American colonies and the process of negotiating a new federalist republican government there. The recurrent constitutional deliberations of successive governments in France from 1789 were even more wide-ranging. The sequence of new constitutions in 1791, 1793 and 1795 marked major changes in the theoretical framework of government, forcing both the French national assemblies and the wider public to learn about constitutional law and the foundations of citizenship. Notions of representation underwent profound change, from the elaborate and surprisingly inclusive indirect elections for the Estates General in the spring of 1789 and the more restrictive electoral system of 1791, to the universal male franchise of 1793, reversed again by 1795. Successive assemblies argued over their own role, changing from being representatives of a notional national interest to mandatories subject to popular scrutiny and possible denunciation or deselection. In terms of innovative fiscal and monetary policies, much less was achieved, despite significant attempts at a national redistribution of property and redeployment of the extensive theoretical fiscal understanding inherited from the old order.

The exercise of executive power changed dramatically with each consecutive upheaval in French politics, from the first attempts at creating a constitutional monarchy (1789–91), through what was meant to be a genuinely open republican regime (from September 1792), then into the Terror (from the summer of 1793) and the anarchic White Terror (after Thermidor). The overthrow of the monarchy, and in particular the formal trial and execution of the king, had a huge impact on European political opinion, but also forced the supporters of continuing revolution within France to think hard about what they were trying to achieve. Although the impact varied enormously across France, almost all the institutions and frameworks of public life were affected by successive phases of revolution. In Paris and other cities, the power of the Catholic church was destroyed, starting with the confiscation of its property assets from late 1789 and culminating in the bitter dechristianisation campaigns of the autumn of 1793. Political clubs and societies changed at a bewildering speed, ranging right across the political spectrum. Some of these organisations openly incorporated women, although rarely in a key role. The urban middling and lower sorts (the ubiquitous *sans-culottes*) made dramatic assertions of power in recurrent *journées révolutionnaires*, but their organisational structures were systematically dismantled in 1794 and effectively eliminated by 1795. The peasantry, who broke into open rebellion across parts of France in the summer of 1789, were consistently ignored by politicians, their interests relegated to the bottom of the political agenda. Military conscription was totally reorganised, laying the foundations for a colossal war effort run under a new command structure supposedly based on merit and motivated by heavy-handed propaganda promoting the defence of 'la patrie' (the fatherland).

Public discussion in France was achieved partly through print, in the form of newspapers, pamphlets, revolutionary songs, broadsheets, patriotic stories, official proclamations or detailed reports. But we also need to remind ourselves more than ever that political discourse could be transmitted in many different ways. The great outpouring of grievances and demands written into the thousands of *cahiers de doléances* during the process of elections to the Estates General in 1789 were very rarely printed,[1] yet are vivid testimony to the scope and range of political

---

[1] There is evidence that printed checklists for those drafting the *cahiers* were pre-circulated. The abbé Sieyes was commissioned by Orléans to write one of these, the *Délibérations à prendre dans les assemblées de bailliages*, published in Paris, February 1789, immediately after his more famous pamphlet *What is the Third Estate?* See also G. A. Kelly, 'The

discussions triggered across the whole country by the prospect of new political solutions. No doubt some of the ideas raised in the electoral meetings were also reflected in the huge outpouring of pamphlets that had started in the autumn of 1788 and lasted right through the spring and beyond. Yet much of the language of revolution originated in the speeches and arguments which took place in electoral assemblies, local meetings and other public places – language which we cannot track reliably, though we may assume it was imitated to some extent in polemical texts. But there were other ways of proclaiming new political concepts. Visual symbolism became more prominent and important: the new national festival first held on 14 July 1790 (the first anniversary of the fall of the Bastille) created endless scope for what became an annual refashioning and visualisation of national myths to suit the rapidly shifting political leadership. Soon, public squares and buildings were redesigned, streets renamed and celebratory public buildings planned (though not always built). A new hall for the national parliament itself, long overdue and designed to improve daily debate, was inaugurated in May 1793 – sadly too late to mitigate the bitter factionalism of the beleaguered National Convention. Both the ideal and the real manifestations of public opinion(s) were noted. Active popular participation was encouraged both in abstract theory and sometimes in direct street action. Revolutionary ideals were represented physically in many other ways: in the *bonnet rouge* (the red hat of galley slaves adopted as an emblem of freedom); the cockade and other symbols, represented through forms of national dress for a new egalitarian society and in the great symbolic pageantry designed by the artist Jacques-Louis David; or experienced in the new styles of revolutionary theatre, music and opera, and much else. Revolutionary discourse changed decisively, becoming loaded with new words and meanings. As denunciation of conspiracy developed into a national obsession, the symbolism and language of revolution quickly became a minefield for the unwary.

Inevitably, therefore, printed texts can never be regarded as more than a representation, or proxy description, of the real political culture enacted in halls, streets and public spaces. Judging from letters and other manuscript sources, verbal political discourse was always more diverse and from 1791 more extreme, at least in Paris. Substantive discussion tended to become overshadowed by simplistic rhetoric: for example, many Parisian newspapers were increasingly intent on projecting the prejudices and obsessions of the writer or publisher, rather than providing accurate

machine of the Duc d'Orléans and the new politics', *Journal of Modern History*, 51 (1979), 667–84. For the *cahiers* as a whole, see J. Markoff, *The abolition of feudalism: peasants, landlords and legislators in the French Revolution* (Philadelphia, 1996).

reporting. Nevertheless, those papers which attempted to exercise independent judgment (sometimes continuing to do so even into the period of
Terror government) provide material by which we can gauge not just
revolutionary discourse itself, but also the scope for public discussion
concerning the purpose and effectiveness of republican government, and
political imagination more broadly. In the rest of Europe, newspapers
initially provided factual summaries, often sympathetic to reform.
However, this changed from early in 1792, as the threat of war loomed
ever larger and opinions both within France and elsewhere polarised.

Women in Politics and Print

Before 1789, only a small minority of women, in special circumstances, had
any direct influence on collective decision-making and policy anywhere in
Europe. The most obvious way was through rioting – making the most of
a passing opportunity to join one of the recurrent food riots amongst the
poorer sorts in the unstable years of the seventeenth century, in the severe
famines from the 1690s to 1709 and again during the early 1770s across
many parts of Europe. In the repression that would follow such rioting,
women were sometimes treated more leniently, either on the assumption
that they were less violent, or that they were primary carers looking after the
interests of their family and so had acted only out of desperation. Recurrent
economic instability and unrest in the later 1780s, and the visible aggrava-
tion caused by the poor harvest of 1788, was bound to give women further
opportunities for such traditional activism. Whether they had also acquired
a political voice in *ancien-régime* France, however, was less clear.

Far removed from the food rioters, both in terms of social status and
primary interests, were the few elite women able to host their own salon as
a venue for free intellectual discussion. These almost legendary cultural
hostesses, active in Paris, Berlin, London and other major cities in the
later eighteenth century, may appear to have been path-breakers of female
self-improvement and empowerment, controlling and inspiring intellectual sociability. Salons certainly attracted enlightened writers and free
thinkers who either were already part of the leisured elite, or who hoped to
gain support, pensions and rewards for their efforts. But recent research
on salon culture both in France and elsewhere has questioned the extent
to which the great salon hostesses could genuinely control and direct the
intellectual agenda of these gatherings.[2] In any case the salons were by

---

[2] A. Lilti, *Le monde des salons: sociabilité et mondanité à Paris au xviiie siècle* (Paris, 2005);
U. Weckel, 'A lost paradise of a female culture? Some critical questions regarding the
scholarship on late eighteenth and early nineteenth-century German salons', *German*

definition private and exclusive – guests were admitted by invitation or through private contacts. Ideas arising from such polite conversation are impossible to document and were hardly ever disseminated in print in anything resembling their original form. That does not mean that salons were ineffective on their own terms: no doubt they created an environment in which guests could explore new ideas and even read out draft manuscripts. But it would have been extremely bad taste, and an abject admission of failure, to cite salon conversation in published work in such a way that it could be attributed. Madame Roland, in her fragmented secret diary mostly written in the months before she was guillotined, described the dinners she hosted while her husband was still active in government in 1792: she noted with scorn how Robespierre occasionally attended, rarely said anything useful, but might well reuse what he had heard in a political speech the next day.[3]

The revolutionary mood of the early 1790s undoubtedly encouraged some exceptional women to break free from the restrictive social and gender norms of their age. Despite being excluded from voting, a few groups of third-estate women gathered to compile their own unofficial *cahiers de doléances* (lists of grievances) for submission to local electoral assemblies in the run-up to the meeting of the Estates General in May 1789. Women also compiled petitions to the crown asking for protection of any economic rights they already held. In conformity with accepted practice in the French monarchy, however, such demands were not part of a public negotiation and were therefore not disseminated through print.

Of course women were capable of expressing more complex grievances, as became apparent during the women's march of 5–6 October 1789. The Parisian women first invaded the Hôtel de Ville (city chambers), not only demanding immediate action on the price of bread and against market malpractices, but also confronting the municipal bureaucracy by ransacking documentary material and setting fire to some of it in the entrance hall. Multiple grievances were at issue, ranging from inadequate enforcement of food-marketing regulations to accusations of negligent or foot-dragging civic administration. Eventually, the women were persuaded to go to Versailles to bring their grievances direct to the National Assembly and the king. The resulting march turned into a significant demonstration of power: the women dragged along two cannons, on the way threatened several military commanders with violence and subsequently deployed

History, 18 (2000), 310–36; U. Wyrwa, 'Berlin and Florence in the age of Enlightenment: Jewish experience in comparative perspective', *German History*, 21 (2003), 1–28.
[3] E. Shuckburgh (ed.), *The memoirs of Madame Roland* (London, 1989), 81.

other unmistakeable symbols of empowerment. None of this had been pre-planned, however, so there was no direct attempt by the women to influence wider opinion by means of print and no immediate follow-up to consolidate their political role.[4] Here we are up against a recurrent problem in the 1790s: how to reconstruct the political world of those social groups who rarely created their own written records and were even less likely to publish them. Clearly, printed texts cannot fully reflect the authentic voice or real intent of political change when many writers were themselves also engaged in apparently escalating cycles of revolutionary action.

During the period 1788–91, discussion in print tended to stay within the conventional bounds of the political agenda set out by the Estates General (National Assembly) in the summer of 1789. Despite urgent economic and fiscal challenges, the Assembly focused on giving France a constitutional government matching the Declaration of Rights of 26 Aug 1789. The most significant critique of that Declaration from outside government, however, came from a butcher's daughter, Olympe de Gouges. Her (now iconic) pamphlet, *Les droits de la femme* (no date or place of publication, but probably printed in Paris in 1791),[5] was much more than a mere rewording of the official Declaration to include women and deserves closer scrutiny. She framed her version of the Declaration within longer introductory and concluding sections, giving the whole pamphlet a unique slant. She started with a dedication to Marie-Antoinette, as queen of France and mother – itself an unexpected gesture given that the queen's reputation had been in steep decline in recent years. She also directly addressed her intended readers, calling on men to accept women as equal partners, rather than sexual slaves, and calling on women to wake up to their own potential. She pursued this further in her Postscript, which offered a clearer indication of her strategy. Observing that 'le marriage est le tombeau de la confiance et de l'amour' ('marriage is the tomb of trust and love'), she set out the terms for a new social contract between man and woman – an elective marriage alliance which either party could terminate if it no longer served mutual interests, on condition that the rights of both parties would be fully respected and all property divided in recognition of the interests of any children. She

---

[4] For examples of written accounts and legal transcripts arising from the October march, see D. G. Levy, H. B. Applewhite and M. D. Johnson (eds.), *Women in revolutionary Paris 1789–1795* (Urbana, IL, 1980), 13–50. The October march clearly went far beyond the traditional and accepted female activism of market women or food rioters.

[5] Levy et al., *Women in revolutionary Paris*, 87–96, cites this now iconic text in full in translation; the version used here is the French original, in Gallica, (http://catalogue .bnf.fr/ark:/12148/cb36057180p); see also J. W. Scott, *Only paradoxes to offer: French feminists and the rights of man* (Cambridge, MA, 1996), 19–56.

reinforced this message by calling for the abolition of slavery itself, arguing that a true revolution should focus on turning fraternity and equality into reality.

This powerful line of argument gave a clear context for the central part of de Gouges's pamphlet, in which she reworked the seventeen clauses of the official Declaration of Rights. She deliberately mirrored the style and key concepts of the original, but fundamentally shifted the emphases. In clause 3 she defined the nation as 'the re-union of woman and man', while the following clause noted that the 'exercise of the natural rights of woman has no limits other than the perpetual tyranny which man imposes on her' – a turn of phrase totally different from the original wording outlining the reciprocal and equal rights of man as defined in law. In clause 6 de Gouges demanded the right for all women to consent explicitly to the law, as expressed through the general will. No less dramatic were her demands for equal treatment before the law, including equal punishment (clauses 7–9). The simple assertion of freedom of opinion and expression in the original Declaration was turned by de Gouges into something much more specific: the right of a mother to name the father of her child, without the need to hide the truth. Finally, clauses 13–15 demanded that women be given equal responsibilities and equal rights of accountability in fiscal and all other public financial matters – a demand which, to be effective, would necessitate women having full access to public offices and an equal share in public administration itself. To emphasise her point, de Gouges called for her version of the Declaration to be adopted as an official statement of principle of the Revolution itself, a symbol of the new order.

The pamphlet by de Gouges stands out not just because of its radical re-interpretation of revolutionary principles to secure tangible benefits for women, but also because of the specific ways in which it reshaped a text which was itself already the most widely printed and disseminated statement of revolution. Unfortunately we can only guess at the impact of her pamphlet, but in light of the relative scarcity of surviving copies and the lack of citation by others, we may assume it did not have a large print run. Yet de Gouges had clearly understood the potential power of print and had realised how an emblematic text could itself be used as a vehicle for change. Few other writers matched her inventiveness in using universal concepts relevant to all levels of society, and we struggle to find other examples of authors forcing gender issues beyond the bounds of tradition and cultural indoctrination.[6] From amongst the intellectual elite we note

---

[6] See for example in Prudhomme's newspaper *Révolutions de Paris*, discussed by D. G. Levy, 'Women's revolutionary citizenship in action, 1791: setting the boundaries', in R. Waldinger, P. Dawson and I. Woloch (eds.), *The French Revolution and the meaning of citizenship* (Westport, CT, and London, 1993), 169–84.

the international feminist reformer Etta Palm d'Aelders, Condorcet and his wife Sophie de Condorcet, who published extensively under the auspices of the Cercle Social and its printing press. The Cercle Social clearly served as a focal point for debates which gave due prominence to women's education and their social role and welcomed visiting foreigners such as Mary Wollstonecraft.[7] But ultimately the Cercle Social did not constitute a coherent political lobbying group and its members seem to have preferred acting as individuals rather than as a collective leadership or political caucus. It was much easier for male polemicists to use Rousseau, combined with cultural clichés, as justification for relegating women to the domestic sphere. And as Wollstonecraft noted in her own contribution to public discussion in Britain, taking on Rousseau while appearing not to challenge the social conventions of gender inequality so fundamentally as to lose your readers was a balancing act that proved extremely challenging.[8]

This may explain why much of the printed legacy of gender awareness in the Revolution is so cautious. A good example is the published regulations of the Société des citoyennes républicaines révolutionnaires de Paris (the Society of Revolutionary Republican Women – SRRW). Founded and officially registered in May 1793 by a group of women activists around Pauline Léon and Claire Lacombe, this society had close links with the long-running Cordeliers Club and some Paris sections. Yet in its printed regulations (dating from July) it tried to avoid open controversy. It stated that is aims were self-educational, encouraging women to organise support for the Revolution, defend the constitution and uphold the law, while looking after their domestic responsibilities. Although article 1 of the regulations noted that women could choose to carry arms, all the rest of the text reinforced the image of a cautious organisation conducting orderly discussion in committee meetings, electing office-holders, keeping accurate records and financial accounts. The Society confirmed it would admit as members only those women who had a good reputation.[9]

---

[7] G. Kates, '"The powers of husband and wife must be equal and separate": the Cercle Social and the rights of women, 1790–91', in H. Applewhite and D. Levy (eds.), *Women and politics in the age of the democratic revolution* (Ann Arbor, 1990), 163–80. It is worth remembering that women's education rarely provided proper training in writing: the Cercle Social's insistence on educational reform was therefore an essential component in women's emancipation.

[8] M. Wollstonecraft, *A vindication of the rights of men* (London, 1790), was one of the earliest polemics against Burke, followed by her more substantial text, *A vindication of the rights of woman* (London, 1792). This second book was reprinted in London in 1796, and also had printings in Philadelphia in 1792 and 1794, in Boston in 1792 and in Dublin in 1793. There were translations into French (1792), German (1793), Dutch (1796) and Danish (1801–2).

[9] Regulations of the SRRW, cited in Levy et al., *Women in revolutionary Paris*, 161–5.

However, as the divisions in the Revolution became ever more bitter during the summer of 1793, the Society became increasingly linked to the *enragés* (a loose group of radicals criticising the government, demanding better enforcement of market regulations and systematic assistance for the poor).

The summer of 1793 marked the high point of political participation by women, anywhere. The challenge to male control of the public sphere was so effective that the Jacobin leadership felt a need to infiltrate the Society, disrupt it and ultimately use disputes as an excuse to formally ban all clubs and popular societies for women (30 October 1793). Such tactics were characteristic of an increasingly inward-looking and violent Jacobin leadership trying to tighten Terror government. But in undermining the women's organisations, the government was in effect dismantling a hugely energetic and decentralised form of popular support which they could ill afford to lose. Women had taken a wide range of initiatives in forming societies, participating in revolutionary *journées,* listening in the galleries of the National Assembly and demanding more pro-active policies from administrative authorities. They had also engaged in more traditional female roles as volunteers to help with poor relief and provide assistance for the very large French armies. It would seem that most politicians were too stuck in traditional ways of thought, or too devoted to Rousseau, to be able to acknowledge all this.

That, however, did not stop female writers going into print much more frequently in the early years of the Revolution than they had in the last decades of the *ancien régime.* Carla Hesse has done a detailed quantitative study of female authors across different genres, noting that although women accounted for a very small proportion (less than 5 per cent) of the total French printed output of the 1790s, they remained significant during the Terror and continued after 1795. Their contribution to political discussion mostly took the form of historical writing or even journalism. In both of these Louise-Félicité de Kéralio (1757–1821) excelled. She had already been active as a translator (including of Richard Price) and as an editor of women's writings, but in 1789 broke new ground by founding and producing the *Journal du Citoyen,* which she continued under a new title, the *Mercure National,* in partnership with her father and her new husband François Robert. Louise de Kéralio-Robert (as she was known after her marriage) campaigned for freedom of the press and was involved in other political activism. She also authored a vigorous attack on Marie-Antoinette issued anonymously by the publisher Louis Prudhomme in 1791: unlike the kind of sexualised diatribe against the queen typical of the last years of monarchy, this book raised substantive questions about the political role of women over an extended historical period.[10]

Changes in vocabulary in the titles of French-language publications do reflect some recognition of the potential participation of women in political life, as represented for example in the frequency of distinctive words such as *citoyenne* (citizeness) by 1793. But we can also observe change through the writings of foreign visitors to Paris. A number of British women who witnessed events in France published accounts and analyses which often cut across the policies of their own government. If Mary Wollstonecraft's *A vindication of the rights of woman* (1792) was only in general terms inspired by what she had seen in Paris, her subsequent work *An historical and moral view of the French Revolution* (1794)[11] was more openly political. Anna Barbauld (1743–1825) was highly critical of the war against France, for example in her *Sins of government, sins of the nation* (1793),[12] written not out of enthusiasm for what was happening across the Channel, but to counteract the false nationalism that the British government was propagating. Both writers were trying to create a new understanding of gender roles, yet Barbauld was particularly significant because she minimised the significance of gender in her political arguments, calling for an equality where women as well as the poor would be true citizens. She also campaigned vigorously (in print) for the repeal of the Test and Corporation Act and for reform of the slave trade. Many other women writers engaged with big political issues in the 1790s.[13] Amongst those who gained a thorough understanding of the French Revolution by living through most of it was Helen Maria Williams (1762–1827) whose serialised (and variously titled) *Letters from France*, first published between 1790 and 1795, gained a wide following and were reprinted in various collections.

[10] Anon [Louise de Kéralio], *Les crimes des reines de la France depuis le commencement de la monarchie jusqu'à Marie Antoinette* (460 pages, Paris, 1791; reprinted in 1793). This is one of the case studies in C. Hesse, *The other Enlightenment: how French women became modern* (Princeton, 2001), which also has a full bibliography of French Women 1789–1800, 157–220, including format and publisher details.

[11] Wollstonecraft was not only one of the first to attack Burke's view of the French Revolution (in her tract of 1790, *A vindication of the rights of men*), but also had measurable success as an author with a wider political message. *An historical and moral view of the origin and progress of the French Revolution*, first published in 1794, went through three editions in London (all published by Joseph Johnson in London), as well as printings in Dublin and Philadelphia.

[12] A. L. Barbauld *Sins of government, sins of the nation* (1793) was a pamphlet of just 42 pages, but still appears to have reached four editions. Joseph Johnson was again the publisher, as he had been for her poems and children's stories since 1773 and continued to be until 1800.

[13] See A. Craciun, *British women writers and the French Revolution* (Basingstoke, 2005).

Democratising the 'Political Nation': Paris Radicals

During the later eighteenth century, most writers continued to use the core political terminology inherited from Plato. As we noted earlier, Hobbes, Spinoza and Locke all discussed forms of democracy and all noted how difficult it was to make it work. In the *Encyclopédie*, Jaucourt observed that:

Democracy is one of the simple forms of government, in which the people as a body hold sovereignty. Every republic where sovereignty resides in the hands of the people is a democracy; and if sovereign power is located in the hands of merely a part of the people, it is an aristocracy. Although I do not think that democracy is the most convenient or the most stable form of government, and although I am sure it is disadvantageous for large states, nevertheless I believe it to be one of the oldest forms of government amongst those nations who have adopted as equitable the maxim that 'that in which the members of society have an interest, should be administered by all in common'.

In accordance with eighteenth-century enlightened consensus, Jaucourt goes on to note that in a democracy sovereign power does not reside in everyone as individuals, but rather in a single general assembly of the people convened according to the law; and that decisions should be reached by majority, since unanimity is unattainable. However, the people cannot necessarily either legislate directly, or implement decisions: this may need to be done by an assembly and by magistrates, respectively. And as Spinoza had also made clear nearly a century earlier, Jaucourt noted that for democracy to work citizens needed to be virtuous – meaning that they would be educated, understand frugality, equality, and the law, and always place the collective public interest above their own.[14] In short, it was widely recognised that, while a simple theoretical definition of democracy was easy to formulate, making such a system of government work would be much more complicated and would place very great demands on the people themselves.

If the general theory of democracy was familiar to philosophers, practical experience was non-existent in most parts of later eighteenth-century Europe.[15] Great city republics such as Venice or Hamburg had emphatically hierarchical patrician forms of government; equally, in those states that still had some form of representative parliament, the electorate was always narrow and often uneven, exclusively male and based on property

---

[14] 'Démocratie', in the *Encyclopédie*, vol. 4 (1754), 816.
[15] There were very substantial and unresolved discrepancies in interpretation of key concepts surrounding democracy and representation: J. Innes and M. Philp (eds), *Reimagining democracy in the age of revolutions* (Oxford, 2013); J. Markoff, 'When and where was democracy invented?', *Comparative Studies in History*, 41 (1999), 660–90.

qualifications which were neither fair nor consistent. For most readers, Montesquieu's intermediate powers and balancing institutions may well have been regarded as a more practicable compromise, approximating the real power structures of 'aristocratic' government to which everyone was accustomed. Rousseau had provided what was meant to be a far more democratic theory of government, but no specific or practicable means of making it work anywhere except in very small city-states. In any case Rousseau's concept of the general will seemed much closer to Hobbes's sovereign body than to Spinoza's genuine democracy. In short, a number of key problems relating to a functioning democracy had been recognised but not resolved: universal direct democracy as against indirect representative systems; the need for separate branches of government clearly separated from the executive power; universal respect for the law, including by government itself; some degree of transparency and access to reliable information to ensure citizens could make informed choices. To that list of democratic prerequisites, we might add one that became crucially important in the French Revolution: recognition that differences of opinion might be valid and should be respected, even if parliamentary decisions go against some. We might also note that the option of calling a referendum to resolve particular issues might not always work in the best interests of the nation as a whole.

A few deputies in the National Assembly in France did press for greater democracy when the new constitution of 1791 was being drafted and some had their speeches or pamphlets published to reach a wider audience. But parliamentary debates were chaotic: the detailed work was done in committee, where populist rhetoric was muted and where no-one believed in direct democracy. The decision made already in October 1789 to divide citizens into 'active' and 'passive' categories excluded a large proportion of adult men from voting, let alone standing for election – a step which, as populist writers were quick to point out, seemed deliberately retrograde even by the standards of the 1789 elections to the Estates General. After the fall of the monarchy, universal male franchise was adopted, but even so referenda were used selectively, turnouts in elections were poor and the representative system of the National Assembly had to rely heavily on committees in order to function at all.

Parliaments everywhere, including both the British House of Commons and the French national assemblies, were in effect anti-democratic. The political writer and campaigner John Thelwall (1764–1834) made the point very succinctly with regard to Britain, in September 1795:

The plain and simple fact is, that the government of this country, practically speaking, is no longer either a democracy, or a monarchy, nor a mixture of monarchy and democracy; but a usurped oligarchy, constituted by a set of borough-mongers, who have stolen at once the liberties of the people, and abused the prerogatives of the crown. To these men every species of reformation, every species of discussion, seems equally abhorrent and frightful.[16]

Most deputies, being predominantly part of the propertied elite, tended to distrust popular participation in any kind of politics. They were equally reluctant to recognise the potential of print to improve public understanding of what they were doing, or even to provide detail over and above brief formal proclamations. The most democratic of the French assemblies, the National Convention of 1792–5, was almost as socially exclusive as its predecessors and very well aware of its inability to command genuine popular support. Each French parliament of the 1790s had difficult relations with other representative organisations such as the Paris Commune, let alone the more populist activists amongst the *sans-culottes*.

As we will see shortly, independent newspaper reporting was also discouraged. However, in Paris, elections to the Estates General in the spring of 1789 had generated enough political momentum within some of the electoral districts to sustain not only a new form of permanent representative municipal government, meeting in the Hôtel de Ville, but also more decentralised local political activity arising from the sixty electoral assemblies. The most lively area was the Cordeliers district, the densely populated area of central Paris immediately south of the Île de la Cité, on the left bank, with its narrow streets, mixed population of traders and artisans, middling sorts and university students. Many of the most outspoken early revolutionary leaders lived there, including Danton, Desmoulins, Marat – as well as Royou, the editor of the ultra-royalist paper *L'Ami du Roi*.[17] Conveniently, the Cordeliers district also had a high concentration of printing workshops and booksellers.

When the electoral districts of Paris were reorganised into sections in 1790, the new Théâtre-Français section, which included the Cordeliers area, continued to sustain an exceptionally lively political culture, often determinedly independent both of the Paris communal assembly and of the National Assembly itself. A group of activists there constituted themselves as the Société des amis des droits de l'homme et du citoyen (Society of the Friends of the Rights of Man and the Citizen, often simply called the Cordeliers Club). Its membership fee was extremely low and, in

[16] John Thelwall, *The Tribune*, 25 (1795), cited in G. Claeys (ed.), *The politics of English jacobinism: writings of John Thelwall* (University Park, PA, 1995), 217.
[17] The geography of Paris naturally played a big role at key stages in the popular revolution and in the *journées révolutionnaires* (revolutionary days of action) themselves: see M. Rapport, *Rebel cities: Paris, London and New York in the age of revolution* (London, 2017), 201–35 and 261–96.

contrast to the Jacobin Club, it served as a training ground for populist democrats, grass-roots activists and radical reformers scrutinising and often criticising policies adopted by the mayor of Paris, Bailly, and by successive national assemblies and governments. The Cordeliers welcomed women (including for example Louise de Kéralio) and soon established links to various other sectional societies, including the Société Fraternelle des deux Sexes (from 1790). Significantly in the present context, the Cordeliers used print extensively, publishing speeches and reform proposals, sometimes using their own imprint (the Cordeliers Press). Already from October 1789 they also published extracts and registers of their deliberations, underlining their formal status by printing the names of the presiding officers: Danton, Prudhomme and others appeared in that capacity. Some of their publications appear to have been serialised, and at times they issued a form of political journal.[18]

From the start, the Cordeliers set new standards in the imaginative combination of intense verbal controversy and popular dissemination by print. However, we cannot track all of its activities well, as many of the manuscript records were destroyed in the Commune fire of 1871 and the published records leave a great many questions unanswered. The Cordeliers appear to have met at least once a week, sometimes daily, but the format of the meetings is not always clear. Although the membership soon amounted to several hundred, with activists joining from across the city, it is difficult to see who were the real drivers. The number of publications that can be linked to the Cordeliers Club is significant, if we include not just texts which specifically mention the Cordeliers, but also publications by individuals who are known to have been active in the club. Marat for example was a compulsive polemicist, sometimes signing himself as 'citizen of the Cordeliers district',[19] and openly exploiting his membership of the club for his own safety and reputation. The Cordeliers saw themselves as critical spokesmen for the popular revolution and (as the Society's formal name would suggest) as activists demanding rigorous implementation of the Declaration of the Rights of Man itself. A wide range of issues

---

[18] *Journal général, dédié au district des Cordeliers* (September 1789); and later the *Journal du Club des Cordeliers*, printed by the Cordeliers member Antoine-François Momoro in the Rue Serpente, who proudly proclaimed himself 'the first printer of liberty'. Momoro's venture only lasted ten issues (June–August 1791), with other issues seized when Momoro was arrested on 13 August as part of the clampdown after the Champ de Mars. Further documentation is found in A. Mathiez, *Le club des Cordeliers pendant la crise de Varennes et le massacre du Champ de Mars* (Geneva, 1975, reprinting the original 1910 edition).

[19] As in his *Appel à la nation* (Paris, 1790), a typically confrontational 67-page attack on the government.

were aired in print: the need for a new national treasury; complaints that food prices had not been brought under control; proposals for a reorganised citizens' militia (starting already in August 1789, so probably part of the discussions of the new National Guard); as well as attacks on the celibacy of priests. Interestingly, the Cordeliers were amongst the first to denounce the double-dealing corruption of Mirabeau during his funeral in 1791.[20] They also had to confront allegations of physical harassment in recurrent disputes with the Paris communal assembly or the National Assembly itself. The Cordeliers used a wide range of dissemination strategies: all kinds of printed material, but also petitions to higher authority, demonstrations and other forms of direct action. As we know, the Cordeliers took a lead in 1791 in the organisation of the republican petition at the Champ de Mars, were outraged when the National Guard opened fire on the demonstrators and protested vigorously in print when arrests were subsequently made.[21]

We should of course not assume that the Cordeliers had a coherent or even necessarily very precise agenda, but they were probably one of the most successful and consistently democratic (often oppositional) pressure groups in the critical years of the Revolution – 'democratic' in the sense of encouraging active political engagement amongst the middling and lower sorts who had had no say in politics before 1789 and who were meant to be 'passive' citizens under the new restrictive electoral rules of the National Assembly. The Cordeliers had far stronger grass-roots connections than the more elitist associations such as the Cercle Social or the Jacobin Club. Rachel Hammersley has analysed the ideological roots of the Cordeliers in depth, noting how they tried to resolve some of the inherent contradictions in Rousseau by updating and reusing other republican texts. In the process, she has revised our understanding of the origins of French republicanism as a whole, and its particular language, drawing our attention to extensive links with English republican thinking from Milton, Harrington and Nedham, through Algernon Sidney and Toland, to late eighteenth-century dissenting writers such as Richard Price. Significantly, already from the 1760s a number of French intellectuals had absorbed these texts enthusiastically: the baron d'Holbach had secretly organised a large number of translations into French, and Mirabeau had been keenly interested. Marat had studied

---

[20] *Addresse aux patriotes, sur les funérailles de Honoré Riquetti Mirabeau*, a short speech denouncing his corruption, delivered by an unnamed member in the Cordeliers and published under their imprint.

[21] *Arrestation nocturne de plusieurs membres du club des Cordeliers* (8 pages: Imprimerie de la liberté, Rue Serpente, Paris, 1791). There were a number of other publications arising directly from the Champ de Mars.

the texts when he was in England before the Revolution. One of the Cordeliers, Théophile Mandar, in 1790 published an actual translation of Nedham's *The excellence of a free state* (first published in London in 1656, but itself derived from editorials he had written in the Commonwealth paper *Mercurius Politicus*). The Cordeliers thus used English texts to help construct their own very influential radical political agenda.[22]

One of the fundamental concerns of the Cordeliers was how to make Rousseau's idealised small-scale participatory democracy work in larger states. Rousseau himself had tried to get round this problem in his *Considerations on the government of Poland,* but had done so by accepting a number of practical compromises, including recommending very cautious and gradual change to allow for the extreme inequalities in Polish society. In Paris from 1789, Hammersley argues, the Cordeliers adapted English republican thought to find ways of extending Rousseau and implementing a more democratic general will for the whole of France. In his newspaper *Révolutions de France et de Brabant,* Camille Desmoulins proposed shorter parliaments, stricter mandates for the deputies (requiring them to speak directly for their constituents) and of course full accountability and transparency. He and the Cordelier Réné Girardin also argued for new laws to be formally ratified by popular referenda – a demand that became all the more urgent when the king's aborted flight to Varennes (21 June 1791) failed to convince the National Assembly that the French monarchy was now demonstrably counter-revolutionary.[23] Varennes, and the resulting peaceful demonstration which turned into a massacre of unarmed citizens in Champ de Mars a few weeks later, galvanised not only the Cordeliers: newspaper editors such as Hébert, members of political societies and clubs, and much of the Jacobin and Cercle Social leadership now all had to confront this fundamental political problem.[24] For a while after Champ de Mars, political meetings were banned, and some controversial political publications were suppressed

---

[22] R. Hammersley, *French revolutionaries and English republicans: the Cordeliers Club, 1790–1794* (Woodbridge, 2005); R. Hammersley, *The English republican tradition and eighteenth-century France: between the ancients and the moderns* (Manchester, 2010).

[23] Hammersley, *French revolutionaries,* 32–55 and *passim.*

[24] Changes in normative political language are visible even in the titles of publications. We note a huge increase in titles which include variants of the word 'republican' – quite rare in 1790, but predictably becoming a flood from 1792 onwards, partly for polemical reasons, partly just as an obvious normative word in the political language of the revolutionary regime. Variants of 'democracy' were used in titles throughout the Revolution, but significantly more frequently in 1790 and from 1794. By contrast, the politically sensitive word 'mandataire' as applied to deputies (mandated to speak for those they had been elected to represent) was used sparingly in the years 1789–94 and disappears from 1795 onwards.

and their authors harassed. But the outbreak of war in April 1792, followed by successive and visible failures in government and the overthrow of the monarchy on 10 August, fostered a revival of popular political organisations accompanied by more aggressive newspaper reporting and pamphleteering.

The impact of French republican thinking on other parts of Europe was at first highly variable. Historians have tended to analyse it mostly within the confines of the histories of individual national cultures, often without comparative context. This has certainly brought out the fragmented and ambivalent nature of much contemporary comment, often reflecting the particular conditions under which texts were written and disseminated, within different jurisdictions. However, as always, we lack full access to popular opinion (in verbal discussion) amongst those who took an interest in events in France. A common assumption is that, in many parts of Europe, reports of events in France were initially welcomed with variable degrees of enthusiasm, but soon, especially with the start of war in April 1792, turned to alarm and cultural disassociation, at least in print.

In Britain, public reactions were compounded by the activities of a growing number of radical societies as well as counter-revolutionary loyalist organisations competing for public attention within the bigger cities in Britain. The Society of the Friends of the People, established in April 1792 by members of the political elite, adhered to a programme of moderate reform which might pre-empt more serious challenges. Their aims were promoted by seasoned campaigners and pamphleteers such as Christopher Wyvill, who published *A defence of Dr Price* (1792) and *A state of the representation of the people of England* (1793), advocating cautious political reform. More challenging was the populist London Corresponding Society (LCS), founded in January 1792 by the shoemaker Thomas Hardy (1752–1832). With a very low membership fee (a penny a week), it had a broad base among skilled craftsmen, artisans and shopkeepers, who addressed each other (in French style) as 'citizen'. Its membership grew rapidly, reaching 180 by April 1792 and an estimated 650 members later that year and through 1793.[25] It allowed for rapid expansion by creating subsidiary divisions for every twenty members: meeting weekly, these divisions stayed in close touch with the organisation as a whole through frequent elections of officeholders, correspondence and personal attendance.

---

[25] M. Thale (ed.), *Selections from the papers of the London Corresponding Society 1792–1799* (Cambridge, 1983), xxiv; see also M. Thale, 'London debating societies in the 1790s', *The Historical Journal*, 32 (1989), 57–86.

The LCS also fostered a network of affiliated societies across cities in England and lowland Scotland, with active cells in Sheffield, Manchester, Edinburgh and elsewhere – tactics that gave it a better chance of evading government reprisals than the Cordeliers had in Paris and made it very difficult for the government to monitor effectively. Extensive use of printed posters, pamphlets and newspaper advertising helped to ensure that the Society remained both visible and accessible, but also meant it was very exposed to infiltration by government spies (who soon reported systematically on all their activities and in due course could serve as prosecution witnesses in the trial of the leaders). The exceptional oratorical and polemical skills of key LCS members such as John Thelwall (1764–1834) and Maurice Margarot (1745–1815) ensured that the Society continued to attract substantial public support amongst the middling and lower sorts. It survived sustained attempts by the government to disrupt its meetings, prosecute individuals on charges of seditious libel (in print or word) and intimidate those who let meeting space to the Society. The government acted even more harshly in Scotland: following a Convention of reform societies in Edinburgh in December 1792, the activist lawyer Thomas Muir (1765–99) was accused of sedition, ostensibly for criticising the government in public meetings and encouraging people to read Paine's *Rights of man*. Muir, as the most powerful voice of reform in Scotland, was found guilty in August 1793 by a carefully chosen jury and sentenced to fourteen years' transportation.[26] Margarot and Joseph Gerrald (1763–96) were arrested when they went north to participate in the third Edinburgh Convention for constitutional reform in November, and both were convicted and also deported to Botany Bay.

In England, the continued success of the London and other Corresponding Societies persuaded the government to attempt progressively stronger proclamations against seditious meetings, and eventually take the drastic step of suspending Habeas Corpus (May 1794). A number of LCS leaders including Hardy and Thelwall could then easily be arrested and detained for months without charge. Other critics of the

---

[26] Disseminating Paine's work was by this stage in itself seditious, since Paine himself had been found guilty in December 1792 and his book banned. The prosecution, however, left little to chance: two weeks later, the Unitarian minister Thomas Fyshe Palmer was also found guilty of sedition, on much flimsier evidence, and given a seven-year sentence, with no right of appeal. Muir's trial, in particular, was reported extensively in print. However, lacking political or literary journals, Scottish readers otherwise lacked relevant reading: John Millar's few publications were quite general, and works such as James Mackintosh's response to Burke, *Vindiciae gallicae: defence of the French Revolution and its English admirers* (London, 1791), was never printed in Scotland. See also A. Plassart, *The Scottish Enlightenment and the French Revolution* (Cambridge, 2015); and R. B. Sher, *The Enlightenment and the book: Scottish authors and their publishers in eighteenth-century Britain, Ireland and America* (Chicago, 2006).

government who were not LCS members were also arrested, including the now veteran John Horne Tooke of the Society for Constitutional Information. Hardy and Thelwall were finally brought to trial in November 1794, on charges of high treason, but the prosecution over-reached itself in insisting on such a severe charge and spectacularly failed to secure convictions. In order to leave less room for uncertainty, further repressive legislation was passed, including the Sedition and Treason Acts (Two Acts) of December 1795, which extended the definition of treason and undermined the activities of nearly all political societies. Continuing tensions across Britain, food riots 1795–6, naval mutinies and, not least, the revolt in Ireland in 1798 gave the government excuses for further repressive measures. The LCS found it increasingly difficult to meet, let alone publish anything, but did not go completely underground until it was formally proscribed in 1799.[27]

Given its rapidly growing membership and sophisticated use of net-works, it is not difficult to see why the LCS was perceived by the British government as a major political threat, or portrayed as a British exten-sion of the French Cordeliers Club encouraging a form of *sans-culotte* activism. Its supporters published statements, addresses and reports and, although its parliamentary petitions were carefully moderated to minimise risks, the intentions of the Society were clear. The LCS also reprinted older texts such as *The Englishman's right* by John Hawles (first published in 1680) and *Constitutional maxims* by Charles Jenkinson (1757). From the start, the LCS campaigned for democratic change, including universal male suffrage, reform of parliamentary constituency boundaries and more frequent elections. Its *Address to the nation at large* (24 May 1792) linked the unnecessary burdens of taxation directly to the lack of political representation for the great majority of the 'indus-trious inhabitants of Great Britain', and bluntly noted that the 'constitution . . . has, by the violence and intrigue of criminal and design-ing men, been injured and undermined in its most essential and impor-tant parts'. Openly critical of the corruption of ministers and members of parliament, the *Address* made clear that the LCS would continue to meet as long as its grievances had not been resolved and would form open alliances with other organisations with similar aims. Members of the LCS were explicitly reminded that it was in the interest of all citizens to reverse the many restrictions on their political rights created over hundreds of years: the unreasonable raising of the franchise threshold; higher property qualifications for parliamentary candidates; longer intervals between parliamentary elections; and a disproportionately

---

[27] Thale, *Papers of the LCS*, editorial Introduction, xv–xxix, and *passim*.

low and very unevenly distributed electorate.[28] The ability of the LCS to win popular support for its radical politics throughout the period 1792–5, its strategy of holding well-organised and frequent meetings and its open sponsorship of a range of carefully prepared printed texts clearly had the British government rattled.

As with the Cordeliers, it is unclear how much of the LCS impact was achieved through print, how much through its many meetings. Indeed in such volatile political contexts, it makes little sense to distinguish print from oral communication. Nowhere is this more clearly illustrated than in the periodical publication *The Tribune*, largely written and published by John Thelwall, and running to fifty issues between March 1795 and April 1796. Some of the issues indicate (on the title page) that the text consisted of lecture transcripts taken down in shorthand by a friend of Thelwall and revised by him for publication. There is no reason to doubt this, since the text often includes explicit rhetorical devices, where Thelwall called on his audience as 'Citizens', or drew them in by markers such as 'Now, Citizens, I will come, if you please, to...' It appears from some of the issues that *The Tribune* was offered for sale at his lectures and also in bookshops, making these texts a convincing bridge between print and oral communication – much like influential parliamentarians in London or Paris having their speeches printed, except that in the case of Thelwall this was a continuous serial publication process. And since Thelwall (unlike his contemporary Thomas Paine) was by all accounts a very powerful and shrewd orator, easily able to organise a whole raft of political issues clearly for his audiences, his lectures do give us a real impression of what you could say at public meetings. Thelwall also gained a reputation for presenting forceful ideas in such a way that government spies and police agents consistently failed to have sufficient grounds to arrest him on the spot: in short, he was one of the most formidable subversive political polemicists of his age.

Thelwall was openly critical of the government both for fighting an unjust war against France (denying there was any threat to Britain's security) and for ignoring the heavy social and economic costs borne by the working population. He lamented the violence which had erupted in the French Revolution, but also used sometimes detailed discussion of French politics to make dangerous comparisons with the British government. Thus in a lecture delivered in May 1795, Thelwall said:

---

[28] Thale, *Papers of the LCS*, 11–14. This volume provides a thorough overview of the different types of printed publications issued by the Society and how spies reported in writing to the government.

I admit, and I think I shall by and by prove, that there were in the character of Robespierre many as great qualities, as magnificent virtues as ever adorned a human being; unfortunately, however, none of those great qualities and virtues were of that description that led to moderation. He had no philosophy, he had no social affections, he had none of those tender sympathies which soften the rugged character of the politician ... without which no character, however splendid, can either command or deserve the general admiration of mankind.

Thelwall then went on to elaborate on the flaws of Robespierre as a political leader, including references to Machiavelli, Danton and Desmoulins, noting how Robespierre above all hated those who simply did not agree with him. Describing the overthrow of the French monarchy on 10 August 1792 as a defeat for despotism and as a brave (if violent) defence of republican constitutionalism, Thelwall finished his lecture with a lengthy and blistering comparison of Robespierre with 'the immaculate minister of this country', William Pitt, whose government was silencing dissent, undermining the constitution and in effect behaving like the Terror government of Robespierre. Thelwall almost taunted the government by referring to his own earlier imprisonment:

I know well, citizens, what dangerous ground I tread upon: I know well that though treason *once meant compassing and imagining the death of the king*, it now means telling truth to the shame and confusion of Ministers ... I have no doubt, either, that there are persons here of various opinions: some of them, perhaps, good pious men, who, when they say their prayers, forget the name of God, and whisper Pitt.[29]

Even though this lecture was delivered well after the fall of Robespierre, such an extraordinary comparison of Robespierre and Pitt could hardly be ignored, given the size of audiences that Thelwall continued to attract.

But as Mark Philp argued some years ago, there were several different (and sometimes incompatible) ideologies of reform within the various radical groups in Britain. These created obstacles to collaboration between clusters such as the respectable Whigs of the Society for Constitutional Information, the followers of Tom Paine, those who wanted a French-style international revolution and various activists in the London, Sheffield or Manchester Corresponding Societies.[30] Since everything written for public dissemination was more muted and ambivalent than what was really intended, we can be sure that their real differences of aims and tactics were substantial. Such differences (explicit,

---

[29] *The Tribune*, issue 11 (23 May 1795), cited in Claeys (ed.), *The politics of English jacobinism*, 116–37.
[30] M. Philp, 'The fragmented ideology of reform', in M. Philp (ed.), *The French Revolution and British popular politics* (Cambridge, 1991), 50–77.

implicit, or invented by opponents) inevitably undermined any co-ordinated campaigns for reform and made it easier for conservatives to blame them all as irresponsible revolutionaries. Once Britain was involved in war, and government propaganda could make the most of national jingoism, political dissenters were more easily silenced. As in modern Britain before and after the Brexit referendum of 2016, meaningful discussion and reasoned evaluation were drowned out by emotional slogans, misinformation and crude oversimplifications.

By late 1792, however, a number of political societies had appeared in London and elsewhere protesting unconditional loyalty and defence of property. With a legacy of extra-parliamentary activism from Wilkes onwards, and knowledge of what the Cordeliers and others were doing in Paris, it was natural for British political organisations right across the spectrum to use a combination of meetings, newspaper reporting and pamphlet publications to broadcast their message. Accordingly, efforts were made to counteract proposals for reform by publishing hostile texts which linked radical reformers directly to French revolutionary upheaval, including its crowd violence, the trial of the king and the emergence of Terror government. In November 1792 John Reeves (1752–1829) founded and organised the Association for the Preservation of Liberty and Property against Republicans and Levellers, the initial purpose of which appears to have been to promote violence against anyone who could be labelled as radical and hence pave the way for the police to make arrests. Historians have disagreed about how strong the conservative arguments really were,[31] but there is no doubt that funding by the British government, combined with real concern over the violence in France, ensured overwhelming loyalist public support from an increasingly polarised public.

Keyword searches on the titles of English-language publications indicate that loyalist tracts of various kinds appearing throughout the 1790s became more outspoken late in 1792 specifically against demands for constitutional reform. The word 'constitution' occurred in the titles of no less than eighty-six items published in London in 1792, including a broadsheet from November 1792 produced by a 'Society for discouraging and suppressing seditious publications'. During 1793 more than a dozen printed addresses, petitions and polemics included effusive declarations of loyalty to the existing political regime. Some naturally also adopted a religious dimension: an anonymous pamphlet of 1793, ascribed to Thomas Witherby, purported to defend Christianity against

---

[31] M. Philp, *Reforming ideas in Britain: politics and language in the shadow of the French Revolution, 1789–1815* (Cambridge, 2014), 40–101.

Joseph Priestley,[32] whose sustained campaign to secure toleration and civic rights for dissenters was still causing controversy. However, as with traditional policies of censorship, it proved difficult for conservatives to make an intellectually strong case for tradition without engaging in the kind of detailed political discussion that they wanted to avoid. Few loyalists of the middling sorts, let alone the aristocratic political elite, had any desire to educate, or engage with, the 'industrious' or lower levels of society, fearing that would merely release a Pandora's box of insubordination and popular violence. An anonymous publication (London, 1794) offered *An account of the treason and sedition committed by the London Corresponding Society, the Society for Constitutional Information [and other named societies]* based on reports to Parliament.

Those who advocated loyalty and respect for the existing political order, however, soon developed more sophisticated ideas and strategies.[33] Patriotism, civil order and preservation of the 'constitution' often had a strong emotional component which could be used to close down actual balanced discussion. Respect for political and religious tradition did not require rational explanation, but exploited strong resonances within British society, especially as the contrasts with France became increasingly apparent. Authors such as Hannah More (1745–1833) took it upon themselves to write small and cheap publications for readers of limited means, encouraging traditional order without pursuing the more aggressively chauvinist tactics of some of her contemporaries. Reeves himself pushed political tradition to its limits when he published *Thoughts on English government* (1795), which defended royal prerogative so vociferously that it was rejected by senior politicians including the long-serving prime minister, Pitt. But a much more subtle and entertaining confirmation of traditional values was encapsulated in the brilliant satirical cartoons of James Gillray (1756–1815), whose

---

[32] [Thomas Witherby], *To the great and learned among Christians, the humble petition of a number of poor, loyal, unlearned Christians. Together with plain questions, stated for direct and unequivocal answers, to Joseph Priestley, LL.D. F.R.S. And other the champions of what they call reformation. The whole intended to represent these innovators to public view in their true colours, And to shew that attachment to the Christian religion, as recorded in the sacred scriptures, is the best preservative to the peace of the state, and the welfare of mankind* (London, 1793), 76 pages in octavo format, cost one shilling. Priestley, already one of the main targets of the 'Church-and-King' riots in Birmingham in July 1791, where his house was burnt down, had resettled in London but remained committed to the cause of constitutional and religious reform. He migrated to the United States in 1794.

[33] M. Philp, 'Vulgar conservatism, 1792–93', *English Historical Review*, 110 (1995), 42–69; M. McCormack, 'Rethinking "loyalty" in eighteenth-century Britain', *Journal for Eighteenth-Century Studies*, 35 (2012), 407–21; on the many-layered identities discernible in this period, see L. Colley, *Britons: forging the nation 1707–1837* (London and New Haven, CT, 1992); and C. Evans, *Debating the revolution: Britain in the 1790s* (London, 2006).

imagery summed up with extraordinary and powerful simplicity many of the current controversies in British political and social life, in ways that must have attracted viewers from right across the political and social spectrum. Gillray's mastery of visual symbolism (visual rhetoric) was far too sophisticated for viewers to regard him as merely a government propagandist, and few would have found his portrayal comforting. But he does remind us that political controversies in Britain in the 1790s cannot always be fitted neatly within 'conservative' and 'radical' labels and that the participants knew how to exploit the complex emotional as well as intellectual dimensions of contemporary controversies.

If both Paris and London produced a wealth of political material in the 1790s, we also need to recognise that print continued to be heavily self-censored: in both cities, if for different reasons, authors had to tread with great caution to avoid reprisals either from government or from vigilante crowds. Political activism may at first have found freer expression in meetings and informal discussion, with less risk than in print. But from 1794 there was good reason to worry about riots, as full-scale economic crisis and acute food shortages compounded the burden of war. In Britain, the government exploited fears of unrest in order to create support for the suspension of Habeas Corpus and then made generous use of treason charges against reform-minded individuals, notably those involved in the Conventions for reform in Edinburgh in 1793 and many relatively moderate reformers in London in 1794. In France, the policies of the Terror government of 1793–4 were designed not just to achieve forced unity behind the war effort, but also systematically to undermine freedom of expression, intimidate political opponents by denunciations of conspiracy and increasingly use short-circuited judicial procedures to apply the death penalty without appeal. After Thermidor, the dismantling of Parisian sectional assemblies, and more particularly the suppression of the *sans-culotte* riots in Germinal and Prairial of Year III (April–May 1795), made any popular revolutionary movement unsustainable. By that stage, in any case, the real military threat from France had reduced the domestic opinion in most of Europe into something powered by nationalism and wartime propaganda.

Further Responses in Print

If democracy might ideally be characterised not only by regular elections but also by meaningful and well-informed political discussion conducted in the spirit of freedom of opinion and expression, then clearly by 1794 both the French and the British governments were utterly resistant to moving in that direction. But for historians, the repressive policies of both governments tend to create a potentially misleading impression of the impact of popular politics, making it difficult to ascertain whether the alleged links between texts and political activism was anything more than scare-mongering. John Barrell has provided a multi-layered discussion of the ways political division pervaded Britain in the years 1792–5 and the many levels at which political culture could operate. His thorough exploration of the subtly changing and contested interpretations of the Statute of Treason (dating back to 1351) not only takes us through the extensive material arising from the sedition and treason trials of 1793–4, but also explores the battles over words and interpretations. Disputed interpretations were a crucial component of the political imaginary and imagination, and of public political discourse more generally, during these troubled years. He notes how fears for the life of George III were understandable enough, especially given the impact in Britain of the trial and execution of Louis in France, as reflected in words and cartoons. Barrell also shows how public opinion genuinely tended to side with the government, no doubt for the sake of preserving what was portrayed as a precarious but stable constitution and political culture.[34]

But compared with France, the threat of revolutionary republican radicalism in Britain was never more than hypothetical. The small group of radicals involved had no prospect of initiating the violent revolution that the government feared. In reality, neither radical challenges nor the aggressive government response in Britain can be compared to the extreme confrontations in France both during the Terror and in the anarchy after Thermidor. Yet, as both London and Paris experienced deeper political divisions than anywhere in Europe in the 1790s, it is tempting to speculate how far readers in one city could access the polemics and evolving political cultures of the other, and might even learn from what they read.

As we will note below, digests and reports in the newspapers in either city did not offer anything remotely resembling a reliable impression of the true political currents of the other. And although the educated elite in both countries no doubt had access to primary texts in the language across the Channel, it is unlikely that language skills amongst the middling sorts or lower would be up to such reading. Even so, both Joseph Priestley and Thomas Paine were already sufficiently familiar to French readers to be nominated and elected as deputies to the French Convention in September 1792. Significantly, Priestley declined on the grounds that

---

[34] J. Barrell, *Imagining the king's death: figurative reason, fantasies of regicide 1793–1796* (Oxford, 2000); and his *The spirit of despotism: invasions of privacy in the 1790s* (Oxford, 2006).

his command of French was not up to the challenge. Perhaps Paine should have made the same decision, as his understanding of French seemed little better. But the charges brought against him in Britain in May 1792 (over part 2 of his *Rights of man*) turned his visit to France into permanent exile, so he accepted a seat in the Convention. In part because of his poor grasp of French, his few substantive speeches in the French parliament (translated by friends and read out on his behalf) led to very serious and fundamental misunderstandings and political misjudgments on his part, and his influence on French politics became counter-productive.[35] His later publications, notably his powerful pamphlet on the *Decline and fall of the English system of finance* (1796) and the extremely controversial *Agrarian justice* (1797), were written for the English and American market. French renditions of these books appear to have had only limited dissemination and negligible impact.

How widely was Paine read in English? We can readily discount the over-generous estimates of his friends, but even on the more rigorous assumptions of William St Clair, the *Rights of man* may have sold more than 20,000 copies[36] – probably as many as Burke's *Reflections on the Revolution in France* (1790), to which Paine was trying to respond. It is impossible to estimate the print run of Paine's *English system of finance* and his *Agrarian justice*, but each of them may have run to a dozen reprints (in London, Dublin and in America). The *English system of finance* attacked the speculative nature of British government finance and the irresponsi-bility of banks in sustaining artificial credit – Paine used language that would not be out of place to modern readers after the 2008 credit crunch. The text was well enough buttressed by means of selective quantitative evidence that the British government felt obliged to commission explicit rebuttals. But even though he was in Paris, Paine made few explicit references to French political ideas, focusing instead on the need for social and institutional reform to help reduce poverty and inequality. For Thelwall, the choice of argumentative strategy may have been differ-ent: he was more inclined to consider the democratic potential of sub-stantive political reform and clearly knew about developments in France, but rarely used that knowledge in his lectures, no doubt because he recognised it could be counterproductive.

Paine was by French standards very moderate and was focusing on generic issues of good government, social fairness and fiscal responsibility.

---

[35] T. Munck, 'The troubled reception of Thomas Paine in France, Germany, the Netherlands and Scandinavia', in S. P. Newman and P. S. Onuf (eds.), *Paine and Jefferson in the age of revolutions* (Charlottesville, 2013), 161–82; but see also C. Lounissi, *Thomas Paine and the French Revolution* (Basingstoke, 2018).

[36] W. St Clair, *The reading nation in the Romantic period* (Cambridge, 2004), 624.

In France, the spectrum of political opinion was much wider and the political extremism of 1792–4 was clearly visible in print, not least in the newspapers. Significantly, the last of the outstanding thinkers of the French Enlightenment also tried to influence public opinion: Condorcet worked intermittently on his *Outline of an historical view of the progress of the human mind,* still incomplete at the time of his arrest and death in March 1794 but published posthumously in 1795.[37] Amongst the Thermidorians, we might note the writings of the last major popular revolutionary, François-Noël [Gracchus] Babeuf (1760–97), who continued to call for the restoration of true democracy and a genuine implementation of the socially levelling policies implied in the Declaration of Rights of 1793. He launched his *Tribun du Peuple* late in 1794 (as a continuation of his periodical *Journal de la Liberté de la Presse*), but his enthusiasm for a revival of Terror policies and for substantive property redistribution earned his Society of Equals such a reputation that he was arrested in May 1796 on charges of conspiracy, and eventually brought to trial and executed a year later. His extreme political views made it easy for the government to secure his conviction, in effect ending any hopes of radical reforms in France for another generation.

Everywhere in Europe, the French Revolution jolted opinion and alerted readers to the need for change, but reactions in print were mostly subdued and cautious. The Dutch, whose lively political culture in the 'patriot times' of the 1780s had created a substantial and distinctive print output, had no way of avoiding entanglement in the new French developments. Much more research is needed on print in the Netherlands in the 1780s and 90s, but so far it seems that Dutch political caution may have been accentuated as a result of the economic and diplomatic setbacks of the 1780s – the Anglo-Dutch War of 1780–4 and the Prussian military occupation that brought the Patriot revolt to a sudden end in 1787. Van der Capellen's polemic of 1781, *Address to the people of the Netherland,* was not reprinted until 1795, even though a few authors did respond in separate publications.[38] Other writers such as Adriaan Kluit had some success with discussions of commercial policies and good government. In the print titles of the early 1790s, it is interesting to observe certain expressions becoming more frequent, including 'rights

---

[37] [Jean-Antoine-Nicolas de Caritat, marquis de] Condorcet, *Esquisse d'un tableau historique des progrès de l'esprit humain* (Paris, Year III, 1794/95). At nearly 400 pages in octavo, this was never likely to be a bestseller, but significantly it was published with a state subsidy in France in 1795 and also attracted immediate interest in the English-speaking world, with printings in London, Dublin and Philadelphia (1795–6).

[38] Joan Derk Van der Capellen, *Aan het volk van Nederland* (Ostende, 1781; reprinted Amsterdam, 1795; also English translation of the first printing, with the title as given here, London, 1782).

of man' (in connection with Thomas Paine's work, and later), and 'liberty' (predictably clustered around discussion of French ideas and the constitutions of 1793 and 1795). Keeping watch on developments in France soon acquired overwhelming importance, as French troops were in the Austrian Netherlands in 1793 and more permanently in 1794. Those Dutch patriots who from 1787 had fled south naturally supported the programme of French revolutionary 'liberation' of neighbouring countries (proclaimed in November 1791) and so became part of a new revolutionary agenda. Patriot writers such as Gerrit Paape (1752–1803) used print to disseminate a new consensus-based republican thinking which secured broad popular support for the overthrow of the moribund stadtholderate of William V. So although the Batavian Republic was established with French assistance in January 1795, and turned the Dutch into a 'sister republic' of the French state, it had genuinely widespread support amongst Dutch republicans[39] and, as demonstrated in the elections of 1796, a more genuinely democratic foundation than what had been achieved even in France itself by that stage.

It is instructive to see how print was used elsewhere, in the 1790s, to help bolster political stability within a variety of different governmental structures. Already in 1772, Sweden had turned back on its short-lived abolition of censorship, as part of the authoritarian policies of Gustavus III. His enthusiasm for French culture did not extend to its subversive elements, and the outbreak of revolution in France merely confirmed his reactionary politics. His assassination in 1792 was used as justification for tighter control of what could be published in print. In quite striking contrast, Denmark-Norway moved in the opposite direction: the resourceful reformist ministerial team of 1786, although in charge of ostensibly the most centralised of all the absolute monarchies, took an unusually relaxed attitude to open discussion of political and social reform, at least until 1795 – with very sparing use of legal prosecution or censorship and only for a few extreme cases. Significantly, although power-sharing was never on the agenda, public discussion of enlightenment and moderate reform in Copenhagen remained lively well into the 1790s.[40]

No such generalisations are possible for the German lands, since conditions for the discussion of political questions varied enormously. As in

---

[39] A. Jourdan, 'The Netherlands in the constellation of the eighteenth-century Western revolutions', *European Review of History*, 18 (2011), 190–225; W. R. E. Velema, *Republicans: essays on eighteenth-century Dutch political thought* (Leiden, 2007); see also N. van Sas, 'The Netherlands, 1750–1813', in H. Barker and S. Burrows (eds.), *Press, politics and the public sphere in Europe and North America, 1760–1820*' (Cambridge, 2002), 48–68.

[40] T. Munck, 'Public debate, politics and print: the late Enlightenment in Copenhagen during the years of the French Revolution 1786–1800', *Historisk Tidsskrift*, 114 (2014), 323–52.

Britain and elsewhere, the early stages of French constitutional parliamen-
tarianism were cautiously welcomed. But crowd violence and *sans-culotte*
activism were almost universally condemned, and German writings tried to
avoid anything that might resemble '*sans-culotte*' demands or denunciations. Historical accounts of the Revolution were a favoured form of writing, whereby different strands could be emphasised (or ignored). Already
in 1790, for example, Ernst Brandes published his first account of the
French Revolution, explaining that he assumed his readers had followed
developments in the newspapers but were looking for an analysis of
whether a revolution in France was necessary at all and whether it could
have been achieved without popular violence. Brandes also asked what the
Revolution might mean for the German lands, but carefully evaded any
precise answer by noting that opinions would differ widely and that he was
merely seeking ways of securing freedom.[41] By 1792 he had published
another volume, which he felt obliged to revise and reprint the
following year, adding an outright condemnation of the aggravated violence in France from August 1792 onwards. He explained defensively that,
as an employee of the administration of Hannover, he was totally content
with the policies of that state and its overlord, the British crown.[42] Brandes
also noted that the impact of the French Revolution on public opinion
differed across the Holy Roman Empire and that amongst the thousands of
German writers engaging with events in France, there was little agreement.
He noted that the only text that could lay claim to being a 'democratic
gospel' (*Evangelium*) was Thomas Paine's *Rights of man,* which Brandes
thought was weak by comparison with some of the work produced by the
French themselves.[43]

Several interesting techniques were used by German writers to convey
some of the complexity of what was happening in France to their respectable reading public. A professor of philosophy at Halle, Johann August
Eberhard, published a two-volume compendium on government and constitutions, arranged under keywords so as to make a convenient political
reference work. Again it was not a large book, so he no doubt intended it for
students and general informed readers. Using the flexibility of separate
entries, Eberhard could tackle a range of subjects, from actual constitutions, the legal framework needed for civic society, equality (with

---

[41] E. Brandes, *Politische Betrachtungen über die französische Revolution* (Jena, 1790) –
a modest volume of 152 pages in octavo, so no doubt intended for a general audience,
though not a populist one.
[42] E. Brandes, *Ueber einige bisherige Folgen der französischen Revolution, in Rücksicht auf
Deutschland* (Hanover, 1792) with the revised edition (Hanover, 1793) carefully explaining in its preface that the author was addressing some issues raised by readers.
[43] Brandes, *Folgen,* 112–19.

a reference to Condorcet), despotism, as well as *Volksdespotismus* (popular despotism), and of course enlightenment and stability.[44] A more conventional moralising approach was adopted by the prolific writer Johann Ludwig Ewald,[45] while by the mid-1790s Christoph Girtanner adopted a more anecdotal approach, in what he called an Almanac, which, generously printed and nearly 400 pages long, was clearly intended for a more discerning readership.[46] Many authors adhered to a predominantly philosophical and moralistic discussion of the 1790s, but that did not preclude controversy. Thus the ageing Osnabrück official Justus Möser tried to defend the old hierarchical order and its inherent social inequality, but also (with his friend, the Berlin publisher Nicolai) became involved in a bitter dispute with the formidable philosopher Kant over issues of reasoning and moral principles.[47] Reactions to the French Revolution clearly took many forms and could be argued at different levels, but most commentators assumed that German political structures were sufficiently robust and diverse to withstand challenges from France.

Only a few German texts promoted an openly radical or subversive line of argument. One such work, attributed to Andreas Georg Friedrich Rebmann in 1796, was published under the pseudonym Huergelmer, with a strange title which can be translated as *Political zodiac*. This was a long-winded and florid text, loosely organised into twenty-four sections, but clearly conveying a Jacobin message attacking aristocracy, hypocrisy and the exploitative elite all over Europe, not least in Germany. The book expressed regrets that simple and pure values in human existence had been forgotten, including liberty itself. It also provided an index of the sins of war, aligned with the misguided priorities of rulers. It is difficult to see what kind of readership such a book might have been intended for, but at 544 pages it can hardly be described as a populist pamphlet, especially taking into account the difficult economic environment and sluggish book market.[48]

Some readers may have been more interested in pursuing the long-running discussion of natural rights and the law. Ludwig Höpfner had published a text in 1780 which had been reprinted regularly as a textbook and reached

[44] J. A. Eberhard, *Ueber Staatsverfassung und ihre Verbesserung: ein Handbuch für deutsche Bürger und Bürgerinnen aus den gebildeten Ständen* (2 vols., 143 and 134 pages, Berlin, 1793–4).

[45] J. L. Ewald, *Über Revolutionen* (Berlin, 1793).

[46] C. Girtanner, *Almanach der Revolutions-Character für das Jahr 1796* (Chemnitz, 1796).

[47] J. B. Knudsen, *Justus Möser and the German Enlightenment* (Cambridge, 1986), 164–86, has a brief overview of some of these disputes. See also P. E. Selwyn, *Everyday life in the German book trade: Friedrich Nicolai as bookseller and publisher in the age of Enlightenment* (University Park, PA, 2000).

[48] Huergelmer [A. G. F. Rebmann], *Der politische Thierkreis oder die Zeichen unserer Zeit* ('Strasburg' [Altona?], no date but probably 1796). There were other animal allegories in this period, often intended as a way of disguising the true meaning to avoid prosecution.

its fifth edition in 1790. Texts of this kind typically covered the whole period from the Reformation onwards: significantly, Höpfner provided commentaries on a number of key figures in natural law, from Buchanan, Grotius and Selden, through Hobbes, to Thomasius, Burlamaqui and others, giving an interesting overview of individual rights, law and rights in civil society while summarising balanced and law-bound governance. The book did not delve into problem areas and was obviously meant as a safe guide rather than as something that would trigger discussion.[49] There were many other books on natural rights in civil society, for example by L.F. Fredersdorff (1790) and by K.J. Wedekind (1793), indicating substantial demand at least in the German academies. Rather less conventional were the works in which authors began to explore the connections between natural rights and human rights in a more imaginative way. Thus Johann Georg Heinzmann in 1795 published a very substantial volume construed as an *Address to my nation,* where he discussed how best to spread knowledge and understanding of the 'freedom and rights of mankind', noting the importance of translators, book-traders, freedom of the press and reprintings.[50] By then, in part thanks to the controversies created by Paine, the term *Menschenrecht* (right of man, human right)[51] had become part of the political and natural law debate across Europe. There were also new German translations and reprints in the 1790s of works by Rousseau, Paine and others, and a more successful translation (by Christian Garve) of Adam Smith's *Wealth of nations.* Significantly, the first ever German translation of Hobbes's *Leviathan* was published in 1794–5 (using the Latin version of 1668, but without its uncompromising Appendix).

Making and Shaping the News

The French Revolution provided a huge and seemingly unending flow of extraordinary news for papers all over Europe. Political weekly and monthly journals struggled to contain the large volume of material from France within their compact format. Even literary reviews responded by

---

[49] L. J. F. Höpfner, *Naturrecht des einzelnen Menschen, der Gesellschaften und der Völker* (Giessen, 1790).

[50] J. G. Heinzmann, *Appel an meine Nation: über Aufklärung und Aufklärer* (546 pages, published at the author's expense, Bern, 1795), which was also an attack on what he saw as the predominance of rationalism and commercialism in the north-German book market.

[51] Exact translations can be problematic in the case of concepts which are as context-sensitive as this. The German word *Menschenrecht* was often used in the singular, but plural forms (*Rechte*) also occur, as in Heinzmann's works cited above. In French and German, the discussion usually pivoted on the assumption of composite 'rights of man' (*droits de l'homme*).

commenting on the many writings with a revolutionary dimension, such as travel accounts, histories, academic publications and even fiction. Because of the importance of France as a major power, and the resulting demand for information, new paper and journal titles appeared in most major cities, some of them gaining a permanent footing. London, Paris, Amsterdam, Hamburg and a number of cities along the main trade routes of north-western Europe thus became effective news hubs. Many smaller provincial towns started to produce their own local papers, often relying on summaries or reports lifted from bigger papers, and surviving if they could sell a few hundred copies. In France itself, many newspapers relied on quarterly or annual subscriptions for much of their revenue, but as they typically cost 30 livres in annual subscription, they were beyond the means of workers on a basic wage of 400 to 450 livres per annum. However, some papers adopted a different strategy to increase their sales: thus the very informative *Feuille Villageoise* simplified distribution by being weekly rather than daily, and at just over 7 livres annually (post free) could reach modest-income readers, including groups in towns and villages who took out joint subscriptions. In bigger cities across Europe, newspapers were routinely available in coffee houses to anyone who could afford to buy a refreshment.[52]

As we noted in the previous chapter, the 1763 peace settlement and the revolt of the American colonies had already provided large amounts of news and a significant expansion of the newspaper industry. In Britain, the American revolt inevitably divided public opinion, but for most Europeans the political earthquake of the French Revolution was of a totally different order of magnitude. Such immediacy also created its own complications, as newspaper editors everywhere struggled with the domestic political fallout within both the governments and the political elites of France's neighbours. When military conflict started to engulf the major powers between April 1792 and February 1793, domestic reactions put enormous pressure even on moderate discussion, let alone dissent. Some governments (including the British) reacted very aggressively against independent-minded editors, while others used more subtle ways of discouraging newspaper interest in democracy or radical reform. It is far beyond the scope of this chapter to attempt an overview of the press in Europe in the 1790s, but select case studies may give some impression of what readers could find in the major papers of the time.

Within France itself, the initial collapse of censorship and print regulation not only made the publishing business much more competitive, but

---

[52] A useful overview of the costs and sales of newspapers is found in H. Gough, *The newspaper press in the French Revolution* (London, 1988), 195–228.

also encouraged some journalists to experiment in their style of writing and presentation.[53] Some deputies, such as Mirabeau, tried their hand at self-promoting newsletters which were nominally intended for their constituents. Some previously marginal writers tried to gain influence by attempting a political account, or by experimenting with single-sheet papers that could be run off on a small press two or three times a week. The more substantial daily *Journal de Paris,* which had started back in 1777, continued to provide local and commercial information. But the most ambitious new paper was the *Gazette Nationale* (also known as the *Moniteur Universel*), launched in November 1789 as an attempt by Panckoucke to sustain his former privileged status as purveyor of official news. Printed in folio format in three columns, the *Moniteur* was designed to appear distinctive and soon established itself as the most factually informative political newspaper in revolutionary France. Concentrating on high-level national politics, it gave detailed accounts of parliamentary proceedings and other major events, published transcripts or summaries of significant parliamentary speeches and provided a contextual survey of international news. Later, it even added retrospective issues back to May 1789, in order to create a daily narrative of the Revolution as if the paper had started then.

Other writers ventured into more troubled waters. The best-known was Jean-Paul Marat, who had spent ten years in England, and from 1777 earned a reputation in Paris as a medic and scientific writer, before turning to politics and joining the Cordeliers Club. Determined to make an impression, he launched a newspaper in September 1789 under the title *L'Ami du Peuple* (*Friend of the People*). Apart from a few gaps when Marat had to hide from the authorities, the paper appeared daily until September 1792 (when as newly elected deputy to the Convention, he launched another journal). From the start Marat experimented with

[53] The French newspaper press of the 1790s has understandably been more fully researched than that of any other part of Europe. Good starting points include J. R. Censer, *Prelude to power: the Parisian radical press 1789–1791* (Baltimore, 1976); J. D. Popkin, *The right-wing press in France 1792–1800* (Chapel Hill, NC, 1980); W. J. Murray, *The right-wing press in the French Revolution 1789–92* (Woodbridge, 1986); Gough, *The newspaper press in the French Revolution*; J. D. Popkin, *Revolutionary news: the press in France 1789–1799* (Durham, NC, 1990), who looks more closely at the journalists, printing workshops, readers and market factors shaping the newspaper industry in the 1790s; H. Chisick (ed.), *The press in the French Revolution* (*SVEC* 287, Oxford, 1991); J.-P. Bertaud, 'An open file: the press under the Terror', in K. M. Baker (ed.), *The French Revolution and the creation of modern political culture*, vol. IV (Oxford, 1994), 297–308. See also the comprehensive background information in J. Sgard (ed.), *Dictionnaire des journaux (1600–1789): édition électronique revue, corrigée et augmentée* (online at http://dictionnaire-journaux.gazettes18e.fr), and in J. Sgard (ed.), *Dictionnaire des journalistes 1600–1789* (Oxford, 1999).

a highly personal and recognisable style of journalism which, much like pamphleteering, was meant to appeal directly to a wider Parisian readership. He did include political news, but often used it as a lead into aggressive and personalised invective against public figures, sometimes calling for popular action against conspirators and corrupt aristocratic parasites exploiting 'the people'. *L'Ami du Peuple* is estimated to have had a circulation of 3–4000 copies by January 1791 and was pirated several times. After Marat's murder on 13 July 1793, other journalists adopted his title and style of writing.

Unlike Hébert's very successful *Le père Duchesne* (September 1790 to March 1794), Marat's paper did not use deliberately coarse language or ostentatious vulgarisation, preferring blunt provocation instead.[54] A typical example is the way he responded to the declaration by the National Assembly that the king's attempted flight to Varennes (20–21 June 1791) had in reality been a treasonous kidnap. Marat described this declaration as 'odious', deflecting blame from the 'infamous monarch':

It is not enough, for these infidel declaration-forgers, to ensure the impunity of this conspirator-king, they also deprive the nation of the right to deny him their confidence which he has lost for all time. They cover him in a mantel of innocence, and replace him, on their private authority, on the throne which he has abdicated. They call him back to the centre of the legislative body, [with] all of whose laws he has trampled underfoot. They place him at the head of the people he has betrayed, and on whom he has brought all the disasters of civil war. They go further, and presume to impose silence on the nation. . .[55]

The ultra-royalist *Les Actes des Apôtres* responded rather differently to this same crisis. The paper, which appeared irregularly (usually two or three times weekly) from November 1789 to January 1792, was edited by a group around Jean-Gabriel Peltier – allegedly sometimes scribbled on a table cloth as they drank a few glasses. They included some political news, but usually in order to mock radical politics and resist popular activism. The issues were not all dated, but in the summer of 1791, around the same time as Marat's denunciation above, number 272 of *Les Actes des Apôtres* noted ironically that after merely two years of anarchy since October 1789, the king would soon be restored to his rightful place,

---

[54] Both Marat and Hébert have been studied extensively, but their styles of journalism are succinctly analysed in Popkin, *Revolutionary news,* 146–68.

[55] Marat, *L'Ami du Peuple, ou le publiciste Parisien, journal politique et impartial,* issue 502, Sunday 26 June 1791, p. 7. Both Marat and Hébert excelled at denunciation, both of general conspiracies and of personal enemies: see A. de Baecque, 'La dénonciation publique dans la presse et le pamphlet (1789–1791)', in Chisick (ed.), *The press in the French Revolution,* 261–79.

the army returned to discipline, state finances revived by a constant renewal of trustworthy treasury staff and public opinion brought back under the control of public administrators – at which point 'without any doubt the memory of our convulsions, our destructions, our massacres and our penury will soon fade from our minds ... and we will also agree that we are wiser than we were during this interregnum to which our constitution will bring an eternal end. Amen.'[56]

Far less provocative, and more informative, was *La Feuille Villageoise*, a weekly started in September 1790 and edited by Joseph-Antoine Cerutti, Rabaut St Etienne, Pierre-Louis Ginguené and others. Being intended as a summary of information for provincial and rural France, it evidently filled a real gap, gaining very wide circulation (claimed to be 15,000 copies at its best).[57] Impressively, and perhaps because of its moderation and political adaptability, it survived right through the revolutionary period. Its reporting of major national events was detailed and thorough, without being sensationalist. The reporting of the trial of the king, for example, started on 13 December 1792 with a short notice that the Convention had heard a number of points of view of how to proceed, and on 6 December had approved a decree accepting the recommendations of its special commissions, allowing it to confirm a formal timetable to hear the charges against Louis Capet and his responses to a set of predetermined questions. Since that hearing had already taken place (on 11 December) the paper could provide a report of Louis's defence, which it considered important enough to print in full, even though it suggested the facts of the case were clear. It also reported the questioning of Louis before the Convention, printing a full transcript including Louis's rather short and mostly evasive answers. To these were added the specific questions regarding the documentary evidence which had been laid before Louis, again with his evasive answers. The president of the Convention was thus reported as asking Louis: 'Do you not recognise your handwriting and your signature? Louis: No. The president: The seal has the coat of arms of France? Louis: Many individuals had [use of] it.'[58]

In subsequent issues, the four roll-call votes were duly reported, with summaries of the main arguments and tallies of the votes cast. *La Feuille*

---

[56] Issue 272 of *Les Actes des Apôtres*, 6–7. Openly right-wing newspapers disappeared or were suppressed in August 1792, at the fall of the monarchy, though as noted by Popkin, *The right-wing press in France*, 84–99, new papers developed ways of criticising the government that were less vulnerable to government reprisals.

[57] M. Edelstein, 'La Feuille Villageoise and rural political modernisation', in Chisick (ed.), *The press in the French Revolution*, 237–60, discusses the likely readership and distribution of this unusual journal and the reasons for its success.

[58] *La Feuille Villageoise*, vol. III, issue 11 (13 Dec 1792), 256–9 and issue 12 (20 December 1792), 267–84.

Villageoise noted that a whole parliamentary session was devoted to checking the precise number of votes cast on each question, whereby 'it was found that the number of deputies voting for the death penalty amounts to 394, with a majority (previously reported as merely five votes) on the contrary confirmed as 26'. The paper noted the formal verdict pronounced against Louis. It described the subsequent requests made by Louis to a delegation charged by the Convention to visit him in his prison cell – requests which were granted, except for his wish for a three-day postponement. Finally it detailed events of the day leading up to the execution and burial. The paper reminded its readers that 'whatever opinion one may have on this large question', there were three fundamentally clear points: that the whole Convention had agreed almost unanimously that Louis had conspired against the liberty and security of the state, for which the law prescribed the death penalty; that any decision to the contrary could be argued solely on grounds of political expediency, which meant that the Convention might be deemed imprudent, but not unjust; that whatever opinion one might have had of those who voted for the death penalty, a great number were 'enlightened men, honest people and true patriots, who cannot be suspected of having been guided by any motive other than those of justice and the safety of the Republic'[59] In short, *La Feuille Villageoise* provided its readers with a report which was sufficiently detailed and factually accurate to enable readers to judge for themselves and as neutral as one could expect from any paper at the time. The paper lasted until August 1795, accepted as a genuinely useful weekly.

The Revolution continued to produce new styles of journalism, even during the dark years of the Terror. Amongst the most outspoken was *Le vieux Cordelier,* a political journal run by the Convention deputy Camille Desmoulins from December 1793 until his arrest and execution by the Terror regime (alongside Danton, 30 March to 5 April 1794). It only had six issues, the seventh remaining in proofs when Desmoulins was arrested (and eventually published long after Thermidor, in 1795). The title itself hinted at the hope of a return to the fundamental political values of the early Cordeliers Club, which, as noted earlier, was itself based on major republican writings. Initially Desmoulins appears to have had the support of his friend Robespierre, but as the paper became more critical of the authoritarian Terror regime, the two fell out. It is not difficult to see why: *Le vieux Cordelier* was never a populist paper like Marat's. Its style and language was clearly intended for an educated and politicised readership and was totally at odds with, for example, the demagoguery of Hébert's *Le*

---

[59] *La Feuille Villageoise*, issue 17 (24 January 1793), 402–7.

père Duchesne. Desmoulins used extensive references to republican Rome as a means of advocating democratic government in revolutionary France, free speech and individual rights.[60] He used characters from ancient history as referents for the current leaders of the revolutionary government, though he also increasingly appealed directly to them by name. In issue 5 (25 December 1793), a much longer piece, he was openly and self-consciously challenging the Committee of Public Safety, obstinately courting retribution.

By the time Desmoulins was arrested, he had corrected the proofs of issue 7, so we can read that text as an example of what was unpublishable. Most of this lengthy issue (which should have appeared early in February 1794) was written as a dialogue between Desmoulins and an old Cordelier, discussing how war has distorted and corrupted the principles of open republican government. But Desmoulins also wrote out what was presumably intended as a supplement to be added to the text, outlining two polarised forms of government: monarchies where fear and hope of favour drove men into slavery, as against republics where citizens are equal and powers are divided, so that 'if the nation lacks virtue, as in monarchies, at least there can be a balance of vices'. He then summed up his criticism of members of the two powerful committees running revolutionary government by asking:

> Already, no matter how indifferent they are to ambition, ... can you find a single nomination [for office], a single draft law proposed by the committee, that has met with the slightest opposition, a single error [by the government] that has been picked up either by the Convention or in a newspaper? In such difficult times ... is this silence, this absence of any criticism of the actions of the Committee not the strongest criticism in the eyes of republicans, and proof of the oppression of public opinion? Even if the Committee of Public Safety was at one and the same time composed of a Nestor, Aristides, Pericles, Sully, Richelieu, Colbert and a Louvois, yet amongst a free people it would still face criticism, both because of freedom of opinion, and because careful scrutiny often reveals something not apparent from a broad overview.[61]

It is clear from incidental and scattered information that some of the revolutionary newspapers were virtually one-man enterprises. However,

---

[60] R. Hammersley, 'Camille Desmoulins's *Le vieux Cordelier*: a link between English and French republicanism', *History of European Ideas*, 27 (2001), 115–132, notes a number of key works and translations that helped the early Cordeliers ground their thinking firmly in a democratic republican tradition going back to the English Commonwealthmen. See also Hammersley, *French revolutionaries and English republicans* (2005) and Hammersley, *The English republican tradition and eighteenth-century France* (2010).

[61] Issue 7 of *Le vieux Cordelier*, with Desmoulin's manuscript additions added to the proofs, as cited in the modern edition: Camille Desmoulins, *Le vieux Cordelier* edited by P. Pachet (Paris, 1987), 141–2.

a daily newspaper could not be maintained on that basis for any length of time, especially if it exceeded the size of a single sheet (folded once or twice, to make four or eight sides). Most papers involved collaboration between one or more editors and a printer, sometimes using a few freelance journalists to gather more stories. Bigger papers might have a separate publisher, sponsor or even owner and some relied on protection or connections in higher places in order to survive the challenges of revolutionary change. Considerable profits could be made if the paper gained enough readers; equally, government sponsorship (often undeclared) could be hugely beneficial. Hébert's *Le père Duchesne* was for a while deemed appropriate for government-funded distribution to the armies, giving it an almost official propaganda role. Throughout the revolutionary years, many Parisian newspapers were distributed to the provinces, either by private subscription or through the far-flung Jacobin club network. Although there were significant local papers in the bigger towns, they made almost no reciprocal impact on the capital and rarely tried to compete in terms of radical language.

In the rest of Europe, most newspapers had to stay within tighter traditional bounds, both to attract as wide a readership as possible and to avoid intervention by the authorities. Everywhere, however, events in France provided rich material for everyone else, readily deployed either as incentives for reform or as warnings against any change. Second to Paris, the London newspapers were probably the most diverse, but while they could be openly critical of French political developments, they had to be cautious on the domestic front. As we noted for other kinds of print, all discussion of politics in Britain became polarised from the autumn of 1792 onwards, with reform-minded journalism increasingly subject to both government harassment and strongly worded loyalist responses. The London Corresponding Society was unable to sustain a journal (except Thelwall's *Tribune*, surviving for a year from March 1794). Their counterparts in Manchester did slightly better and until 1794 the Sheffield Corresponding Society benefited from the success of the fortnightly periodical *The Patriot*, run by Joseph Gales (until he felt so threatened that he emigrated). Generally speaking, however, radical societies in Britain had to rely more on the general press and on pamphlets.

Despite a lively provincial newspaper industry, London remained the main exchange for most British reporting of international news and political commentary. Many Scottish writers habitually used London publishers, and Scottish newspapers and journals relied heavily on London sources for their own stories. Even Dublin, although becoming a highly productive and independent centre for printing of all kinds, was under increasingly close scrutiny by the government from the early 1790s onwards, especially once the Society of United Irishmen was formed in 1791 around Theobald Wolfe Tone (1763–98) and others. Their focus on parliamentary reform, 'the promotion of Constitutional knowledge, the abolition of bigotry in religion and politics, and the equal distribution of the Rights of Man through all Sects and Denominations of Irishmen', was reported from the start in British newspapers.[62] At this stage, although their agenda was clear, they were not yet openly calling for assistance from revolutionary France, nor advocating independence from Britain (as happened in the Irish rebellion of 1798). Nevertheless, most reporting in the English newspapers rapidly turned hostile already from 1793, as it did in respect of the Edinburgh Conventions for constitutional reform. No doubt the growing strength of political loyalism, combined with strong support from the established church, ensured that the British press generally did more to shore up traditional politics than to encourage real discussion. As so often in major political crises, polarised and emotional assertion displaced any substantive discussion of political options.[63]

In the early 1790s, newspapers published in north-western Germany could afford to take a more detached view of events in France. The *Hamburgische Correspondent* provided very extensive coverage of high-level politics in Paris, with the violent events of August and September 1792 taking up whole issues at the expense of news from any other parts of Europe. The trial of the king later that year was predictably also reported in detail. News from France figured prominently in Schirach's monthly *Politisches Journal*, which as we noted had been openly conservative from its launch in 1781. It reported the 'critical conditions' in France already in January 1790, castigating the National Assembly's failure to organise even its own debates in an orderly manner. By April, the journal reviewed the first year of French upheaval by referring to a checklist provided by one of the French deputies, the lawyer Gui Target, who observed how much remained to be done: a reorganisation of justice; the completion of the civil constitution of the clergy; reform of the army and the national guard; comprehensive financial reform; clarification of the rights of man; reorganisation of the legislative and executive branches of government; reform of many remaining features of feudal rights; the creation of a new magistracy for Paris; liquidation of

---

[62] This quotation is from the London *Morning Post*, Thursday 15 December 1791, quoting a resolution agreed at a Society meeting in Dublin on 9 November.

[63] On Scotland, see B. Harris, 'Scotland's newspapers, the French Revolution and domestic radicalism (c.1789–1794)', *The Scottish Historical Review*, 84 (2005), 38–62; and for the wider context, B. Harris, *Politics and the rise of the press: Britain and France, 1620–1800* (London, 1996).

compensations for abolished venal offices; new agrarian and commercial law; reform of education; and clarification of the freedom of the press itself. Such a comprehensive list of outstanding issues was clearly meant to speak for itself.[64] Schirach noted that the National Assembly was costing 50,000 livres a day and suggested (without providing details or evidence) that each promulgated decree cost even more, both in committee time and printing and dissemination costs. By 1792, the tone of the *Politisches Journal* became highly alarmist, with a subtitle already in March announcing 'French Anarchy, Insurrection, Tumult, Civil War'.[65]

Some German newspapers greeted the French Revolution more positively, in line with the range of opinions voiced in the pamphlets and detailed accounts we noted earlier. The rationalist writer August Adoph von Hennings (1746–1826), already active both in the Danish government and as an exponent of economic reform, launched a new monthly journal in Altona (near Hamburg) in 1794, entitled *Genius der Zeit*. This prioritised optimistic rationalism, including a positive view of civil society and calls for religious toleration. Hennings wrote about the connection between Enlightenment and revolution, noting that there was no historical evidence for a causal connection, but urging readers to see the positive scope in reform. In June 1794, *Genius der Zeit* provided a report on the trial of Thomas Muir in Scotland, juxtaposing efforts to achieve electoral and constitutional reform in Britain with the nature of the charges and form of prosecution brought against him.[66] Such a pragmatic approach was entirely in line with the continuing interest amongst journalists in northern Germany and Denmark to maintain some public discussion of the scope for moderate and gradual reform, while of course condemning violence and radical subversion. Many assumed (rightly, as it turned out) that revolution beyond the borders of France could be avoided, provided moderate public discussion was preserved and sensible reform implemented.[67]

Language and the Creation of 'National' Understanding

The political landscape of the 1790s may, to contemporary observers, have looked at times like an earthquake zone, both conceptually and in practical terms. It certainly had a new or evolving political vocabulary. The optimism of 1789 lasted for a few years in those parts of Europe

---

[64] *Politisches Journal nebst Anzeige von gelehrten und andern Sachen*, Jahrgang 1790, issue 4 (April 1790), 376–83.
[65] *Politisches Journal*, Jahrgang 1792, issue 3 (March), 276.
[66] *Genius der Zeit*, vol. II (June 1794), 176–236.
[67] Munck, 'Public debate, politics and print', 323–52.

where stability was maintained, but there is no doubt that for many readers both in Paris and in London the rapidly growing political polarisation soon cast long shadows over the future. Some responded positively: Paine clearly showed no signs of loss of momentum, despite his imprisonment in Paris, and John Thelwall continued to campaign for electoral reform until he gave up in 1798. Others found the political environment more discouraging: Condorcet had given up writing his *Esquisse* by the time he fled from his place of hiding in Paris (just before his death in March 1794), Desmoulins was guillotined and Priestley emigrated from England a few weeks later. Those who avoided personal misfortune might still be alarmed by the factional political climate, the disappearance of rational and informed public discussion, and the kind of unpredictable violence which made the political middle ground difficult to hold. The outbreak of war, directly affecting much of Europe from 1792–3 onwards, inevitably made rational public debate far more difficult. But there may also have been alarming signs that *ancien-régime* civil society, imperfect as it had been because of elite patronage and chaotic administrative systems, was giving way to a new more centralised order, where politics was even more brutal, public accountability only skin-deep and social deprivation ever-present, all veiled behind patriotic propaganda where freedom of expression was not valued.

Print was of course just a vehicle for dissemination, but it was a hugely versatile one, capable of fostering and standardising different kinds of discourse across a very wide political spectrum. As we have seen, print could enhance the impact of any text, from extreme populist politics to constitutional innovation, through cautious democratic idealism and inclusivity, as well as satirical criticism, loyalism, elitist conservatism and even (where appropriate) unapologetic or entrenched royalism. Publication in itself helped to create more colourful but also more standardised use of all the main languages in those parts of Europe that had a lively print culture. But as always in such situations, not everything was visible in print or in extant reports of political meetings: both self-censorship and the pressures of conformism continued to play a major role in determining what could be published and what should be read. In France, formal censorship, working alongside the restrictions imposed by printing cartels and guild regulations, had been swept away, only to be replaced by less familiar controls exercised through denunciation, destructive vigilante crowds, or prosecution in law courts of questionable reputation. In Britain the loyalist reaction relied on both populist and government support to disrupt public meetings and thereby obstruct meaningful discussion of reform, political rights or even just freedom of expression. In both countries, political rhetoric loaded with inflammatory language could easily drown out moderate counsel and newspapers struggled even to claim editorial independence. In most other parts of Europe reporting tended to appear slightly more detached, even though some pamphleteers continued to experiment with innovative ways of discussing political issues.

Within France itself, the potential for misunderstandings between centre and periphery became a more serious problem. Large areas of France relied either on distinct languages (such as Breton or Catalan) or such strong dialects (notably across much of the south) that Parisian French was not always comprehensible. These areas typically had a much less developed print culture, but effective dissemination was also curtailed for other reasons: incompatible legal and fiscal systems in different parts of the kingdom; variant local government structures left over from the traditional *pays d'états* and *pays d'élection*; not to mention the remote isolation of mountainous areas. The administrative reorganisation undertaken from 1790, setting up more uniform *départements* and systems for electing local officials, created a potential framework for a unifying national administration. But it is clear that some parts of France remained almost untouched by the Revolution, beyond the reach of the new printed texts. Proposals to institute systematic translation of government proclamations to match the needs of recipients seem to have been implemented only minimally. More seriously, the provincial revolts and civil wars that hit France by 1793 demonstrated the gap between theory and reality, emphasising the urgent need for improved communications. Deputies who were sent out as *représentants en mission* by the National Convention in the autumn of 1793 regularly reported that in remoter parts they found extraordinarily high levels of apparent ignorance and disinformation, not just regarding government policies but also the fundamentals of revolutionary ideology. Clearly dissemination by the national newspapers and the growing network of Jacobin clubs was extremely uneven.

Some contemporary observers took it upon themselves to investigate ways of improving the language of political communication, recognising both print and education as essential means of forging a basic coherent political culture to help modernise France. One of the key activists in this respect was the deputy to the First Estate (the clergy) in the Estates General in 1789, Henri Grégoire (1750–1831). He had been a keen reformer from the very start, took the oath of loyalty to the Civil Constitution of the Clergy (which he had helped to draft) and was also active in the movement to abolish the slave trade and secure toleration for Jews. As constitutional bishop he was well acquainted with weaknesses in the provincial education system and already in 1790 launched detailed enquiries to map out local dialects and levels of linguistic common ground. Elected once more as deputy to the Convention, he remained a consistent and prominent reformer while maintaining his strong local interests. In June 1794 he presented a full report to the Convention, noting that a quarter of the population of France did not speak French and another quarter only imperfectly. Unlike the very inadequate work of the revolutionary lexicographers we noted in Chapter 4, Grégoire's research was as thorough and detailed as he could make it. He too believed that all *patois* (local dialects) were a legacy of rustic backwardness which needed to be eradicated, so that everyone could unite behind a shared national outlook. Such an approach remained broadly acceptable to the majority of the Convention, not least because it absolved them from the need to scrutinise the divisive effects of their own policies.

Such concerns about language, communication and dissemination may at first sight appear reasonable. But David Bell, Patrice Higonnet and others have reminded us that Grégoire's campaign for linguistic modernisation had various subtexts. Significantly, those who shared his enthusiasm for educational reform did not see language as a real problem: Condorcet, for example, was less alarmist, suggesting that knowledge of standard French was reasonably widespread, while Barère considered *patois* an indicator primarily of wilful resistance to national assimilation. We now know that both Grégoire and Barère were fundamentally wrong in directly linking linguistic and political deviance, but they clearly liked the simplicity of their explanation. Bell argues that Grégoire exaggerated the level of linguistic disunity because he was heir to a long-running programme to reform religious education. Under the influence of Jansenist and even Protestant ideas, he wanted to achieve linguistic unity in order to remove the superstitions and local traditions that he felt impeded integration of essential Christian values within the new republic. Barère, on the other hand, seems to have used *patois* speakers as a convenient target to strengthen his own revolutionary credentials. Higonnet has emphasised the underlying tensions between a modernised Parisian urban political culture and a traditional rural peasant culture with very different core assumptions. Appropriately presented, the standardisation of language could seem a benevolent push for social levelling and integration, even though in reality it could also serve as a means of undemocratic (and perhaps culturally damaging) political and social control.[68]

[68] D. A. Bell, 'Tearing down the tower of Babel: Grégoire and French multilingualism', in J. D. Popkin and R. H. Popkin (eds.), *The abbé Grégoire and his world* (Dordrecht, 2000), 109–28; D. A. Bell, 'Lingua populi, lingua Dei: language, religion and the origins of French Revolutionary nationalism', *American Historical Review*, 100 (1995), 1403–37; P. L. R. Higonnet, 'The politics of linguistic terrorism and grammatical hegemony during the French Revolution', *Social History*, 5 (1980), 41–69; M. de Certeau, D. Julia and

In short, the language issue was part of a more complicated problem at the very heart of revolutionary ideology. The Revolution needed a clear definition, and revolutionary discourse (verbal and textual) was the only reliable way of formulating and projecting one. Some years ago, Mark Olsen alerted us to the need to analyse linguistic usage, and in particular the collocation of certain sensitive terms, in order to understand why key concepts caused so much difficulty and argument.[69] We may now go further and suggest that the real and frustrating disunity of French political culture was not just the result of different voices appropriating common words for different purposes. More alarmingly, words and whole phrases could be used as tools to denounce critics and opponents in deliberately divisive ways. Politically 'correct' language became a test of conformity to a hypothetical general will, and speech acts became tools by which you could cut down political rivals and marginalise erstwhile friends while claiming you were acting solely in the interests of public morality and revolutionary virtue.[70] A key aim of many revolutionaries had been to break emphatically with the corrupt factions of the *ancien régime*, so much so that they now focused obsessively on the risks of deception, conspiracy and (after the outbreak of war) the understandable threat of 'foreign plots' and suspect enemy aliens.

If learning to manipulate revolutionary language became a necessary skill for leaders during the Revolution, conceptual clarity was often sacrificed in the process. Robespierre himself was a master of florid speeches, generalising about virtue and the people, but almost invariably also giving dark and unspecific warnings of revolutionary conspiracies by enemies of the general will. He was a notoriously inexhaustible speaker who somehow managed to hold the attention of his listeners even when saying nothing new.[71] From the first year of the Revolution, he and many others

---

J. Revel, *Une politique de la langue: la Révolution française et les patois* (Paris, 1975), which includes source material.

[69] M. Olsen, 'Enlightened nationalism in the early Revolution: the *nation* in the language of the *Société de 1789*', *Canadian Journal of History*, 29 (1994), 24–50; for the language of higher education itself, see for example J. Langins, 'Words and institutions during the French Revolution: the case of "revolutionary" scientific and technical education', in P. Burke and R. Porter (ed.), *The social history of language* (Cambridge, 1987), 136–60.

[70] N. Hampson, *Prelude to terror: the Constituent Assembly and the failure of consensus 1787–91* (Oxford, 1988); M. Linton, *Choosing terror: virtue, friendship and authenticity in the French Revolution* (Oxford, 2013); J. Guilhaumou, 'Fragments of a discourse of denunciation (1789–1794)', in K. M. Baker (ed.), *The French Revolution and the creation of modern political culture*, vol. IV, 139–55; J. Guilhaumou, *La langue politique et la révolution française* (Paris, 1989); the impact of Rousseau in France was opened up for wider discussion by C. Blum, *Rousseau and the republic of virtue: the language of politics in the French Revolution* (Ithaca, NY, 1986).

[71] A skill graphically described by Jean-Baptiste Louvet, in his dramatic denunciation of Robespierre in the Convention on 29 October 1792. For a broader study of political

recognised the effectiveness of such rhetoric, both when deployed in the Assembly, for the public in the galleries, or if published selectively as pamphlets or in the newspapers. It is interesting to note that Danton had a reputation for masterly rhetoric, yet he hardly ever made it into print, perhaps because his political philosophy did not hang together when written out. By contrast, Marat appears to have been so melodramatic and hysterical a speaker that his impact on an audience was limited or even counterproductive, yet in print seems to have been able sway his readers. Marat's and Hébert's newspapers acquired political influence by their systematic use of colourful and increasingly violent language, often deployed specifically to denounce 'enemies of the people'. Such divisive tactics were much lamented by everyone,[72] but acquired irresistible momentum, and denunciations became a civic duty during the Terror. As we noted earlier, even Desmoulins used a series of more erudite references to classical Rome to construct elaborate criticisms of those in power, reaching a climax in his last publications just before he was arrested and executed in the spring of 1794. Ultimately, it was not revulsion against the Terror itself, but rather a combination of alleged conspiracies, mutual recriminations and denunciations that triggered the coup of Thermidor.

Ancien-régime etiquette and decorum had understandably been rejected by those revolutionaries who wanted to replace 'aristocratic' intrigue with honesty and plain language. Initially, greater freedom of information and discussion had created considerable opportunities for reform and political restructuring, but it is safe to assume that from the spring of 1793 to Thermidor (and beyond) a growing proportion of what was said and discussed in high-level politics outside the assembly was unlikely to be noted in writing, let alone printed. Differences of opinion were increasingly liable to be construed as deviations from the general will and

---

rhetoric, see E. Négrel and J.-P. Sermain (eds.), *Une expérience rhétorique: l'éloquence de la Révolution* (*SVEC* 2002: 02, Oxford, 2002).

[72] For an overview of Jacobin ideology, see notably P. L. R. Higonnet, *Goodness beyond virtue: Jacobins during the French Revolution* (Cambridge, MA, 1998). On the significance of conspiracy theories and social-political denunciations in the Revolution, including undermining the status of foreigners who had come to France, see C. le Bart, 'L'imputation: un outil pour l'analyse des mentalités révolutionnaires', *Revue Historique*, 282 (1989), 351–65; C. Lucas, 'The theory and practice of denunciation in the French Revolution', *Journal of Modern History*, 68 (1996), 768–85; M. Linton, '"The Tartuffes of patriotism": fears of conspiracy in the political language of revolutionary government, France 1793–1794', in B. Coward and J. Swann (eds.), *Conspiracies and conspiracy theory in early modern Europe* (2004), 235–54; M. Linton, '"Do you believe that we're conspirators": conspiracies real and imagined in Jacobin politics', in P. R. Campbell, T. E. Kaiser and M. Linton (eds.), *Conspiracy in the French Revolution* (Manchester, 2007), 127–49.

denounced as such. Even so, we should not underestimate the scope for innovative political analysis. Members of successive national assemblies engaged with the public not just in the speeches they delivered (with the public listening in the galleries), but (more rarely) also by going into print while sitting as deputies. Amongst the members of the National Constituent Assembly who also went into print we note for example Grégoire, Pierre-Samuel Dupont (who later emigrated to America) and Robert-Thomas Lindet. It is interesting to note that Lindet rarely spoke, early in his parliamentary career, but seems to have preferred to publish instead.

During the first year of the French National Convention of 1792–5, many perceptive speeches were delivered by deputies with impressive analytical powers who clearly recognised both the dangers threatening the Revolution and its most promising opportunities. When we read the detailed reports of these Convention debates, as printed in the *Moniteur*, we encounter both visionary ideals and many practical legislative and administrative proposals. Amongst the most active speakers in the critical first eight months of the Convention (from late September 1792 to June 1793) was Pierre Cambon, who spoke almost weekly, often lucidly, on financial reform and planning. Jean Maihle spoke less frequently, but as chair of the Legislative Committee worked hard to combine legally sound governance with pragmatism. Others, including the tactically agile Bertrand Barère, were on their feet regularly, trying to shape their own version of politics. Not only were the speeches reported in full in the *Moniteur* (more summarily in other quality papers), but many were also published separately, alongside government reports.[73]

The very active hard-line revolutionary Billaud-Varenne demonstrated how much influence one might gain from combining all kinds of communication strategies: a former schoolmaster and lawyer, he had published a three-volume work on the *Despotisme des ministres de France* (1789) and a number of speeches he made in the Jacobin and Cordeliers clubs (both of which he attended early in the Revolution). When elected to the Convention as left-wing deputy for Paris, he continued to use his strong *sans-culotte* base to become a member of the Committee of Public Safety, and a number of his reports and speeches to the Convention were published officially. As one of the Thermidorians

---

[73] This discussion is based on the daily reports in the *Moniteur*. These also reveal that leaders of the 'factions' (notably Danton and Robespierre, and amongst their Girondin opponents notably Brissot, Buzot and Barbaroux) seemed to be more interested in denouncing each other in lengthy speeches that contrasted with the short and pointed interventions of men such as Jacques Thuriot. But what is significant is how many deputies took an active part, many of them from a position of factional neutrality.

who helped to overthrow Robespierre, he continued to support the extreme policies of the Terror, publishing several further polemics until he was arrested and deported after the Germinal riots.[74]

The stabilising effect print could have had in creating an informed public may well have been negated both by the increasingly bitter polemics found in newspapers and pamphlets and the recurrent confrontations over even the most fundamental political ideals. Over six years (1789–95) three radically different Declarations of Rights were compiled and widely published, and as many constitutions. The second Declaration of Rights (1793), originally formulated by a cross-party committee and then extensively rewritten by the Jacobin leadership, was hurriedly locked away with the Constitution for the duration of the war and never implemented. Such declarations of revolutionary principles were undoubtedly significant in setting an officially approved agenda for government and disseminating the elementary ideas to a wider public. But good governance is never created merely by means of lofty general principles: the devil is always in the detail and the practicalities of effective implementation. We may well assume that the failure to create satisfactory stable institutions of government during the early republic was not because the Convention lacked imaginative ideas, or there was insufficient published information, but rather that political leadership was disastrously divided.

Publishing and Revolutionary Politics

In France, from June 1793 if not before, public opinion was increasingly constrained by the emergencies of war and the resulting gradual but extreme centralisation of executive power. But there are a number of other factors that may help explain why political reality increasingly failed to match revolutionary ideals. Few would doubt that fiscal irresponsibility, unstoppable inflation, institutional chaos in central government, as well as the economic pressures that all European governments faced in the 1790s all took their toll. But in addition, historians have for many years noted the growing violence and bitterness generated by political disappointment, clearly visible for example in the diary notes of Madame Roland already after the king's attempted flight in June 1791 and much

---

[74] Jacques-N. Billaud-Varenne, *Despotisme des ministres de France* (3 vols., Amsterdam [Paris], 1789); idem, *Les elemens du républicanisme* (Paris, first year of the French republic [1793]); idem, *Principes régénérateurs du système sociale* (Paris, Year III [1795]); see also J. M. Burney, 'The fear of the executive and the threat of conspiracy: Billaud-Varenne's terrorist rhetoric in the French Revolution, 1788–1794', *French History*, 5 (1991), 143–63.

more strongly a year later. To her, as for Robespierre and some other would-be visionaries, compromise of any kind was unacceptable, since it would require a softening of revolutionary ideals and an abandonment of Rousseau's illusory principles.

The changing role of print in the unstable and complex political and cultural life of revolutionary France deserves closer attention. Basic educational provision suffered severe setbacks in the early years of Revolution, partly because of the nationalisation of the church and its assets, and partly because the substantive proposals for reorganisation by Condorcet, Grégoire and others took time to implement. At a higher level, we might also note the closure of official academies (confirmed in the decree of 8 August 1793): not many would have lamented the end of the venerable but sclerotic Académie Française, but the loss of the Academy of Sciences and many other institutions was more serious, and creating effective new state institutions was bound to take time. Local or church libraries were threatened with confiscation and selective weeding, and there were even some book-burnings, as had been suggested in 1771 by Mercier in his *L'an 2440* (we may note that in 1792 Mercier was elected to sit in the Convention, but his impact as a deputy was minimal). Great uncertainties also threatened public and private archives.[75] Although some forms of cultural vandalism (Grégoire's word) were avoided because of bureaucratic inefficiency and local resistance, the damage to the cultural heritage of France was considerable. In July 1793 Grégoire was commissioned to do a full report on the promotion of the sciences and arts, but he did not complete his task until well over a year later, in October 1794, by which time much of the damage had been done.[76] The Revolution not only changed the tone and language of political controversy and analysis: it also tried to change the visual symbolism, musical and theatrical representations, public architecture and public festivals, all in an effort to consolidate its new political and social ideals. Inevitably, books, manuscripts, authors, publishers and ultimately readers were all substantially and materially affected.

The impact may well have been made worse by actual changes in the conditions under which the publishing industry had to operate from around 1792. Although some printing firms were able to benefit from the

---

[75] Much work remains to be done, assessing the scale of change, destruction or preservation of French cultural heritage in the early 1790s: see E. Kennedy, *A cultural history of the French Revolution* (New Haven, CT, 1989).

[76] Henri Grégoire, *Rapport sur les encouragements, récompenses et pensions à accorder aux savants, aux gens de lettres et aux artistes* (Imprimerie Nationale, Paris, year III [1794–5]), discussed by C. Hesse, *Publishing and cultural politics in revolutionary Paris, 1789–1810* (Berkeley, 1991), 140f.

growing demand for government printing (legislation, proclamations and other circulars, significant speeches and much else), most of the evidence we have suggests that independent commercial printing dropped severely during the Terror. Without detailed information on all types of publication it is not yet possible to provide a full explanation. We may assume that the political climate was simply becoming too unpredictable and repressive. There may also have been serious economic and structural changes which restricted the effective dissemination of the kinds of lively, diverse and often irreverent publications that had previously been such a characteristic feature of the Parisian scene. Many independent newspapers ceased publication, either from loss of readers or because they were harassed by the authorities. State subsidies were of course available only for those papers deemed to strengthen civic morale (for example *Le père Duchesne,* until February 1794), or providing relatively neutral information judged to be in the public interest (notably the upmarket *Moniteur*). At a more basic practical level, independent printing suffered when a number of presses were requisitioned for official purposes and brought under the centralised state printing office in Paris in December 1793.

Historians have long since recognised that the decline in commercial printing from around 1792 through to the later 1790s was exceptionally precipitous, affecting pamphlets and books, including new texts as well as reprints. Some years ago Carla Hesse uncovered additional evidence identifying some ill-considered changes in policy and copyright law that may have been crucially important in causing this sudden decline. De-regulation of copyright and the removal of the corporate structures of the print industry were no doubt unavoidable, since both were deemed incompatible with the ideological principles of 1789–91. But the resulting regulative confusion created endless scope for lawsuits and disputed publishing rights, and may have contributed to a significant number of bankruptcies amongst printers (particularly high already between 1789 and 1792, under the constitutional monarchy). Public subsidies did not offer sufficient compensation and were in any case heavily politicised and susceptible to sudden changes in direction: for example, Roland's attempt to subsidise certain publications through his Bureau de l'Esprit Public in the Ministry of the Interior (autumn 1792) came to an abrupt end when he was hounded out of office and fled in January 1793.

There were other fundamental issues, too. New legislation, notably the law of 19 July 1793 regarding author's rights, may have had serious unintended consequences. The law did recognise intellectual and literary property rights, but on such limited terms that the incentives to publish new specialist books or reprint classics were severely reduced. This law became the long-term basis for French copyright, but did not at first resolve the conflict between author's rights and the national interest – between the legitimate claims of individuals to maintain their intellectual property rights, as against the desire to make all useful knowledge a form of open-access national asset. Significantly, the law was not even debated in the Convention in any depth, suggesting either that politicians had more immediate worries, or that this was one of the areas where revolutionary principles were in fact ultimately self-contradictory. The resulting confusion, aggravated by inadequate enforcement, seems to have increased the risks of piracy and plagiarism. More seriously, slower-selling or ambitious books became less commercially viable, adding a further disincentive for already disillusioned authors who might otherwise have aimed to advance scientific knowledge or contribute to constructive discussions on major social, economic and political issues of the day. By 1794, Hesse suggests, 'book publishing was at a near standstill'.[77]

This takes us towards some unexpected conclusions. In Chapter 2 we noted how the English Revolution of the 1640s led to a huge growth in innovative print which reached an unprecedented wider reading public and contributed directly to a rich and diverse religious, political and social debate. Much of this legacy laid the foundations for further gains in social and political understanding during the Enlightenment, accessible to the European reading public thanks to a creative publishing industry. The American Revolution more than a century later demonstrated similar links between a lively print culture and creative nation-building, but within a moderate and cautious political environment. France after 1789, however, went much further, ending up in a series of consecutive revolutionary upheavals which created so many internal contradictions that stability seemed almost unattainable. A huge range of issues were raised: some, such as the potential emancipation and political integration of women discussed in this chapter, were promoted by means of the dissemination of texts, but other issues, such as social inequality and the imbalance of economic power, were not. France did explore the potential of full-scale democracy, including universal male franchise, but failed to provide the educational and social foundations for this to work well. The Cordeliers pushed political activism as far as they could, using older English republican ideals to generate a real if somewhat uncontrollable form of political accountability, but as Desmoulins made clear, they, too, were sidelined. In the midst of all this, newspapers and pamphlets initially provided plenty of food for thought, from ultra-conservative to provocatively iconoclastic, but only a few provided the quality of information that would have strengthened public debate and reduced the risk of violent extremism.

---

[77] Hesse, *Publishing and cultural politics*, 127–35 and *passim*.

Rousseau himself had offered no guidance as to the means whereby a notional general will could be stabilised, and no-one quite had the nerve to try the more extreme solutions offered by either Hobbes or Spinoza. The first three years of parliamentary government in revolutionary France may have been inspired by the ideas of Locke and Montesquieu, but were sabotaged by a fundamentally inept and moribund monarchy. It is worth reminding ourselves that the declaration of war, with all its domestic consequences, was intuitively backed by the king and (for different reasons) approved by the Legislative Assembly. Yet as indicated in this chapter, the political problems cannot just be blamed on the war and may well have had much deeper roots. Political culture, and political awareness amongst the broader population, did not develop the way any of the revolutionary leaders had predicted or hoped: the reasons for this are very complex, but the setbacks to commercial and independent printing and publishing certainly did not help. The printing and publishing industry was too complex to cope with extreme and unpredictable political change. Perhaps public opinion itself became too divisive and unpredictable for either authors or printers to get the best texts on the market at the right time.

Despite the fears of most governments, there was no comparable political and cultural upheaval anywhere else in Europe. The legislative and repressive reactions to developments in France varied hugely and were mostly not synchronised to events in Paris. We have noted that the British government exploited news from France as an excuse for wildly exaggerating the threat posed by what were essentially very modest proposals for democratic reform with minimal connection to events across the Channel. As both the German and Scandinavian examples have shown, government reactions there were also determined primarily by domestic political factors rather than genuine French 'contagion'. More detailed studies of print culture are needed, both in France and in other parts of Europe in the 1790s, to understand the full range of public reactions in print. Such studies may work even if confined to individual political cultures, but evaluation of impact and dissemination can be more effective if tackled from a transnational comparative perspective, in which influences, selective adaptations and negative reactions are more readily apparent, and the wide range of contrasting opinions becomes more clearly visible. There was a wide diversity of responses to, and reinterpretations of, news from France and some of these responses throw fresh light back on the Revolution itself and on the variant readings of political culture attempted all over Europe.

Conclusions

Searching for the 'origins' of the Enlightenment may resemble searching for the end of a rainbow – at least when the focus is on politics. Systematic analysis of good governance in civic society goes back to Plato or earlier, and any form of social community requires some use of power and authority. Given the huge political upheavals in the 1640s and 50s, and the intense discussion of religious and political ideals that resulted, it makes no sense to see either Spinoza or Locke as originators of new 'enlightened' systems of political thought. Hobbes would have a stronger claim, not least because he was an inescapable influence on everyone who studied politics after 1651. But Hobbes, too, was part of a continuing search for answers going back through the Levellers, Grotius, Calvinist resistance theory and the ideal of a true 'commonwealth', all influenced by long-running controversies revived during the movements for religious Reformation of the early sixteenth century. This book has tried to show how a detailed study of print, both as a form of material culture and as a mechanism for dissemination and public controversy, can help us understand why and how discussion of civil society, good governance and legitimate political authority developed so rapidly and profoundly in the period 1635–1795. It has also tried to show that the political parameters of the middle decades of the seventeenth century were very different from those of the mid-eighteenth century, let alone the revolutionary decade from the late 1780s.

Print had demonstrated its effectiveness as a major tool for religious propaganda during the Reformation, with ideas disseminated in sermons, visual material, devotional texts and sectarian pamphlets. From the 1630s it became at least as significant in providing a means of disseminating fundamental arguments and ideas in political culture. In central Europe during the Thirty Years War, images probably had more impact than texts; but during the English civil wars, even though printed images remained very important, it is clear that various forms of textual publication could convey much more detail and analysis. Those who experienced the divisive conflicts of the 1640s found most of their assumptions about the nature of civil society profoundly challenged. In the struggle to make some kind of sense of it all, everyone needed information and perhaps new answers. Print became a key tool for broadcasting alternative visions of civil society, power and authority to anyone who could read, or who was prepared to learn how. The dramatic and totally unprecedented increase in the scale and range of unauthorised publications, particularly those dealing with religion and politics, turned England into a huge experiment, where those previously outside the 'political nation' could now access alternative models of governance ranging from the ultra-royalist arguments of Charles I to the levelling arguments of radical groups and the near-anarchic model of the Quakers in the 1650s. Observers in the Netherlands and France followed these developments with great interest, while adding thoughts of their own; in the rest of Europe others also took notice from the perspective of their often concurrent political troubles.

The evidence of dissemination and transnational adaptation of texts and ideas in the early modern period suggests that the political impact of print did not increase in a linear pattern, but was (as we would expect) driven by particular circumstances and specific contexts. The time span covered by this book starts and ends with eruptions of extraordinary political innovation, visible both in the conceptual languages that developed in each of the two big revolutions, but also in techniques of outreach, dissemination and public controversy. Printed texts of course do not represent the totality of political culture in early modern Europe, but there is no doubt that print was the most effective way of reaching beyond the limits of verbal communication – the only obvious way of creating the broad political consensus that everyone wanted. In short, new work in the history of print has laid the foundations for a major reassessment of public discussion and public opinion in the early modern period.

This book has argued that a major and fundamental change in the use of print occurred during the English civil wars and Commonwealth period. Print was used in innovative ways for petitions, pamphlets, news transmission and other forms of communication intended for a much more inclusive urban readership. We are only beginning to understand how the collapse of regulation affected the market for print, allowing a much greater diversity of opinions to be disseminated. But it is already abundantly clear that political culture was far more complex than, for example, traditional histories of the English civil wars and the 1649 revolution have suggested. No-one can now claim that 'radicals' were merely a sideshow to the big confrontation between a very blinkered monarch and an increasingly authoritarian parliament. And it is now very difficult to categorise the many strands of argument – religious, social, deferential, irreverent, utopian or even pragmatic – into coherent intellectual blocks that would have been recognised as such by contemporary readers, let alone fit modern categories of 'authoritarian', 'democratic', 'parliamentarian' or 'dictatorial'. One of the great delights of working in the history of print is to encounter the extraordinary range of writers explaining in their own words what they thought they wanted to say to readers whom they did not know – a cacophony of voices often violently disagreeing with each other, but not always sure what they could say and how they could express it. The development and dissemination of a more sophisticated political and conceptual language was one of the striking features of the 1640s and 50s. And even if we cannot be sure who the actual readers were, the texts themselves give clear indications that a much wider readership was both intended and actively engaged.

The profound changes in political discourse in France in the early 1790s constitute an obvious end point for this book. The cumulative effect, both in rhetoric and in print, was debated almost immediately after Thermidor, and has been the focus of widely divergent interpretation almost ever since. This book has not attempted to resolve these disagreements, but has pointed to evidence suggesting that, as in the English civil wars, new forms of vocabulary and new authorial techniques were exploited consciously to create new forms of political culture. It is remarkable (but perhaps not surprising) how many of those who wanted to disseminate ideas on good governance, reformed power relations in society, the scope for democratic consultation and reconsideration of social and gender inequality often relied on an extensive range of older printed material – their heritage of political culture – even when they tried to break with the past. Hobbes and Spinoza may have been misused by late eighteenth-century writers, just as Locke and Montesquieu were no longer read with the attention to detail they might have deserved. But there is no doubt that long-running discussions of republicanism, representation, civil society and legitimate authority were both revived and refashioned to suit the increasingly complex political debates of later eighteenth-century France and Europe – often in direct response to events in Paris.

A traditional approach to the history of ideas used to concentrate on analysing a few particular texts in detail, attempting to pin down the origin of key ideas and their potential impact – a kind of 'lineage' of ideas and concepts. This may still work adequately as a starting point for some forms of the history of philosophy and the history of science. But in terms of politics, civil society and concepts of good governance, such an approach on its own is no longer sufficient to explain the reconfiguration of republican and commonwealth thinking, levelling, mass petitioning (such as that of the 1640s in London), millenarianism – or for that matter, divine-right monarchy, the concept of a 'general will', or the many notions of natural law and natural rights informing readers from the mid-seventeenth century through to the 1790s. Much political negotiation was done by verbal and gestural means, now largely beyond our reach; and handwritten forms of political bargaining (for example petitions) indicate many levels of political engagement taking us into areas other than print. But even if we stay with print and public dissemination, the huge volume of texts produced in north-western Europe from the middle decades of the seventeenth century to 1795 are far too cacophonous to indicate lineages or simple influences in the emergence of new political ideas. We struggle to see comprehensive or convincing explanations – a struggle already familiar to avid collectors and readers of pamphlets at the time, such as the woodturner Nehemiah Wallington in London during the 1640s and 50s. We are slightly closer to understanding precisely how and why Hobbes arrived at his stark analysis of power in his *Leviathan,* and we now have a thorough understanding of how the book was written, disseminated and rendered into Latin many years later by Hobbes himself. We know a good deal about when and why Locke tried to describe what eventually became a moderate consensus political view, but we can no longer take for granted precisely what influenced him, nor can we assume that the positions he took in his publications from 1689–95 exercised a direct and major influence on the middle ground of the European Enlightenment later on.

The development of new research methods and approaches in the history of print and dissemination is not only changing the way we locate individual texts in the wider public debates taking shape at the time of publication. It also has direct repercussions on how we might now broadly characterise the intellectual and political revolutions of the seventeenth century, or the Enlightenment. Some critics have argued that the term 'Enlightenment' has been used by historians, philosophers, social scientists and literary scholars for so many different aspects of late seventeenth-and eighteenth-century cultural life as to be meaningless. But that kind of criticism perhaps merely shows up differences of approach between different academic disciplines and misunderstands why historians use broad labels to help identify extremely complex periods of change. No-one who has studied seventeenth- and eighteenth-century published texts, or followed discussions in the journals, would claim there was any coherent 'programme' or agenda amongst even the most prominent intellectuals at any stage: indeed to look for such a coherent programme would be to fundamentally misunderstand one of the key features of public debate both in the seventeenth and eighteenth centuries. We may get a clearer overall understanding if, instead, we examine the questions that were asked, the methods used to try to find answers, the formats in which debates were conducted and the intentions that underpinned efforts to reach a broader readership. If we allow a moment of generalisation, historians might now argue that during much of the seventeenth century the idea of absolute certainty (including a divinely ordained truth) was one of the key focal points for discussion, while the eighteenth-century Enlightenment was more about understanding the fundamentals and contradictions within existing forms of civil society, including its imperfections and at least some of its failings. Hobbes, Locke, Beccaria, Diderot and Condorcet did not focus on the same challenges, but they did all try to analyse power and civil society in ways that might help emancipate everyone from ingrained prejudices and lazy intellectual habits.

How public consensus and stability might be achieved, however, could never be agreed, even within individual linguistic communities or national cultures. Categorising published writings and trends of thought in terms of 'national Enlightenments' (French, Scottish, German, or other) does not work even for what was once regarded as the 'canon' of famous texts or great writers of the period. It makes even less sense now that we are able to identify and understand the circumstances surrounding the publication of more obscure, neglected, anonymous, translated or illegal works. Instead, we need a more meticulous mapping of a much wider range of printed material, from pamphlets and polemics to major analytical or theoretical works, recognising the quantitative evidence of distribution, reprinting and dissemination within specific cultural and social contexts, and noting the variable chronology and duration of any impact. With more thorough analysis of transnational dissemination through translations, adaptations and additional reprinting, we will have a better understanding of communication strategies across Europe.

As indicated in Chapter 1 of this book, compilation of comprehensive short-title catalogues of all printed material is still work in progress and may not yet give us a complete or accurate picture, but the data is of fundamental importance in understanding the changes we are discussing here. Print remained the only mechanism of reliable and consistent communication, even though other media (such as music, art, and oratory) could offer different perspectives. Printed texts were never cheap, but they became by far the most readily available source of ideas, controversy, discussion and imaginative thinking. The huge but uneven growth in printed output across many of the larger cities in Europe during the period 1635 to 1795 can now be measured and analysed in ways that do not always give fully accurate results, but which certainly indicate that, during key periods of major political change, authors and publishers really were imaginative in meeting growing market demand. The periods of substantive growth in political print are clear: first the 1640s and 50s in the more politically advanced parts of Europe, then the longer period of disturbances almost everywhere from around 1685 to 1715 or 1721, followed by a slightly quieter couple of decades before the flood of radical thinking led by French writers from 1748 onwards and the more polarised print culture of the French Revolution itself from the late 1780s to 1795 and beyond. The detailed geography and chronology of substantive political discussion varied enormously across Europe, depending on national and regional politics, the strength or otherwise of religious authorities, the mechanisms for censorship, the scope for prosecutions for libel and breach of copyright, and of course the self-censorship and cultural conditioning of writers and publishers themselves.

What is really striking about the whole period covered by this book is the way print facilitated socially diverse and faster political engagement and at times almost democratised political debate. We are acquiring a better grasp of how much print was produced, what it was about, how it was marketed, whether and where it was in sufficient demand to merit reprinting, and how far other writers felt compelled to respond, criticise or review. We can readily identify which texts met with sufficient recognition abroad to gain translation into other languages and what adaptations were required for such cultural translation to work reasonably well (or at least have a chance of covering its own costs). We can begin to compare the impact of different genres, recognising for example that fiction became an important (and very accessible) medium for speculation about civil society and power. We can observe how most of the newspaper industry had to restrict itself to 'safe' reporting, in order to survive – often using derivative and supposedly factual material rather than attempting politicised editorials, yet continuing to meet (and in turn generating) growing interest and a surge in demand. Even the success of journals and periodicals (though not the most obvious reading material for the general public) can now be explained in terms of the mechanisms of debate and communication. Scientific, literary, and cultural journals proliferated at an impressive rate during the later eighteenth century and yield rich insights into what editors thought were the most important new ideas, discoveries and interesting books of their time. In effect, the old exclusive republic of letters was being superseded (though not entirely displaced) by a much wider 'imagined community' of readers and writers.

This leads us to the broader question of how public opinion was enhanced through open contestation. Public opinion has always existed in some form, but print was by definition a public statement, duplicated in order to reach more readers and formally or even ostentatiously breaking out of the bounds of private communication. As we have noted throughout this book, print could serve all kinds of political purposes, but could never be regarded as private or confidential. Many authors developed techniques specifically to extend the limits of what could be said in public and how you might say it while trying to limit the risks of reprisals, censure or prosecution. The stakes were extremely high and the context all-important. As we noted in Chapter 2, Milton, Hobbes and Spinoza faced personal charges of heresy and blasphemy, the penalty for which could have been death. Throughout the period up to and including the 1790s and beyond, countless others faced prosecution, exile, imprisonment and other forms of severe personal punishment. Printers risked having their equipment destroyed and their business ruined by imprisonment and punitive fines. Any critical reading of a text must therefore fully recognise the limitations on what the author could say. It is clear that in no part of Europe was any general right of freedom of opinion recognised, let alone sanctioned by government or in law. Even the experiments from the 1760s to abolish censorship in Sweden and Denmark were of limited duration and questionable legal precision.

It is testimony to the strength of feelings and commitment, right across the political spectrum, that no amount of repressive action against print seems to have worked as intended. On the contrary, already in the 1640s and 1650s many polemicists were venturing into new territory, undeterred, as first-time authors. Print clearly fostered participation and engagement across a wider social spectrum, even if it rarely extended to the poorest levels of society. Naturally, members of the elite frequently railed against uneducated individuals writing on subjects they might not understand – a complaint that continued right through the eighteenth century and featured very prominently in the early years of the French Revolution. No-one knew what would happen if knowledge and analysis fell into the hands of individuals who had never before been part of the 'political nation'. Moderates such as Locke and Montesquieu were at first challenged for being too subversive, but may later have seemed too exclusive, elitist or even irrational to some readers. Yet such open resentments might also raise further questions, creating discussion of fundamental inequalities in European society, or even reconsideration of whose opinions counted in public and political life, and on what terms. The discussion of acceptable use of power, and claims to legitimate authority, were occurring in a rapidly changing environment, and some governments even began to recognise that a moderate and coherent public opinion could be a useful stabilising resource.

Whether readers liked or disliked what they saw in print, public opinion was becoming both visibly malleable and inherently irrepressible. The outraged attacks on Hobbes, Spinoza and their generation were mirrored in the extreme reactions confronting La Mettrie and Helvétius, or the bitter disputes surrounding Lessing before and after his death. In the 1790s, the loyalist crowds burning Priestley's house, or trying to silence those calling for electoral reform in London and Edinburgh, were perhaps just a counterpart to the irresponsible outbursts of Marat in his notorious newspaper, or the mob violence in the prison massacres in Paris in September 1792. It is not at all clear whether these ideological confrontations were moving away from core religious beliefs to more secular politics: there is plenty of evidence to the contrary, right up to the campaign of dechristianisation in revolutionary France in 1793. Print (and especially some of the Parisian newspapers) undoubtedly fuelled the violence and polarisation of opinion. Nevertheless those who saw repression as the obvious response may have been trying to shoot the messenger rather than confront the message. By then, all over Europe, political culture had come to include a much wider reading public, and print had become the most important tool of communication and dissemination.

Select Bibliography (Works Published after 1800)

NOTE: publications printed before 1800 are recorded in the text and footnotes.

The serial *Studies on Voltaire and the Eighteenth Century* is abbreviated to *SVEC*. It changed its numbering system in 2000 (with volume 381 followed by 2000: 01) and in 2014 changed its title to *Oxford University Studies in the Eighteenth Century* (listed below accordingly).

Adams, C., Censer, J. R. and Graham, L. J. (eds.), *Visions and revisions of eighteenth-century France* (University Park, PA, 1997).

Adams, G., *The Huguenots and French opinion 1685–1787* (Waterloo/Ontario, 1991).

Akkerman, F. and Steenbakkers, P. (eds.), *Spinoza to the letter: studies in words, texts and books* (Leiden, 2005).

Amelang, J. S., *The flight of Icarus: artisan autobiography in early modern Europe* (Stanford, 1998).

Anderson, B., *Imagined communities: reflections on the origin and spread of nationalism* (London, 1983; rev. edn 2006).

Andries, L., Ogée, F., Dunkley, J. and Sanfey, D. (eds.), *Intellectual journeys: the translation of ideas in Enlightenment England, France and Ireland* (*SVEC* 2013: 12, Oxford, 2013).

Applewhite, H. B. and Levy, D. G. (eds.), *Women and politics in the age of the democratic revolution* (Ann Arbor, 1990).

Asch, R., *Sacral kingship between disenchantment and re-enchantment: the French and English monarchies 1587–1688* (New York, 2014).

Astigarraga, J., *The Spanish Enlightenment revisited* (*Oxford University Studies in the Eighteenth Century*, 2015: 02, Oxford, 2015).

Aylmer, G. E. (ed.), *The Levellers in the English Revolution* (Ithaca, NY, 1975).

Baker, K. M., *Condorcet* (Chicago, 1975).

Baker, K. M., 'Public opinion as political invention' in his *Inventing the French Revolution* (New York, 1990).

Baker, K. M. (ed.), *The French Revolution and the creation of modern political culture*, 4 vols. (Oxford, 1987–94).

Bancarel, G. and Goggi, G. (eds.), *Raynal: de la polémique à l'histoire* (*SVEC* 2000: 12, Oxford, 2000).

Bannister, M., 'Mazarinades, manifestos and mavericks: political and ideological engagement during the Fronde', *French History*, 30 (2016), 165–80.

Barber, G., *Studies in the booktrade of the European Enlightenment* (London, 1993).

Barker, H., *Newspapers, politics and English society 1695–1855* (London, 2000).

Barker, H. and Burrows, S. (eds.), *Press, politics and the public sphere in Europe and North America, 1760–1820* (Cambridge, 2002).

Barnard, J. and McKenzie, D. F. (eds.), *The Cambridge history of the book*, vol. IV: 1557–1695 (Cambridge, 2002).

Barnes, D. G., *Epistolary community in print, 1580–1664* (Farnham, 2013).

Barnett, S. J., *The Enlightenment and religion: the myths of modernity* (Manchester, 2003).

Barrell, J., *Imagining the king's death: figurative reason, fantasies of regicide 1793–1796* (Oxford, 2000).

Barrell, J., *The spirit of despotism: invasions of privacy in the 1790s* (Oxford, 2006).

Bauer, V. and Böning, H. (eds.), *Die Entstehung des Zeitungswesens im 17. Jahrhundert* (Bremen, 2011).

Baumgold, D., 'The difficulties of Hobbes interpretation', *Political Theory*, 36 (2008), 827–55.

Beales, D., 'Joseph II, petitions and the public sphere', in H. Scott and B. Simms (eds.), *Cultures of power in Europe during the long eighteenth century* (Cambridge, 2007), 249–68.

Behringer, W., 'Communications revolutions: a historiographical concept', *German History*, 24 (2006), 333–74.

Behringer, W., *Im Zeichen des Merkur: Reichspost und Kommunikationsrevolution in der frühen Neuzeit* (Göttingen, 2003).

Behrisch, L., *Die Berechnung der Glückseligkeit: Statistik und Politik in Deutschland und Frankreich im späten Ancien Régime* (Ostfildern, 2016).

Beik, W., *Urban protest in seventeenth-century France* (Cambridge, 1997).

Bell, D. A., 'Lingua populi, lingua Dei: language, religion and the origins of French Revolutionary nationalism', *American Historical Review*, 100 (1995), 1403–37.

Bell, D. A., *The cult of the nation in France: inventing nationalism 1680–1800* (Cambridge, MA, 2001).

Bellingradt, D., *Flugpublizistik und Öffentlichkeit um 1700: Dynamiken, Akteure und Strukturen im urbanen Raum des Alten Reiches* (Stuttgart, 2011).

Bercé, Y.-M., *Revolt and revolution in early modern Europe* (New York, 1987).

Bergin, J., *The politics of religion in early modern France* (New Haven, CT, 2014).

Bevilacqua, A., *The republic of Arabic letters: Islam and the European Enlightenment* (Cambridge, MA, 2018).

Biederbeck, F., Dingel, I. and Li, W. (eds.), *Umwelt und Umweltgestaltung: Leibniz' politisches Denken* (Göttingen, 2015).

Birn, R., 'Book censorship in eighteenth-century France and Rousseau's response' (*SVEC* 2005: 01, Oxford, 2005), 223–45.

Birn, R., *Royal censorship of books in eighteenth-century France* (Stanford, CA, 2012).

Black, J., *The English press in the eighteenth century* (London, 1987).

Blanning, T. C. W., *The culture of power and the power of culture: old regime Europe 1660–1789* (Oxford, 2002).

Blockmans, W., Holenstein, A. and Mathieu, J. (eds.), *Empowering interactions: political cultures and the emergence of the state in Europe, 1300–1900* (Farnham, 2009).

Blum, C., *Rousseau and the republic of virtue: the language of politics in the French Revolution* (Ithaca, NY, 1986).

Boberg, S., *Gustav III och tryckfriheten 1774–1787* (Göteborg, 1951).

Bödeker, H. E. and Herrmann, U. (eds.), *Über den Prozess der Aufklärung im Deutschland in 18. Jhrh.* (Göttingen, 1987).

Böning, H., *Periodische Presse: Kommunikation und Aufklärung, Hamburg and Altona als Beispeil* (Bremen, 2002).

Böning, H. and Moepps, E., 'Die vorrevolutionäre Presse in Norddeutschland. Mit einer Bibliographie norddeutscher Zeitungen und Zeitschriften zwischen 1770 und 1790', in A. Herzig (ed.), *Sie, und nicht Wir: die Französische Revolution und ihre Wirkung auf Norddeutschland* (Hamburg, 1989).

Bowie, K., *Scottish public opinion and the Anglo-Scottish Union, 1699–1707* (Woodbridge, 2007).

Bowie, K. and Munck, T. (eds.), 'Early modern political petitioning and public engagement in Scotland, Britain and Scandinavia', *Parliaments, Estates and Representation*, 38 (2018), 271–391.

Boys, J. E. E., *London's news press and the Thirty Years War* (Woodbridge, 2011).

Braddick, M. J. (ed.), *The Oxford handbook of the English Revolution* (Oxford, 2015).

Brewer, D. and Hayes, J. C. (eds.), *Using the Encyclopédie: ways of knowing, ways of reading* (*SVEC* 2002: 05, Oxford, 2002).

Brooks, C. W., *Law, politics and society in early modern England* (Cambridge, 2008).

Brown, G. S., 'Reconsidering the censorship of writers in eighteenth-century France: civility, state power and the public theater in the Enlightenment', *Journal of Modern History*, 75 (2003), 235–68.

Brown, S. W. and McDougall, W. (eds.), *The Edinburgh history of the book, vol. 2: Enlightenment and expansion 1707–1800* (Edinburgh, 2012).

Brown, K. M., 'Toward political participation and capacity: elections, voting and representation in early modern Scotland', *Journal of Modern History*, 88 (2016), 1–33.

Brown, K. M. and Mann, A.J. (eds.), *Parliament and politics in Scotland 1567–1707* (Edinburgh, 2005).

Brunner, O., Conze, W. and Koselleck, R. (eds.), *Geschichtliche Grundbegriffe: historisches Lexikon zur politisch-sozialen Sprache in Deutschland* (8 vols., Stuttgart, 1972–97).

Brunot, F., *Histoire de la langue française des origines à 1900* (13 vols., Paris, 1905).

Burke, P., *Languages and communities in early modern Europe* (Cambridge, 2004).

Burke, P., *Popular culture in early modern Europe* (London, 1978).

Burke, P. and Po-Chia Hsia, R. (eds.), *Cultural translation in early modern Europe* (Cambridge, 2007).

Burkhardt, J. and Werkstetter, C. (eds.), *Kommunikation und Medien in der Frühen Neuzeit* (*Historische Zeitschrift*, Beiheft 41; Munich, 2005).

Burney, J. M., 'The fear of the executive and the threat of conspiracy: Billaud-Varenne's terrorist rhetoric in the French Revolution, 1788-1794', *French History*, 5 (1991), 143–63.

Burrows, S., *Blackmail, scandal and revolution: London's French libellistes, 1758–82* (Manchester, 2007).

Burrows, S., 'French banned books in international perspective 1770-1789' (SVEC 2013: 15, Oxford, 2013), 19–45.

Burrows, S., *The French book trade in Enlightenment Europe II: Enlightenment bestsellers* (London, 2018).

Campbell, P. R., 'The politics of patriotism in France (1770–1788)', *French History*, 24 (2010), 550–75.

Campbell, P. R., Kaiser, T. E. and Linton, M. (eds.), *Conspiracy in the French Revolution* (Manchester, 2007).

Caplan, J., *Postal culture in Europe 1500–1800* (*SVEC* 2016: 04, Oxford, 2016).

Caradonna, J. L., *The Enlightenment in practice: academic prize contests and intellectual culture in France 1670–1794* (Ithaca, NY, 2012).

Carrier, H., *La Fronde: contestation démocratique et misère paysanne*, 2 vols. (Paris, 1982).

Carrier, H., *La presse de la Fronde (1648–1653): les Mazarinades*, 2 vols. (Geneva, 1989–91).

Carrier, H., *Le labyrinthe de l'état: essai sur le débat politique au temps de la Fronde* (Paris, 2004).

Castiglione, D. and Sharpe, L. (eds.), *Shifting the boundaries: transformation of the languages of public and private in the eighteenth century* (Exeter, 1995).

Censer, J. R., *Prelude to power: the Parisian radical press 1789–1791* (Baltimore, 1976).

Censer, J. R., *The French press in the age of Enlightenment* (London, 1994).

Censer, J. R. and Popkin, J.D., *Press and politics in pre-revolutionary France* (Berkeley, 1987).

Champion, J., *Republican learning: John Toland and the crisis of Christian culture, 1696–1722* (Manchester, 2003).

Champion, J., *The pillars of priestcraft shaken* (Cambridge, 1992).

Chartier, R., *Lectures et lecteurs dans la France d'ancien régime* (Paris, 1987).

Chisick, H. (ed.), *The press in the French Revolution* (*SVEC* 287, Oxford, 1991).

Ciosáin, N. O., *Print and popular culture in Ireland 1750–1850* (Basingstoke, 1997).

Claeys, G., *Thomas Paine* (London, 1989).

Clegg, C. S., *Press censorship in Jacobean England* (Cambridge, 2001).

Colley, L., *Britons: forging the nation 1707–1837* (London and New Haven, CT, 1992).

Como, D. R., *Radical parliamentarians and the English civil war* (Oxford, 2018).

Como, D. R., 'Secret printing, the crisis of 1640, and the origins of civil war radicalism', *Past & Present* 196 (2007), 37–82.

Considine, J., *Dictionaries in early modern Europe: lexicography and the making of heritage* (Cambridge, 2008).

Coupe, W. A., *The German illustrated broadsheet of the seventeenth century* (Baden-Baden, 1961).

Coward, B. and Swann, J. (eds.), *Conspiracies and conspiracy theory in early modern Europe* (Aldershot, 2004).

Craciun, A., *British women writers and the French Revolution* (Basingstoke, 2005).

Cressy, D., *Dangerous talk: scandalous, seditious and treasonable speech in pre-modern England* (Oxford, 2010).

Curelly, L. and Smith, N. (eds.), *Radical voices, radical ways: articulating and disseminating radicalism in seventeenth- and eighteenth-century Britain* (Manchester, 2016).

Curran, M., *Atheism, religion and Enlightenment in pre-revolutionary Europe* (London, 2010).

Curran, M., 'Beyond the forbidden best-sellers of pre-revolutionary France', *Historical Journal*, 56 (2013), 89–112.

Curran, M., *The French book trade in Enlightenment Europe I: selling Enlightenment* (London, 2018).

Cuttica, C. and Burgess, G. (eds.), *Monarchism and absolutism in early modern Europe* (London, 2012).

Cuttica, C. and Mahlberg, G. (eds.), *Patriarchal moments: reading patriarchal texts* (London, 2015).

Darnton, R., *Edition et sédition: l'univers de la littérature clandestine au xviiie siècle* (Paris, 1991).

Darnton, R., *George Washington's false teeth* (Norton, 2003).

Darnton, R., *The business of the Enlightenment: a publishing history of the Enclyclopédie 1775–1800* (Cambridge, MA, 1979).

Darnton, R., *The forbidden best-sellers of pre-revolutionary France* (London, 1996).

Darnton, R., 'The forbidden books of pre-revolutionary France', in C. Lucas (ed.), *Rewriting the French Revolution* (Oxford, 1991), 1–32.

Darnton, R., *The great cat massacre and other episodes in French cultural history* (London, 1984).

Darnton, R., 'The high Enlightenment and the low-life of literature in pre-revolutionary France', *Past & Present* 51 (1971), 81–115.

Darnton, R. and Roche, D. (eds.), *Revolution in print* (Berkeley, 1989).

Dawson, R .L., *Confiscation at customs: banned books and the French booktrade during the last years of the ancien régime* (*SVEC* 2006: 07, Oxford, 2006).

de Champs, E., *Enlightenment and utility: Bentham in French, Bentham in France* (Cambridge, 2015).

de Madariaga, I., *Russia in the age of Catherine the Great* (London, 1981).

de Vivo, F., *Information and communication in Venice: rethinking early modern politics* (Oxford, 2007).

der Weduwen, A., *Dutch and Flemish newspapers of the seventeenth century*, 2 vols. (Leiden, 2017).

Deen, F., Onnekink, D. and Reinders, M. (eds.), *Pamphlets and politics in the Dutch Republic* (Leiden, 2011).

Devine, T. M. and Young, J. R. (eds.), *Eighteenth-century Scotland: new perspectives* (East Linton, 1999).

Dickinson, H. T., *The politics of the people in eighteenth-century Britain* (Basingstoke, 1994).

Dickinson, H. T. (ed.), *Britain and the American Revolution* (London, 1998).

Dickinson, H. T. (ed.), *British pamphlets on the American Revolution 1763–1785*, 4 vols. (London 2007).

Dixon, S., *The modernisation of Russia 1676–1825* (Cambridge, 1999).

Doering-Manteuffel, S., Mancal, J. and Wüst, W. (eds.), *Pressewesen der Aufklärung: periodischen Schriften im alten Reich* (Berlin, 2001).

Donald, D., *The age of caricature: satirical prints in the reign of George III* (New Haven, 1996).

Donoghue, F., *The fame machine: book reviewing and eighteenth-century literary careers* (Los Angeles, 1996).

Dooley, B. (ed.), *The dissemination of news and the emergence of contemporaneity in early modern Europe* (Farnham, 2010).

Dooley, B. and Baron, S. (eds.), *The politics of information in early modern Europe* (London, 2001).

Doyle, W., *Jansenism: Catholic resistance to authority from the Reformation to the French Revolution* (Basingstoke, 2000).

Dubray, J., *La pensée de l'abbé Grégoire: despotisme et liberté* (*SVEC* 2008: 02, Oxford, 2008).

Duchhardt, H. and Espenhorst, M., *August Ludwig (von) Schlözer in Europa* (Göttingen, 2012).

Dukes, P., *Catherine the Great's Instruction (Nakaz) to the Legislative Commission, 1767* (Newtonville, MA, 1977).

Dunstan, V., 'Glimpses into a town's reading habits in Enlightenment Scotland: analysing the borrowings of Gray Library, Haddington, 1732–1816', *Journal of Scottish Historical Studies*, 26 (2006), 42–59.

Duthille, R., *Le discours radical en Grande-Bretagne, 1768–1789* (*SVEC* 2017: 11, Oxford, 2017).

Eagles, R., *Francophilia in English society, 1748–1815* (London, 2000).

Echeverria, D., *The Maupeou revolution: a study in the history of libertarianism, France 1770–74* (Baton Rouge, 1985).

Edelstein, D., 'Enlightenment rights talk', *Journal of Modern History* 86 (2014), 530–65.

Edelstein, D., *The Enlightenment: a genealogy* (Chicago, 2010).

Edelstein, D., *The terror of natural right: republicanism, the cult of nature and the French Revolution* (Chicago, 2009).

Eger, E. et al. (eds.), *Women, writing and the public sphere 1700–1830* (Cambridge, 2001).

Eisenstein, E., *The printing press as an agent of change : communications and cultural transformations in early-modern Europe* (Cambridge, 1979).

Engelhardt, J., 'Borgerskab og fællesskab: de patriotiske selskaber i den danske helstat 1769–1814', *Historisk Tidsskrift*, 106 (2006), 33–63.

Eriksson, J., *Carl Christoffer Gjörwell som aktör på den svenska bokmarknaden 1769–1771* (Uppsala, 2003).

Erskine, C. and Mason, R. A. (eds.), *George Buchanan: political thought in early modern Britain and Europe* (Farnham, 2012).

Evans, C., *Debating the revolution: Britain in the 1790s* (London, 2006).

Fabian, B., 'English books and their eighteenth-century German readers', in P. J. Korshin (ed.), *The widening circle: essays on the circulation of literature in eighteenth-century Europe* (Philadelphia, 1976), 119–96.

Fabian, B., *The English book in eighteenth-century Germany* (London, 1992).

Farge, A., *Subversive words: public opinion in eighteenth-century France* (Cambridge, 1994).

Félix, J., 'The financial origins of the French Revolution', in P. R. Campbell (ed.), *The origins of the French Revolution* (Basingstoke, 2006), 35–62.

Ferret, O., *La fureur de nuire: échanges pamphlétaires entre philosophes et antiphilosophes 1750–1770* (*SVEC* 2007: 03, Oxford, 2007).

Ferrone, V., *The Enlightenment: history of an idea* (Princeton, 2015).

Fischer, E., Haefs, W. and Mix, Y.-G. (eds.), *Von Almanach bis Zeitung: ein Handbuch der Medien in Deutschland 1700–1800* (Munich, 1999).

Forster, A., 'Review journals and the reading public', in I. Rivers (ed.), *Books and their readers in eighteenth-century England* (London, 2001).

Fox, A., *Oral and literate culture in early modern England 1500–1700* (Oxford, 2000).

Foxley, R., *The Levellers: radical political thought in the English Revolution* (Manchester, 2013).

Freedman, J., *Books without borders in Enlightenment Europe: French cosmopolitanism and German literary markets* (Philadelphia, 2012).

Friedeburg, R. von (ed.), *'Patria' und 'Patrioten' vor dem Patriotismus: Pflichten, Rechte, Glauben und die Rekonfigurering europäischer Gemeinwesen im 17. Jhrh* (Wiesbaden, 2005).

Frimmel, J. and Wögerbauer, M. (eds.), *Kommunikation und Information im 18. Jhrh: das Beispiel der Habsburgermonarchie* (Wiesbaden, 2009).

Furrer, N., *Die vierzigsprachige Schweiz: Sprachkontakte und Mehrsprachigkeit in der vorindustriellen Gesellschaft (15.–19. Jahrhundert)*, 2 vols. (Zurich, 2002).

Gantet, C., *La paix de Westphalie (1648): une histoire sociale, xviie–xviiie siècles* (Paris, 2001).

Garrioch, D., *Neighbourhood and community in Paris 1740–90* (Cambridge, 1986).

Garrioch, D., *The Huguenots of Paris and the coming of religious freedom 1685–1789* (Cambridge, 2014).

Garrioch, D., 'The police of Paris as enlightened social reformers', *Eighteenth-century Life*, 16 (1992), 43–59.

Gaskill, H. (ed.), *The reception of Ossian in Europe* (London, 2004).

Gatti, H., *Ideas of liberty in early modern Europe from Machiavelli to Milton* (Princeton, 2015).

Gawthrop, R. and Strauss, G., 'Protestantism and literacy in early modern Germany', *Past & Present*, 104 (1984), 31–55.

Gentles, I., 'The *Agreements of the people* and their political contexts, 1647–1649', in M. Mendle (ed.), *The Putney debates of 1647: the army, the Levellers and the English state* (Cambridge, 2001), 148–74.

Gestrich, A., *Absolutismus und Öffentlichkeit: politische kommunikation in Deutschland zu Beginn des 18. Jhrh* (Göttingen, 1994).

Gestrich, A., 'The public sphere and the Habermas debate', *German History*, 24 (2006), 413–29.

Gibbs, G. C., 'Government and the English press, 1695 to the middle of the eighteenth century', in A. C. Duke and C. A. Tamse (eds.), *Too mighty to be free: censorship and the press in Britain and the Netherlands* (Zutphen, 1987), 87–105.

Goldenbaum, U. (ed.), *Appell an das Publikum: die öffentliche Debatte in der deutschen Aufklärung 1687–1796*, 2 vols. (Berlin, 2004).

Goldsmith, E. C. and Goodman, D., *Going public: women and publishing in early modern France* (Ithaca, NY, 1995).

Goodwin, A., *The friends of liberty: the English democratic movement in the age of the French Revolution* (London, 1979).

Gordon, D., *Citizens without sovereignty: equality and sociability in French thought, 1670–1789* (Princeton, 1994).

Gordon, D. (ed.), *Postmodernism and the Enlightenment: new perspectives on eighteenth-century French intellectual history* (New York and London, 2001).

Gough, H., *The newspaper press in the French Revolution* (London, 1988).

Green, A., *Cultural history* (Basingstoke, 2008).

Green, T. A., *Verdict according to conscience: perspectives on the English criminal trial jury 1200–1800* (Chicago, 1985).

Grell, O. and Porter, R. (eds.), *Toleration in Enlightenment Europe* (Cambridge, 2000).

Grosclaude, P., *Malesherbes, temoin et interprète de son temps* (Paris, 1961).

Gross, J.-P., 'Progressive taxation and social justice in eighteenth-century France', *Past & Present*, 140 (1993), 79–126.

Guilhaumou, J., 'Fragments of a discourse of denunciation (1789–1794)', in K. M. Baker (ed.), *The French Revolution and the creation of modern political culture*, vol. IV (Oxford, 1994), 139–55.

Guilhaumou, J., *La langue politique et la révolution française* (Paris, 1989).

Haakonssen, K. and Olden-Jørgensen, S. (eds.), *Ludvig Holberg (1684–1754): learning and literature in the Nordic Enlightenment* (London, 2017).

Habel, T., *Gelehrte Journale und Zeitungen der Aufklärung: zur Entstehung, Entwicklung und Erschliessung deutschsprachiger Rezensionszeitschriften des 18. Jahrhunderts* (Bremen, 2007).

Habermas, J., *Strukturwandel der Öffentlichkeit* (Neuwied, 1962); translated as *The structural transformation of the public sphere: an enquiry into a category of bourgeois society* (Boston and Oxford, 1989).

Hammersley, R., 'Camille Desmoulins's *Le vieux Cordelier*: a link between English and French republicanism', *History of European Ideas*, 27 (2001), 115–132.

Hammersley, R., *French revolutionaries and English republicans: the Cordeliers club 1790–94* (Woodbridge, 2005).

Hammersley, R., *The English republican tradition and eighteenth-century France: between the ancients and the moderns* (Manchester, 2010).

Hampsher-Monk, I., *History of concepts: comparative perspectives* (Amsterdam, 1998).

Hampson, N., *Prelude to terror: the Constituent Assembly and the failure of consensus 1787–91* (Oxford, 1988).

Hanley, W., *A biographical dictionary of French censors*, vols. 1–II (Ferney-Voltaire, 2005–16).

Harris, B., *Politics and the rise of the press: Britain and France, 1620–1800* (London, 1996).

Harris, B., 'Scotland's newspapers, the French Revolution and domestic radicalism (c.1789–1794)', *Scottish Historical Review*, 84 (2005), 38–62.

Harris, B., 'The Enlightenment, towns and urban society in Scotland c.1760–1820', *English Historical Review*, 126 (2011), 1097–1136.

Harris, J. A., *Hume: an intellectual biography* (Cambridge, 2015).

Harris, R., *A patriot press: national politics and the London press in the 1740s* (Oxford, 1993).

Harris, T., *London crowds in the reign of Charles II: propaganda and politics from the Restoration until the exclusion crisis* (Cambridge, 1987).

Harvey, D. A., *The French Enlightenment and its others: the mandarin, the savage and the invention of the human sciences* (New York, 2012).

Haug, C., Mayer, F. and Schröder, W. (eds.), *Geheimliteratur und Geheimbuchhandel in Europa im 18. Jahrhundert* (Wiesbaden, 2011).

Hazard, P., *La crise de la conscience européenne 1680–1715* (Paris, 1935); translated as *The crisis of the European mind* (London, 1953).

Hellmuth, E., 'Enlightenment and freedom of the press: the debate in the Berlin Mittwochsgesellschaft, 1783–1784', *History (The Historical Association)*, 83 (1998), 420–44.

Helmers, H. J., *The royalist republic: literature, politics and religion in the Anglo-Dutch public sphere, 1639–1660* (Cambridge, 2015).

Hessayon, A. and Finnegan, D. (eds.), *Varieties of seventeenth- and early eighteenth-century English radicalism in context* (Farnham, 2011).

Hesse, C., *Publishing and cultural politics in revolutionary Paris, 1789–1810* (Berkeley, 1991).

Hesse, C., *The other Enlightenment: how French women became modern* (Princeton, 2001).

Higonnet, P. L. R, *Goodness beyond virtue: Jacobins during the French Revolution* (Cambridge, MA, 1998).

Higonnet, P. L. R, 'The politics of linguistic terrorism and grammatical hegemony during the French Revolution', *Social History*, 5 (1980), 41–69.

Hoppitt, J., 'Political arithmetic in eighteenth-century England', *Economic History Review*, 49 (1996), 516–40.

Horstbøll, H., 'Bolle Luxdorphs samling af trykkefrihedens skrifter 1770–1773', *Fund og forskning i det Kongelige Biblioteks samlinger*, 44 (2005), 371–412.

Horstbøll, H., *Menig mands medie: det folkelige bogtryk i Danmark 1500–1840* (Copenhagen, 1999).

Horstbøll, H., 'Trykkefrihedens bogtrykkere og skribenter 1770–1773', *Grafiana* (2001), 9–25.

Houston, R. A., *Literacy in early modern Europe: culture and education 1500–1800* (London, 1988; new edn 2002).

Hudson, D., 'In defense of reform: French government propaganda during the Maupeou crisis', *French Historical Studies*, 8 (1973), 51–76.

Hughes, A., *Gangraena and the struggle for the English Revolution* (Oxford, 2006).

Hughes, A., 'Gender politics in Leveller literature', in S. D. Amussen and M. A. Kishlansky (eds.), *Political culture and cultural politics in early modern England* (Manchester, 1995), 162–88.

Hunt, A., 'Recovering speech acts', in A. Hadfield, M. Dimmock and A. Shinn (eds.), *The Ashgate research companion to popular culture in early modern England* (Farnham, 2014), 13–29.

Hunt, L., Jacob, M. C. and Mijnhardt, W., *The book that changed Europe: Picart and Bernard's Religious ceremonies of the world* (Cambridge, MA, 2010).

Hunt, T., *Defining John Bull: political caricature and national identity* (Aldershot, 2003).

Hunter, M., 'Pitcairneana: an atheist text by Archibald Pitcairne', *The Historical Journal*, 59 (2016), 595–621.

Hunter, M., (ed.), *Printed Images in early modern Britain: essays in interpretation* (Farnham, 2010).

Ihalainen, P., *Agents of the people: democracy and popular sovereignty in British and Swedish parliamentary and public debates, 1734–1800* (Leiden, 2010).

Innes, J. and Philp, M. (eds.), *Re-imagining democracy in the age of revolutions* (Oxford, 2013).

Israel, J. I., *Radical Enlightenment: philosophy and the making of modernity 1650–1750* (Oxford, 2001).

Jacob, M. C., *The radical Enlightenment: pantheists, freemasons and republicans* (London, 1981).

Jacob, M. C., and Mijnhardt, W. W. (eds.), *The Dutch Republic in the eighteenth century: decline, Enlightenment and revolution* (Ithaca, NY, 1992).

Jarrick, A., 'Borgare, småfolk och böcker i 1700-talets Stockholm', [Swedish] *Historisk Tidskrift* (1990), 191–227.

Johannes, G. J., *De barometer van de smaak: tijdschriften in Nederland 1770–1830* (The Hague, 1995).

Johns, A., *The nature of the book: print and knowledge in the making* (Chicago, 1998).

Jouhaud, C., *Mazarinades: la Fronde des mots* (Paris, 1985).

Jourdan, A., 'The Netherlands in the constellation of the eighteenth-century Western revolutions', *European Review of History*, 18 (2011), 190–225.

Kafker, F. A., *The Encyclopedists as a group: a collective biography of the authors of the Encyclopédie* (*SVEC* 345, Oxford, 1996).

Kafker, F. A. and Kafker, S. L., *The Encyclopedists as individuals: a biographical dictionary of the authors of the Encyclopédie* (*SVEC* 257, Oxford, 1988).

Kainulainen, J. *Paolo Sarpi: a servant of God and state* (Leiden, 2014).

Kelly, G., *Revolutionary feminism: the mind and career of Mary Wollstonecraft* (Basingstoke, 1992).

Kelly, G. A., 'The machine of the Duc d'Orléans and the new politics', *Journal of Modern History*, 51 (1979), 667–84.

Kennedy, E., *A cultural history of the French Revolution* (New Haven, CT, 1989).

Kennedy, M., *French books in eighteenth-century Ireland* (*SVEC* 2001: 07, Oxford, 2001).

Kidd, C., *The forging of races: race and scripture in the Protestant Atlantic world, 1600–2000* (Cambridge, 2006).

Kingdon, R. M., *Myths about the St. Bartholomew's Day massacres 1572–76* (Cambridge, MA, 1988).

Kitromilides, P. M. (ed.), *From republican polity to national community: reconsiderations of Enlightenment and political thought* (*SVEC* 2003: 09, Oxford, 2003).

Knachel, P. A., *England and the Fronde: the impact of the English civil war and revolution on France* (Ithaca/NY, 1967).

Knights, M., *Representation and misrepresentation in later Stuart Britain: partisanship and political culture* (Oxford, 2005).

Knudsen, J. B., *Justus Möser and the German Enlightenment* (Cambridge, 1986).

Koenigsberger, H. G., *Estates and revolutions: essays in early modern European history* (Ithaca, NY, 1971).

Kontler, L., *Translations, histories, enlightenments: William Robertson in Germany 1760–95* (Basingstoke, 2014).

Kors, A. C., *D'Holbach's coterie* (Princeton, 1976).

Koselleck, R., *Critique and crisis: Enlightenment and the pathogenesis of modern society* (Oxford, 1988).

Kozul, M., *Les lumières imaginaires: Holbach et la traduction* (*Oxford University Studies in the Eighteenth Century*, 2016: 05, Oxford, 2016).

Krefting, E., Nøding, A. and Ringvej, M. (eds.), *Eighteenth-century periodicals as agents of change: perspectives on northern Enlightenment* (Leiden, 2015).

Krieger, L., *The politics of discretion: Pufendorf and the acceptance of natural law* (Chicago, 1965).

Kümin, B. (ed.), *Political space in pre-industrial Europe* (Ashgate, 2009).

Kümin, B. and Würgler, A., 'Petitions, *gravamina* and the early modern state: local influence on central legislation in England and Germany (Hesse)', *Parliaments, Estates and Representation*, 17 (1997), 39–60.

Kwass, M., *Privilege and the politics of taxation in eighteenth-century France: liberté, égalité, fiscalité* (Cambridge, 2000).

Lake, P. and Pincus, S. (eds.), *The politics of the public sphere in early modern England* (Manchester, 2007).

Landes, J. B., *Visualising the nation: gender, representation and revolution in eighteenth-century France* (Ithaca, NY, 2001).

Lauzon, M., *Signs of light: French and British theories of linguistic communication 1648–1789* (Ithaca, NY, 2010).

La Vopa, A. J., 'Conceiving a public: ideas and society in eighteenth-century Europe', *Journal of Modern History*, 64 (1992), 79–116.

le Bart, C., 'L'imputation: un outil pour l'analyse des mentalités révolutionnaires', *Revue Historique*, 282 (1989), 351–65.

Leith, J. A., *Space and revolution: projects for monuments, squares and public buildings in France, 1789–1799* (Montreal, 1991).

Levy, D. G., *The ideas and careers of Simon-Nicolas-Henri Linguet: a study in eighteenth-century French politics* (Urbana, IL, 1980).

Levy, D. G., Applewhite, H. B. and Johnson, M. D. (eds.), *Women in revolutionary Paris 1789–1795* (Urbana, IL, 1980).

Lifschitz, A., *Language and Enlightenment: the Berlin debates of the eighteenth century* (Oxford, 2012).

Lilti, A., *Le monde des salons: sociabilité et mondanité à Paris au xviiie s.* (Paris, 2005).

Lindemann, M., *Patriots and paupers: Hamburg 1712–1830* (Oxford, 1990).

Lindemann, M., *The merchant republics: Amsterdam, Antwerp and Hamburg 1648–1790* (Cambridge, 2015).

Linton, M., *Choosing terror: virtue, friendship and authenticity in the French Revolution* (Oxford, 2013).

Linton, M., *The politics of virtue in Enlightenment France* (Basingstoke, 2001).

Loretellli, R., 'The first English translation of Cesare Beccaria's On Crimes and Punishments: uncovering the editorial and political contexts', *Diciottesimo Secolo*, 2 (2017), 1–22.

Lough, J., *The Encyclopédie* (London, 1971).

Lucas, C., 'The theory and practice of denunciation in the French Revolution', *Journal of Modern History*, 68 (1996), 768–85.

Lukowski, J., *Disorderly liberty: the political culture of the Polish-Lithuanian Commonwealth in the eighteenth century* (London, 2010).

Lukowski, J., 'Recasting Utopia: Montesquieu, Rousseau and the Polish constitution of 3 May 1791', *The Historical Journal*, 37 (1994), 65–87.

Lüsebrink, H.-J. and Reichardt, R., *Die Bastille: zur Symbolgeschichte von Herrschaft und Freiheit* (Frankfurt am Main, 1990); translated as *The Bastille: a history of a symbol of despotism and freedom* (Durham, NC, 1997).

Macleod, E., *British visions of America 1775–1820* (London, 2013).

Madi, C., 'Pour une étude des choix de langue en milieu plurilingue: représentations et pratiques en Bohême à l'époque des lumières', *Revue historique*, 315 (2013), 637–59.

Mahlberg, G. and Wiemann, D. (eds.), *European contexts for English republicanism* (Farnham, 2013).

Malcolm, N., *Aspects of Hobbes* (Oxford, 2002).

Malcolm, N., 'Hobbes and Spinoza', in J.H. Burns (ed.), *The Cambridge history of political thought 1450–1700* (Cambridge 1991), 547–55.

Malcolm, N. (ed.), Thomas Hobbes: *Leviathan* (3 vols., Oxford, 2012).

Mann, A. J., *The Scottish book trade 1500–1720* (East Linton, 2000).

Mansfield, A., *Ideas of monarchical reform: Fénelon, Jacobitism and political works of the chevalier Ramsay* (Manchester, 2015).

Marker, G., *Publishing, printing and the origins of intellectual life in Russia 1700–1800* (Princeton, NJ, 1985).

Markoff, J., *The abolition of feudalism: peasants, lords and legislators in the French Revolution* (Philadelphia, 1996).

Markoff, J., 'When and where was democracy invented?', *Comparative Studies in History*, 41 (1999), 660–90.

Marshall, J., *John Locke, toleration and the early Enlightenment culture* (Cambridge, 2006).

Martin, H.-J., *Livre, pouvoirs et société à Paris au xviie siècle* (Geneva, 1969).

Martin, H.-J., Chartier, R. and Vivet, J.-P. (eds.), *Histoire de l'édition française*, vol. 2: *Le livre triomphant, 1660–1830* (Paris, 1984).

Mason, H. T. (ed.), *The Darnton debate: books and revolution in the eighteenth century* (*SVEC* 359, Oxford, 1998).

Mathias, P., 'The social structure in the eighteenth century: a calculation by Joseph Massie', in his *The transformation of England* (London, 1979), 171–89.

Mathiez, A., *Le club des Cordeliers pendant la crise de Varennes et le massacre du Champ de Mars* (Geneva, 1975, reprinting the original 1910 edition).

Matytsin, A. M., *The specter of skepticism in the age of Enlightenment* (Baltimore, 2016).

Maza, S., *Private lives and public affairs: the causes célèbres of prerevolutionary France* (Berkeley, 1993).

McCormack, M., 'Rethinking "loyalty" in eighteenth-century Britain', *Journal for Eighteenth-Century Studies*, 35 (2012), 407–21.

McElligott, J., *Royalism, print and censorship in revolutionary England* (Woodbridge, 2007).

McKitterick, D., *Print, manuscript and the search for order 1450–1830* (Cambridge, 2003).

McLeod, J., 'Provincial book trade inspectors in eighteenth-century France', *French History*, 12 (1998), 127–48.

Medlin, D. and Merrick, J. (eds.), *André Morellet: texts and contexts* (*SVEC* 2003: 10, Oxford, 2010).

Merrick, J., 'Subjects and citizens in the remonstrances of the Parlement of Paris in the eighteenth century', *Journal of the History of Ideas*, 51 (1990), 453–60.

Merrick, J. and Medlin, D. (eds.), *André Morellet (1727–1819) in the republic of letters and the French Revolution* (New York, 1995).

Midgley, C., *Women against slavery: the British campaigns, 1780–1870* (London, 1992).

Mintz, S., *The hunting of Leviathan: seventeenth-century reactions to the materialism and moral philosophy of Thomas Hobbes* (Cambridge, 1962).

Möller, H., *Aufklärung in Preussen: der Verleger und Geschichtsschreiber Friedrich Nicolai* (Berlin, 1974).

Möllney, U., *Norddeutsche Presse um 1800: Zeitschriften und Zeitungen in Flensburg, Braunschweig, Hannover und Shaumburg-Lippe im Zeitalter der französische Revolution* (Bielefeld, 1996).

Mulsow, M., *Enlightenment underground: radical Germany 1680–1720* (Charlottesville, VA, 2015).

Munck, T., 'Absolute monarchy in later eighteenth-century Denmark: centralized reform, public expectations and the Copenhagen press', *Historical Journal*, 41 (1998), 201–24.

Munck, T., 'Eighteenth-century review journals and the internationalization of the European book market', *The International History Review*, 32 (2010), 415–35.

Munck, T.,'Music', in H. Scott (ed.), *The Oxford handbook of early modern European history 1350–1750* (Oxford, 2015), vol. II, 111–40.

Munck, T., 'Petitions and "legitimate" engagement with power in absolutist Denmark 1660–1800', in *Parliaments, Estates and Representation*, 38 (2018), 378–91.

Munck, T., 'Public debate, politics and print: the late Enlightenment in Copenhagen during the years of the French Revolution 1786–1800', *Historisk Tidsskrift*, 114 (2014), 323–52.

Munck, T., *The Enlightenment: a comparative social history 1721–1794* (London, 2000).

Murray, W. J., *The right-wing press in the French Revolution 1789–92* (Woodbridge, 1986).

Muthu, S., *Enlightenment against empire* (Princeton, 2003).

Nadler, S., *A book forged in hell: Spinoza's scandalous treatise and the birth of the secular age* (Princeton, 2011).

Négrel, E. and Sermain, J.-P. (eds.), *Une expérience rhétorique: l'éloquence de la Révolution* (*SVEC* 2002: 02, Oxford, 2002).

Newman, S. and Onuf, P. S. (eds.), *Paine and Jefferson in the age of revolutions* (Charlottesville, 2013).

Niethammer, O., *Autobiographien von Frauen im 18. Jahrhundert* (Tübingen, 2000).

O'Brien, K., *Women and Enlightenment in eighteenth-century Britain* (Cambridge, 2009).

O'Gorman, F., *The long eighteenth century: British political and social history 1688–1832* (London, 1997).

Olden-Jørgensen, S., 'Robert Molesworth's *An account of Denmark as it was in 1692*: a political scandal and its literary aftermath', in K. Haakonssen and H. Horstbøl (eds.), *Northern antiquities and national identities* (Copenhagen, 2007), 68–87.

Olsen, M., 'Enlightened nationalism in the early Revolution: the *nation* in the language of the *Société de 1789*', *Canadian Journal of History*, 29 (1994), 24–50.

Oz-Salzberger, F., 'The Enlightenment in translation: regional and European aspects', *European Review of History*, 13 (2006), 385–409.

Oz-Salzberger, F., *Translating the Enlightenment: Scottish civic discourse in eighteenth-century Germany* (Oxford, 1995).

Ozouf, M., *Festivals and the French Revolution* (Cambridge, MA, 1988).

Paas, J. R., 'The changing images of Gustavus Adolphus on German broadsheets, 1630–33', *Journal of the Warburg and Courtauld Institutes*, 59 (1996), 205–44.

Paas, J. R., *The German political broadsheet 1600–1700*, vols. I–XIII (Wiesbaden, 1985–2016).

Parkin, J., *Taming the Leviathan: the reception of the political and religious ideas of Thomas Hobbes in England 1640–1700* (Cambridge, 2007).

Parrish, D., *Jacobitism and anti-jacobitism in the British Atlantic world 1688–1727* (London, 2017).

Peacey, J., *Print and public politics in the English Revolution* (Cambridge, 2013).

Peacey, J., (ed.), *The print culture of parliament 1600–1800* (Edinburgh, 2007).

Peters, K., 'The Quakers and the politics of the army in the crisis of 1659', *Past & Present*, 231 (2016), 97–128.

Pettegree, A., 'Centre and periphery in the European book world', *Transactions of the Royal Historical Society*, 18 (2008), 101–28.

Pettegree, A., *The book in the Renaissance* (New Haven and London, 2010).

Pettegree, A., *The French book and the European book world* (Leiden, 2007).

Philp, M., *Reforming ideas in Britain: politics and language in the shadow of the French Revolution 1789–1815* (Cambridge, 2014).

Philp, M., *The French Revolution and British popular politics* (Cambridge, 1991).
Philp, M., 'Vulgar conservatism 1792–93', *English Historical Review*, 110 (1995), 42–69.
Plassart, A., *The Scottish Enlightenment and the French Revolution* (Cambridge, 2015).
Pocock, J. G. A., 'The concept of language and the *métier d'historien*: some considerations on practice', in A. Pagden (ed.), *The languages of political theory in early modern Europe* (Cambridge, 1987), 19–38.
Pocock, J. G. A., *The Machiavellian moment: Florentine political thought and the Atlantic republican tradition* (Princeton, 1975).
Pollmann, J, *Memory in early modern Europe 1500–1800* (Oxford, 2017).
Popkin, J. D., *News and politics in the age of revolution: Jean Luzac's Gazette de Leyde* (Ithaca, NY, 1989).
Popkin, J. D., 'Pamphlet journalism at the end of the old régime', *Eighteenth-century Studies*, 22 (1989), 351–67.
Popkin, J. D., 'Political communication in the German Enlightenment: Gottlob Benedikt von Schirach's *Politische Journal*', *Eighteenth-century Life*, 20 (1996), 24–41.
Popkin, J. D., *Revolutionary news: the press in France 1789–1799* (Durham, NC, 1990).
Popkin, J. D., 'The German press and the Dutch patriot movement, 1781–1787', *Lessing Yearbook*, 22 (1990), 97–111.
Popkin, J. D., *The right-wing press in France 1792–1800* (Chapel Hill, NC, 1980).
Popkin, R. H., *The history of scepticism from Erasmus to Spinoza* (Berkeley, 1979).
Porter, R., *Enlightenment: Britain and the creation of the modern world* (London, 1990).
Porter, R. and Teich, M. (eds.), *The Enlightenment in national context* (Cambridge, 1981).
Prak, M., *Citizens without nations: urban citizenship in Europe and the world c.1000–1789* (Cambridge and New York, 2018).
Raffe, A., *The culture of controversy: religious arguments in Scotland 1660–1714* (Woodbridge, 2012).
Rapport, M., *Rebel cities: Paris, London and New York in the age of revolution* (London, 2017).
Raven, J., *Judging new wealth: popular publishing and responses to commerce in England 1750–1800* (Oxford, 1992).
Raven, J., *The business of books: booksellers and the English book trade 1450–1850* (Yale, 2000).
Raymond, J., *Pamphlets and pamphleteering in early modern Britain* (Cambridge, 2003).
Raymond, J., *The invention of the newspaper: English newsbooks 1641–49* (Oxford, 1996).
Raymond, J. (ed.), *News, newspapers and society in early modern Britain* (London and Portland, OR, 2000).
Raymond, J. (ed.), *The Oxford history of popular print culture*, vol. 1: *Cheap print in Britain and Ireland to 1660* (Oxford, 2011).
Rea, R. R., *The English press in politics 1760–1774* (Lincoln, NE, 1963).
Real, H. J. (ed.), *The reception of Jonathan Swift in Europe* (London, 2005).

Reichardt, R., Lüsebrink, H.-J. and Leonhard, J. (eds.) *Handbuch politisch-sozialer Grundbegriffe in Frankreich 1680–1820*, vol. I–XXI (Munich/Berlin, 1985–2017).

Reinders, M., *Gedruckte chaos: populisme en moord in het rampjaar 1672* (Amsterdam, 2010).

Reinert, S. A., *Translating empire: emulation and the origins of political economy* (Cambridge, MA, 2011).

Richter, M., *The history of political and social concepts* (Oxford, 1995).

Rigogne, T., *Between state and market: printing and bookselling in eighteenth-century France* (*SVEC* 2007: 05, Oxford, 2007).

Robertson, J., *The case for the Enlightenment* (Cambridge, 2005).

Robertson, J., *The Enlightenment: a very short introduction* (Oxford, 2015).

Robertson, R., *Censorship and conflict in seventeenth-century England* (Philadelphia, 2009).

Roche, D., *Le siècle des lumières en province: académies et académiciens provinciaux, 1680–1789*, vols. I–II (Paris, 1978).

Rogers, G. A. J. and Schuhmann, K. (eds.), *Thomas Hobbes Leviathan*, 2 vols. (London, 2003).

Roper, D., *Reviewing before the Edinburgh, 1788–1802* (London, 1978).

Rosenberg, D., 'Louis-Sébastien Mercier's new words', *Eighteenth-century Studies*, 36 (2003), 367–86.

Rospocher, M. (ed.), *Beyond the public sphere: opinions, publics, spaces in early modern Europe* (Bologna and Berlin, 2012).

Schilling, M., *Bildpublizistik der frühen Neuzeit: Aufgaben und Leistungen des illustrierten Flugblatts in Deutschland bis um 1700* (Tübingen, 1990).

Schlaak, A., 'Overloaded interaction: effects of the growing use of writing in German imperial cities', in J. P. Coy, B. Marschke and D. W. Sabean (eds.), *The Holy Roman Empire reconsidered*, (New York, 2011), 35–47.

Schmidt, J., 'The question of Enlightenment: Kant, Mendelssohn and the Mittwochsgesellschaft', *Journal of the History of Ideas*, 50 (1989), 269–91.

Schmidt, J. (ed.) *What is Enlightenment? Eighteenth-century answers and twentieth-century questions* (Berkeley, CA, 1996).

Schnakenbourg, E., 'Les chemins de l'information: la circulation des nouvelles depuis la périphérie européenne jusqu'au gouvernment française au début du xviiie siècle', *Revue historique*, 308 (2006), 291–310.

Scott, H. (ed.), *The Oxford handbook of early modern European History 1350–1750*, 2 vols. (Oxford, 2015).

Scott, J. W., *Only paradoxes to offer: French feminists and the rights of man* (Cambridge, MA, 1996).

Seaward, L., 'Censorship through cooperation: the Société typographique de Neuchâtel and the French government', *French History*, 28 (2014), 23–42.

Seaward, L., 'The Société typographique de Neuchâtel (STN) and the politics of the book trade in late eighteenth-century Europe, 1769–1789', *European History Quarterly*, 44 (2014), 439–57.

Seelig, S. C., *Autobiography and gender in early modern literature: reading women's lives, 1600–1680* (Cambridge, 2006).

Selwyn, P. E., *Everyday life in the German book trade: Friedrich Nicolai as bookseller and publisher in the age of Enlightenment* (University Park, PA, 2000).

Sennefelt, K., 'Citizenship and the political landscape of libelling in Stockholm, c.1720–70', *Social History*, 33 (2008), 145–63.

Sennefelt, K., 'The politics of hanging around and tagging along: everyday practices in eighteenth-century politics', in M. J. Braddick (ed.), *The politics of gesture: historical perspectives* (*Past & Present* Supplement 4, 2009), 172–90.

Sgard, J., *Dictionnaire des journalistes, 1600–1789* (Oxford, 1999).

Sgard, J. (ed.) *Dictionnaire des journaux (1600–1789): édition électronique revue, corrigée et augmentée* (online at http://dictionnaire-journaux.gazettes18e.fr). Date last accessed 21 January 2019.

Shapiro, G. and Markoff, J., *Revolutionary demands: a content analysis of the cahiers de doléances of 1789* (Stanford and Cambridge, 1998).

Sharpe, K., *Image wars: promoting kings and commonwealths in England 1603–1660* (New Haven, CT, 2010).

Sharpe, K., *Reading authority and representing rule in early modern England* (London, 2013).

Shaw, E. P., *Problems and policies of Malesherbes as Directeur de la Librairie* (New York, 1966).

Sheehan, J., *The Enlightenment Bible* (Princeton, 2005).

Shennan, J. H., 'The rise of patriotism in eighteenth-century Europe', *History of European Ideas*, 13 (1991), 689–710.

Shepard, A. and Withington, P. (eds.), *Communities in early modern England* (Manchester, 2000).

Sher, R. B., *The Enlightenment and the book: Scottish authors and their publishers in eighteenth-century Britain, Ireland and America* (Chicago, 2006).

Shevlin, E. F. (ed.), *The history of the book in the west 1700–1800*, vol. III (Farnham, 2010).

Skinner, Q., *The foundations of modern political thought*, 2 vols. (Cambridge, 1978).

Skinner, Q. and van Gelderen, M. (eds.), *Freedom and the construction of Europe*, 2 vols. (Cambridge, 2013).

Skuncke, M.-C., 'Press and political culture in Sweden at the end of the age of liberty', (*SVEC* 2004: 06, Oxford, 2004), 81–101.

Skuncke, M.-C. and Tandefelt, H. (eds.), *Riksdag, kaffehus och predikstol: Frihetstidens politiska kultur 1766–1772* (Stockholm, 2003).

Smith, H., *'Grossly material things': women and book production in early modern England* (Oxford, 2012).

Smith, J. M., 'No more language games: words, beliefs and the political culture of early modern France', *American Historical Review*, 102 (1997), 1413–40.

Smyth, A., *Autobiography in early modern England* (Cambridge, 2010).

Soll, J., *The information master: Jean-Baptiste Colbert's secret state intelligence system* (Ann Arbor, 2009).

Søllinge, J. D. and Thomsen, N., *De danske aviser 1634–1989*, vol. I (Odense, 1988).

Sommerville, C. J., *The news revolution in England* (Oxford and New York, 1996).

Soulard, D., 'The Christ's copy of John Locke's *Two Treatises of Government*', *Historical Journal*, 58 (2015), 25–49.

Spalding, P., *Seize the book, jail the author: Johann Lorenz and censorship in eighteenth-century Germany* (Purdue, 1998).

Spierenburg, P., *The prison experience* (New Brunswick and London, 1991).

St Clair, W., *The reading nation in the Romantic period* (Cambridge, 2004).

Stapelbroek, K. and Marjanen, J. (eds.), *The rise of economic societies in the eighteenth century: patriotic reform in Europe and North America* (Basingstoke, 2012).

Stafford, J. M., *Private vices, publick benefits? The contemporary reception of Bernard Mandeville* (Solihull, 1997).

Steinmetz, W., Freeden, M. and Fernández-Sebastián, J. (eds.), *Conceptual history in the European space* (New York and Oxford, 2017).

Sternberg, G. S., 'Epistolary ceremonial: corresponding status at the time of Louis XIV', *Past & Present*, 204 (2009), 33–88.

Stewart, L., *Rethinking the Scottish revolution: covenanted Scotland 1637–51* (Oxford, 2016).

Stijnman, A., *Engraving and etching 1400–2000: a history of the development of manual intaglio printmaking process* (London, 2012).

Stock, B., *Listening for the text: on the uses of the past* (Baltimore, 1990).

Stollberg-Rilinger, B., *The emperor's old clothes: constitutional history and the symbolic language of the Holy Roman Empire* (New York and Oxford, 2015).

Stuurman, S., *François Poulain de la Barre and the invention of modern equality* (Cambridge, MA, 2004).

Sutherland, J., *The Restoration newspaper and its development* (Cambridge, 1986).

Swann, J. and Félix, J. (eds.), *The crisis of the absolute monarchy: France from old regime to revolution* (Proceedings of the British Academy, 184, Oxford, 2013).

Swiggers, P., 'Préhistoire et histoire de l'*Encyclopédie*', *Revue historique*, 271 (1984), 83–92.

te Brake, W. P., *Regents and rebels: the revolutionary world of an eighteenth-century Dutch city* (Cambridge, MA and Oxford, 1989).

te Brake, W. P., *Shaping history: ordinary people in European politics 1500–1700* (Berkeley, 1998).

Temple, K., *Scandal nation: law and authorship in Britain, 1750–1832* (Ithaca, NY, 2003).

Terrall, M., *The man who flattened the Earth: Maupertuis and the sciences in the Enlightenment* (Chicago, 2002).

Thale, M., 'London debating societies in the 1790s', *The Historical Journal*, 32 (1989), 57–86.

Thale, M. (ed.), *Selections from the papers of the London Corresponding Society 1792–1799* (Cambridge, 1983).

Thomas, D. O., Stephens, J. and Jones, P. A. L., *A bibliography of the works of Richard Price* (Aldershot, 1993).

Thomas, P. D. G., *John Wilkes: a friend of liberty* (Oxford, 1996).

Thomson, A., *Bodies of thought: science, religion and the soul in the early Enlightment* (Oxford, 2008).

Thomson, A., *L'âme des lumières: le débat sur l'être humain entre religion et science Angleterre-France, 1690–1760* (Seyssel, 2013).

Thomson, A., Burrows, S. and Dziembowski, A. (eds.), *Cultural transfers: France and Britain in the long eighteenth century* (*SVEC* 2010: 04, Oxford, 2010).

Tolkemitt, B., *Der Hamburgische Correspondent: zur öffentlichen Verbreitung der Aufklärung in Deutschland* (Tübingen, 1995).

Towsey, M., *Reading the Scottish Enlightenment: books and their readers in provincial Scotland, 1750–1820* (Leiden, 2010).

Tricoire, D., 'Attacking the monarchy's sacrality in late seventeenth-century France: the underground literature against Louis XIV, Jansenism and the dauphin's faction', *French History*, 31 (2017), 152–73.

Tuck, R., *The sleeping sovereign: the invention of modern democracy* (Cambridge, 2016).

Underdown, D., *Revel, riot and rebellion: popular politics and culture in England 1603–1660* (Oxford, 1985).

Upton, A. F., *Charles XI and Swedish absolutism* (Cambridge, 1998).

Upton, A. F., 'The Riksdag of 1680 and the establishment of royal absolutism in Sweden', *English Historical Review*, 103 (1987), 281–308.

van Bunge, W. (ed.), *The early Enlightenment in the Dutch Republic 1650–1750* (Leiden, 2003).

van Gelderen, M. and Skinner, Q. (eds.), *Republicanism: a shared European heritage*, 2 vols. (Cambridge, 2002).

Van Kley, D., 'Religion and the age of "patriot" reform', *Journal of Modern History*, 80 (2008), 252–95.

Van Kley, D., *The religious origins of the French Revolution: from Calvin to the civil constitution, 1560–1791* (New Haven, CT, 1996).

Van Ruymbeke, B. and Sparks, R.J. (eds.), *Memory and identity: the Huguenots in France and the Atlantic diaspora* (Columbia, 2003).

Vardi, L., *The physiocrats and the world of the Enlightenment* (Cambridge, 2012).

Velema, W. R. E., *Enlightenment and conservatism in the Dutch Republic: the political thought of Elie Luzac, 1721–1796* (Assen, 1993).

Velema, W. R. E., *Republicans: essays on eighteenth-century Dutch political thought* (Leiden, 2007).

Verbeek, T., *Spinoza's Theologico-political treatise* (Farnham, 2003).

Vernon, E. and Baker, P., 'What was the first Agreement of the People?', *The Historical Journal*, 53 (2010), 39–59.

Waldinger, R., Dawson, P. and Woloch, I. (eds.), *The French Revolution and the meaning of citizenship* (Westport, CT and London, 1993).

Walsham, A., *Catholic reformation in Protestant Britain* (Farnham, 2014).

Wangermann, E., *Die Waffen der Publizität: zum Funktionswandel der politischen Literatur unter Joseph II* (Vienna, 2004).

Weckel, U., 'A lost paradise of a female culture? Some critical questions regarding the scholarship on late eighteenth and early nineteenth-century German salons', *German History*, 18 (2000), 310–36.

Welke, M., 'Die Legende vom "unpolitischen Deutschen": Zeitungslesen im 18. Jahrhundert', *Jahrbuch der Wittheit zu Bremen*, 25 (1981), 161–88.

Wiemann, D. and Mahlberg, G. (eds.), *Perspectives on English revolutionary republicanism* (Farnham, 2014).

Wilson, K., *The island race: Englishness, empire and gender in the eighteenth century* (London, 2003).

Wilson, K., *The sense of the people: politics, culture and imperialism in England, 1715–1785* (Cambridge, 1995).

Winton, P., *Frihetstidens politiska praktik: nätverk och offentlighet 1746–1766* (Uppsala, 2006).

Wittman, R., *Geschichte des deutschen Buchhandels* (Munich, 1991).

Wolff, C., *Vänskap och makt: den svenska politiska eliten och upplysningstidens Frankrike* (Helsinki, 2005).

Wolff, L., *Inventing eastern Europe: the map of civilization on the mind of the Enlightenment* (Stanford, 1994).

Wootton, D., *Paolo Sarpi: between Renaissance and Enlightenment* (Cambridge, 1983).

Würgler, A., *Unruhen und öffentlichkeit: städtische und ländliche Protestbewegungen im 18. Jahrhundert* (Tübingen, 1995).

Würgler, A., 'Voices from among the "silent masses": humble petitions and social conflicts in early modern central Europe', *International Review of Social History*, 46, Supplement 9 (2001), 11–34.

Wyrwa, U., 'Berlin and Florence in the age of Enlightenment: Jewish experience in comparative perspective', *German History*, 21 (2003), 1–28.

Yeo, R., 'Encyclopaedism and Enlightenment', in M. Fitzpatrick, P. Jones, C. Knellwolf and I. McCalman (eds.), *The Enlightenment world* (London, 2004), 350–65.

Young, J. R., *The Scottish parliament: a political and constitutional analysis* (Edinburgh, 1996).

Zagorin, P., *Rebels and rulers 1500–1660: society, states and early modern revolution* (Cambridge, 1982).

Zaret, D., *Origins of democratic culture: printing, petitions and the public sphere in early modern England* (Princeton, 2000).

Index